Law and the Postmodern Mind

## Law, Meaning, and Violence

The scope of Law, Meaning, and Violence is defined by the wide-ranging scholarly debates signaled by each of the words in the title. Those debates have taken place among and between lawyers, anthropologists, political theorists, sociologists, and historians, as well as literary and cultural critics. This series is intended to recognize the importance of such ongoing conversations about law, meaning, and violence as well as to encourage and further them.



*Narrative, Violence, and the Law: The Essays of Robert Cover,* edited by Martha Minow, Michael Ryan, and Austin Sarat

*Narrative, Authority, and Law,* by Robin West

*The Possibility of Popular Justice: A Case Study of Community Mediation in the United States,* edited by Sally Engle Merry and Neal Milner

*Legal Modernism,* by David Luban

*Surveillance, Privacy, and the Law: Employee Drug Testing and the Politics of Social Control,* by John Gilliom

*Lives of Lawyers: Journeys in the Organizations of Practice,* by Michael J. Kelly

*Unleashing Rights: Law, Meaning, and the Animal Rights Movement,* by Helena Silverstein

*Law Stories,* edited by Gary Bellow and Martha Minow

*The Powers That Punish: Prison and Politics in the Era of the "Big House," 1920–1955,* by Charles Bright

*Law and the Postmodern Mind: Essays on Psychoanalysis and Jurisprudence,* edited by Peter Goodrich and David Gray Carlson

# Law and the Postmodern Mind

## Essays on Psychoanalysis and Jurisprudence

PETER GOODRICH
*and*
DAVID GRAY CARLSON,
*Editors*

*Ann Arbor*
THE UNIVERSITY OF MICHIGAN PRESS

Published in the United States of America by
The University of Michigan Press
Manufactured in the United States of America
⊗ Printed on acid-free paper

2001 2000 1999 1998 4 3 2 1



*A CIP catalog record for this book is available from the British Library.*

Library of Congress Cataloging-in-Publication Data

Law and the postmodern mind : essays on psychoanalysis and
jurisprudence / Peter Goodrich and David Gray Carlson, editors.
p. cm. — (Law, meaning, and violence)
Includes bibliographical references and index.
ISBN 0-472-10841-7 (cloth : acid-free paper)
1. Law—Philosophy. 2. Law—Psychology. 3. Psychoanalysis.
I. Goodrich, Peter, 1954– . II. Carlson, David (David Gray)
III. Series.
K346.L38 1998
340'.1'9—dc21 97-33739
CIP

# Contents

# Introduction

*Peter Goodrich and David Gray Carlson*

The history of modern legal thought has been concerned predominantly with an external and objective conception of law. In its most extreme manifestations, the study of law has been conceived as a science, and law itself as a system of exterior norms or rules. Even where the sources of such rules have been recognized as being plural, and their substantive content contradictory, the textual or evident character of law and the public quality of its representations have remained the exclusive focus of traditional and even radical expositions. To become a lawyer, or even a teacher of law, has meant to enter an exterior world, to engage in a distinct vocation, to learn an art that is distant from the self. Law, within this modern tradition, is cold, most usually rational, and intrinsically political; it is written, it legislates, it is an exterior fate, a foreign or institutional will inscribed on the soul.

The modernist concern to make law an affair of the surface, to make its justice visible, its reason apparent, its rules and other institutions distinct and exclusive, has been increasingly subject to challenge. There are always flaws or fault lines within the modernist tradition. The complexity of legal history and the plurality of legal jurisdictions and rules always threatened to explode the boundaries of doctrine and the strict limits of judgment.

The postmodern legal mind can be characterized best as having shifted the focus of legal analysis away from the flaws or simple indeterminacies of the modernist tradition. Postmodernity has been witness to the blooming of a thousand flowers.[1] In jurisprudential terms, the

1. A few are collected in Gary Minda, *Postmodern Legal Movements: Law and Jurisprudence at Century's End* (1995). *See also* Costas Douzinas and Ronnie Warrington, "Justice Miscarried: Ethics and Aesthetics in Law," in *Legal Studies as Cultural Studies* (Jerry Leonard ed., 1994).

various and numerous "other dimensions" of law have formed the basis of a series of alternative species of legal analysis and the representation of different forms of law or plural jurisdictions. The postmodern legal mind is radical primarily in its return to the roots of the legal tradition in an endeavor to recover the "dynamic"[2] or creative resources of a plurality of laws. The postmodern is not merely the contradiction or antithesis of the modernist tradition. Easy though it may be to classify and counterpose the two rather vague epistemic categories of modernity and postmodernity, and to oppose positivism to criticism, law to psychoanalysis, or repression to hedonism, such oppositions are only momentary interventions in the path of a developing interdisciplinary and profoundly affective rewriting of the power, potential, and parameters of legal studies and legal practices.

The postmodern legal recourse to other disciplines, to sociology, philosophy, economics, history, or literature, represents much more than a simple proliferation of academic concerns or a mere inversion of precedence and establishment. At an institutional level it represents the symbolic collapse of the concept and practice of any singular or sovereign jurisprudence. The postmodern legal mind introduces a series of "minor jurisprudences" or partial forms of legal knowledge that both compete with and subvert the lingering and far from exhausted modernist conception of a unitary system or notionally complete totality of legal rules. In place of the essentially scholastic representation of the identity of a legal system in the form of some emblem of unity or similarity, and in opposition to the universal subject and abstract rule of law, postmodernity recalls the difference and the otherness without which the sameness or precedence of law could not be built. In substantive terms, other disciplines have been the means of representing other experiences and other constructions of law and of its impositions. Combining literature and law, to take one example, and particularly the focus upon the narrativity of both justificatory reason and legal texts, has been a primary occasion of introducing the experience of women and of race into the analysis of doctrine.[3] Sociology has allowed for an

2. The term *dynamic jurisprudence* is elaborated in Arthur J. Jacobson, "Hegel's Legal Plenum," in *Hegel and Legal Theory* (Drucilla Cornell et al. eds., 1990).

3. See specifically, on the use of narrative, Derek Bell, *Confronting Authority* (1995); Patricia Williams, *The Alchemy of Race and Rights* (1992). In more academic terms, Richard Delgado, "Story-Telling for Oppositionists and Others: A Plea for Narrative," 87 *Mich. L. Rev.* 2411 (1989).

oppositional account of the impact of legal rules upon disparate economic and ethnic groups. The return of rhetoric and hermeneutics within jurisprudence has equally been the occasion of critically representing the class character and elite audience of the bulk of legal rules. The examples could be multiplied and crosscut by academic genres such as feminist legal studies, critical race theory, legal semiotics, or aesthetics of law that again provide resources and impetus to experiences that transgress the norms and boundaries of public space and displace the purported universality, abstraction, or sameness of legal rules.

The essays collected in the present volume address what is arguably the most fundamental or structural of interdisciplinary encounters, namely that of psychoanalysis and law. While psychoanalytic interpretations of law and of legal judgments are by no means a novelty within common law jurisprudence, the extent and the possibilities of the terrain opened up by psychoanalysis as a minor jurisprudence in its own right have yet to be extensively addressed. In a philosophical sense, psychoanalysis is an exemplary postmodern discipline, and not least for this reason it is arguably the antithesis of modern jurisprudence. In a preliminary and somewhat superficial sense, psychoanalytic interpretations of subjectivity are the inverse of its legal definitions. The intentional subject and the "reasonable man" are disassembled in psychoanalysis to reveal a chaotic and irrational libidinal subject, a sexual being, a body and its drives. Behind the mask of reason, the unconscious plays the role of law and emotion determines both judicial judgment and the subject's deeds. Psychoanalysis in this sense might be taken to represent law's unconscious, its "other scene," and, at least in this regard, as the shadow, underside, or "backface" of law, it constitutes an exorbitant threat to the order and reason of the legal system. The unconscious, in other words, presses constantly against the barrier of biography, the repressed threatens inexorably to return, and desire—which in legal terms is paradoxically the most undesirable of forces—holds center stage.

The interpretation of psychoanalysis as a theoretically dangerous discipline, as an "undesirable text,"[4] "repressed discipline,"[5] or "China

4. The notion of undesirable texts is taken from Pierre Legendre et al., *Leçons IV. Le Dossier occidental de la parenté. Textes juridiques indésirables sur la généalogie* (1988).

5. Pierre Legendre, *L'amour du censeur* (1974).

within,"[6] has a lengthy and elaborate history.[7] As with any disciplinary tradition, it is important to note that psychoanalysis also has a series of nonconfrontational or adaptive uses, that it is not necessarily a radical threat or unsettling to the dogmatic tradition. Psychoanalysis can and does adapt the subject to the institution and in Freud's terms repression can account for the origin of law. In the context of postmodernity, however, psychoanalysis is to be understood rather as another domain or dimension of legal practice, as a minor jurisprudence or further and plural territory of law. It is in this sense, as a discipline that comes "after law" or in the wake of the dogmatic tradition, that psychoanalysis can play a radical role in legal analysis. At the risk of a massive oversimplification, three dimensions of psychoanalytic jurisprudence have already made a mark upon legal studies. These may be grouped loosely in terms, first, of psychoanalytic techniques of reading legal speech, its texts, and its institutions. A symptomatic reading of legal representations leads to a second concern, that of the power or role of the image in the institution, and specifically of the fantasm in the subject's identification with or attachment to law. A third and no less demanding avenue of analysis combines the first two approaches and directly confronts the place of the subject in legal knowledge, of eros in law.

First, and most obviously, psychoanalysis is a theory of meaning, and its history has been that of the development of techniques of attending to the signs of psyche and of eros, of the soul and of desire, in speech.[8] In relation to the predominantly scriptural tradition of modern law, its principal discovery has been that of providing a novel technique of textual interpretation, a radical hermeneutic that allows for symptomatic readings of the causes or motives of legal judgment. While legal realism had already observed the importance of personality to decision and of affectivity to judgment, postmodern jurisprudence has used psychoanalysis more systematically to read legal texts in symptomatic terms as expressions of what might be called the "work of

6. Julia Kristeva, *In the Beginning Was Love: Psychoanalysts and Faith* 35 (1987) ("Is psychoanalysis perhaps also our China Within?").

7. See Sherry Turkle, *Psychoanalytic Politics* (2d ed. 1993); *see also* Drucilla Cornell, "What Takes Place in the Dark," in Cornell, *Transformations* (1994). The most comprehensive history of post-Freudian psychoanalytic politics is to be found in Elizabeth Roudinesco, *Jacques Lacan and Co: A History of Psychoanalysis in France, 1925–1985* (1990).

8. For two very different but equally powerful analyses of this theme, see Julia Kristeva, *New Maladies of the Soul* ch. 1 (1995); Klaus Theweleit, *Object Choice: All You Need is Love* (1994).

legal culture."[9] The gaps, slips and other condensations of the text, of case law and judgment, are taken as expressions of a textual unconscious, of an unwritten history of legal affections and repressions as they motivate both judgment and law. The interpretation of individual biography as the cause of a subject's repetitions or patterns of behavior is replicated jurisprudentially through a genealogical analysis of legal texts.[10]

More than other disciplines, law has developed historically around figures of denial, prohibition, and interdiction. These suggest that the repetitions of precedent are not innocent, that they are analytically comparable to traumas, that they conceal as much as they reveal, that their presence is the sign of a repression or more simply of an absence.[11] In accounting for the work of law, psychoanalysis not only examines the lack or absence that motivates the text but equally charts the positive representation of desire within legal institutions. Although much of the affective content of law is expressed in indirect or abstract forms and is present primarily in the negative mode of denial, a second phase of psychoanalytic analysis seeks to reconstruct the positive imaginary or fantasmatic structure of law. The shift in the object of analysis can be characterized loosely as that from the professional persona to the cultural presence of law. The denial, distance, or unemotive and uncaring persona of the lawyer, the "withdrawn self" or narrow and emaciated mind,[12] is contrasted here to the cultural imaginary that attaches law to national identity and the subject to its paternity, its father the state. There is, in short, something that approaches a positive unconscious of law, a domain of attachment or of political desire in which

---

9. The expression is taken from Ganeth Obeyeskere, *Interpretation and Culture* (1990).

10. This genealogical approach to legal analysis is elaborated most expansively in the work of the French jurist and psychoanalyst Pierre Legendre. See particularly Pierre Legendre, *Leçons IV. L'Inestimable objet de la transmission. Etude sur le principe généalogique en Occident* (1985). For a critical introduction to this analysis, see Alain Pottage, "The Paternity of Law," in *Politics, Postmodernity and Critical Legal Studies* (Costas Douzinas et al. eds., 1994). Further commentaries on Legendre, and by Legendre, appear in this volume.

11. This theme is developed at length in Gilles Deleuze, *Difference and Repetition* (1994). For a legal analysis that makes use of the play of trauma and repetition, see William MacNeil, "Borderlines: Law/History," 5 *Law and Critique* 143 (1995).

12. See Peter Gabel, "The Phenomenology of Rights Consciousness and the Pact of Withdrawn Selves," 62 *Tex. L. Rev.* 1563 (1986). Pierre Legendre talks more succinctly of the "sophisticated imbecility of jurists," in *Paroles poétiques échappées du texte,* at 7 (1982).

images and other fantasmatic representations tie the subject and correlatively the polity to its destiny or fate. This "obscene 'nightly' law that necessarily accompanies, as its shadow, the 'public' law"[13] reflects both the paucity of the exterior law and the limits of law's reason. The rites and ceremonies of law, its architecture, art, and other public displays, its languages and its images, all combine to stage the fantasmatic power or figure of identification to which the subject of law adheres.[14]

While law may seem a surprising object of desire, its zone of safety no more than a theater of cruelty or asylum of loss, the recuperation of the positive imaginary of law, of the staging of power, is a necessary moment in the reexamination of the relation of law to the real. The objectivity of public law, in this account, can be understood as a more or less direct projection of the subjective laws of intimate or erotic association. We desire order, we love our country, we identify with the images or faces of authority in far more complex, ambivalent, and profound ways than law has hitherto imagined. Psychoanalysis provides one highly significant avenue of exploration of the desires that found the attachment of the subject to institution and to law. More than that, however, psychoanalysis disturbs legality by finding an active subjectivity within the logic of rules, by discovering an affectivity internal to normativity, a desire or delirium at the heart of legislation.

The focus of the present collection of essays upon desire as an inner law, upon love as an interior idiom of legality, represents a significant and at times surprising development of the psychoanalytic analysis of legality. Each contribution rests directly and at times elaborately upon the theme of eros in law.

In his essay "A Unique and Different Subject of Law," Alain Pottage, inspired by the work of Luce Irigaray, polemically tenders the promise of displacing a dead and static legal idiom with a creative and dynamic source of subject creation—one that honors sexual (and other) difference. The source is what Irigaray calls *admiration*—a relation that unifies the irreducible uniqueness of the other with the equally irreducible uniqueness of the self. If successful, the idiom of law might be transformed from something static and spiritless into the site of a genuine dialogue with the other, a space of desire and of becoming. In a

13. Slavoj Žižek, *Metastases of Enjoyment* 54 (1994).

14. For a dramatic analysis of the political uses of identificatory phantasms, see Renata Salecl, *The Spoils of Freedom* (1994).

future and fluid form, the science of law and the passive study of rules would be displaced by an art of justice and an idiom of passion.

A similar theory—one proffered in the work of Bernard Williams—is criticized by Henry Staten in his essay, "The Deconstruction of Kantian Ethics and the Question of Pleasure." According to Staten, Williams's new theory of ethical desire aligns Williams with Nietzsche and Aristotle in finding moral character to be inherited and imposed—a Law of the Father. The location of ethics in desire, however, simply replicates the ascetic ethics of Kant, Staten suggests. Nevertheless, pleasure is always the "arch-supplement" of ascetic ethics, "the noxious freebie (noxious to ascetic metaphysics, that is) that always turns up as the extra element added on" to ethical activity.

In "Why Does the Law Need an Obscene Supplement?" Slavoj Žižek suggests that identification of the legal subject with an ideology depends upon a spacing of the subject from the ideology, so that, in the end, distance from the ideology *is* the very essence of ideology—its condition of possibility. On this view, nothing is more subversive than the ideologue who follows the letter of the law in all its absurdity. The *unwritten rules* are the condition of possibility for any ideology. Law cannot survive and, in any event, cannot hope to achieve self-regulation.

Jeanne L. Schroeder, in "The Vestal and the Fasces: Property and the Feminine in Law and Psychoanalysis," describes the parallel between the Lacanian subject as lack and Hegel's concept of property in *The Philosophy of Right.* Both serve the logical function of radical other, which subjects "trade," and by their trades establish a community in which subjectivity can sustain itself. A key to this essay is to understand that Lacan abstracts gender from its biological context. Subjectivity is itself the feminine, which sacrifices itself on behalf of masculine community. In structural terms, the feminine is thus the space that makes property and the market possible. In a subtle elaboration of a Lacanian axiom, Schroeder proposes that woman is the negativity that sets both desire and subjectivity in motion, and in consequence to understand property in a critical manner is to analyze the structure of attachment to objects and the erotics of their exchange.

In "Love Me, Love My Dog," Renata Salecl discusses the case of Oleg Kulik, a Russian performance artist whose show consisted of having a dog kennel built in a gallery and then behaving like a dog and living in the kennel for the duration of the show. On two occasions, Kulik began biting visitors to the show. In a subtle and amusing Lacanian analysis of Kulik's performance, Salecl suggests that the desire to be a dog must fail because, like all desire, it is focused upon an impossible object. Kulik's performance is of no interest to animals—no dogs run to see the show—and the reason for this is precisely what distinguishes the animal from the human. Human desire is predicated upon a lack that cannot be filled. In attempting to portray a dog, Kulik's performance is of interest in its exemplification of the general structure of desire, namely, that only a human would or could wish to be a dog.

Michel Rosenfeld, like Schroeder, emphasizes the parallels of Lacan and Hegel in "The Identity of the Constitutional Subject." Also borrowing from Lacan and Hegel, Rosenfeld describes the creation of the legal subject as an exercise of negation, metaphor, and metonymy—a formulation that lawyers, upon reflection, will find very descriptive indeed of ordinary practice both in constitutional law and other fields. Rosenfeld concisely states his thesis:

> Negation is crucial to the extent that the constitutional subject can only emerge as distinct, through exclusion and renunciation. Metaphor or condensation, on the other hand, which proceeds by stressing similarities at the expense of differences, plays a key unifying role, in producing partial identities around which constitutional identity can revolve. Finally, metonymy or displacement, with its emphasis on continuity and context, is essential to guard against the constitutional subject fixating on identities that remain so condensed and abstract as to gloss over the differences that must be taken into consideration if constitutional identity is genuinely to encompass both self and other.

According to Rosenfeld, the subject is a discursive figure and so bound to the dialectic of its representation. A figure is proposed. Then it is negated. Then it exists as a dialectical structure that is a unity of the two previous stages. By this means the legal category of personhood is constructed.

Perhaps the most important task that we have set for ourselves in this volume is to introduce and celebrate the heretofore underappreciated worth of Pierre Legendre, the author of some twelve books on law and psychoanalysis. In pursuit of this task, we are pleased to present an essay by Legendre himself: "The Other Dimension of Law." This "other dimension" is

> that dimension which, by taking into account the biological and social elements of subjectivity, forces us to consider the function of the institution as a bond, which integrates the elements of subjectivity, the subject and its unconscious representations.

It is Legendre's argument that the legal construction of subjectivity, law's institution of life, is the key to understanding the historical and contemporary significance of the Western juridical tradition. The normative enterprise of legality can only be understood critically in terms of its essentially mythological fabrication of the human subject as a subject of law. The "other dimension" of law—what Legendre elsewhere refers to as the lawyer in the unconscious—is that of the symbolic construction of subjectivity and of the social institution of desire through which the individual comes to recognize the authority or paternity of the social and to identify with its images of power. It is psychoanalysis that allows us to trace the manner in which the subjects of law come to "love the censor" and to "desire the absolute."

Anton Schütz compares the work of Legendre with that of Saint Paul in "Sons of the Writ, Sons of Wrath: Pierre Legendre's Critique of Rational Law-Giving." In Schütz's account, Legendre's psychoanalytic approach to legal study is driven by an anti-imperialistic ethic. Thus, Western universalism is nothing but a Western particularism. The story of law is the story of institutions dispossessing individuals of their genealogy. These individuals are portrayed, in Pauline language, as "sons of wrath," i.e., of irrationality. In the theater of reason created by law, reborn individuals, newly manageable and governable under law's sovereignty, are promised free will but "at the price of a giant sell-out of individuality, and of individual difference." We are left with a question formulated by Joyce, namely, "who is the father of any son that any son should love him or he any son?"[15]

Peter Goodrich recalls, in "Translating Legendre, or the Poetical Sermon of a Contemporary Jurist," contributing an essay on Legendre to a prestigious English law journal, only to be accused of fabricating

15. James Joyce, *Ulysses* 257 (1965).

the very existence of the man and his work. Goodrich is able to salvage from this culturally charged experience the insight that, after all, these editors received the message of Legendre's work. Legendre's goal, according to Goodrich's account, is to place fiction at the very core of legal interpretation. By bringing forth fiction as the law's originary core, Legendre shows the fundamentally satiric structure that legal critique must have, if it is to enjoy some limited immunity from its own reflexive character.

We conclude this volume with two eminent essays critical of the Lacanian project for being insufficiently true to its premises. Drucilla Cornell, in her essay "Rethinking the Beyond of the Real," sides with the view that makes of Lacan a practitioner of classic logocentric metaphysics. On her reading of Lacanian theory, Lacan attempts to place subjectivity beyond the realm of the symbolic, but the attempt is a failure—a disguised exemplar of identity logic that suppresses *différance.* In Cornell's account of Lacan, the subject is as much a signifier as the signifiers to which it refers. Her criticism of Lacan therefore echoes Hegel's criticism of Kant, according to which the "thing-in-itself" is just as much a phenomenon as the phenomena against which it is supposed to stand. To be sure, Cornell sees that Lacan sees the impossibility of the project of "naming" the "Thing" without transforming the Thing. Nevertheless, Cornell complains, "The Real *appears* in Lacan; it is given form. It is the appearance of the Real, its identification with its representation as lack, that Lacan analyzes." The Real mandates a law, Cornell argues. The law should not be permitted to inscribe a domain for the Real.

Finally, Jacques Derrida contributes his personal and professional encounters with Jacques Lacan in "For the Love of Lacan." Derrida recalls speaking with Lacan in Baltimore, the City of Death and of Poe. There, Lacan speaks of the binding that will hold his *Ecrits* together—of how, within this binding, Lacan would be read after his death, and of whether the proposed binding of his works would hold. Derrida thus found Lacan obsessed with a reconstruction of psychoanalysis at a time when philosophy called for deconstructive questioning. Derrida also recalls Lacan's disinclination to be "with" a philosopher charged with such a questioning. Thus, following the conversation just described, Lacan is quoted as dismissing Derrida as someone who did not deal with "people who are suffering." Some years later, in an expurgated portion of a seminar transcript, Lacan attempts a joke at Derrida's expense by insinuating that Derrida was in the charge of an analysand—an unfair remark, but one perhaps revealing of who precisely Lacan was inclined to be with, if not with the philosophers.

Across all of the essays in this volume, psychoanalysis is used first to impel law toward an encounter with desire and latterly to trace what Alain Pottage poetically depicts as "[w]hat seems most unthinkable," namely, "the very notion of a liberating or fulfilling juridical personality." What is most crucially at issue in this formulation of affectivity in law is not simply the attempt to locate legal relations within the subjective realities of race, gender, or class. Across the entire range of intersections of eros and law, the issue is a more personal one. Psychoanalysis offers a technique, a practice, of analysis that refuses to tolerate the abstraction or denial that constitutes the dogmatic discourse of law in an exteriority for which the lawyer pretends to be unaccountable. In place of the distance or defense of the legal persona, psychoanalysis addresses the unthinkable, the repressed discourses, the desires, of the subjects of law, specific individuals, specific legal actors.

The uniqueness of desire does not preclude the generic significance of its representations but rather the opposite: the uniqueness of desire is the reality of its representation. The fantasms of law, the images by means of which lawyers think as lawyers and judges judge as sovereigns, are both singular and exemplary. What is novel in contemporary uses of psychoanalysis in law, and what can be traced most radically in the essays in the present volume, is a very personal honesty or murmur of authenticity. The essays discuss themes of friendship, sexual relation, desire, love, admiration, and other personal utopias. To locate such concerns in the real is to inscribe them both in social discourse and in the self; it is to represent the emotions that attach to institutional relations, and the subjectivity of their law. Thus, what Legendre has termed the capture of the subject by the institution does not eradicate the subjectivity or potential of institutional being, nor does it preclude the building of a life that transgresses the boundaries of institutional or legal norms. The focus of psychoanalysis upon relationship is in this sense a focus upon the spaces, the intensities, durations, and desires that exist in between institutional subjects, between and across the sexes, and in the diverse colors of the flesh. It is to these other spaces, this subjective time, of institutional being that the psychoanalytic elaboration of eros in legality attends.

*Chapter 1*

# A Unique and Different Subject of Law

*Alain Pottage*

Might an idiom of love be instituted in law? This question is posed by Luce Irigaray's ethics of sexual difference, which, in the guise of a critique of law, depicts the elements of a semantic or symbolic structure of a law that articulates an ethical relation of love—not love as *caritas* but love as *eros*. This implausible association of love and law seeks to institute an immediate and idiomatic relation within the axiopoietic order of law. Irigaray's *J'aime à toi* prescribes a set of basic rights that law—in its role as cultural tutor—might institute as the basic marker of a new model of sexuate subjectivity. The rights in question are described as civil rights—symbolic markers around which the fabric of a new, differentiated, subjective identity might be fashioned.[1] To redefine and rewrite rights on the basis of sexual difference would be not only to invent new symbols but also a new symbolism for law. Hence, it is not surprising that Irigaray should present this ostensibly "concrete" concern for law as a continuation of the project initiated by *Speculum: De l'autre femme*.[2] The demand for rights would be unintelligible or simply unremarkable were it not for the unique theoretical sensibility that it expresses and that is concerned to map out the possibility of beginning with something other than the formulas that currently measure the values of equality and difference. This essay develops the question of uniqueness and difference by manufacturing a conversation between Emmanuel Lévinas and Irigaray. The suggestion is that a careful reading of some aspects of the philosophy of Lévinas offers a particularly

1. Luce Irigaray, *Je, tu, nous: Pour une culture de la difference* 109 (1990).
2. *Id.* at 102.

productive way of uncovering the unique theoretical imagination that infuses the work of Irigaray.

Section I introduces the idea of a relation to others, characterized by a peculiar experience of surprise or a peculiar mode of apprehending the uniqueness of a neighbor. This relation—which for Lévinas is "obsession" whereas for Irigaray it connotes "*admiration*"—is the model of a style of ethics that is refractory to the all-encompassing principle of individuality prescribed by liberal or juridical models of ethics. In section II the relation of obsession is described more amply, with particular emphasis upon the manner in which it isolates the self as *soi-même,* fissioned by a responsibility that has no origin and that can never be discharged. Section III contrasts this model of an ethical countercurrent with Irigaray's model of *admiration* as the vehicle of a sort of chromatic fluidity: a relation of *eros* rather than *caritas.* This is followed in section IV by an account of the eroticism or *amor* that suffuses Lévinas's ethical model of maternity, in which an irredeemable debt to the flesh is converted into an unending responsibility. Sections V and VI return to Irigaray's scheme of color and attempt to convey a sense of the imagination that infuses Irigaray's references to the chromosomatic patrimony of a "natural" genealogy, suggesting that the apparent naïveté of Irigaray's reference to "nature" disguises a quite novel and distinctive philosophical sophistication. In section VII, this theme is developed through a discussion of Irigaray's account of the intrication of breath and communication, through which a utopian temporality of intersubjectivity is articulated. The final section describes how Irigaray weaves this model of recognition—as a "*toucher à*"—into a new symbolism of law, which would offer an alternative principle for the creation and cultivation of subjectivity.

## *I*

For Irigaray the quality of difference consists of an experience of negativity, one that was "unknown to Hegel."[3] The aim is to rediscover a negativity that is not wrapped in a dialectical movement, but that instead retains its ability to surprise.[4] *Surprise* here refers to an intrigue

3. Luce Irigaray, *J'aime à toi* 32 (1992) (my translation). At the time of publication, this text was unavailable in English translation. Translations of extracts from this book and of quotations from other original French texts are my own.

4. Emmanuel Lévinas, *Autrement qu'être ou au delà de l'essence* 59 (1974).

of otherness; the "extraordinary ambiguity of a relation ruptured by the difference between its terms, where this difference is not indifference, and where rupture connotes obsession,"[5] or, in the idiom of difference, *admiration.*[6] Each of these readings of the intrigue of otherness depicts an encounter that is utopian in the sense of being placeless: an encounter that can take place only in a "place" apprehended otherwise than according to the luminosity of geometry.[7]

Difference therefore connotes incomprehensibility: "*non-savoir qui n'est pas cependant absence de relation.*"[8] The encounter with an ethical neighbor is characterized as an experience of wonder or astonishment. It leaves both *ego* and *alter* unfettered by any grid of comprehension, and therefore unique. For Lévinas, this uniqueness is also experienced in the curious "pathos of liberalism."[9] In seeking to manufacture difference out of similarity, the business of conferring human rights gives rise to a strange paradox:

> [Human rights], because they do not depend upon any act of conferment, . . . express the alterity or absoluteness of each human being, the suspension of any *reference:* an extraction from the determining order of nature or the social, in which, for all other purposes each of us is quite obviously implicated; the alterity of that which is *unique* and incomparable, which is attributable to the suspension of each person in the human genre, which, *ipso facto and paradoxically,* abolishes itself so as to leave each human being *unique in his own genre.* An extraction or suspension—a freedom—which is not some form of abstraction, but which marks the absolute identity of the person as noninterchangeable, incomparable and unique. A uniqueness beyond the individuality of the individuals who belong to a genre. A uniqueness which is not due to any distinguishing mark which might make a specific or individuating difference.[10]

5. *Id.* at 133 (my translation).

6. *See* Luce Irigaray, "L'admiration," in *Éthique de la différence sexuelle* 75–84 (1984).

7. *See Autrement qu'être, supra* note 4, at 20–25.

8. Emmanuel Lévinas, *La Mort et le temps* 21 (1992). The vital question follows directly: "can this relation be described?"

9. Emmanuel Lévinas, *Totalité et infini* 125 (1991) (where the original French speaks of "*le pathétique du libéralisme*").

10. Emmanuel Lévinas, *Hors Sujet* 176 (1987) (my translation).

> It is as if a multiplicity of persons—might this not be the very meaning of the personal?—were the condition of plenitude or "absolute truth," as if each person, through their uniqueness, assured the veneration of a unique aspect of truth, and as if some of those aspects might never have been revealed had certain persons been missing from humanity.[11]

Read in this "Talmudic" or "hermeneutical" style,[12] the paradox of human rights hints at the beauty of a relation in which the logic of categories is suspended, leaving each person unique in the world. This uniqueness connotes surprise and wonder at the world, or a continuously interrogatory relation to things. The world is encountered as though it were irrepressibly spontaneous, as though every encounter was the first. It is therefore encountered through a temporal medium that is not measured "chronometrically," and that cannot be bound in the strands of a temporal flux. As such, the world is also the unquenchable source of a responsibility that can never be discharged because it is as infinite as this spontaneity is incessant. Uniqueness thus consists in a certain authenticity of accountability: the self is characterized as the sincerity of an ever-belated, and therefore infinite, effort to account for an uncontracted and unquantifiable debt.

Paradoxically, in this ethical scheme, to "belong" to the human race is also not to belong. Each individual is not simply the individuation of a concept or *genre.* This subscription to and yet subtraction from the *genre* is granted by the experience of encountering an absolute neighbor: an other who remains unthematized and unindividuated—unbound, either by concept or pronoun. Uniqueness arises from being with this neighbor in the manner of an encounter of *transascendence,*[13] an opposition that is also a peculiarly oblique or orthogonal a-position. The self encounters *autrui* in a moment of revelation that is neither the appropriational relation of knowledge (as a measure of adequacy or correspondence), nor a relation of desire (as a mimetic identification as a dual impulse of being and having). Lévinas's version of a "metaphys-

11. Emmanuel Lévinas, *L'au delà du Verset: Lectures et discours Talmudiques* 143 (1982) (my translation).

12. *See generally* Marc-Alain Ouaknin, *Concerto pour quatre Consonnes sans Voyelles: au-delà du principe d'identité* 207–10 (1991); Marc-Alain Ouaknin, *Méditations Érotiques: Essai sur Emmanuel Lévinas,* 144–68 (1992).

13. *Totalité et infini, supra* note 9, at 24.

ical" relation is one of absolute difference, an engagement with an Infinity that is radically aconceptual, exceeding as it does the *ideatum* of the idea we have of it.[14] This adventure of subjectivity suggests the possibility of "a nonadditive multiplicity of unique beings,"[15] or the utopia of a perpetually unfinished community of absolute neighbors.

Law, or the light that guides juridical techniques of comparison and judgment, all but stifles this possibility. Legal judgment gathers all its subjects into a single or synchronic horizon:

> With the comparison of incomparables there emerges the latent birth of re-presentation, *logos,* consciousness, work, and that neutral notion: being. All things are co-present, one can move from one to another, and from other to one, relating things, judging, knowing, and asking how or why things are as they are . . . ; one can transform matter . . . . Justice requires the contemporaneity of representation. A *Dire* is frozen as a *Dit,* is written with precision, and turns itself into a book, a law and a science.[16]

The individual appears in this neutral light only as *individuum*—the irreducible remainder of the division of a larger mass. This basic and indivisible unit is produced by an identical operation of individuation. The subjectivity dispensing machinery of culture stamps each coin with an identical mark, instituting multiplication without genuine multiplicity. The only otherness permitted is the difference in identity of *ego* and *alter.* Precisely because *alter* is another *ego,* another originary source of meaning or intention, he or she is said to be irreducible to the form that appears on *ego*'s map of the world; he or she remains genuinely *alter* to *ego.*[17]

---

14. *Id.* at 40–41, 123–24.

15. *Hors Sujet, supra* note 10, at 177 (my translation).

16. *Autrement qu'être, supra* note 4, at 247 (my translation).

17. Both Lévinas and Irigaray refuse to explore the productivity of this paradox. For a quite different view, see Jacques Derrida, *L'Écriture et la Différence* 117–228 (1967).

> If the other [written here as the *autrui,* or *alter huic,* a peculiarly nameless substantive] were a real moment of my egological life, if "the inclusion of another monad in mine" were real, I would perceive it *originaliter.* Husserl continually emphasises that this is an absolute impossibility. The other as alter ego is the other as other, as irreducible to *my* ego, precisely because it is ego, because it has the form of the ego.

This extension of "objective space" and "objective time" denies uniqueness. The unity of analogy replicates "a unity or community which drags us in, gathering us together as though we were galley slaves chained one to the other, constituting a proximity devoid of meaning. Any effort to undo this conjunction and conjuncture would be heard only as a creaking of chains."[18] However much it is emphasized that *alter* is unattainable as an originary source of experience, the light of judgment discerns only relations that are inscribed in the geometric grid that precedes them. The beauty of the world as incessant event is lost: subjectivity is indeed no adventure because "it is never dangerous. It becomes self-possession, sovereignty, *arche.* All unpredictable aspects of its experience are revealed in advance, made manifest, and accommodated to the shape of existing knowledge, and thereby rendered incapable of provoking absolute surprise."[19]

Participation in the logic of the same initiates a movement from the similar to the same, from *ipse* to *idem:*

> [T]o indicate a here and a now is to presuppose a reference to the *situation* in which, from outside, the movement of the index is identified. The identity of the individual does not consist in being similar to itself, but in being the same—in being its self, or in identifying itself from within.[20]

This specularity structures a curiously triangular relation with *alter*, a "strange symmetry in which I know myself to be the other of another."[21] This is an identification that is "simultaneously marked with the sign of hatred, a non-bond with the other, and the sign of the positive, peaceful bond with the other."[22] The subject sees itself from "outside," from the neutral or objective standpoint of the law or the concept, which gives rise to the triangulation structure of mimetic desire, according to which the other person is desirable only because he or she "has" more or less of whatever is valued according to a singular

*Id.* at 184 (my translation). This "transcendental symmetry between two empirical asymmetries" then yields the possibility of thinking the violence of homologation in other terms, as the originary violence that is also the possibility of ethics. *Id.*

18. *Autrement qu'être, supra* note 4, at 279 (my translation).

19. *Id.* at 157 (my translation).

20. *See Totalité et Infini, supra* note 9, at 14 (my translation).

21. *L'Écriture et la différence, supra* note 17, at 188 (my translation).

22. Mikkel Borch-Jacobsen, *The Freudian Subject* 222 (Catherine Porter trans., 1988).

law or economy of desire. This is a relation of jealousy, sustained by the impulse of a rival who wishes to be with the being-with enjoyed by the object with which he identifies: "*[ô]te-toi que je m'y mette.*"[23] This double bind, the unbinding bond of René Girard's fraternity of jealousy, supplies the formula of the jealous contract of liberal thought; the thought of a "social order mended by violence."[24]

Irigaray's critique of homologation develops some of these themes. Homologation is diagnosed as a violence of subjection, where subjection connotes both subjectification and subjugation. Homologation therefore preserves the reproduction of culture in the image of a masculine morphology—a morphology sculpted and sustained through techniques of identification and attachment that institute a self predicated upon the denigration of otherness; or, specifically, an otherness that has been attributed a feminine gender. The violence of subjection is therefore the denial of the possibility of a specific feminine *genre,* and hence of the possibility of a specific feminine culture.[25] Irigaray addresses those modes of attachment: the temporality or transitivity of the abstracted subject of law, or the modes of being and having that are implicit in the liberal scheme of rights and that define the interactions of subjects between themselves and with the world at large.

Against these processes of homologation or individuation, Lévinas and Irigaray offer utopian ethical schemes for the recovery or cultivation of an experience of uniqueness and difference—an experience of proximity that preserves the strangeness and wonder of the advent of otherness.

For Irigaray an ethical relation of sexual difference would "consist" in sustaining a question between subjects; the temporality that is proper to what we now know as law would, through the promulgation of sex specific rights, be undone by attributing to members of each sex the rights appropriate to them as members of *genres* defined by sexual difference.[26] These rights would not—and could not—be inscribed in any historically or sociologically conceivable form of law; accordingly, the project is "not just a matter of changing this or that aspect of a pre-

23. *Id.* at 45.

24. Gillian Rose, *The Broken Middle: Out of Our Ancient Society* 309 (1992).

25. Luce Irigaray, "L'amour de soi," in *Éthique de la différence sexuelle* 70 (1984) (my translation).

26. The feminine rights in question are rather minimally and cryptically defined: "a right to physical and moral inviolability"; the "right to choose whether to become a

defined horizon of human culture, but of the changing the horizon itself."[27] Without this change in the horizon of inscription and interpretation, rights written to secure sexual difference would inevitably erase themselves in the very movement of their inscription.

## *II*

Lévinas's model of obsession might be described as a relation to death, where the question of death is not so much the question of *la mort*—death in general—as a question of *le mort*—the death of a neighbor. It involves death as the scandal that leaves the survivor with an unbearable burden of guilt or responsibility. In other words, death is a "prototype" of what for Lévinas is a privileged relation: a relation that takes the form of a question, thereby showing "deference to the unknown."[28] Lévinas's motto of uniqueness in difference—which might be written as *l'accentuation de l'imprévisible*[29]—expresses the unremitting intensity of obsession: "obsession runs through consciousness in a countercurrent, registering itself as something alien: as imbalance, delirium, dethematization; as an escape from any principle, will, or *arche* produced in the light of consciousness."[30] The intrigue of alterity is thereby communicated as a primordial restlessness: a moment of rupture that jolts the philosophical subject from the stifling monotony of self-identity and that is figured in the experience of death as an experience of the absolutely other. The temporality of being toward death is redrawn as the inexorable approach of an always imminent threat of "absolute violence"; an event of violence that is not comprehensible within any spatiotemporal horizon of experience. The unthinkable (un)certainty of death, which eludes even the radical alternative of being or nothingness, places it "beyond" the beyond of any horizon of intentionality. Death springs from a time that is wholly other to the temporality of intentionality; it is unlike "all those moments of my life which are spread out between my birth and my death, and which can either be

mother"; "a right to . . . languages, religions, sciences, or arts [which would be] appropriate to a feminine identity"; and a right intended to safeguard the relationship between mothers and their children. *J'aime à toi, supra* note 3, at 205–6 (my translation).

27. *Id.* at 40 (my translation).

28. *La Mort et le temps, supra* note 8, at 43 (my translation).

29. For the basis of the motto "*l'accentuation de l'instant*" see *Hors Sujet, supra* note 10; for the theme of the *imprévisible,* see generally *Totalité et Infini, supra* note 9, at 111–200.

30. *Autrement qu'être, supra* note 4, at 159 (my translation).

recalled or anticipated."[31] This intentionality, which is predicated on the possibility of repeating or re-presenting a punctual present, necessarily projects a spatiotemporal extension that cannot in any sense comprehend or apprehend the event of death. The self as an intending self is faced with a future moment that will abolish the stance of protension within which that moment is anticipated; the very horizon within which such an event is supposed to be comprehensible will already have been abolished in and by that very event. This peculiar overlapping of noncommunicating temporal moments accounts for the implausible élan of an appetite for life, the *jouissance* that asserts itself because the adversary that opposes it is always infinitely postponed, being apprehended only in the mode of an indefeasible "not yet."

Death is depicted as the absolute adversary because it epitomizes the metaphysical version of war as an encounter of adversaries that cannot be resolved into an economy of finite forces or strategies. In war, the moves of one's adversary simply cannot be anticipated; each event of violence emerges from a point that cannot be plotted or predicted through any sectoring of time and space. Adversaries do not occupy mutually limiting zones of cartographic or chronometric space; between them, there is no line of demarcation, if by that one means a line registering the tension separating and uniting counterposed forces. In war, adversaries remain self-confident and self-sufficient, separated only by a sort of no-man's-land, an imperceptible, incomprehensible, and unbridgeable distance that expresses a paradox of disengagement within engagement. This no-man's-land is a place that simply does not belong in any form of dialectic or *différend;* it is a suspended moment of equivocation, the "between" of an encounter that has no "between." It is a line beyond which there is a "beyond" unrepresentable within any horizon of thought. "Beyond" it, there lies an adversary with whom one is engaged but whose strategies cannot be deciphered. This elusive figure of an interval that unceasingly sculpts itself, untrammelled by any predrawn geometry, describes the metaphysician's version of uniqueness in difference.

Uniqueness emerges from a movement of ever-accentuated solitude in the face of *autrui,* which, being infinite—ever-different, persistently and spontaneously other than what might be anticipated, never comprehensible—instills a constant restlessness in the *soi-même,* a rest-

31. *Totalité et Infini, supra* note 9, at 261 (my translation).

lessness that is experienced as inadequacy. Thus, the passion of proximity engenders a peculiarly solipsistic "ethical" experience. Obsession unceasingly fissures the *soi-même* as an "atomic" self: "a self with no rest in itself, because it is 'more and more one' [*de plus en plus un*]—to the point of explosion or fission."[32] Rather than a process of additive or sequential alteration, this demultiplication of the *un* is a movement elicited in the *soi-même*'s witnessing of the absolute infinity of *autrui,* which as *infini* is neither a version of Hegel's false infinity nor a figure of "positive infinity."[33] Infinity is not presented as the sublation of finitude, but rather as a moment that, as with the movement of being toward death, recedes unceasingly even as it inexorably approaches: "the Other does not become an Other similarly; the end is not born again, but, with each stage of its approach, becomes more and more distant."[34]

## *III*

Irigaray's sense of surprise is described as a rereading of *admiration,* Descartes's *passion première.*[35] For Irigaray *admiration* describes the impulse of an intentionality that encounters the world as a renewed

32. *Autrement qu'être, supra* note 4, at 169 (my translation).

33. This would imply an ever-receding idea.

34. *Autrement qu'être, supra* note 4, at 149 n.1 (my translation).

35. "When we are surprised by our first encounter with some object, and when we consider it to be novel, or very different from what we knew beforehand, or from what we supposed that it ought to have been, we come to wonder at it [*nous l'admirons*] and to be surprised by it; and because this can happen before we have any knowledge as to whether this object is agreeable to us or not, it seems to me that wonder [*l'admiration*] is the first of all passions, and that it has no opposite, because, if the object which appears has in itself nothing which surprises us, we are not at all moved by it, and we consider it without passion." *L'admiration, supra* note 6, at 20, *quoting* René Descartes, *Passions de l'âme* art. 53, *reprinted in* 1 René Descartes, *The Philosophical Work of Descartes* 358 (Elizabeth S. Haldane and G. R. T. Ross trans., 1978) (my translation). Although "wonder" is by now the standard translation of Descartes's *admiration,* I have chosen here to retain the original French; the word *admiration* has the virtue of avoiding the banality of the common use of "wonder" as a "wondering about" something, which describes nothing other than an experience of speculation which takes place within a conventional horizon of intentionality. Equally, it may be that "wonder" as an encounter with something "wondrous" connotes *émerveillement* rather than *admiration,* and so approaches what for Descartes is *étonnement*—astonishment—the speechlessness that overtakes apprehension through a paradoxically immediate category, an apprehension through or of which one can say nothing.

"advent or event of the other" [*l'avènement ou l'événement de l'autre*].[36] *Admiration* describes a "temporality" of spontaneity, which shares with the mode of obsession the experience of an unceasing *accentuation de l'instant;*[37] as does obsession, *admiration* meets the approach of the encountered object as a source that "burns without consuming itself,"[38] the source of a continually renewed experience of surprise. However, where obsession is utter passivity, transfixed by the unflinching and unremitting demand of the other, *admiration* takes more lightly to heart the injunction that "it is forbidden to be old."[39] If being "old" in this context means being deaf to the question asked by the one's ethical neighbor, this injunction is not, in *admiration,* taken to prescribe submission to the command of the other. Rather, it is the command to live not in passivity but in passion, to cultivate the fecundity of difference, and to discover in proximity a passion for life as living rather than mere survival ("*survivre = vivre plus, et non vivoter*").[40]

*Admiration* is an essentially shared passion:

> Our tradition usually restricts the sphere of sensibility to that of the solitary subject. It does not recognize the fact that sensibility is often shared between two subjects. And, where this dimension is taken into account, it is treated in the mode of passivity–activity, agent–object, a mode which does not begin to address the interaction of *two* free subjects. Hence the paradox of a thought within which passions remain solitary.[41]

The energies that are conveyed, exchanged, and produced in this encounter are neither entirely psychic nor entirely somatic. Descartes's text offers a palimpsest that is scratched and scraped so as to fashion a private frame of reference not unreflectively indebted to the conven-

36. "L'admiration," *supra* note 6, at 77 (my translation) (advent—*avènement* rather than *avenir*—because *admiration* is an impulse animated by interrogation rather than anticipation; event—*événement*—because it is an experience of moments that are unique, irreplaceable, and irreversible, which are not memorizable in the trace of a temporal flux).

37. *See Hors Sujet, supra* note 10, at 21; *Totalité et Infini, supra* note 9, at 65 ("*d'une reprise* incessante *des instants*").

38. *Totalité et Infini, supra* note 9, at 243 (my translation).

39. Referring to the Hassidic formula. *Cf. Autrement qu'être, supra* note 4, at 86–90 (on the question of senescence).

40. For this untranslatable rendition of Nietzsche, see Luce Irigaray, "L'amour de l'autre," *in Éthique de la différence sexuelle* 136 (1984)

41. *J'aime à toi, supra* note 3, at 68 (my translation).

tional psychoanalytical vocabulary of desire, instinct, or drive. Rather, it serves as the medium of another return to Freud, or a return to a problem of the body that was so elegantly sublimated by Lacan but that is more immediately and disruptively present in Freud's "hydraulic" metapsychology.[42] This reference to the passions of the soul therefore tempers the insights of psychoanalytic theory with the imagery of a long tradition of speculation on the nature of the passions—the indeterminate vapors that were held to suffuse the world with the colors of the flesh. The point is to produce a semantic depth of field that would allow the ethics of sexual difference to recover some sense of what persists as "the flesh of our passions."[43]

The passion of *admiration* is "at once active and passive:"[44] although the passions are excited or drawn forth by correlative actions, each passion is itself active, being a movement toward "all that which occurs or that happens anew."[45] In Irigaray's appropriation of this scheme the separation of "agent" and "recipient" that for Descartes marks each side of an indissoluble unity of action and passion[46] is liquefied. The receptive activity of passion in its "movement toward" becomes the action that excites or draws forth a corresponding passion, so that the scheme of simple opposition is fashioned as an incessant flux of *admiration.* The insurmountable difference and inexhaustible novelty of sexual difference thereby generates and sustains a continuously reflexive passion. It is no longer possible to impose temporal or logical priorities: the impulse of *admiration* is somehow "no longer in the past and not yet in the future."[47]

The attempt to color the media of intersubjective communication with the textures of the body (or to otherwise mobilize the body)

---

42. Indeed, in retrospect, Descartes might be said to have anticipated the scheme of Freud's "mystic writing pad." *Admiration* as an effect of surprise is the experience of an event that is unrecognizable because it finds no receptive traces upon the surface of the brain. This topography of memory as the condition of repetition and receptivity is echoed by Freud's model of the economy of resistance and receptivity that structures the neuronal grids that are the surface of memory. *See* 19 Sigmund Freud, "The Ego and the Id," *in The Standard Edition of the Collected Psychological Works,* 226–32 (James Strachey ed., 1961). *Cf. L'Écriture et la différence, supra* note 17, at 293.

43. Luce Irigaray, *Sexes et parentés* 69 (1985).

44. "L'admiration," *supra* note 6, at 76 (my translation).

45. Descartes, *supra* note 35, at 331 (Article I).

46. *Id.* ("the action and the passion are always one and the same thing") (my translation).

47. *Id.* at 77.

involves an attempt to represent the sensuous dimension of the body in terms other than those exemplified by Descartes's account of the passions:

> For Descartes, the surface upon which [*admiration*] is registered is to be found only in the brain. It is an effect of surprise, the suddenness of the impact of rare and extraordinary objects which register themselves in some untouched part of the brain. A part which is still tender, not yet hardened by the impact of past impressions, which are often stirred up, and which processes of repetition have rendered incapable of being further affected or impressed. . . . [*Admiration*] is not, then, supposed to be a modification of the heart or the blood. . . . It is supposed to remain a pure cerebral inscription, purely a matter of knowledge. . . . It is an appetite for knowing who or what awakens our appetite.[48]

Irigaray attempts to exchange the equivocation or ambiguity that structures Descartes's reading for a more liquid and mobile scheme of apprehension. For Descartes, the dimension of passion is the vector or axis along which the relation between body and soul is negotiated, and along which one might mark an interval between activity and passivity, soul and body, or body and environment. In this scheme of oppositions, priority is accorded to the soul; yet the membrane between soul and body is extraordinarily permeable. The soul itself occupies no place other than the body; it is coextensive with, but not localizable in, the physical body. It is in some sense a libidinal idea of the body, the medium of representation being the dimension of the passions that somehow equivocate between body and soul.[49] For example, Descartes marks the boundary between soul and body as the point of a change in physical substance. The body, which is self-sufficiently fuelled by "the heat of the heart"[50] meets the soul at the point where the most "subtle" and "agitated" qualities of the blood vaporize,[51] generating the "animal spirits" that sustain the passions. Here, the equivocation between body

48. "L'admiration," *supra* note 6, at 79–80.

49. So, for example, the passions are said to be irresistible; and yet the specific responses or reflexes that are motivated by passion can be learned and unlearned through force of will.

50. Descartes, *supra* note 35, at 334 (Article VIII).

51. *Id.* at 335 (Article X)

and soul condenses into the innominate fluid dimension that is according to Irigaray the fabric of subjective identity.

Irigaray's rereading of Descartes diverges from the latter in valorizing *admiration* as a relation that continually rememorizes the flesh. The flesh is resistant to any sort of memorization or temporalization; the flesh retains no imprint, but subsists as a source of innocence and enthusiasm, the spontaneity and fluidity of natural energies. In and by the same movement as it respects the spontaneity of the "objects" that it approaches, *admiration* leaves the energies that it conveys unfettered and unspecified in their becoming. *Admiration* is a modality of desire in which desire is not yet a directional or repetitive impulse; it is, rather, the latent impulse of a desire that is not dedicated to the movement of a *Trieb* or *pulsion*. This culture of the spontaneity of the flesh, or of capacities that are idiomatically "archived" in the flesh, implies the cultivation of psychic and corporeal energies, knitting the rhythms of one into those of the other, creating a life that is always open to the novelty of an event [*vie toujours offerte à l'événement*].[52]

The flux of *admiration* sketches a sublimation of the flesh that is implausibly faithful to the body. In those terms, the bodily aesthetic of Greek antiquity, as it is described in the project of a proper *usage des plaisirs*, appears to be a denial of the body.[53] In the relation of *enkrateia*, the body was that which was most deeply private, the source of needs and desires that would, if unmastered, threaten to enslave the person. Moreover, one who had not transcended the demands of private desire and whose relations with others would be modeled by this enslavement to the forces of the body would be unfit to govern others. This stylization of the self was a relation within a relation; the exercise of a power over oneself that unfolded within the power that one exercised over others[54] or, more generally, a relation to oneself constituted within one's relation to others or to external forces.[55] This aesthetic or ascetic stylization of the self is no more a fulfillment of *admiration* than the exercise of sculpting or styling "another" body so as to stage and cho-

52. Luce Irigaray, "Fécondité de la caresse," in *Éthique de la Différence Sexuelle* 174 (1984).

53. From a nonutopian perspective things seem very different; the scheme of Michel Foucault, *L'Usage des Plaisirs* (1984) assumes the inscription in history of any project of rememorization of the self and is therefore committed to history and sociology in a style that Irigaray cannot follow.

54. *See id.* at 205–48 (chapter 4).

55. *See generally* Gilles Deleuze, *Foucault* 55–130 (1986).

reograph the enigmatic double of body and soul—a maneuver exemplified in the role of dance as a movement fashioned in the image of the soul, a passion or performance in which the profane body is made a sublime soul.[56]

Against these modes of transcending the body, the ethics of sexual difference cultivates a modality of the caress. This caress is inspired and deciphered by the tactility of *admiration.* It is an uncovering that is not a discovering; neither a charting of the unknown nor a memorization of the successive moments of the trajectory of the caress. Rather, it is an evanescent touch that traces no trajectory in memory and leaves no train of impressions behind it, but is inscribed and effaced in the same moment and movement, encountering and awakening an experience of continuous alteration. Temporality and memory are suspended without any equivocation between passivity and activity or between recall and anticipation, yielding an idiomatic experience:

> [A] vertiginous experience of losing one's footing, to such an extent that one is immersed in something that has as yet no proper form, an experience of returning to the deepest depths of an elemental flux in which the event of birth has not yet been sealed in an identity. Any subjectivity would lose its mastery and its method in this experience.[57]

This describes a joint rememorization of the flesh, the unfurling of an experience of "*eros* before any *eros* which is defined or framed as such."[58] The touch of an other summons this incessant and imperfect refashioning of the flesh, sustaining an intrigue in which the admirer respects and cultivates the mystery of his or her other. The passion and intentionality of *admiration* is this dissolute stance of wonder and surprise. It is simultaneously a bonding and an unbinding, issuing an invitation to the other to be ever-otherwise and to become through *admira-*

56. *See generally* Pierre Legendre, *La Passion d'être un autre: Étude pour la danse* (1978).

57. "Fécondité de la caresse," *supra* note 52, at 176. The very intensity of this encounter might identify it as a preference for a heterosexually ethical relation, in which the genealogy of gender serves to deconstruct and rematerialize a heterosexual difference. *Cf. J'aime à toi, supra* note 3, at 82 ("The relation between man and woman is paradigmatic, it is the groundless ground of communication: a space which is at once generative and creative, natural and spiritual, passive and active" [my translation]).

58. "Fécondité de la caresse," *supra* note 52, at 173.

tion a *visage sans habitudes,* "allowing oneself to be seen so as to be reborn beyond that which has already been."[59]

## *IV*

How do these valorizations of difference diverge? The divergence might be represented as a difference between fluidity and equivocation. For Lévinas, the beauty of revelation is experienced as a rupture of synchronic order of the *Dit;* the ethical relation is experienced only as disruption or countercurrent. This equivocation consists in a peculiar enjoyment of the femininity of phenomena, an appreciation of the impossible simultaneity of light and dark or activity and passivity.

For Lévinas, the ethical relation of uniqueness in difference, the ethical self (the *un*) is realized as an undoing; undone in the sense of being absolved from the bonds of a relation occupying the predefined coordinates of space.[60] There are many forms of this undoing. Ethically, it is felt in an experience of temporal sympathy that springs from beneath the temporality of the codes that make communication possible. Existentially, it is a moment of revelation, the moment of hope or astonishment in which a ray from a utopian future penetrates the obscurity of subjectivity. This experience of revelation might be felt in "the way in which a leaf stirs in the breeze, in the beauty of a melody, the face of a young girl, a child's smile, or in a single word."[61] In each case, what is experienced is a basic experience of equivocation—an experience of the otherwise-than-temporality of obsession or proximity—which is "a disruption of memorizable time" [*dérangement du temps remémorable*],[62] a moment that is recoverable neither as "time's other" (which might, perhaps, be the "eternity" that makes time possible) nor as memorized or anticipated history. Obsession is engendered in a passivity that consists in—or, rather, is undone in—a moment that is before any beginning, and therefore before any chosen engagement in the activity of re-presenting the world as a memorizable order. In

59. *Id.* at 178 (my translation).

60. Though not undone in the sense in which something which was previously self-identical might be undone; rather it is the interminable undoing of a self which was always-already-undone, whose offering of its self to an absolute neighbor is neither gift nor renunciation, springing as it does from a moment anterior to any horizon of action or choice.

61. *La Mort et le temps, supra* note 8, at 117.

62. *Autrement qu'être, supra* note 4, at 142.

obsession, the *soi-même* is passive, obedient to a command that permits no work of understanding, in which being unique is not a labor of action, but a matter of being solely and uniquely accountable for the wrongs of the world: a hostage whose uniqueness consists in being the sole focus of the world's persecution. In this relation, the self "ruptures under a weight of years, and irreversibly tears itself from the present as re-presentation."[63] The deepening of anxiety in the ethics of Lévinas is thought of as the excavation of an interval, which is not a mediating third, between two moments.

For Lévinas, the original equivocation[64] represented by the incarnated subject is eroticized as a relation to a world that is obliquely or equivocally framed, leaving the subject suspended between engagement and abandon, enjoying transgression without peril. This erotic framing of the world amounts to another form of misrecognition; the equivocation or oscillation that passes over the no-man's land renders that void habitable. The diagnosis of *essence* more directly recognizes the void only so as better to overlook it; the irruption of the an-archic and incarnated is recovered as a formal ethical experience. This "otherwise than being" does indeed risk being nothing other than than a "being otherwise."[65]

The movement of eroticization originates in the bipolarity of activity and passivity that characterizes the "autochthonous" self; a self that is "grounded in that which it is not, and which, despite and because of this grounding, is independent and separate."[66] This essential equivocation of the autochthonous self is reproduced as a paradoxical veiling–unveiling of the world, a "flickering" or "alternation" of meaning [*clignotement de sens*],[67] or an erotic oscillation between disclosure in light and nocturnal concealment. This prescribes the phenomenology of the caress, a movement that uncovers the world obliquely, an ambiguous touch that is as much a releasing as it is a grasping:

> Voluptuousness, as profanation, uncovers the hidden as hidden. This conjunction accomplishes an exceptional relation, which according to formal logic could only be contradictory. That which

63. *Id.* at 88 (my translation).

64. *Totalité et Infini, supra* note 9, at 177.

65. *See generally L'Écriture et la Différence, supra* note 17, at 117–228.

66. *Totalité et Infini, supra* note 9, at 152 (my translation).

67. *Autrement qu'être, supra* note 4, at 238.

> is uncovered does not lose its mystery through being uncovered, that which is hidden is not revealed, the night is not dispersed.[68]

> The caress reaches beyond consensus or willing agreement, towards that which is not yet, that which is less than nothing, which lies enclosed and dormant beyond the future and, consequently, dormant otherwise than as possibility which might be given to anticipation. The profanation which is insinuated into the caress is in tune with the originality of this dimension of absence.[69]

The "response" of the caress produces and uncovers the world, not as a domain deployed according to the temporality or luminosity of intelligible appearing, but as that which is ever-mysterious, beyond apprehension or thematization. The touch of the caress encounters things as a single surface, behind which there are no other sides that could be recovered in successive profiles; there is only the unfathomable depth of the "element"[70] from which the things are detached by touch as an instance of "*le fini sans infini*."[71] This describes "the fact of originating nowhere, in 'something' that is not, of an appearance in which nothing appears, and, therefore, the fact of always originating, without my being able to possess its source."[72]

The phenomenology of the caress is not, therefore, one that would progressively "zero in" on its object, nor is the infinity of its trajectory that of an ever-tightening, but never quite closed, temporal knot. The caress lacks the guiding idea of an object that, even as it recedes in a movement of positive infinity, is represented as something to be reached toward. The equivocation of the caress—a holding that is also a releasing—encounters the object as unpredictably lost in the depth or "nocturnal extension"[73] of the elements. The resulting inability of a temporal horizon to enclose or encircle an object, even through protension, means that things are never simply hidden from light. The disjunction or discontinuity "between" light and dark cannot be spread

68. *Totalité et Infini*, *supra* note 9, at 291 (my translation); *see also id.* at 192 (referring to Freud's account of dream work).

69. *Id.* at 288 (my translation).

70. *See generally id.*

71. *Id.* at 143.

72. *Id.* at 150 (my translation) (where the quality is described in the original French as that of "*venir de nulle part, . . . et par conséquent, de* venir toujours").

73. *Id.* at 151.

out as a sequence of monochromatic gradations; it cannot be described as though things were more or less clear, as though darkness were simply the absence of light, or as though things that are obscure are simply things that are not yet illuminated. Rather, light and dark are peculiarly simultaneous or equiprimordial.

The movement of the caress is not the grasp of the *main-tenant*,[74] or the hold of the eternal present; the caress is not the action of reaching toward practical theoretical possibilities.[75] The equivocal trajectory of the caress defines the response or experience of the subject, which in unfolding this flickering framing of the world remains as unformed and seductive as the clandestine world it unveils. An experience of the world as something inexhaustibly alien supports an oscillating movement in which the self is erotically other to itself—or, an experience in which the self is always poised as a yet-to-be. This oscillation of disengagement within engagement constructs a peculiarly oblique being with the world, an unfamiliarity that is enjoyed as such, in which the subject is never exposed to the risk or terror of a no-man's-land, but remains always in a condition of transition or transgression. This eroticization of the world—a framing that never quite encloses what it represents[76]—renders the void bearable and even enjoyable by offering a vision that attributes a transparent clothing to the world "so as not to see that it cannot see everything."[77]

## *V*

This scheme of ethical eroticization and equivocation offers another facet of the infinite inadequacy of the subject. This inadequacy is thematized by Lévinas as the absence of any authorship or origin of the self, and is therefore depicted as a constant spiraling return to an 'origin' that cannot be recovered as such. The experience of the *soi-même* is sustained by the absolute memory of an origin that is satisfied by inverting the order of things so as to make oneself the origin of things,

74. *Méditations Érotiques, supra* note 12, at 45; *Concerto pour Quatre Consonnes sans Voyelles, supra* note 12, at 28.

75. *Totalité et Infini, supra* note 9, at 290.

76. There may be more to be said about the resemblances between this framing of the world and the obliqueness of the "looking awry" which describes this erotic misrecognition in psychoanalytical terms. *Cf.* Slavoj Žižek, *Looking Awry: An Introduction to Jacques Lacan Through Popular Culture* (1991).

77. "Fécondité de la caresse," *supra* note 52, at 176 (my translation).

"mother" to a world for which one is thereby rendered infinitely responsible. For Irigaray, in contrast, this valorization of maternity would be seen as the effective denial of the maternity of the flesh. This debt to the flesh haunts the attempt to find an origin within the articulation of thought and accompanies every gesture of thought. The truly "ethical" response is not to unravel thought by reversing or inverting the phantasm of origin, but by undoing the phantasm altogether; by beginning, that is, to acknowledge the corporeality of thought and the debt owed to the maternity of the corporeal-carnal.

The recourse to the metaphor of maternity in expressing the condition of the *soi-même* captured in an intrigue of proximity could scarcely be innocent. For Lévinas, "maternity" describes the condition of the subject as *sub-jectum,* bearing the weight of a world for which it is uniquely responsible: "Responsibility for others is signified in maternity—to the extent of a substitution for others or to the extent of suffering both from the effects of persecution and from the persecution in which the persecutor is made destitute."[78] Responsibility as an ethical, presocial relation of obsession is an inverted bond of maternity, prescribing "the gestation of the other in the self."[79] To assume these burdens of maternity is to unravel oneself in an unceasing movement of extrusion, constantly offering yet more of a self that one has never possessed, tearing bread from one's own mouth to give to the other.

In this relation, activity and passivity are composed otherwise. The movement of the Möbius band closes, unraveling in an inverse movement; whereas the movement of *auto-affection* twists exposure into closure, gathering in passivity as a moment or product of activity. The intrigue of obsession knits activity and passivity together, seeking to construct the impossible movement of undoing in which the *soi-même* exposes itself more and more while remaining one: closure twisted into exposure. The seamless centripetal movement of the Möbius becomes a centrifugal trajectory that nonetheless returns just as surely to its starting point—or rather to a moment before its starting point:

> [T]he recursivity of the self [*la récurrence à soi*] cannot describe a return to the self, but a return to a point before the self, a return to a point before which occurs *within* a movement of recursivity to

78. *Autrement qu'être, supra* note 4, at 121 (my translation).

79. *Id.* at 167 (my translation).

> self. A does not return to A [*ne revient pas à A*] as in a relation of identity, but retreats to a point before its starting point.[80]

The self is locked into a constant movement of undoing, which is not an action or intention because it is not the undoing of what was once self-identical, but rather a process of constant displacement to a point before any beginning, or a point that because it infinitely regresses, cannot be recollected as a beginning. The *soi-même* is always and already exiled from itself.[81] The utter passivity of the subject of obsession is simply this movement of accounting for a debt that is exacted by a command heard only in the act of executing it. The *soi-même* is a being that is unique in its ability to sustain the authenticity of accountability through its ability to contain more than it can hold.

Thus the figure of maternity stands for the devotion that is implicit in the experience of being uniquely responsible for the world, held hostage to the sins of the world. It is a devotion that turns an indefensible or unboundable local space into an incomplete totality. The ethics of proximity is a more richly aestheticized version of nostalgia. It more closely and yet more blindly retraces the contours of the imprint left by absolute memory, more directly revealing and yet remaining within a boundary that is drawn by and within thought. This ethical or aesthetic appropriation of a role of maternity is a moment of sacrificial identification with an ineradicable symptom; the anxiety of thought's repeated boundary is relived and explored through a sacrificial identification with the mother, an identification with maternity that is made so as both to repeat and deny it. In thus recovering anxiety as an ethics of proximity, Lévinas more acutely remembers the moment of maternity (the better to forget it). The work of remembering reaches the memory of an unchosen birth [*naissance non-choisie*]—an unmemorizable and unthematizable debt that precedes and undoes any active authorship of life. This authorship is problematic, requiring one "to be author of something which, unknown to me, has been breathed into me—to have received that which I have authored from an unknown source" [*être auteur de ce qui m'avait été* à mon insu *insufflé—avoir reçu, on ne sait d'où, ce dont je suis*

80. *Id.* at 180 (my translation) (where "*revenir à*" connotes both "returning to" and "amounting to").

81. There is in this no memory of original unity.

*l'auteur*].[82] And yet this anarchic moment is recovered only to be represented in the model of a "second" or "latent" birth:

> [Proximity] is the latent birth of the subject. A birth which is latent because it is before any origin, before any initiative, before any present which could be designated or undertaken, even through memory; an anachronistic birth, anterior to its own present, a non-beginning, anarchy; a birth which is latent and never present, which excludes the present of self-identity because it is *in contact,* within sensibility, within vulnerability, exposed to the other's offence.[83]

The absolute memory of the flesh can no more be recovered or rememorized in the ethics of obsession than it can in *auto-affection.*

This ethics of maternity is accompanied by another denial of the feminine. The equivocation described in section IV describes the ground of equivocation as a ground veiled in a feminine tenderness—a diaphanous and yet opaque veil spread across the otherwise terrifying things of the world.[84] This veiling and unveiling through the agency of a feminine principle leaves the instance of the feminine as "the possibility of seduction, the wondrous irruption into human life of an irreducible alterity, which might take the form of a gesture, a face, a word, an object, or a prophetic dream."[85] This valorization of the feminine as the source of "*une défaillance délicieuse dans l'être*"[86] denigrates the "natural" otherness of the feminine. It yields an eroticism that reduces the *amante* to an *aimée:*

> The *aimée* is introduced into a world which is not hers, allowing the *amant* to dally, gathering his strength for a journey towards autistic transcendence. Dispensing him, in his quest for an already written but still mute God, from the task of realising the ethical locus of the act of love? A seducer, seduced by the solemnity of the other [*la gravité de l'Autre*], only carelessly addressing the feminine other.

82. *Autrement qu'être, supra* note 4, at 232 (my translation).
83. *Id.* at 218–19 (my translation).
84. *Totalité et Infini, supra* note 9, at 289.
85. *Méditations Érotiques, supra* note 12, at 22 (my translation).
86. *Totalité et Infini, supra* note 9, at 166.

> Stealing her light so as to illuminate his own path, showing no respect for what shines resplendently between him and her.[87]

This overlooking of sexual difference, or corporeo-carnal difference, denies what would otherwise be recognized: that the body as a whole exists as *visage*—or as the advent of "a *morphé* in continuous gestation, whose movements unceasingly remodel its incarnation"[88]—and that body and flesh are sculpted in the encounter of *admiration.*

The love of the absolute neighbor is itself purely ethical or intelligible, an encounter with another who remains disincarnated. Despite the observation—made contra Heidegger—that Dasein never goes hungry,[89] and despite the insistence that the *soi-même* is "skin and face, a skin which is always the alteration of a face, a face which is burdened with skin,"[90] the body simply becomes the medium of that erotic equivocation. The *visage* itself is not of this world, and certainly not of the world of corporeo-carnal existence. The absolute neighbor is projected as the *très-haut* where the prefixed superlative indicates the projection of the *visage* beyond even an equivocal engagement with the world in which one is incarnated.[91] This leaves the ethics of proximity as a relation that, although claimed to be prenatural, and therefore precedent to our engagement with things,[92] is in fact the return of the natural through the morphological imprint left on the flesh by absolute memory. This reproduces a relation of "love as perpetual tragedy, dismal charity, or acquisitive devotion; a form of *agape* without *eros.*"[93] This relation is forgetful of incarnation. It represents a God who can be reached only through spiritual supplication and who could never be imagined as "tactile pleasure," as that which "envelops, surrounds, and cradles," loving "carnally and erotically."[94] This results in an ethics that only obliquely recognizes the debt that it strains to acknowledge; it "recognizes only the wrongs which it openly produces. It turns on itself,

87. "Fécondité de la caresse," *supra* note 52, at 193.
88. *Id.* at 176 (my translation).
89. *Totalité et Infini, supra* note 9, at 142 (*"Le Dasein chez Heidegger n'a jamais faim"*).
90. *Autrement qu'être, supra* note 4, at 135 (my translation).
91. *See generally Totalité et Infini, supra* note 9, at 203.
92. *Id.* at 161.
93. "L'amour de soi," *supra* note 25, at 70 (my translation, text modified slightly).
94. *Id.* at 153 (my translation).

within itself, in ignorance of its hidden wrongs or the invisibility of the wrong it commits."[95]

## *VI*

As distinct from this relation of equivocation and obsession, the relation of *admiration* articulates a fluid process of natural and cultural creation. This fluidity connotes a dissolution of the distinctions, gradations, and tensions that are sublimated in the ethical maternity of the *soi-même.* The culture of nature fashioned by the relation of *admiration* is represented as the foundation of an alternative principle of subjective authorship: "[m]ost societies, at least those which are composed of relations between men, organize themselves against nature, despite nature, by sacrificing nature by not remaining rooted within it so as to cultivate it."[96]

Irigaray's depiction of a dimension of chromatic fluidity begins with a critique of the process of continuity that masculine thought attempts to recreate through the articulation of conceptual distinctions. Her critique addresses the model of *auto-affection* that serves to sculpt and sustain the morphology of the masculine subject. *Auto-affection* is a process of self-definition realized in a movement that turns activity and passivity into continuity. This aspiration is well expressed in the model of the Möbius strip or, more specifically, Lacan's presentation of that peculiar topographical paradox as an *esthétique transcendentale.*[97] In this topographical model, *recto* and *verso* of the strip communicate seamlessly across a unilateral surface; *verso* is assumed or subsumed into the movement by which *recto* is retraced. In other words, there are two sides to a Möbius strip, distinguished by a difference that is realized only temporally: two cycles will return one to the point at which one started; a single cycle leaves one on the "other" side. This temporal difference within the continuity of a single spatial extension deploys the structure of the re-presented present: the oscillation of time as it repeats itself backward; the self-temporalization of monotonous being; the repetition of—and yet difference within—an "eternal" present.

95. Luce Irigaray, *Questions à Emmanuel Lévinas* 914–15 (1990) (my translation).

96. Luce Irigaray, *Egales à qui?* 436 (1987) (my translation).

97. A useful account of this is to be found in Jeanne Granon-Lafont, *La Topologie ordinaire de Jacques Lacan* (1988); it may be that my own extrapolations of Lacan's topology risk taking Lacan's prescription—*il faut en user bêtement*—rather too straightforwardly.

The morphology of this movement is expressed in the gesture of *auto-affection* with which the masculine subject attempts to construct a conceptual dwelling for itself. Irigaray's model of *auto-affection* develops, from a psychoanalytical perspective, an earlier philosophical model of self-definition:[98]

> The operation of hearing oneself speak [*s'entendre-parler*] is an *auto-affection* of an absolutely unique kind. On one hand, it operates within the medium of universality; the signifieds which appear must be idealities which one can repeat or transmit *idealiter*, as being indefinitely the same. On the other hand, the subject can hear itself or speak to itself, allowing itself to be affected by the signifier which it produces without any detour through the instance of exteriority, of the world, or of otherness in general. All other forms of *auto-affection* must either be mediated by otherness or renounce universality.[99]

This operation of *auto-affection* is reformulated; hearing oneself speak, or seeing oneself being seen, becomes a movement in which the power of difference is deployed as a morphological gesture. Language becomes a substitute for the primary dwelling in the flesh; or, rather, it recreates an experience which is given not in accessible memory but only in the nostalgic impression left by an absolute memory, an archaic archive which is so thoroughly severed from memory that its contents cannot be forgotten. *Auto-affection* is therefore "a way of putting activity and passivity back together again,"[100] a way of turning a movement of idealized repetition and re-presentation into a fluid continuum. A natural or idiomatic fluidity is recreated as a conceptual continuity in which the duration and gradation of words and numbers—the temporality and transitivity of *essence*[101]—is substituted for the spontaneous and extensible fluidity of the corporeal-carnal dimension of life. *Auto-affection* is an endeavor to recover or recollect in thought that which makes thought possible, and thus to turn thought into something that

98. *See* Jacques Derrida, *La Voix et le Phénomène* 83–84 (1967) ("*un* contre . . . *à la fois au sens du* tout-contre *de la proximité et de l'*encontre *de l'op-posé*").

99. *Id.* at 88 (see also chapter 6 in general).

100. Luce Irigaray, "L'invisible de la chair," *in Éthique de la Différence Sexuelle* 145 (1984) (my translation).

101. In the sense which is developed in *Autrement qu'être,* especially in chapter 2.

would recover or rememorize the nostalgic impression of a primary dwelling.

The movement of *auto-affection* remains a gesture in which an impression of being in contact is reflected as a sense of being intact. Otherness is opposed and recovered in an operation of inversion, turning dependence into independence, and invisibility into visibility:

> The seer [*le voyant*] attempts to put activity and passivity back together again, to overcome the invisibility of and within the other, which constitutes an obscurity which his gaze would have to reduce in order to compose its field of vision. He tries to establish a *continuum* or duration between utter passivity and utmost activity. But he cannot do so. Not least because he lacks any memory of that primary event in which he was encircled—touched by a tangible invisibility from which his eyes were themselves formed, but which he will never see.[102]

This reflexive vision appropriates the sensual or material dimension of the things it illuminates: the invisible or nocturnal substrate that incarnates both viewer and viewed is twisted outside-in, fashioning an experience of "being oneself while inhabiting the other" [*être* moi *tout en vivant dans l'*autre].[103] The things of the world are gathered in and embraced by the luminosity and intentionality of this vision, which enfolds and encircles them within itself, fashioning a flesh held together and articulated by the essential connective tissue of vision. The achievement of this gaze would be to give birth[104] to itself as much as to the things that it embraces. Thus, the domain of the visible is bathed in the active light of a gaze that is recovered or reflected as the passivity of being touched. The seeing of the subject is returned as touch: visibility is made tactility, a touch that "feels and envelops, alloying itself with things," discovering them "as though it already knew them,"[105] yielding or expressing a secret complicity between world and subject. In this complicity or alliance of touching and being touched, activity switches into passivity and back again. The gesture of touch is experienced through a morphology that equivocates between activity

102. "L'invisible de la chair," *supra* note 100, at 145 (my translation).
103. *Totalité et Infini, supra* note 9, at 121 (my translation).
104. "L'invisible de la chair," *supra* note 100, at 145.
105. *Id.* at 150 (my translation).

and passivity—an ambiguity that is awakened and returned with each encounter, so that with each gesture self encounters and touches itself in a movement of *auto-affection*, reducing the otherness of the world to the inert and invisible medium traversed by this equivocal gesture. Nature is denatured; that which is always before any beginning is postponed to the initiative of action.[106]

Sight turns itself into an experience of continuous touch, where continuity also connotes extensibility—the substitution in thought of the *lieu du lieu*[107] as that which assures the sculpting of the viewer's morphology. This continuity is reproduced as the paradoxical topography of the Möbius strip. The gaze that is made connective tissue returns to a self-referential source. The self encounters itself as other. And yet the medium that permits this operation is not itself visible: "the in between, the middle or *medium*, of the caress is unseen."[108]

The return of this repressed invisibility is precisely what prevents the sublimation of flesh in thought. The repressed returns as an impression that paradoxically persists as memory precisely because it is not within memory. It is so radically uncoupled from the "archives of the flesh"[109] that whatever is archived therein cannot be rememorized or decathected: "How, so long as there persists the mystery of a touch which exceeds any touching of or the intention of any gesture, can one recall this permanence? Or become it by memorising it? Or fashion time from this foundation of time?"[110] How could one be the original author or sculptor of one's self?

In place of this, Irigaray proposes a new culture of nature. The relation of *admiration* consists in the recognition or cultivation of "natural" sexual difference; the "physiological and morphological complementarity of the sexes."[111] This complementarity realizes a difference inscribed in nature: contra Hegel, this nature cannot be represented as purely or simply immediate because it discovers within itself, in the difference between masculine and feminine, an experience of limitation and negativity.[112] It is far from straightforward to ask what is natural

106. Creating a thought that is necessarily—and perhaps unashamedly—*antérieure postérieurement. Totalité et Infini, supra* note 9, at 183.

107. Luce Irigaray, "Le lieu, l'intervale," *in Éthique de la Différence Sexuelle* 41 (1984).

108. *Id.* at 152 (my translation).

109. *Id.* at 158.

110. *Id.* at 178 (my translation).

111. *Sexes et Parentés, supra* note 43, at 121 (my translation).

112. *J'aime à toi, supra* note 3, at 75.

about the nature that is at stake here. "Nature" can only be an enigmatic or refractory motif in Irigaray's scheme of sexual difference. It is enigmatic because the model of culture as fidelity to nature cannot itself do otherwise than play on the enigmatic difference between the factual and factical. It is refractory because nature is written in the utterly naive and yet extravagantly sophisticated style that characterizes Irigaray's version of *admiration*. "Nature" is at once a naive appeal and a rhetorical motif that renders ironic the very notion of the naive.

The boundary between mind and body—or indeed the libido or *pneuma* that mediates between the two or that forms a supplement with which each is infused or suffused—is dissolved to leave a spatiotemporal field upon which the colors of the flesh are played out according to the rhythms of a *temps sensible*.[113] The dimension of passion becomes the medium that spans what is for Descartes a difference between mind and body; those polarities themselves are dissolved. The point is to exchange a perspective from which the soul is recognized as incorporated for one that sees the corporeality of the soul. The chromo-somatic medium of passion extends a surface of "mucosity" [*le muqueux*].[114] The culture of the sensuous proportions of the body through a style of psychosomatic "painting" offers the dimension of color as essential to "the spatial representation of the body, voluptuousness and sensuality."[115] This dimension is not only a resource for the development of a sexed subjective identity, but is also the medium of an intersubjective flux of passion. The movement of *admiration* that sustains a particular adventure of subjectivity also unfolds a dimension between subjects. It models a continuous relation of non-indifferent difference in which the other remains absolutely strange and unfamiliar, but still mine according to an intentionality of recognition. Passion therefore offers an essentially shared rememorization of the self. The fluid dememorization and rememorization of *admiration* denies the psychoanalytical version of the memory that forms subjectivity. No longer is memory simply the persistence of a sedimented or encrypted trauma.

This dimension of corporeal color is elaborated through a complex culture of voice and speech. The ethics of sexual difference develops a

113. The phrase is from Proust via Kristeva. *See* Julia Kristeva, *Le temps sensible: Proust et l'expérience littéraire* (1994).

114. Luce Irigaray, "La différence sexuelle," in *Éthique de la Différence Sexuelle* 24 (1984).

115. *Sexes et Parentés*, *supra* note 43, at 173 (my translation).

discipline or aesthetic of the chromatic sonority of the voice. "In each sex there is an entire range of tones whose chords, medians, and harmonies might inexhaustibly be discovered or recovered within individual equilibrium or within a relation to another."[116]

Descartes's passions fulfill a peculiar complicity between words and the hydraulic mechanism of the body: words "excite movement" in the soul, although "so far as the institution of nature is concerned, [they] do not represent to the soul more than their sound when they are uttered by the voice."[117] This expresses an essential indeterminacy of the voice. Indeed, the ethical or intersubjective complexity of speech is an enduring theme: the voice being "that other point where mind and physical reflex met in the body."[118] The colors and modulations of the voice combine the essential substance and semantic spirit of speech, and the point of the ethics of sexual difference is to recover those colors from subjection to the code of a monotone language, to recover what persists despite the authority of the rhythm of writing as the originary template of speech. These colors are, for Irigaray differently from Descartes, the vehicle of the blood: "the marks of writing try to contain and repress the blood [whereas] painting and color attempt to give voice to it [*essaient de le dire*]."[119]

Nature might, perhaps, be associated figuratively with the dimension of color as that which exceeds and eludes the monochromatic gradations fashioned by conceptual difference. The excessive reality or givenness of the natural is allied to the mysterious "talisman" of color, which, even in the hands of philosophy, conjures up the irreducible intimacy and interiority of a natural fluid dimension. Color is "a given which is beyond any subjective imperium, which immerses the subject in an invisible dwelling within the visible, an unmasterable dwelling [*séjour immaîtrisable*], infernal or celestial, anterior or posterior to any incarnation determined by a dualism of subject and object."[120] However oblique or allusive the attempts to rememorize the sensations of color, whether it is recovered in a structure of grids or gradation or in the framing of "intervals *between*, or

---

116. *Id.* at 172 (my translation).

117. Descartes, *supra* note 35, at 355 (Article L).

118. Peter Brown, *The Body and Society: Men, Women and Sexual Renunciation in Early Christianity* 134 (1988).

119. *Sexes et Parentés, supra* note 43, at 173 (my translation).

120. "L'invisible de la chair," *supra* note 100, at 147 (my translation).

differences and successions,"[121] color returns as that which is irrepressibly fluid and fugitive. Beneath or beyond the conceptual apprehension of color there is the material or textural dimension of things, which is alienated in thought, but which, as the naïveté of the natural, remains unsublimated. Color, alloyed to nature in the color of the eyes, is that which is "as unmodifiable as a genealogical inheritance";[122] or rather, as unmodifiable as a genealogical heritage is thought to be, because nature and color are invoked against the violence of juridically ordered genealogies. Whether it is named color or nature, what is at issue is the enigma of absolute memory that leaves thought "harassed by repetitions and reproductions," impressed with an imprint "which is erased and yet returns": a "double nature, or a nature which is resurgent in language."[123]

### *VII*

This cultivation of the naive and native is fulfilled not only in touch but in the breathing of a new style of communication, motivated by the impulse of *admiration* rather than an operation of recognition. The ritual of repetition proper to *auto-affection,* in which the subject makes itself the voice of, or a voice addressed to the O/other, renders the sterile paradox of a speech that is too full because it is empty and empty because it is too full.[124] It is a speech that serves "not to enable one to communicate or encounter, but to speak to oneself," and that offers no "becoming, other than one which is already closed" and "no air, other than the exhalation of an already spoken and already existing word."[125] Where communication is twisted into recognition, speech serves only to smother the element that is most indispensable to life; "in the forgetting of being there is a forgetting of air [*l'oubli de l'air*], of that primary fluid which is freely and unilaterally given in a mother's blood."[126]

*Admiration* is fashioned in the cultivation of a certain rhythm of listening, speaking, and breathing, in which the articulation of speech and

121. *Id.* at 149 (my translation).
122. *Id.* at 146 (my translation).
123. *Id.* at 134 (my translation).
124. *See* Mikkel Borch-Jacobsen, *Lacan: The Absolute Master* 96–167 (1991).
125. "L'invisible de la chair," *supra* note 100, at 166 (my translation).
126. *Id.* at 122 (my translation).

breath would be the medium of an ethical and corporeo-carnal relation whose articulations of subject and world subvert the repetition of the punctual present:

> [A] present which is supposed to displace itself while remaining the same. A sort of puncturing of the fabric of the world, between the fabric of the world and that of the subject, between the fabric of language and the thread of the subject, each alternating and exchanging places with the other, like a sewing machine or a machine tool which takes one step forwards and one backwards, one backwards and one forwards, indefinitely. With neither creation, invention, event, nor risk beyond this interminable movement.[127]

The culture of sexual difference offers a spiritualization of breath which dissolves this antagonism of breathing and speaking. In the moment of exhalation, breath is asphyxiated by the closure of a speech, and the exposure of inhalation is passed over as nothing more than a preliminary to speech.

Irigaray's diagnosis of this monotony is in some sense paralleled by the experience of the *soi-même* as it is described in Lévinas's account of respiration:

> That the void of space should be filled with invisible air—unperceived, other than in the caress of the wind or the threat of a storm—unperceived, but penetrating to the folds of my interiority; that this invisibility or this void should be at once breathable and horrific; that this nonindifferent invisibility should obsess me even before any act of thematization, that a simple *ambiance* should impose itself as an *atmosphere* to which the subject is delivered and exposed, to the depths of its lungs, prior to any goal or intention; that the subject should, in the depths of its substance, be a lung: all this suggests a subjectivity which, in suffering, and before losing its footing in being, offers itself as passivity and as utter *sub-jectum*.[128]

---

127. *Id.* at 166 (my translation).
128. *Autrement qu'être, supra* note 4, at 276 (my translation).

An entire ethical experience of proximity is expressed in this absolute diachrony of inhalation and exhalation; two self-sufficient moments, separated by an instant that belongs neither to one nor the other, yielding again the equivocation of the subject exiled within itself by a no-man's-land. An equivocation "between" the naive and unchosen moment of passive exposure—inhalation as the movement of "displacing oneself to the extent of departing one's self"[129]—and the active pole of exhalation, in which the self closes in on itself—no longer offering itself as exposure, but folding the moment of unchosen dependence into the self-assertion of a speech act. This leaves the subject as dirempted self, exiled within itself, its internal membranes or surfaces signifying immersion within an external and unfathomable element. Paradoxically, the element is that which is most deeply and trustingly internalized and yet which leaves the subject exposed, fissured "down to the resisting kernel of the self, to the indivisible core of its individuality."[130] This is the most tangible or physical *frisson* of the countercurrent of obsession, the incorporation of this equivocation within the self. To cultivate breath ethically would be to pay attention to the moment of accusation within breath, to heed the *Dire* which persists within the *Dit*, turning the diachrony of inhalation/exhalation into a continuous inhalation of and for the other, so that the alternation of breath is experienced as an unending undoing. The breath of exhalation is a breath yielded to other; it is a breath offered to the other in a spirit of responsibility, an offering that subsists in the moment of inhalation that offers yet more. In this way the oscillation of breath is fashioned as exposure without closure. One again uncovers the movement of a Möbius strip turned contrary-wise; running as a seamless undoing even as it unceasingly closes in on itself.

For Irigaray, breath is not rendered as the fealty of an already subjected subject; the diachrony of breath is instead articulated with speech as dialogue. As with Lévinas, the fact of dependence on respiration communicates, within and despite the repetitions of the *Dit*, something that refuses to be asphyxiated by speech. The repetitions of the *Dit* are therefore figured as a perilous exercise in "navigation" backward and forward, in which "the element which supports the boat is precisely the element which submerges and threatens to engulf it."[131] This primary,

129. *Id.* at 279 (my translation).
130. *Id.* at 277 (my translation).
131. *Id.* at 278 (my translation).

elemental dimension is the medium that assures and cultivates the permeability of air to speech and simultaneously realizes the relation between receptivity and activity, or between speaking and listening, which defines the fecundity of *admiration:*

> The intention . . . is to move [*émouvoir*] the other through the medium of a communicating *with,* the medium of the heart and of a speech which remains sensual. [The moment of] inhalation seeks to awaken an exchange in which the word is born and is maintained between two bodies, sustained within each while respecting their differences, spiritualising them without drawing them out of their flesh.[132]
>
> This speech is also tactile. It is not in the designation of any sort of reality, truth, or object external to the body. It is not submitted to possession, or to the acquisition of a good outside itself. Nor is it reduced to a supposed appropriation of speech by itself, to a precoded truth. Nor yet is it the exteriorization of a univocal sentiment. Speech is for communicating between selves [*à communiquer entre soi*].[133]

This describes a work of intercomprehension in which speech and breath are articulated as a unique and idiomatic temporality between self and other. Speech is punctuated not only by the syntax of grammatical usage or by the production of the self through speech acts, but by the material or sensual qualities and effects that are attributable to the rhythms and textures of breath. Even in the apparent simplicity of silence, there is the possibility of a "cultural ethos" of silence[134] in which the qualities and meanings of silence would be modeled according to the duration and context of an encounter. In the culture of sexual difference, this is worked into a sensuality of silence and speech. The cultivation of the sensual impressions offered and experienced in the accents and modulations of speech and silence, in which the cultivation of a sense of timing that is habitually learned as a pattern of corporeal *hexis,*[135] would be learned and unlearned in the immediacy of an

132. *J'aime à toi, supra* note 3, at 194 (my translation).

133. *Id.* at 193 (my translation).

134. *See* Michel Foucault, "The Minimalist Self," in *Michel Foucault: Politics, Philosophy, Culture* 3–16 (Laurence Kritzman ed., 1988).

135. *See* Pierre Bourdieu, *Le sens pratique,* 111–34 (1980).

encounter with a transcending other. *Admiration* would maintain a question between, a relation that would carry an intersubjective temporality—a *temps sensible,* or an idiomatic time of love—flesh made word in the *toucher à.*[136] This discipline would be imposed not as the precoded and prearticulated grammar of instrumental speech, but rather the cultivation of an idiom of *admiration,* an "alliance" in which "flesh is made word—annunciation, question, dialogue, mercy—in the poetry of an encounter."[137]

### *VIII*

The fluidity of this *temps sensible* is the medium of an alternative relation between subjects of law. This "reinterpretation of the notion of nature"[138] seeks to recover nature not as a specifically or essentially feminine dimension, but rather as an irrepressible "double" of the semantic structure of homosocial law. This double might be incorporated or metabolized as the medium of a symbolism or syntax of sexual difference, supporting and articulating two symbolic markers or, more specifically, two generic juridical identities. Patriarchy is a myth in action,[139] and this new symbolism would undo the replication of masculine morphologies and engender a specifically feminine subjectivity, remedying a cultural arrangement in which women "are not yet born as women."[140] Law, in its capacity as a secular "tutor,"[141] would, through the deployment of feminine and masculine rights, offer the essential elements of a symbolic repertoire through which feminine selves might be engendered. This implies a different authorship of the self; the recreation or generation of subjects of law otherwise than as replicas of a textual prototype, but rather as mutually created natural-cultural artifacts.

The intentionality of *admiration* remains an intentionality—the production of a self; there can be no unmediated reception of nature. The cultivation of *admiration* through the recognition of the otherness of the other sex is "neither a simple projection nor natural immediacy," but

136. *See generally J'aime à toi, supra* note 3, at 187–99.
137. *Id.* at 192 (my translation).
138. *Sexes et Parentés, supra* note 43, at 16 (my translation).
139. *Égales a qui?, supra* note 96, at 423.
140. *Sexes et Parentés, supra* note 43, at 78 (my translation).
141. *J'aime à toi, supra* note 3, at 93.

"an adjustment of intentions to reality."[142] This project of recognition is, moreover, characterized as "initiating a passive and retroactive intentionality: of becoming aware of being a woman or a man, and of willing to be so."[143] Admiration would be retroactive not only in the sense that it might be figured as a return to reality, but also in the sense that it constitutes the very reality to which it returns. The reality of difference here figures rhetorically to dissolve the ostensible naturalness of a juridically ordered genealogy, the genealogical replication of a paternally instituted *dramatis personae,* in which equality could mean only equality in being a functionary of the genealogical order. The negativity of the natural represents the condition of making good a primary ethical fault:

> [W]omen unfortunately are the first to say that woman does not exist and cannot exist. Which is to say that they deny a generic identity for the feminine. This negation abolishes the possibility of constituting of a culture of two sexes, two *genres.* We remain within a horizon in which man is the model of the human *genre,* a human *genre* within which there are empirical women or natural entities without an identity of their own.
>
> The emancipation of women, and of humanity, lies by way of the definition of a generic femininity, of woman in general, and not simply this or that woman.[144]

In the name of nature, Irigaray offers the possibility of an identity that would be given not by a singular principle of genealogical reason,[145] but that would instead recognize a specifically feminine *genre.* This would remedy the reduction of women to the capacity of being single and substitutable exemplars.

*Admiration* is the medium of a novel articulation of the social body, relaying the domains of "body, home, and city."[146] The idiomatic immediacy of proximity is nonetheless mediated by a porous and cross-permeable boundary between neighbors that is diffracted into the thresh-

142. *Id.* at 71 (my translation).

143. *Id.* (my translation).

144. *Id.* at 111 (my translation).

145. *See generally* Pierre Legendre, *Leçons IV: L'Inestimable Objet de la Transmission* (1985). *Cf.* Alain Pottage, "The Paternity of Law," in *Politics, Postmodernity and Critical legal Studies: The Legality of the Contingent* (Costas Douzinas and Peter Goodrich eds., 1994).

146. *J'aime à toi, supra* note 3, at 62 ("*corps, maison et cité sont une oeuvre commune bâtie par hommes et femmes pour le présent et le futur*").

olds between body, home, and city. The replication of this porous relation across the more conventional spheres of private and public, or citizen, state, and nation, unfolds as the replication of a novel mode of being with the world; a mode of intersubjective dialogue and exchange based upon a temporality other than that prescribed by linguistic or juridical syntax. The difficulty lies in describing this utopian temporality, which would be neither the magma of immediacy nor the replication of an eternal present. The possibility of this temporality in turn offers the possibility of a boundary, or between, drawn in terms that would not be reducible to the function of a mediating third. The work of *admiration* in knitting speech to breath, or corporeal impulse to psychic energy, does not mend the bridges between, or equivocate between, differences and distinctions that are established in operations of *différance* or *auto-affection.* In communicating with the archives of the flesh, *admiration* recovers, or sublimates, an already negativized nature. The between that is mediated in the proximity of sexual difference is precisely this negativity of natural difference, a negativity that is cultivated and instituted in an operation of recognition.

Whatever is implied in the suggestion that the work of recognition is a work of "dialectical creativity"[147] it would be misleading to emphasize the Hegelian resonances of Irigaray's reference to recognition. This is not another philosophical or psychoanalytical variant of the master–slave relationship; it is, rather, a commitment in which the otherness of sexual difference is realized. It implies the recognition of the insurmountable limitation and finitude that is notified by the figure of the other *genre.* This idiomatic difference or negativity is inscribed in law in the form of a distinction between two *genres:* an *en soi* comes to be doubled by a *pour-soi,*[148] paradoxically enabling the members of each *genre* to identify themselves as such and yet be left unmediated, free to develop a unique relation of *admiration.* Indeed, the most basic role of law as moral or cultural "tutor"[149] is in notifying each subject of this condition of individuation and limitation. This possibility raises the question of what can be done with or within law without recourse to a mediating and alienating third.

With Irigaray as with Lévinas, the "I" is inevitably instituted within a universal *genre,* but it is "a universal which can be breached in

147. *Id.* at 72 (my translation).

148. *Id.* at 56 (with no explicit reference either to Sartre or Hegel).

149. *Id.* at 93.

thought."[150] The "I" is at once a particular representative of a universal *genre* and the self which is, paradoxically, unique within or despite its *genre.* Nevertheless, for Irigaray the relation of axiom to idiom is not constituted as chiasmus or equivocation; nor does it secretly incorporate a historical mediation which it ostensibly denies. Irigaray does not make even this sort of oblique concession to history or sociology. Where Lévinas exposes the absolute void of the no-man's-land, Irigaray uncovers what is lost to thought or passed over in thought. The fluidity that characterizes the movement of inscription-erasure in the institution of *admiration* is not a moment or movement of equivocation, whether theological or historical; it is not a movement "between" two moments of mastery and subversion, but the nonantagonistic fluidity of the corporeal-carnal. Which would be an inversion and dissolution of the conventional way of thinking the constitution of the juridical *persona;* rather than the civilization of a corporeal or psychosomatic dimension according to an institutional dimension of law, one would have the metabolism of an institutionalized axiom within a corporeal idiom. The movement is not one invented within the formal equivocation of interpretation, but a movement supported by the temporality of the flesh. Through this metabolism of the word in flesh an ethics practiced in private might then become public. The unfolding of *admiration* as the modulation of the boundary between body, home, and city begins with the cultivation of a desire which itself begins and ends with a private passion of proximity rather than a collective passion of a public participation (in which privacy might be registered only as deprivation).[151]

This allusion to a temporality of the flesh is essential. Recognition in *admiration* involves the weaving of an idiomatic syntax of intersubjectivity. This weaving is not an oscillation or repetition backward and forward; nor is it fashioned as the return of a singular project to itself so

150. *Autrement qu'être, supra* note 4, at 218 (my translation).

151. "To live an entirely private life means above all to be deprived of things essential to a truly human life: to be deprived of the reality that comes from being seen and heard by others, to be deprived of an 'objective' relationship that comes from being seen and heard by others, to be deprived of an 'objective' relationship with them that comes from being related to and separated from them through the intermediary of a common world of things, to be deprived of the possibility of achieving something more permanent than the life itself. The privation of privacy lies in the absence of others; as far as they are concerned, private man does not appear, and therefore it is as though he did not exist." Arendt, *supra* note 164, at 58.

as to bind one subject to the other in a reciprocal but not other affecting interlocking—an intrication of involuted loops, each defining and defending its own local space.

The difficulty is to realize a boundary or medium between self and other that would retain the porosity and spontaneity of the difference made by *admiration;* to write in law a *genre* that would not be a mediating third. Rights would be written in the flesh to form a relation "founded in an unfounded foundation" [*a lieu sur fond d'un fond sans fond*],[152] or in an immediacy in which no institution could take root. Nevertheless, this nature is not simply immediate, being already fissured by the originary difference between masculine and feminine.[153] It is the irreconcilability of what is fissured in nature, the maintenance of a mysterious "between" that permits an identification that is also a dissolution of identities. The negativity of nature forbids the assertion of any property or propriety, leaving a subject that is already disappropriated, somehow already a stranger to the world. This disappropriation need not entail disappointment; rather, it elicits the passion of *admiration.* The negativity or transcendence of the other to the self is precisely that incomprehensible excess that, through *admiration,* I see as "something insurmountable or mysterious, a freedom which will never be mine, a subjectivity which will never be mine, something of mine which will never be mine."[154]

This gives some sense of Irigaray's utopian project for law. How could each local idiomatic "we" relate to a larger public "we"? The structure of this porous and diaphanous boundary between is a ground that might be cultivated not as ownership and obligation but as interrogation, so as to realize the surprise of the negative that is diffracted and sustained through the spheres of body, home, and city, dissolving the impersonal "us" or "we" of the "neutral" community.

This proposes a community of aconceptual *genres,* and invokes the notion (not taken from Lévinas) of a relation of belonging to a *genre* that does not reduce the adherent to a mere exemplar. Metabolized in *admiration,* the juridical *persona* becomes the diaphanous and ever-rewoven clothing of the subject as a subject of *admiration;* it is dissolved into the medium of a culture of *admiration,* a clothing bestowed by admiration. The subject does not, at least not in any conventional sense, recognize

152. *Id.* at 169 (my translation).

153. *Id.* at 65–76.

154. *Id.* at 162 (my translation).

itself in or identify itself with its *genre;* the *genre* is not the operator or medium that assures the movement through the boundaries between body, home, and city. The interiority and externality of those boundaries is thought otherwise. The indefinite shape or imprint of the subject's interiority and identity is the "impression" left and erased by its encounter with a paradoxically universal other. This capacity to sustain a question "between" subjects would require nothing less than the rememorizing of the subject; what is at stake is the "becoming of the matter which is our being; the transfiguration of our bodies, our gender, and our history."[155] It requires rememorizing—or, perhaps, dememorizing: overcoming the stupefaction of a framing of the world as repetition. Not so as to stimulate a merely intellectual intrigue, in much the same sense as *admiration* was for Descartes a manner of rejuvenating the brain [*rajeunir le cerveau*],[156] but to begin with what could never "begin": how, indeed, could a memory of the flesh be retained?[157] One is left with a *topos* that is beyond any beyond: a sketch of virtuosity beyond monotony.

155. *Id.* at 197 (my translation).
156. "L'admiration," *supra* note 6, at 75–84.
157. *Id.* at 178.

*Chapter 2*

# The Deconstruction of Kantian Ethics and the Question of Pleasure

*Henry Staten*

This essay is primarily about the recent work of Bernard Williams, who is in my opinion the most radical thinker on the question of ethics in the analytic philosophy camp. In fact, Williams's work tests the limits of what we know as analytic philosophy. His project is rigorously deconstructive, yet it has been developed out of the materials of analytic philosophy quite independently of Derridean deconstruction. Thus, this project is extraordinarily rich in its resonance, and regardless of whether one comes at it from an analytic or a deconstructive background, one is equally likely to find it surprising in its way of slicing through traditional philosophical formulations of the questions at issue. I will argue in the final third of this essay, however, that in contradiction to the preponderantly deconstructive force of his work as a whole, Williams retains one central prejudice of the philosophical ideology he deconstructs: the "ascetic" prejudice (in Nietzsche's sense of "ascetic") that the ethical cannot be motivated by the aim at pleasure. Williams retains this prejudice despite the fact that two of his main influences, Aristotle and Nietzsche, broach a conception of pleasure that is powerfully antiascetic.

The term "Kantian ethics" in the title of this essay is invoked in a very general sense, as a shorthand for certain persistent features or tendencies of ethical theory that Williams, in his influential book *Ethics and the Limits of Philosophy*[1] links primarily, but by no means exclusively, to Kant and his inheritors.

1. Bernard Williams, *Ethics and the Limits of Philosophy* (1985).

For Kant, the moral agent is poised between the awesome majesty of the moral law on one side and the pull of inclination or desire on the other. The individual's relation to the moral law is conceived in terms of something called "obligation" or "duty." It is the job of rationality to recognize moral obligation, and the individual who recognizes it and acts in accordance with it is conceived by Kant as acting "freely" or "autonomously," which for Kant means acting like a rational being and not an animal.

It is essential to this picture of ethics that ethical choice is abstracted from whomever the ethical agent happens to be. The only thing that counts toward the definition of the autonomous moral agent is that aspect of her that is the same for all rational beings. The aim of ethical theory is universality; therefore, it must produce pure general principles to which any rational person can subscribe. It is obviously not only Kantian ethics that dwells at this level of abstraction; ethical theory in general aims at producing universal principles. A corollary of this universality is the tendency of ethical theory to reduce, or attempt to reduce, all ethical motivations to one type and all unethical motivations to another, antithetical type—for example, under the rubrics of the "altruistic" on the one hand and the "self-interested" on the other. Kant himself carries this reductivism to a logical and metaphysical extreme, positing an ontological abyss between the morally good will in its absolute purity on the one hand and egoistic hedonism on the other.

Of course, not many people today would found ethical theory on the claim Kant makes: that a rational agent is essentially a noumenal self, impervious to any of the motivations that drive a worldly, embodied being. Yet it might be argued that modern ethical theory merely fails to follow out the implications of its own universalism, implications that, if pursued to their logical conclusion, would result either in a metaphysics of the Kantian type or in an abandonment of universalism. For example, Rawlsian contractualism presupposes as what Williams calls its "natural constituency"[2] everyone who might be subject to an ethical agreement—any moral agent in general. Utilitarianism, which on its face is distant from Kant, proposes the homogenization of all individual preferences so that an impartial, disinterested, rational calculation might be made by an impartial, disinterested, rational

2. *Id.* at 103.

observer.[3] Like Kantianism, Rawlsian and utilitarian ethics are, as Williams says, "characterless" in that they make no reference to the ethical character of individuals in their social and psychological individuality except as something from which to be abstracted.

What Williams wants to urge against all varieties of universalizing ethical theory is the particularity of individual ethical agents acting within particular, historically constituted communities. The trouble with the republic of rational agents is that by virtue of being no *particular* community at all, the basis for making any decision of practical deliberation is thinned out almost to inanition. It is a mystery structurally similar to the old "mind–body" enigma how the deliberations of an agent qua impartial rational being can make contact with the interests and desires of that same agent considered as an empirical individual. "How," Williams asks, "can an *I* that has taken on the perspective of impartiality be left with enough identity to live a life that respects its own interests? If morality is possible at all, does it leave anyone in particular for me to be?"[4] For Williams, as well as for Hegel, whom he cites in this connection, the starting point of ethical reflection is the *Sittlichkeit* of particular historically constituted communities, as opposed to the *Moralität* dictated by a universal moral law.[5] For Williams, however, there is no question of a harmonious identity between the essence of the self and what Hegel calls the "ethical substance" of the community. Williams takes as fundamental the facts of fragmentation, incoherence, and conflict—both in the structure of society and in the structure of the self. Thus, in his view, the fundamental datum of ethical life is "the primacy of the individual and of personal dispositions."[6] For even if radical structuralist descriptions of society are right, social structures must nevertheless still be *represented* in the desires and habits of individuals. Individual dispositions are the point at which social structures get their purchase on people's behavior.[7]

3. *Id.* at 83–84.

4. *Id.* at 69–70.

5. *Id.* at 104.

6. *Id.* at 201.

7. This sounds like a form of relativism, though in fact Williams finds moral relativism just as untenable as he does moral absolutism, if moral relativism means the belief that the moral judgments of one group apply just to that group. Such a notion projects a picture of groups neatly divided into autonomous systems; but, as Williams notes, in reality we cannot simply draw a line between "us" and "them," because "they" are at varying distances from "us" and our reactions and relations to other groups are themselves part of our ethical lives.

From the standpoint of Kantian ethics, of course, to locate the basic material of ethical reflection in individual dispositions would be disastrous to the pursuit of moral autonomy. Dispositions are a mixed bag that include motives such as desires and concern for the opinions of others. On the Kantian view, to act out of such motives is to be ruled by something other than one's own rational essence, to succumb to heteronomy. Kant thinks that only the purely voluntary is moral, and only the rational can be truly voluntary. Any other motivation is the product of empirical causality and therefore not truly chosen by the moral agent. But Williams argues that the simple split between voluntary and involuntary action is artificial and, indeed, false.[8] If we compare this abstract philosophical picture with the way in which concepts of responsibility actually function in both ancient and modern law, it is obvious that the idea of the voluntary is just one element in the ascription of responsibility. The Kantian might reply that this comparison only shows that the legal concept of responsibility is less perfectly developed than the philosophical concept. Law, of course, cannot develop in response to the sole requirement of theoretical purity and consistency as ethical theory can, and this might generate the illusion that legal thought lags behind the progress of moral thought.

In his most recent book, *Shame and Necessity*,[9] Williams questions whether there has been, in fact, any progress in moral thought. The Kantian picture of moral autonomy underlies a very widespread conception, a "progressivist" conception Williams calls it, of the development of Western culture since the Greeks. This conception relies strongly on the distinction between "shame" cultures and "guilt" cultures, a distinction that embodies in a rough-and-ready, seemingly self-evident fashion the technical Kantian distinction between moral heteronomy and moral autonomy. In the progressivist view of history, Western culture has, since the time of the Greeks, and with the aid of Christianity, gradually evolved from a shame culture to a guilt culture. In the context of such a picture of history, Kant's development of ethics can look like the culminating development of this evolution as the purity of the concept of moral autonomy is finally lifted free of all contamination by heteronomy.

8. Williams, *supra* note 1, at 194.

9. Bernard Williams, *Shame and Necessity* (1993).

*Shame and Necessity* attacks this progressivist view of the history of moral thought, a view Williams believes has given us a completely distorted idea of Greek ethics. Williams seeks to show that the concepts of ethical agency and ethical responsibility embodied in Homer, Greek tragedy, and Greek law manifest a subtlety, complexity, and adequacy to the real conditions of agency that are unmatched by the concepts of guilt and moral autonomy. In particular, Williams attempts to rehabilitate the Greek concept of *aidos,* "shame." Shame, like guilt, involves internalization. However, whereas guilt is supposed to abstract moral ideas from all other kinds of ideas, and also from the expectations of other people, shame packs along all sorts of nonmoral motivations and retains a strong sense of the social other. Far from being weaknesses, Williams argues, these elements constitute the distinctive superiority as an ethical concept of shame over guilt.[10] For the sharp boundary between moral motivations on the one hand, and all other sorts of motivations on the other hand, is an artifact of metaphysics and can lead only to an overly simple conception of ethical life; specifically, a conception that cannot address the situation of individual identity within the *Sittlichkeit* of a community.[11]

In defending shame as an ethical concept, Williams might appear to open the door to a chaos of social and psychological influences large and small—precisely that chaos that it is the purpose of ethical theory to whip into ethical shape. For "the morality system," the "other" to whom one relates morally or ethically is "just a screen for one's own ethical ideas,"[12] which is precisely why this relation does not fall into heteronomy. But in shame, one internalizes as a self-judgment the expectations of an other who "still has some independent identity" and who remains "the locus of some genuine social expectations."[13] Does not shame thus belong to the realm of mere social expectations, to what Kant calls heteronomy and existentialist ethics calls inauthenticity?

Williams must steer a careful course between the either/or that ethical theory seems to force on us here. The internalized other that operates on us in ethical shame is to be thought of as an intermediate

10. *Id.* at 94–95.

11. Williams, *supra* note 1, at 194–95; Williams, *supra* note 9, at 94–95.

12. Williams, *supra* note 9, at 98.

13. *Id.*

construct, neither a mere projection of one's own ethical ideas nor as merely one of "the neighbors." "Those alternatives leave out much of the substance of actual ethical life. The internalized other is indeed abstracted and generalized and idealized, but he is potentially somebody rather than nobody and somebody other than me."[14]

This notion of the internalized other seems to me strikingly sensible and helpful. It is an idealization, thus capable of being distinguished from the shifting infinitude of major and minor pressures that are put on each person by the expectations of those around us; but this idealization is limited to the ethical materials provided by a concrete sociohistorical context. Williams's move involves a "minimum of idealization," to invoke Jacques Derrida's useful notion—just enough idealization to keep us from falling into the binary opposition that metaphysics makes obligatory.[15]

Armed with this minimal idealization, we can begin to rethink the question of the force of ethical motivation, of the ethical "ought." This question involves another aspect of the autonomy/heteronomy binary; at its deepest level the anxiety that afflicts ethical theory has to do not with the influence of "the neighbors," the social "other," but with the force of drive and desire—the "other" within the self. In the conception of the self that is operative here, a conception determined by the hegemony of Christianity over ethical thought, drive and desire are so powerful, so inimical to restraint, so intrinsically "sinful," that the problem becomes, not that the neighbors will influence us too much, but that they cannot influence us enough, that nothing merely sociopsychological can stand up to the force of amoral impulse. In the aftermath of the "death of God," the sense remains that if there is to be ethical life, something must enjoin it that has a force and majesty equal to God's word, for ethics must be something so deeply compelling that we cannot get under it or around it. For Kant, the majesty of the moral law was such that it allowed God himself to be posited on its basis as a reflex of the absolute claim that the moral law makes on a rational being. As he says in the *Dialectic of Pure Practical Reason* in the *Critique of Practical Reason:* "Granted that the pure moral law inexorably binds every man as a command . . . the righteous man may say 'I will that there be a God.'"[16] This is the last stage in the

---

14. *Id.* at 84.

15. On the notion of minimal idealization, see Henry Staten, *Wittgenstein and Derrida* 22–23 (1984).

16. Immanuel Kant, "Dialectic of Pure Practical Reason," in *Critique of Practical Reason* 113, 150 (Lewis W. Beck ed. and trans., 3d ed., Macmillan Publishing Co. 1993) (1788).

movement toward what Nietzsche calls nihilism, before the dam bursts and the question of values can be posed in its most naked form. In its most extreme form, the question of the motive for ethics is posed by modernity as the radical antithesis of the ethical and the nonethical, and the question becomes, "Why should I, or anybody, live ethically at all?" This is the form the question of ethics took in the second half of the nineteenth century in the work of such figures as Nietzsche and Dostoyevski (whose Ivan Karamazov makes the famous declaration that "If there is no God, then everything is permitted"),[17] but it is already implicit in Kant, for whom ethical life has already ceased to be the response to the command of God, and it continues to reverberate today. Thus, Paolo Flores d'Arcais, in a passage that Gianni Vattimo cites and that sets the terms of his further discussion, writes:

> Once God . . . is exiled, we are faced with the following dilemma. As there is only the individual, *One* is master of the law, to the negation of all the others [Flores calls this the "egocratic" sense]. . . . Alternatively, as the individual is *merely* the individual, each is master of the law in the sense that everyone shares in it equally [he calls this the "democratic" sense].[18]

Flores and Vattimo think that there is a terrible dilemma here, that we need to find some compelling way to make humanity decide in favor of democracy and rational debate as against an "egocratic" war of "all against all." Flores thinks that the decision has been made in favor of democracy by the movement of Western history itself; Vattimo rejects this but thinks that Heideggerian "destining" can provide the needed impetus. Thus, a variety of godlike powers continue to be posited in the place that God once held. In the work of Lévinas, too, to give a final and currently very influential example, the notion of the responsibility to the Other seems to be accruing much the sort of transcendental majesty that Kant ascribes to the moral law. Thus, if I understand at all what Lévinas is up to, his approach to ethics belongs to the universalizing tradition that Williams is out to deconstruct, even though, of course, Lévinas's emphasis on love is distinctly un-Kantian.

For Williams, however, there is no question of a transcendental

---

17. Feodor Dostoyevski, *The Brothers Karamazov* (Manuel Komroff ed. and Constance Garnett trans., New American Library 1957) (1880).

18. Gianni Vattimo, *The Transparent Society* 93 (David Webb trans., Johns Hopkins University Press 1992) (1989).

account of the force of ethical motivation because there is no room for the seemingly fundamental question, "Why be ethical?" In order to really pose this question, to pose it as a real choice, one would have to stand outside of ethics, in a position of neutrality with respect to the alternatives. But who could occupy such a position? Only a certain fantasy interpretation of the Nietzschean superman. In this part of his account, Williams agrees with Aristotle. One has either been adequately brought up in an ethical community or one has not. If one has, one cannot help but feel certain ethical desires and dispositions as essential to one's sense of self. If one has not acquired such dispositions, there is no chance that a mere verbal account of the *ought* of moral obligation will exercise the transcendental force over the individual that the proponents of such accounts want to ascribe to them. We are back, then, to Williams's notion of the internalized other who is a limited idealization drawn from the *ethos* of a particular community, or as he calls it, an "abstracted, improved neighbor lodged in one's inner life."[19]

From the standpoint of transcendental ethics it seems that such a locus for the force of the ethical is too superficial, too feeble. Even though Williams rejects relativism, it is hard not to feel the vertigo of complete ethical decentering when one tries to think of the ethical in terms of this other with a very little "o."

In *Shame and Necessity,* however, Williams takes what I would interpret as a profoundly Nietzschean turn, invoking as the deepest motive force of the ethical something very much like *amor fati.* The internalized other, as someone I can respect, is the concrete representation of my own ethical aspirations. To fail to live up to the expectations of this internalized other is identical to failing to live up to my own expectations of myself, and the force of the ethical conceived in this way would seem to be nothing less than what Nietzsche calls *becoming what one is.*[20]

Williams's internalized other is not merely a naive version of Freud's ego ideal, the nucleus of the superego. Nor is the drive to live up to the expectations of the internalized other merely a response to the infantile idealization of the parental figure and the dread of punishment or withdrawal of love by that figure.

No doubt, a fuller development of the notion of the internalized

19. Williams, *supra* note 9, at 98.

20. Friedrich Nietzsche, *Ecce Homo* (Walter Kaufman ed. and trans., Vintage Books 1967) (1887).

other would need to take account of the Freudian aspect of the matter, but it cannot be *reduced* to Freudian terms. Williams's internalized other belongs primarily not to the interiority of the nuclear household and the Oedipus complex, but to the public forum—the place where, regardless of the intricacies of our psychical formation, we assume our properly ethical being. The virtue of psychoanalysis at its best is that it gets behind the hollow professions of cultural ideals and restores to us a sense of the full narrative of personal history, restoring to the subject what Lacan call the "censored chapter" of this narrative.[21] Ideally, psychoanalysis should result in subjects who can pick and choose their cultural ideals, affirming the ones they cathect out of the depths of their libidinal-ethical being rather than mechanically obeying them out of fear of the superego. But the danger of psychoanalysis is that it will enmesh the subject interminably into the folds of the personal narrative, and that the fascination of this narrative will indefinitely defer the movement into ethical life.

Indeed, the Freudian narrative is far more fascinating than any available narrative we have of the nature of ethics. Ethical life outside the home ought to have the power to suck us out of the family romance and its ultimately stifling preoccupation with the miscarriages of Oedipus and pre-Oedipus, but our ethical discourse is too staid and stale to accomplish this, and not only at the degraded level of public pronouncement. Little help is available from the philosophical discourse on ethics, with its search for universal rules of rational agency and its decisive distinction between egoism and altruism.

If we look at what in fact, at the most immediate libidinal level, are the ideal images from the outside world that draw our children and young people, we see that it is images of self-affirmation and, in a word, of *prowess*, broadly conceived to include the sense of mastery of any activity, physical or intellectual. (The appeal of prowess has been less the case for young women than for young men, but with the impact of feminism, that is changing, though the sorts of prowess that impress young women will probably not be so much of the martial arts and professional sports varieties.) But prowess is precisely the sort of thing that plays no role in Kantian, or in general, transcendental or universalizing ethics.[22]

There is a powerful historical reason why this is so; that is, that our

21. Jacques Lacan, *Ecrits: A Selection* 50 (Alan Sheridan trans., W. W. Norton and Co. 1977) (1966).

22. Williams, *supra* note 9, at 92.

ethical theory still lives and breathes the atmosphere of Judeo-Christianity (a fact nowhere more evident than in the case of Kant). In Anglo-American philosophy the emphasis is on rules, duties, obligations, and altruism; in recent continental philosophy (Lévinas, Vattimo, Jean-Luc Nancy), the emphasis is on love or compassion. Neither accords a central role, or any role at all, to the Nietzschean and Aristotelian value of the self-affirmative exercise of prowess.

Williams conceives his inquiry into ethics precisely as post-Christian. His reconsideration of ancient Greek ethics aims to show that in certain fundamental ways, Greek ethics is more realistic, and therefore more adequate, to the demands of ethical reflection than are the idealizations of "the morality system." Shame in Greek ethics functions not only in the negative way that we tend notionally to associate with shame, but positively, as an ethical force that draws the individual up to the stature of the social identity that functions as an ideal for him.

Yet this is not an optimistic philosophy of voluntary self-actualization. On Williams's reading, it is Kantian ethics that despite its ascetic insistence on the unpleasure of obedience to the moral law is optimistic in its voluntarism—its positing of a moral agent who can choose, purely voluntarily, between the alternatives of good and evil.

The Greeks themselves, and Williams following them, trace the implications of their own ethical system into the inescapable contradictions of tragedy. There is, Williams argues, a decisive aspect of *passivity* in our relations to ethics; the passivity of our relation to who we are as what we have become not because we chose freely and rationally between good and evil, but because of how our identity was formed unbeknownst to ourselves.[23]

At certain decisive ethical moments this passivity manifests itself as necessity, the necessity that being who I am, this is what I must do if I am not to die in shame, even if it costs me my life. Thus, in the examples from Greek tragedy Williams discusses, Ajax after slaughtering the herd of sheep in his madness chooses to die rather than live as the man who has done this thing, and Agamemnon sacrifices his own daughter in order that his ships may sail to Troy. Williams's point in these readings is not to commend the actions of Ajax or Agamemnon, or to recommend to us the ethical system that leads to these actions, but to show the *depth* at which the imperatives of their relation to their social identities operates.

23. Williams, *supra* note 1, at 169.

The rigidity of the heroic conception of self, as of the social order within which it functioned, is deplorable to us, and the gap between it and any possible contemporary self-conception might seem unbridgeable. Yet Williams argues that our ideas about ethics are farther from the Greeks than is our actual *Sittlichkeit*.[24] Notionally, we draw a sharp boundary between the moral and the nonmoral, and the claims of our social identity are relegated to the area of the nonmoral. But in practice, the two are inseparably bound, for us as well as for the Greeks. The mixing of altruistic motives with the affirmation of one's social identity is obvious in the case of large-scale philanthropists who go on television with giant-sized checks made out to children's hospitals. But in more subtle ways, it operates on everyone. When I receive an appeal for contributions from Amnesty International, I do not feel compelled to give because the moral law commands it; it is because being who I am, having had the personal history I have had, and occupying the place in a social and economic structure that I occupy, I can do no other.

Yet the morality system makes us think that these intermixed motives are heteronomous, and that our motive in order to be properly ethical ought to be purified of them. In this way, the contours of our actual ethical life are distorted or falsified. (This distortion, incidentally, has *massive* political consequences, determining as it does, for example, the most corrupt and hypocritical aspects of the rhetoric of the Democratic party.)

At the center of the conflict between transcendental morality and Williamsian ethics is the question of desire. Desire is what sutures the self to its minimally idealized social identity and makes it vulnerable to the expectations of the neighbor lodged within the self. But from the standpoint of what I am calling transcendental morality and what Williams calls "the morality system,"[25] desire seems to be something contingent, a quality of the individual and merely empirical existent, and therefore a disturbance, indeed the preeminent disturbance, of rational moral agency as a universal or universalizable faculty. Here again it is Kant who wages the most relentless campaign to drive desire from the scene of moral autonomy, but in less systematic or explicit ways all forms of ethical theory must neutralize desire in order to arrive

24. Williams, *supra* note 9, at 92.

25. Williams, *supra* note 1, at 174–75.

at universality. The morality system involves a strict boundary between the moral and the nonmoral, and the drawing of this boundary involves in a fundamental way the relegation of desire to the nonmoral side of the line. But the larger realm of the ethical, as Williams and the Greeks conceive it, must include desire, and desire of a particularly powerful kind. There are desires that the agent merely happens to have, Williams argues, "but a conclusion of practical necessity could itself be the expression of a desire, if the desire were not one that the agent merely happened to have, but was essential to the agent and had to be satisfied."[26] Thus, the distinction between the necessary and the merely contingent, which in Kantian ethics runs between rationality and desire, is reinscribed by Williams within desire and produces the notion of an *essential or necessary desire.*

An analytic philosopher talking about essential desire! This I find intriguing. But can one talk about such a thing and remain an analytic philosopher, or is it not precisely here that, if one took the notion of an essential desire really seriously, one would begin to speak a different language altogether? I believe such is indeed the case at the present moment, but I do too believe that it is necessarily the case. The methods of analytic philosophy can be and need to be extended into the areas that have been the preserve of poststructuralism. Williams contributes a great deal to such an extension. Yet precisely because Williams is such a subtle, radical, and independent thinker, it is instructive to observe at what point his project stops short in its radicalism. Williams lays waste to the "morality system," deconstructing the boundaries within the larger realm of the ethical, between the moral and the nonmoral, the voluntary and the nonvoluntary, autonomy and heteronomy, guilt and shame. He even attempts to reinstate desire, or at least one kind of desire, at the center of ethics. But we come now to the classical dichotomy that stands firm, or almost firm—at least Williams never unequivocally deconstructs it as he does the other dichotomies. I am referring to the split between an ethical motivation on the one hand and a pleasure-seeking motivation on the other. Williams agrees with Hume and the Greeks, as against Kant, that it is a mark of virtuous character to take pleasure in doing virtuous things. But he thinks this pleasure cannot

26. *Id.* at 189.

be what the virtuous person *aims at* in acting virtuously; the pleasure goes along with the virtuous activity, but it is not performed on account of the pleasure.[27]

Williams is trying to salvage desire as a source, perhaps *the* source, of ethical motivation, but he thinks he can do this only by severing the connection between desire and pleasure. Not all desires aim at pleasure, he argues; there are also what he calls "non-I" or "self-transcending desires," desires for the existence of states of affairs from which the desiring subject is absolutely absent.[28] The distinction between "I" and "non-I" desires is the point at which the architecture of Williams's argument remains bound up with the metaphysics Williams is otherwise so at odds with. Thus, I will need to scrutinize it in some detail.

Let us note first of all that the non-I or self-transcending desires are essentially, as Derrida would say, "testamentary" in their structure.[29] They are desires that aim at the realization of a state of affairs that would obtain in my absence, without my knowledge, or, at the limit, after my death. My absence belongs to what Williams, in an essay from 1973, called the "logical structure" of the thought in which the aim is specified.[30] For instance, he says, the desire might be "that Mary be looked after." Our agent (Williams calls him Paul) could be invited to contemplate two possibilities for a world in which he does not exist: one, a world in which Mary is looked after and the other, a world in which she is not. And in that case, what motivates him is not anything about *him* or *his* desires insofar as these refer back to him, since nothing of the kind occurs in the specification of the state of affairs he desires, but rather "something about Mary."

Now, a non-I desire is not yet an ethical desire. Williams stresses that the desire in question might be capricious or malicious and yet remain structurally a non-I or self-transcending desire. For example, Williams suggests that some eccentric might provide in his will "that a chimpanzees' tea party . . . be held in the cathedral, just because it would be such a striking event," or one might have "the selfless desire

27. *Id.* at 50.

28. *Id.*

29. *Cf.* Jacques Derrida, *The Post Card: From Socrates to Freud and Beyond* 304–5 (Alan Bass trans., University of Chicago Press 1987) (1980).

30. Bernard Williams, "Egoism and Altruism," in *Problems of the Self: Philosophical Papers 1956–1972*, at 250, 265 (1973).

that another be harmed, whether one comes to know about it, or has anything to do with it, or not."[31]

The concept of a non-I desire is thus morally neutral; Williams posits it as the mediating moment by which one could pass from egoism to the possibility of ethics. The structure of the non-I desire, though it may serve nonaltruistic desires, is a condition of the possibility of altruism; once one has taken the step from I desires to non-I desires, one is ripe for the "more general" benevolent dispositions of altruism. The movement from I desire to non-I desire accomplishes the step from "the self to someone else," and it is *this* and not "the Kantian leap from the particular and affective to the rational and universal," that "makes all the difference in moral theory and moral psychology." So Williams argues in the 1973 essay, which he cites in *Ethics and the Limits of Philosophy,* in a passage where he reaffirms the notion of a self-transcendent desire.[32]

Has not Williams now come by a circuitous route back to another version of what he deconstructs? How much difference is there between an ethical non-I desire, a desire wrenched free from pleasure and self, selflessly desiring the good of another, and the purity of the good will in Kant? Is this not another version of what Nietzsche would recognize as ascetic metaphysics?

Williams tells us in *Ethics and the Limits of Philosophy* that he thinks the picture of ethics presented by Aristotle is basically correct.[33] In The *Nicomachean Ethics,* however, Aristotle tells us that the life of virtue is pleasant as such, in its essence.[34] Pleasure is not an incidental add-on; it does not just happen to be the case that acting virtuously is pleasant—"there is no pleasure without activity, and also no perfect activity without pleasure."[35] Thus, there appears to be a fundamental difference between Williams and Aristotle on the question of pleasure, a difference that places Williams on the side of ascetic metaphysics.

The question of exactly what view Aristotle actually held concerning pleasure is complicated. He has been accused of holding an "egoistic" view and thus of falling short of true morality. But more recently, writers like Williams and Julia Annas have stressed the fact that, for Aristotle, all pleasures are not on the same level, that the pleasures

31. *Id.* at 265.

32. Williams, *supra* note 1, at 50.

33. *Id.* at 52–53.

34. Aristotle, *Nicomachean Ethics* 41 (H. Rackham trans., rev. ed. Harvard University Press 1962) (1962).

35. *Id.* at 599.

associated with virtue are internal to the conception of the good that an agent has internalized in the course of her socialization.[36] Aristotle is, therefore, on this view, not a "hedonist" in any interesting sense. When the good person considers possible aims and objects of desires, she does so from a perspective that already conceives of these aims and objects in ethical terms, and she finds pleasure in the ones chosen precisely *because* they are good. On Williams's and Annas's account, even if pleasure and the good are inextricably linked, the good retains primacy, since it is in terms of the good that pleasure is defined.

Stating the matter this way seems to me entirely different from the way Aristotle does it. In order to see the distinctive character of Aristotle's analysis, it is necessary to look at what he means by *arētē,* the Greek word that is standardly translated as "virtue." This translation is highly misleading. The word "virtue" is so thoroughly saturated with ascetic values that the Greek *arētē* is unrecognizable through the veil of this word; in the transition from the Greek word to the English word the Greek value undergoes a sea change—it enters the realm of "morals" proper, and something goes askew in the entire discussion.

Although *arētē* does in fact overlap the field of meaning of "virtue," its fundamental sense is "excellence," "prowess," or, in general, "optimal functioning." The concept of *arētē* is essentially linked to the concept of *energeia,* which is the fulfillment in perfect functioning of the capacity that an existent has by virtue of being the kind of entity that it is. Excellence is essentially action or activity, in accord with the nature or essence of a thing, and Aristotle tells us such activity finds its *telos,* its fulfillment or completion, in *hēdonē,* pleasure. Pleasure is the essential correlate of *telieos energeia,* perfect activity, and to act and enjoy in this way is what Aristotle calls *arētē.* The orientation of Aristotle's ethics on this point is consistent with his metaphysics, which is oriented throughout by the teleological pull of *energeia.* Everything that exists is drawn toward the perfect manifestation in act of its essence.

Whatever one might think about Aristotle's metaphysics in general, in the case of living things we can translate Aristotle's account into respectable modern terms via the notion of a *functional structure.*[37] The

---

36. *See, e.g.,* Julia Annas, "Aristotle on Pleasure and Goodness," in *Essays on Aristotle's Ethics* 285, 285–86 (Amelie O. Rorty ed., 1980).

37. On structure and function in Aristotle, see T. H. Irwin, "The Metaphysical and Psychological Basis of Aristotle's Ethics," in *Essays on Aristotle's Ethics, supra* note 36, at 35, 37–45; Martha C. Nussbaum and Hilary Putnam, "Changing Aristotle's Mind," *in Essays on Aristotle's De Anima* 27 (Martha C. Nussbaum and Amelie O. Rorty ed., 1992).

eye, for example, has a specific organization adapted to the performance of a specific function, and there is an optimal state of this function that Aristotle sometimes describes as "unimpeded activity," a state signaled by the experience of pleasure. If one must squint or strain to see, or if what one sees is repellent or disgusting, this pleasure will be diminished or eliminated. For Aristotle, the functioning of an entire human being in relation both to specific activities and to an entire life is to be understood by analogy with the optimal functioning of an organ such as the eye. There is a function specific to the human species, and to perform this function is to live the life of *arētē*, of full energization of the essence of the human. There are obvious limitations to this account of what analytic philosophers like to call "human flourishing," and I will suggest a bit further on how Aristotle's account can be further developed in terms of Nietzsche's concept of the exercise of power. But for the moment, the point I am making is that this account of functional structure, unimpeded activity, and the completion of activity in pleasure, is *more fundamental* in the architecture of Aristotle's thought than the ethical account of good and bad pleasure. Before pleasures are good or bad in a moralizable sense, they are more or less optimal in a structural/functional sense. To understand Aristotle's ethics in its pre-Christian sense, we must understand it from the bottom up in this way. If we begin with our own moralized concepts of "virtue" and the "good," then we are likely to be troubled by the way Aristotle mixes together what we think of as self-regarding and other-regarding "virtues." Aristotle lists magnificence, ambition, and ready wit as virtues because, as Kathleen Wilkes writes, his "focus [is] on the capacities and competences of the individual," those capacities I summed up earlier under the rubric of prowess.[38]

Thus, we need to grasp the question of pleasure at this pre-ethical or sub-ethical level in order to understand the role it plays in Aristotle's ethics. At the deepest level, pleasure is an energetic phenomenon, an aspect of the self's experience of itself exercising its powers.

Williams and Annas argue that the concept of pleasure is vacuous as an explanation of the aim of activity if it merely identifies anything that an agent does with the goal of pleasure. But Aristotle's account suggests a dialectical concept of pleasure. At the most obvious level, as

38. K. V. Wilkes, "Psuchè Versus the Mind," in *Essay on Aristotle's De Anima, supra* note 37, at 109, 120, See *generally* Kathleen V. Wilkes, "The Good Man and the Good for Man in Aristotle's Ethics," *in Essays on Aristotle's Ethics, supra* note 36, at 341.

Aristotle says, we derive greater pleasure from those activities that we are good at, and because we take more pleasure in them, we tend to spend more time on these activities, which improves our skill, which in turn refines our pleasure. This is a very obvious fact, but its significance is profound in ethics. What is being drawn out or unfolded in this process is the self, a self that discovers its own powers in the process of being drawn out by the pleasure it takes in the exercise of those same powers in increasingly elaborated ways.

Of course this process is not merely an individual dialectic, it is caught in the web of what Lacan calls the symbolic order and in social, political, and economic relations with others. It is this entanglement and these relations that form the condition of possibility for the optimal exercise of the *energeia* of a human being. The functional structure of the human being qua human is determined preliminarily at the biological level, but finally at the cultural and intersubjective level. This thesis is not controversial; no one today doubts that this is the case. But ascetic morality misunderstands this fact, treating the transition to the cultural order as a transition from the merely worldly to the *Geistlich* and imposing on this transition the moral distinctions between prowess and virtue, egoism and altruism, and above all, between pleasure-seeking and non–pleasure-seeking motives. However refined these distinctions may be made by ethical theory, they remain derivatives of the condemnation of what Christianity calls the "natural man." What we need, and what Aristotle helps us pursue, is a nonmoral account of the nature of the ethical *energeia* that is made possible at the point of juncture between the individual and the social-political matrix.

It is true, however, as Williams notes, that we cannot share Aristotle's presupposition of a coherent and unified political community and its harmonious relation to the equally coherent and unified ethical development of the individual.[39] In order to adapt Aristotle's picture of ethics to our very different cultural situation, we need to think our way down into the roots out of which this picture is developed. And at that level, we can get help from Nietzsche toward the necessary further elaboration of Aristotle's notions. Nietzsche's "power," *Macht,* is by no means identical with Aristotle's *arētē,* but it partially overlaps the structural/functional dimension of Aristotle's concept. Just as pleasure is an essential concomitant of the exercise of *arētē,* so it is of the exercise of *Macht,* and pleasurable exercise is in both cases the aim of existence.

39. Williams, *supra* note 1, at 43–48.

Aristotle's notion of perfect activity posits the repose of completion as its goal. This is in line with the comparatively static and well-defined nature of the social organization within which he conceives the exercise of the "virtues" as taking place. Nietzsche's *Macht*, however, is a conflictual and open-ended concept; the essence of *Macht*-pleasure is not the sensation of the mere exercise of power but the sensation of the *increase* of power through the overcoming of obstacles. Once obstacles are removed, of course, activity is "unimpeded." But for Nietzsche, the pleasure of such activity is primarily in the sensation of passage from an impeded to an unimpeded state, the consciousness of difference between the two; and this is a recursive process that is in principle illimitable.

At one level of Nietzsche's thought, this definition of Will to Power manifests itself in the glorification of conquest, appropriativeness, and bellicosity. But when Nietzsche pushes his dialectic to its limit, Will to Power finds its *Aufhebung* as what Zarathustra calls "overcoming oneself" and in the drive to create, or, as Zarathustra puts it, to "bring forth beyond oneself."[40]

Thus, Nietzschean Will to Power issues in an ethical conception that plays a role quite similar to that played in the morality system by the notions of selflessness and altruism. Yet the ethical system by which selflessness and altruism are defined is of a fundamentally different type, for in Nietzsche, the motive to gift-giving remains the stimulation of the pleasurable feeling of power. The transition from the desire to master others to the desire to sacrifice oneself for them does not correspond to any line between self-regarding and other-regarding motivation. "Let your kindness be your final self-conquest," says Zarathustra, "I love him who wants to create over and beyond himself and thus perishes."[41] We could link this with that highest ideal of conduct that Aristotle calls *to kalon*, a word translated in the context of the *Nichomachean Ethics* as "nobility" but which is the Greek word for "the beautiful," so that it means literally "the beautiful as manifested in ethical action." For the sake of *to kalon*, Aristotle says, a man "will surrender wealth and power and all the goods that men struggle to win," and, if necessary, will lay down his life for his friends, since the noble man "would

40. I discuss the intricate ambiguities of Nietzsche on Will to Power in Henry Staten, *Nietzsche's Voice* 86–107 (1990).

41. Friedrich W. Nietzsche, *Thus Spoke Zarathustra* (1892), *reprinted in The Portable Nietzsche* 177 (Walter Kaufman ed. and trans., Penguin Books 1982).

prefer an hour of rapture to a long period of mild enjoyment."[42] This is a stunning moment in the *Nichomachean Ethics,* a moment at which Aristotle abuts on Bataille. Aristotle's normative concept of pleasure as a complete or perfect activity here opens out into a pleasure that is a violent or excessive expenditure, expenditure without reserve. This is not a typical moment in the *Nichomachean Ethics,* but it shows that there is something in the logic of Aristotle's concept of pleasure that is open to development along Nietzschean lines.

What both Nietzsche and Aristotle posit is not precisely that pleasure is the aim of all activity but that *when we probe the idea of an aim deeply enough we always find pleasure there.* It is true, as Williams emphasizes, that the ethical person does not think of pleasure when she desires an ethical goal, that the self and its pleasure are not represented in her consciousness. But it is not true that the self and its pleasure are missing from the "logical structure" of the thought, unless logical structure is going to be identical with what is present to consciousness or at least admissible to consciousness under rules stipulated by the ethical ideology to which that consciousness adheres. If with the help of Aristotle and Nietzsche we push beyond those rules—the rules of ascetic morality—we find that wherever there is a goal, pleasure is nothing but the other side of the coin we are looking at; that pleasure is always there and all we have to do is turn the coin over to find it. *Turning over the coin:* this is the essential move in the unmasking of ascetic morality. In order to perform this role, in order to always be refound at the limit of all striving, the concept of pleasure must be, as Williams and Annas complain, in a certain sense, vacuous. For the absence of determinate content is precisely what enables the concept of pleasure to function as the deconstructive operator, the monkey wrench that is always there to foul the gears of the system of ascetic morality. It is, in Derridean terms, the arch-supplement or *arkhe-pharmakon,* the noxious freebie (noxious to ascetic metaphysics, that is) that always turns up as the extra element added on to the goal of striving, incapable of being accounted for. Hence the odd vacillation of an identical type in both Nietzsche and Aristotle on the question of pleasure. Pleasure in the ordinary sense, as mere sensual gratification, both dismiss out of hand; such gratification is certainly not the universal good.[43] What Aristotle and Nietzsche are

42. Aristotle, *supra* note 34, at 555.

43. Incidentally, this dismissal strikes me as a little too ready and unconsidered. Farther down the road we are traveling in this discussion, the question of sensual pleasure

interested in is not pleasure pure and simple, but the *transformations* of pleasure, its deeper and deeper modes of manifestation, modes that include pain—from the little, rhythmic, sexual pain Nietzsche remarks on all the way up to the ecstatic agony of self-immolation.

Even at the deepest level pleasure seems to be in one sense only an accompaniment, something added on to the "as-such" of the experience of optimal activity; yet at the same time not an add-on, but the very deepest resonance of the essence of the experience. This ambiguity is unresolved by Aristotle and Nietzsche and is, I would argue, unresolvable, because it reflects the functioning of the concept of pleasure, at least of the philosophical concept of pleasure as the *telos* of all activity. It is always open to the philosopher to seize on one side of this oscillation, the side of inessentiality, in order to repress pleasure from his representation of ethical striving. We have seen how even Williams is—can I say "seduced"?—by the illusion of the absence of pleasure.

Williams's antiascetic instincts are strong. Consequently, he attempts to detoxify the notion of a self-transcending desire, to remove what Nietzsche calls its "moraline," by his argument that a self-transcending desire can be malicious as well as benevolent.[44] You will recall the example he gives of someone who provides in his will for a chimpanzees' tea party to be held in a cathedral, or who selflessly desires that someone should be miserable after he himself has died.[45] But this desynonymization of "selflessness" and "benevolence" removes the moraline from one level of the analysis only to hide it more effectively at another level. The apparently Nietzschean indifference of the notion of a non-I desire to the distinction between benevolent and malicious pleasures is only a distraction from the fact that pleasure in general is still, again, being banished from the scene.

We have seen that for Nietzsche and Aristotle, the overcoming or even sacrifice of self can be not the banishment but the consummation of pleasure: the translation of pleasure from the superficial level at which pain and pleasure are opposites, to the level at which certain kinds of pain, undergone for certain purposes, become, if not them-

would have to be taken up again. In order to do this, we would need D. W. Winnicott's help in investigating the way the economy of pleasure is established in the pre-oedipal infant.

44. Friedrich Nietzsche, *The Will to Power* 179 (Walter Kaufman ed., Walter Kaufman and R. J. Hollingdale trans., Vintage Books 1967) (1887).

45. See *supra* note 31 and accompanying text.

selves pleasurable, at least the price that is paid for a deeper pleasure than would otherwise be available.

We will not be able to start clearing the stench of moral tartuffery from our ethical discourse, either at the public or the private level, until we have cleared away the self-deception of the notions of selflessness and altruism, of a motive that could be detached from the aim of pleasure. This is not, of course, to suggest that all pleasures are on the same level, or to deny that one can be misled by the allure of pleasure. But the most seductive and deceitful pleasures of all are those of feeling morally superior to someone else because one is more altruistic, *more selfless,* and of using the rhetoric of selflessness as a bat with which to beat the opposition—a bat which, incidentally, can be used by all parties in the debate, whether right or left.

It was Nietzsche, in *Daybreak*[46] and *Human, All Too Human,*[47] who initiated the critique of the altruistic masks of Will to Power; but we have made little progress along these lines since Nietzsche. I believe Bernard Williams's critique of the "morality system" in general, and his development of the ethical concept of shame in particular, constitute a rare, significant advance in the Nietzschean "transvaluation of values." In this essay I have attempted to sketch the outlines of a further development.

46. Friedrich Nietzsche, *The Dawn of Day* in *The Complete Works of Friedrich Nietzsche* (J. M. Kennedy trans., Russel and Ressel 1964) (1881).

47. Friedrich Nietzsche, *Human, All Too Human: A Book for Free Spirits* (Marion Faber ed., Marion Faber and Stephen Lehman trans., University of Nebraska Press 1985) (1878).

Chapter 3

# Why Does the Law Need an Obscene Supplement?

*Slavoj Žižek*

## I

Perhaps, the truly subversive authors are not direct "transgressors" à la Sade but those (from Pascal through Kleist, Kierkegaard and Kafka to Brecht's learning plays) who belong to the "overconformist" line: authors who subvert the ruling ideology by taking it more literally than it is ready to take itself—the uneasy, disturbing effect on the reader of *Pensées* or *The Prince of Homburg* resides in the fact that they as it were disclose the hidden cards of the ideology they identify with (French Catholicism, the German military patriotism, revolutionary Communism) and thus render it inoperative, i.e., unacceptable for the existing order. These works violently confront us with the fact that ideology requires a distance from itself in order to rule unimpeded: if ideology is to maintain its hold on us, we must experience ourselves as not fully in its grasp—"I'm not merely a direct embodiment of . . . [Jansenism, Prussian patriotism, Communism]; beneath this ideological mask, there lurks a warm human person with his small sorrows and joys that have nothing to do with big ideological issues. . . ." What Pascal, Kleist, and Brecht do is invert this (mis)perception: the apparently nonideological experience of the "warm human person" beneath the ideological mask is in itself false, it is here to obfuscate the fact that the ideological mask effectively runs the game—in Brecht's *Massnahme,* for example, individuals are violently reduced to their "ideological mask," so that the very moment the desperate hero, unable to endure any longer the sight of the suffering of the poor peasants, wants to shed off his mask and show his true face in order to help them, he is denounced as false, as the moment of betrayal of the revolutionary Cause . . .

Another aspect of this subversion was emphasized already by Pascal: one should reverse the Enlightenment notion according to which, to the ordinary people unable to grasp the need for their religious belief, the truth of their religion has to be asserted in an authoritarian way, as a dogma that needs no arguments, while the enlightened elite is able to obey upon being convinced by good reasons (in homology to the children who must learn to obey without any explanation, in contrast to adults who know the reasons to follow social obligations)—the uncanny truth is rather that argumentation is for the crowd of "ordinary people" who need the illusion that there are good and proper reasons for the order that they must obey, while the true secret known only to the elites is that the dogma of power is grounded only in itself: "Custom is the whole of equity for the sole reason that it is accepted. That is the mystic basis of its authority."[1] "It would therefore be a good thing for us to obey laws and customs because they are laws."[2] Ideology is thus not only "irrational obedience" beneath which critical analysis has to discern its true reasons and causes; it is also the "rationalization," the enumeration of a network of reasons, that masks the unbearable fact that Law is grounded only in its own act of enunciation.

Another key philosopher and theologian to be inserted in this series is Nicolas Malebranche, the great Cartesian Catholic who, after his death, was excommunicated and his books destroyed on account of his very excessive orthodoxy. In the best Pascalian tradition, Malebranche laid the cards on the table and "revealed the secret" (the perverted truth) of Christianity: it was not that Christ came to Earth in order to deliver people from sin, from the legacy of Adam's Fall; on the contrary, *Adam had to fall in order to enable Christ to come to earth and dispense salvation.* (Malebranche applies here to God Himself the "psychological" insight that tells us that the saintly figure who sacrifices himself for the benefit of others, to deliver them from their misery, secretly *wants* the others to suffer misery *so that he will be able to help them*—like the proverbial husband who works all day for his poor crippled wife, yet would probably abandon her if she were to regain health and turn into a successful career woman. It is much more satisfying to sacrifice oneself for the poor victim than to enable the other to lose the status of a victim and maybe even to become more successful than ourselves . . .)

1. Blaise Pascal, *Pensées* 46 (Penguin Books 1966).
2. *Id.* at 216.

Malebranche develops this parallel to its conclusion, to the horror of the Jesuits who organized his excommunication: in the same way that the saintly person merely uses the others' suffering to bring about his own narcissistic satisfaction in helping the others in distress, God also ultimately *loves only Himself,* and merely uses man to promulgate his own glory . . . From this reversal, Malebranche draws a consequence worthy of Lacan's famous turnabout of Dostoyevski (*"If God doesn't exist,"* the father says, *"then everything is permitted.* Quite evidently, a naive notion, for we analysts know full well that if God doesn't exist, then nothing at all is permitted any longer"):[3] it is not true that, if Christ were not come to earth to deliver humanity, everybody would be lost—quite the contrary, if Christ were not to come, nobody would be lost, i.e., every human being had to fall so that Christ could come and deliver some of them . . . What further follows from this is the paradoxical nature of predestination and grace: divine grace is contingently disseminated, it has absolutely no correlation with our good deeds. The moment the link between grace and our deeds were to be directly perceptible, human freedom would be lost: God is not allowed to intervene directly in the universe, i.e., grace has to remain masked, nonperceptible as such, as a direct divine intervention, since its direct transparency would change man into a slavish entity subordinated to God like an animal and would deprive him of faith grounded in free choice.[4]

The Jansenist notion of miracle bears witness to this paradox: for Jansenists, a miracle is an event that has the quality of a miracle only in the eyes of the believer—to the commonsense eyes of an infidel, it appears as a purely natural coincidence. It is thus far too simple to read this reluctance of the Church as an attempt to avoid the objective test-

---

3. *The Seminar of Jacques Lacan. Book II: The Ego in Freud's Theory and in the Technique of Psychoanalysis* 128 (1988).

4. A homologous operation of laying the (hidden) cards on the table is performed by Kierkegaard who emphasized that the necessary consequence (the "truth") of the Christian demand to *love one's enemy* is "the demand to *hate the beloved* out of love and in love . . . So high—humanly speaking to a kind of madness—can Christianity press the demand of love if love is to be the fulfilling of the law. Therefore it teaches that the Christian shall, if it is demanded, be capable of hating his father and mother and sister and beloved." Søren Kierkegaard, *Works of Love* 114 (1962). Kierkegaard applies here the logic of *hainamoration,* later articulated by Lacan, which relies on the split in the beloved between the beloved person itself and the true object-cause of my love for him, that which is "in him more than himself" (for Kierkegaard: God)—sometimes, hatred is the only proof that I really love you . . .

ing of the truth of a miracle. The point is rather that the miracle is inherently linked to the fact of belief: there is no neutral miracle to convince cynical infidels. Or, to put it in another way, the fact that the miracle appears as such only to believers is a sign of God's true omnipotence, not of His impotence. However, although the dispensation of Grace is not grounded in our good deeds but disseminated in an utterly contingent way, one should nevertheless endeavor to accomplish as many good deeds as possible—if and when divine Grace touches us, our good deeds make us receptacles for it, they enable us to recognize it and thus to profit from it. The achievement of Malebranche is thus to propose a *materialist theory of Grace:* Grace is distributed in a completely contingent way, not in accordance with human merits but following its own inherent protonatural laws, like (to use a metaphor by Malebranche himself) the rain across a countryside that can either wet a field, thus being spent in a productive way for human purposes, or it can wet a barren hillside nearby and be spent in vain, one never knows, it is blind like fate; and this metaphor also makes it clear why one should nonetheless accomplish good deeds—like the peasant who should cultivate his field, so that when (and if) rain falls, it will bear fruit. In this precise sense, God is the Lacanian big Other: a machine that follows its inherent "natural" laws and is (like Schreber's God) completely ignorant of human affairs.

What lurks in the background is, of course, the fact that the God of Malebranche is Lacan's big Other at its purest: the order that regulates our universe, but remains purely virtual, i.e., is nowhere directly perceptible. The standard reproach to occasionalism (according to which not only is there no proof for occasionalism, but occasionalism even directly contradicts our sensible experience that tells us that physical bodies act directly upon our senses) presents no problem for Malebranche, since it is the key component of his argument *for* occasionalism—his point is that the knowledge of the true order of things (of divine causality) contradicts our sensible experience: if the divine causality were to become directly observable, this would make us slaves of God and change God into a horrifying tyrant (this idea was later taken over by Kant, in his notion that it is only our epistemological limitation—our ignorance of noumenal causality—that makes us free moral beings). One can never experience the symbolic "big Other" *as such:* either—in our "normal" everyday life—we are oblivious of the way it overdetermines our acts, or—in psychotic experience—we become aware of the big Other's massive presence, yet in a "reified" way, not as a virtual Other, but as the materialized, obscene, superego Other (God who bombards us with excessive *jouissance,* who controls us in the Real). The only way to experience the big Other in the Real is thus to experience it as the superego agency, the horrible obscene Thing.

## *II*

This impossibility of experiencing the "big Other" in the real signals the *virtual* character of our symbolic identity. This virtuality is far from limited to theology—it also forms the basis of bureaucratic metaphysics. The Swiss, as one would expect, excel in the delicate art of this metaphysics with its distinctions beyond comprehension for common mortals. A foreigner who wants to teach in Switzerland has to appear before a state agency called *Comité de l'habitant* and to apply for *le certificat de bonne vie et moeurs;* the paradox, of course, is that nobody can *get* this *certificat*—the most a foreigner can get, in the case of a positive decision, is a paper stating that he is not to be refused the *certificat*—a double negation which, however, is not yet a positive decision.[5] This is how Switzerland likes to see a poor foreign worker: your stay there can never be fully legitimized, the most you can get is the admission that allows you to dwell in a kind of in-between state—you're never positively accepted, you're just not yet rejected and thus retained with a vague promise that, in some indefinite future, you stand a chance.

This central place of virtuality also accounts for the elementary trick of bureaucracy (which is not an exception but the very rule of its "normal" functioning): bureaucracy corners the subject into a situation in which, in order to survive, he has to break the (explicit) Law—this violation is then tolerated, but also manipulated as a permanent threat. Whenever one deals with a true bureaucratic machine, one is sooner or later caught in a vicious circle (for the attestation *A* one needs the paper *B;* one cannot get *B* without *C;* and, finally, of course, the circle is closed, *C* cannot be obtained without *A* . . .)—at this point, a bureaucrat displays his so-called human warmth, he mercifully makes an exception, breaks the vicious circle, and gives us the required attestation, although he never forgets to point out that, according to the rules, he should not

5. I owe this information to John Higgins, Capetown University.

do it . . . Bureaucracy literally feeds on this eternal and a priori indebtedness/guilt of the subject.

And, to add the third term to this mysterious complicity between theology and bureaucracy, namely psychoanalysis, this constitutive guilt of the subject is also at work in the psychoanalytic notion of the "subject supposed to know" elaborated by Lacan. In the television series *Columbo,* the crime (the act of murder) is shown in detail in advance, so that the enigma to be resolved is not the usual "whodunit" but how the detective will establish the link between the deceitful surface (the "manifest content" of the crime scene) and the truth about the crime (its "latent thought"), how he will prove to the culprit his or her guilt. The success of *Columbo* thus attests that the true interest of the detective's work is the process of deciphering itself, not its result: the triumphant final revelation "And the murderer is . . ." is completely lacking here, since we know this from the very outset. Even more crucial than this feature is the fact that not only do we spectators know in advance who did it (since we directly see it), but, inexplicably, Columbo himself immediately knows it: the moment he visits the scene of crime and encounters the culprit, he is absolutely certain, he simply knows that the culprit did it, so that his subsequent effort does not concern the enigma "who did it?," but how to prove it to the culprit. This reversal of "normal" order has clear theological connotations: just as in a true religion where I first believe in God and then, on the ground of my belief, become susceptible to the proofs of the truth of my faith, Columbo also *first*—with a mysterious, but nonetheless absolutely infallible certainty—knows who did it, and *then,* on the basis of this inexplicable knowledge, proceeds to gather proofs. And, in a slightly different way, this is what the analyst qua "subject supposed to know" aims at: when the analysand enters the transferential relationship with the analyst, he has the same absolute certainty that the analyst knows his secret (which only means that the patient *is* a priori "guilty," that there is a secret meaning of his acts to be unearthed). The analyst is thus not an empiricist probing the patient with different hypotheses, searching for proofs, etc.—he embodies the absolute certainty (which Lacan compares with the certainty of Descartes's *cogito ergo sum*) about the analysand's "guilt," i.e., his unconscious desire.

In order to be able to determine properly the scope of this Lacanian notion of the *subject supposed to know,* one should bear in mind its second paradoxical feature, i.e., the fact that it occurs in place of *another* notion that is much closer to our symbolic experience, that of the subject supposed to *believe.* The two are not symmetrical, since belief and knowledge themselves are not symmetrical: at its most radical, the status of the (Lacanian) big Other qua symbolic institution is that of belief (trust)—i.e., the big Other involves and relies on a fundamental "trust," reliance—not that of knowledge, since belief is symbolic and knowledge is real. (For that precise reason, Lacan speaks of "knowledge in the real," not of *belief* in the real.) That is to say, belief is always minimally "reflective," a "belief in the belief of the other"[6]—"I still believe in Communism" equals saying "I believe there are still people who believe in Communism," while knowledge is precisely *not* knowledge about the fact that there is another who knows. Another way to put it is to say that belief and knowledge relate to each other as desire and drive: desire is also always reflective, a "desire to desire," while drive is not "drive to drive."

According to a well-known anthropological anecdote, the "primitives" to whom one attributed certain "superstitious beliefs," when directly asked about them, answered that "some people believe . . ."—they immediately displaced their belief, transferring it onto another. Are we not doing the same with our children? We go through the ritual of Santa Claus since our children (are supposed to) believe in it and we do not want to disappoint them. Is this not also the usual excuse of the mythical crooked or cynical politician who turns honest?—"I cannot disappoint them (the mythical 'ordinary people') who believe in it (or in me)." And, furthermore, is this need to find another who "really believes" also not what propels us in our need to stigmatize the Other as (religious or ethnic) "fundamentalist"? In an uncanny way, belief seems always to function in the guise of such a "belief at a distance": in order for belief to function, there *had to be* some ultimate guarantor of it, yet this guarantor is always deferred, displaced, never here *in persona.* How, then, is belief possible? How is this vicious circle of deferred belief cut short? The point, of course, is that the subject who directly believes need not exist for the belief to be operative: it is enough precisely to *presuppose* its existence, i.e., to *believe* in it, either in the guise of the mythological founding figure who is not part of our experiential reality, or in the guise of the impersonal "one" ("one believes . . .").

6. Michel de Certeau, "What We Do When We Believe," in *On Signs* 200 (Marshall Blonsky ed., 1985).

It was again Kierkegaard who rendered the ultimate paradox of belief: he emphasized that the apostle preaches the need to believe and asks that we take his belief upon his word—he never offers "hard proofs" destined to convince nonbelievers. For that reason, the reluctance of the Church when it faces material that may prove or disprove its claims is more ambiguous than it may appear. In the case of the Turin shroud that allegedly contains the contours of the crucified Jesus and thus his almost photographic portrait, it is too simple to read the Church's reluctance to submit the shroud to chemical analysis as expressing the fear that the shroud will turn out to be a later fake—perhaps, it would be even more horrifying if the shroud were proven to be authentic, since this positivist "verification" of the belief would undermine its status and deprive it of its charisma. Belief can only thrive in the shadowy domain between outright falsity and positive truth. (The above-mentioned Jansenist notion of miracle proves that they were fully aware of this paradox of a belief that has to remain unsubstantiated.)[7]

### *III*

All these paradoxes, of course, point toward the fundamental *inconsistency* of the domain of Law (not merely in the restrained legal meaning of the term, but also in the vague and global sense of the symbolic network of rules that regulate our lives), clearly discernible in the functioning of political *power* as a social relation.

When one approaches politics through psychoanalysis, one usu-

7. A further interesting fact concerning the relationship between belief and knowledge is that attempts to "demonstrate the existence of God" (i.e., to confer to our assurance that "God exists" the status of knowledge) as a rule emerge *when nobody seems to doubt His existence* (in short, when "everybody believes"), not in the times of the rise of atheism and the crisis of religion (who is today still seriously engaged in "proving the existence of God"?). One is thus tempted to claim that, paradoxically, the very endeavor to demonstrate the existence of God introduces doubt; in a way creates the problem it purports to solve—in clear contrast to the standard Hegelian notion according to which attempts to prove God's existence by reasoning bear witness to the fact that the Cause (our immediate faith in Him) is already lost, i.e., that our relationship to Him is no longer a "substantial" faith but already a reflectively "mediated" knowledge, reflective knowledge seems rather to have the status of an "excess" we indulge in when we are sure of our Faith (like a person in an emotional relationship who can allow himself to mock gently his partner precisely when he is so sure of the depth of their relationship that he knows such superficial jokes cannot hurt it . . .).

ally focuses on Freud's elaboration of the notion of "crowd" à propos of Army and Church. However, this approach seems to give rise to a justified criticism: are Army and Church not the very examples of the *disavowal* of the proper political dimension, i.e., the two forms of social organization in which the logic of collective deliberation and decision about public affairs that defines the political space is replaced by a clear hierarchical line of command? Is this not a proof by negation that psychoanalysis is unable to define the properly *political* space: the only form of "sociability" it can articulate is the "totalitarian" distortion/ obfuscation of the political? Hannah Arendt seemed to point in this direction when she emphasized the distinction between political power and the mere exercise of (social) violence: organizations run by direct nonpolitical authority—by an order of command that is not politically grounded authority (Army, Church, school)—present examples of violence (*Gewalt*), not of political Power in the strict sense of the term.

However, it would be productive to introduce here the distinction between the public symbolic Law and its obscene supplement: the notion of the obscene superego double-supplement of Power implies that *there is no Power without violence:* Power always has to rely on an obscene stain of violence, political space is never "pure" but always involves some kind of reliance on the "prepolitical" violence. Perhaps, this also accounts for the insufficiency of Arendt's notion of the "banality of Evil" from her famous report on the Eichmann trial, i.e., of how Eichmann, far from being driven by some demonic will to impart suffering and destroy human lives, was simply a model civil servant doing his job, executing orders and not minding about their moral implications: what mattered to him was the pure "boring" symbolic form of the Order, deprived of all imaginary—or, in Kantian terms: "pathological"—vestiges (horrors that its execution will entail, private motifs of financial profit or sadistic satisfaction, etc.). However, the fact remains that the execution of the holocaust was treated *by the Nazi apparatus itself* as a kind of obscene dirty secret, not publicly acknowledged, resisting simple and direct translation into the anonymous bureaucratic machine. In order to account for the way executioners carried out holocaust measures, one should thus supplement the purely *symbolic* bureaucratic logic involved in the notion of the "banality of Evil" with two other components: the *imaginary* screen of satisfactions, myths, etc., which enabled subjects to maintain a distance toward (and thus to "neutralize") the horrors they were involved in and the knowledge they had about it (saying to oneself that Jews are only being transported to some new Eastern camps; claiming that just a small number of them were actually killed; listening to classical music in the evening and thus convincing themselves that "after all, we are men of culture, unfortunately forced to do some unpleasant, but necessary things," etc.); and, above all, the reality of the perverse (sadistic) *jouissance* in what they were doing (torturing, dismembering the bodies, killing them). Of special importance is to keep in mind how the very "bureaucratization" of the crime was ambiguous as to its libidinal impact: on the one hand, it enabled (some of) the participants to neutralize the horror and take it as "just another job"; on the other hand, the basic lesson of the perverse ritual holds also here: this "bureaucratization" was in itself a source of an additional *jouissance* (does it not provide an additional rush if one performs the killing as a complicated administrative-criminal operation? Is it not more satisfying to torture the prisoners as a part of some orderly procedure, say, the meaningless "morning exercises" that served only to torture the prisoners—didn't it give another "kick" to the satisfaction of the guards when they were inflicting pain on their victims not by way of directly beating them up but in the guise of an activity officially designed to maintain their health?).

The same impasse confronts a spectator of Robert Altman's *MASH*, a film that occupies an exceptional place: at the beginning of the director's opus, it negates its basic "tone," so that all his later films can be read as so many attempts to surmount the ideological limitations of *MASH*. That is to say, contrary to the misleading appearance, *MASH* is a perfectly conformist film—through all their mockery of authority, practical jokes, sexual escapades, etc., the members of the *MASH* crew *exemplarily perform their job* and thus present absolutely no threat to the smooth running of the military machine. No wonder that the film served as the base for a long-running and definitely *not* "subversive" television series. In other words, the cliché about *MASH* as an antimilitarist film depicting the horrors of the meaningless military slaughter that can be endured only through a healthy measure of cynicism, practical jokes, laughing at the pompous official rituals, etc., misses the point—this very distance *is* ideology. This dimension of *MASH* becomes even more tangible the moment one compares it to two other well-known films about military life, *An Officer and a Gentleman* and *Full Metal Jacket*. The first two films exhibit the two versions of the perfectly functioning military subject: identification with the military machine is supported either by ironic distrust, indulging in practical jokes, sexual escapades, etc. (*MASH*), or by the awareness that behind the cruel drill sergeant there is a "warm human person," i.e., a helping father-substitute who only feigns cruelty (in *An Officer and a Gentleman,* Louis Gossett Jr. got an Oscar for this role), in strict homology to the—profoundly antifeminist—myth of a hooker who, deep in her heart, longs to be a good mother. *Full Metal Jacket,* on the other hand, successfully resists this ideological temptation to "humanize" the drill sergeant or other members of the crew and thus lays on the table the cards of the military ideological machine: the distance toward it, far from signaling the limitation of the ideological machine, functions as its positive *condition of possibility.* What we get in the first part of the film is the military drill, the direct bodily discipline, saturated by the unique blend of humiliating display of power, sexualization, and obscene blasphemy (at Christmas, the soldiers are ordered to sing "Happy birthday dear Jesus . . .")—in short, the superego machine of Power at its purest. As to the status of this obscene machine with respect to our everyday life-world, the lesson of the film is clear: the function of this obscene underworld of unwritten rituals is not to enable the official "public" ideology to "catch on," to start to function as a constituent of our actual social life, i.e., this obscene underworld does not "mediate" between the abstract structure of symbolic law and the concrete experience of the actual life-world. The situation is rather inverse: we need a "human face," a sense of distance, in order to be able to accommodate ourselves to the crazy demands of the superego machine. The first part of the film ends with a soldier who, on account of his overidentification with the military ideological machine, "runs amok" and shoots first the drill sergeant, then himself—the radical, unmediated identification with the superego machine necessarily leads to a murderous *passage à l'acte.* The second, main part of the film ends with a scene in which a soldier (Matthew Modine) who, throughout the film, displayed a kind of ironic "human distance" toward the military machine (on his helmet, the inscription "born to kill" is accompanied by the peace sign, etc.—in short, it looks as if he stepped right out from *MASH*!), shoots a wounded Vietcong sniper girl—he is the one in whom the interpellation by the military big Other has fully succeeded, he is the fully constituted military subject.

*IV*

The lesson of all this is thus clear: an ideological identification exerts a true hold on us precisely when we maintain an awareness that we are not fully identical to it, that there is a rich human person beneath it—"everything is not ideology; beneath the ideological mask, I am also a human person" is *the very form of ideology,* of its "practical efficiency." A close analysis of even the most "totalitarian" ideological edifice inevitably reveals that in it, not everything is "ideology" (in the popular sense of the "politically instrumentalized legitimization of power relations"): in every ideological edifice, there is a kind of "transideological" kernel, since, if an ideology is to become operative and effectively "seize" individuals, it *has* to parasitize on and manipulate some kind of "transideological" vision that cannot be reduced to a simple instrument of legitimizing pretensions to power (notions and sentiments of solidarity, justice, belonging to a community, etc.). Is not a kind of "authentic" vision discernible even in Nazism (the notion of the deep solidarity that keeps together the "community of people"), not to mention Stalinism? The point is thus not only that there is no ideology without a transideological "authentic" kernel, but rather that *it is only the reference to such a transideological kernel that renders an ideology "workable."*

In one of his speeches to the Nazi crowd in Nuremberg, Hitler made a self-referential remark about how this very reunion is to be perceived: an external observer unable to experience the "inner greatness" of the Nazi movement will see only the display of external military and political strength, while for us, members of the movement who live and breathe with it, it is infinitely more, the assertion of the inner link connecting us . . . Here, again, we encounter the reference to the extraideological kernel. John Deathridge emphasized the remarkable fact that Hitler's favorite Wagner opera was neither the overtly German *Meistersinger* nor *Lohengrin* with its call to arms to defend Germany against the Eastern hords, but *Tristan* with its tendency to leave behind the Day—the daily life of symbolic obligations, honors, debts, etc.—and to immerse oneself in the Night, to embrace ecstatically one's death. This "aesthetic suspension of the political" (to paraphrase Kierkegaard) was at the very core of the fantasmatic background of the Nazi attitude: at stake in it was "something more than politics," an ecstatic aestheticized experience of Community best exemplified precisely by the nightly rituals during Nuremberg rallies. So, paradoxically, the dangerous ingredient of Nazism is not its "utter politicization" of the entire social life, but, on the contrary, the suspension of the political via the reference to an extraideological kernel, much stronger than in a "normal" democratic political order.[8] Therein, perhaps, resides the problem with Judith Butler's question:

> [D]oes politicization always need to overcome disidentification? What are the possibilities of politicizing disidentification, this experience of misrecognition, this uneasy sense of standing under a sign to which one does and does not belong?[9]

Is, however, the attitude of the heroes of *MASH* not precisely that of an active *dis*identification? Of course, one can argue that *this* disidentification is something entirely different than the lesbian parodic imitation-subversion of feminine codes—nonetheless, the point remains that the difference is the one between the two modes of *dis*identification, not between identification and its subversion. Or, to put it in a more precise way: an ideological edifice can be undermined by a too-literal identification, which is why its successful functioning requires a minimum of distance toward its explicit rules. Is not an exemplary case of the subversion-through-identification provided by Jaroslav Hasek's *The Good Soldier Schwejk,* the novel whose hero causes total havoc by simply executing the orders of his superiors in an overzealous and all-too-literal way? Everything hinges on the crucial fact that the Law is already split in itself, which is why a too-direct identification with it cripples its functioning. One can thus clearly perceive the weak point of the standard feminist reasoning as exemplified in Claudia Springer's critical assessment of the television series *Mann and Machine:* "The contradictory messages about gender roles that emerge from the series are signs

8. For that reason, it is also erroneous to dismiss Nazi rituals as an "inauthentic" faked imitation of pagan sacred rituals: Nazism effectively does carry out the "return of the repressed" of Christianity, i.e., of the pagan logic of the "offering to obscure gods": "This, re-enacting the most monstrous and supposedly superseded forms of the holocaust, is the drama of Nazism" (Jacques Lacan, *The Four Fundamental Concepts of Psycho-Analysis* 275 [1978]). In other words, those who lament the loss of the authentic "primitive" relationship to the Sacred in our "rationalist" and "utilitarian" Western civilization have no right to become indignant at the Nazi rituals . . .

9. Judith Butler, *Bodies That Matter* 219 (1994).

that patriarchal ideology in late twentieth century is no longer coherent or consistent and cannot hide the cracks in its reasoning."[10] However, what if certain inconsistencies and "cracks in its reasoning" are, on the contrary, positive conditions of the "normal" functioning of "patriarchal ideology"? (And, incidentally, is this—the unavoidable inconsistency of an ideological edifice, of its line(s) of argumentation—also not the very fundamental lesson of the Derridean deconstruction?)

The inevitable conclusion to be drawn from this paradox is that the feature that effectively sustains identification—the famous Freudian-Lacanian *einziger Zug,* the unary feature—is not the obvious one, the big "official" insignia, but a small feature, even the one of *taking a distance* toward the official insignia. When a lesbian imitates-parodies-repeats-subverts the standard feminine code, does she not thereby, at a "deeper" level, assert her "true" queer identity that requires such an ironic-subverting-parodizing attitude? A different example of the same logic is provided by the "leader caught with his pants down": the solidarity of the group is strengthened by the subjects' common disavowal of the misfortune that laid open the Leader's failure or impotence—a shared lie is an incomparably more effective bond for a group than the truth. When, in an academic department, members of the inner circle around a famous professor are aware of some flaw of his (he is addicted to drugs, a kleptomaniac, a sexual masochist pervert, he has stolen a key line of argumentation from a student, etc.), this very knowledge of the flaw—together with the willingness to disavow this knowledge—is the true feature of identification that keeps the group together.[11] One should introduce here the difference between *S* and *a,* between identification at the level of symbolic and/or imaginary features and its real kernel: a "real" identification requires "something more," some ineffable *je ne sais quoi* that transpires only through the distance toward the "official" symbolic features.

*The Duellists,* Ridley Scott's extraordinary directorial debut (based on a short story by Heinrich Kleist), depicts the lifelong combat between two high-ranking soldiers, a true upper class nobleman and an aspiring officer of middle class origins—what keeps them forever apart is the difference in the way each of them relates to the upper class code of honor. The aspiring middle class officer doggedly follows this code

10. Claudia Springer, *Electronic Eros,* 14 (1996).

11. For a more detailed account of this paradox of the "leader caught with his pants down," see Slavoj Žižek, *The Metastases of Enjoyment,* chap. 3 (1994).

and for that very reason generates the lasting impression of awkward ridicule, while his counterpart, the nobleman, constantly violates the explicit rules of the official code and thereby asserts his true upper-classness.[12] The problem of the aspiring lower middle classes is that they misperceive the true cause of their failure: they think they are missing something, some hidden rule, so that they have to learn to follow even more closely all the rules—what they misperceive is that the mysterious *X* that accounts for the true upper-classness cannot be pinpointed to a specific positive symbolic feature. Here, we encounter again *l'objet petit a:* when we are dealing with two series of behavior that cannot be distinguished by any clearly defined positive symbolic feature, and yet the difference between the two is the unmistakable difference between true high-classness and its clumsy imitation, that unfathomable *X*, the *je ne sais quoi* that accounts for this gap—in short: the object that makes the difference where one cannot establish any positive difference is precisely *l'objet petit a* as the unfathomable object-cause of desire. One can also say that the Lacanian *objet petit a* is the ultimate shibboleth, the element that accounts for the difference where no difference is perceptible. Were the Nazis not all the time in search of a shibboleth that would allow them clearly to identify Jews, like the humans in science-fiction films on the invasion of mimicker aliens who are desperately searching for a tiny feature by means of which one can identify an alien?

When a visitor reaches a local village with its customs, is there anything more racist than his clumsy attempts to demonstrate how he "understands" the local customs and is able to follow them? Does such behavior not bear witness to the same patronizing attitude as the one displayed by the adults who adapt themselves to their small children by way of imitating their gestures and their way of speaking? Are not local inhabitants legitimately offended when the foreign intruder mimics their speech? The patronizing falsity of the visitor does not reside merely in the fact that he only feigns to be "one of us"—the point is

12. This unfathomable distinction between true upper-classness and the false upper-classness of the middle classes is, of course, a constant theme in the work of Pierre Bourdieu. To put it in Hegelian terms, the difference is here between the in-itself and the for-itself: upper classes live their code "in itself," while middle classes which consciously aspire to it relate to it "for itself," in a reflected way, and thus spoil the effect which has to emerge as a "by-product." The same goes for fashion: the aspiring middle classes doggedly follow the fashion and thus always lag behind, while upper classes freely violate the rules of fashion and thus personify its trends. . . .

rather that we establish a true contact with the locals only when they disclose to us the distance they themselves maintain toward the letter of their own customs. There is a well-known anecdote about the Prince Peter Petrovic Njegos, a Montenegro ruler from the first half of the nineteenth century famous for his battles against the Turks as well as for his epic poetry: when an English visitor to his court, profoundly touched by a local ritual, expressed his willingness to partake in it, Njegos cruelly rebuffed him: "Why should you also make a fool of yourself? Isn't it enough for us to play these silly games?" The existing ideological power-edifice can thus be undermined in two complementary ways of overidentification: either we stick to the *letter* of the law, ignoring its obscene underside of unwritten rules, or we focus on this underside and bring it to the light of day—in both cases, the normal functioning of the power-edifice is suspended, its "organic" unity disintegrates.

## *V*

The thesis according to which an explicit ideological edifice is always supplemented by some "inherent transgression" does not amount to a simple commonsense point that a set of values, laws, etc., in order to survive, must accommodate itself to the complexity of real life, tolerate compromises, etc. What distinguishes the shadowy rules from this kind of worldly "wisdom" is that (1) they are experienced as obscene, permeated with enjoyment; in psychoanalytic terms: *superego* rules; and (2) for that reason, they must remain publicly unacknowledged, i.e., their public revelation disintegrates the system. Or, to put it in yet another way, superego shadowy unwritten rules are the remainder of the original lawless violence that founded the rule of Law itself—this violence is not something present only at the beginning, it must be here all the time in order for the rule of law to maintain itself. Superego unwritten rules are the synchronous aspect of the diachronous process of the imposition of law through the lawless act of violence—or, rather, this diachronous process, the story of the "original crime," is the narrativization of the necessary, structural, synchronous incoherence of the law.

In what, precisely, consists the contrast between Law and superego? The public Law "between the lines" silently tolerates, incites even, what its explicit text prohibits (say, adultery), while the superego injunction ordains *jouissance*, but this very direct order hinders the subject's access to it much more efficiently than any prohibition. Let us recall the figure of the father who advises his son on sexual exploits: if the father warns him against it, formally prohibits him dating girls, etc., he, of course, between the lines only propels the son to do it, i.e., to find satisfaction in violating the paternal prohibition; if, on the contrary, the father in an obscene way directly pushes him to "behave like a man" and seduce girls, the actual effect of this will probably be the opposite, son's withdrawal, shame of the obscene father, impotence even . . . Perhaps, the briefest way to render the superego paradox is the injunction "Like it or not, enjoy yourself!"

The obscene superego supplement is also not to be confused with another form of "inherent transgression." In the last decade of ex-Yugoslavia, different forms of "transgressive" identification became a central part of the younger generation's counterculture: in Serbia which felt betrayed by the West—especially by the United States; in Bosnia, where the predominant countercultural obsession is the American cultural imaginary, from hard rock to Rambo-look; in Slovenia, where independence was experienced as the cutting of links with the corrupted, inefficient "Balkan," as regaining our place in *Mitteleuropa,* teenage culture is permeated by a "Balkan" nostalgic wave (Serb rock bands are immensely popular; Yugoslav memorabilia abound). Already before the disintegration of Yugoslavia, when the official Socialist ideology was grounded in its opposition to Fascism as the arch-Enemy, Nazi imagery (looks, gestures) was all-present in children's games. However, what we have here is *not* the open assertion of the obscene "underground" of the official ideological space, but something different: a kind of "imp of perversity," a purely negative gesture of identifying with a position *because and only because* it runs against the hegemonic ideological constellation.

Finally, the point about inherent transgression is not that every opposition, every attempt at subversion, is automatically "coopted." On the contrary, the very fear of being coopted that makes us search for more and more "radical," "pure" attitudes, is the supreme strategy of suspension or marginalization. The point is rather that true subversion is not always where it seems to be. Sometimes, a small distance is much more explosive for the system than an ineffective radical rejection. In religion, a small heresy can be more threatening than an outright atheism or passage to another religion; for a hard-line Stalinist, a Trotskyite is infinitely more threatening than a bourgeois liberal or social democrat. As le Carré put it, one true revisionist in the Central Committee is worth more than thousand dissidents outside it. It was easy to dismiss Gorbachev for aiming only at improving the system, making it more efficient—he nonetheless set in motion its disintegration. So one should also bear in mind the obverse of the inherent transgression: one is tempted to paraphrase Freud's claim from *The Ego and the Id* that man is not only much more immoral than he believes, but also much more moral than he knows—the System is not only infinitely more resistant and invulnerable than it may appear (it can coopt apparently subversive strategies, they can serve as its support), it is also infinitely more vulnerable (a small revision etc, can have large unforeseen catastrophic consequences). Or, to put it in another way: the paradoxical role of the unwritten superego injunction is that, with regard to the explicit, public Law, it is simultaneously transgressive (superego suspends, violates, the explicit social rules) *and* more coercive (superego consists of additional rules that restrain the field of choice by way of prohibiting the possibilities allowed for, guaranteed even, by the public Law). From my personal history, I recall the moment of the referendum for the independence of Slovenia as the exemplary case of such a forced choice: the whole point, of course, was to have a truly free choice—but nonetheless, in the pro-independence euphoria, every argumentation for remaining within Yugoslavia was immediately denounced as treacherous and disloyal. This example is especially suitable since Slovenes were deciding about a matter that was literally "transgressive" (to break from Yugoslavia with its constitutional order), which is why the Belgrade authorities denounced Slovene referendum as unconstitutional—one was thus ordered to transgress the Law . . . The obverse of the omnipotence of the unwritten is thus that, if one ignores them, they simply *cease to exist,* in contrast to the written law that exists (functions) whether one is aware of it or not—or, as the priest in Kafka's *The Trial* put it, law does not want anything from you, it only bothers you if you yourself acknowledge it and address yourself to it with a demand . . .

When, in the late eighteenth century, universal human rights were proclaimed, this universality, of course, concealed the fact that they privilege white men of property; however, this limitation was not openly admitted, it was coded in apparently tautological supplementary qualifications like "all humans have rights, insofar as they truly are rational and free," which then implicitly excludes the mentally ill, "savages," criminals, children, women . . . So, if, in this situation, a poor black woman disregards this unwritten-implicit qualification and demands human rights also for herself, she just takes the letter of the discourse of rights "more literally than it was meant" (and thereby redefines its universality, inscribing it into a different hegemonic chain). "Fantasy" designates precisely this unwritten framework that tells us how are we to understand the letter of Law. The lesson of this is that—sometimes, at least—the truly subversive thing is not to disregard the explicit letter of Law on behalf of the underlying fantasies, but to *stick to this letter against the fantasy that sustains it.* Is—at a certain level, at least—this not the outcome of the long conversation between Josepf K. and the priest that follows the priest's narrative on the Door of the Law in *The Trial*?—the uncanny effect of this conversation does not reside in the fact that the reader is at a loss insofar as he lacks the unwritten interpretive code or frame of reference that would enable him to discern the hidden Meaning, but, on the contrary, in that *the priest's interpretation of the parable on the Door of the Law disregards all standard frames of unwritten rules and reads the text in an "absolutely literal" way.* One could also approach this deadlock via Lacan's notion of the specifically symbolic mode of deception: ideology "cheats" precisely by letting us know that its propositions (say, on universal human rights) are not to be read *à la lettre,* but against the background of a set of unwritten rules. Sometimes, at least, the most effective anti-ideological subversion of the official discourse of human rights consists in reading it in an excessively "literal" way, disregarding the set of underlying unwritten rules.

## *VI*

The need for unwritten rules thus *bears witness to, confirms, this vulnerability:* the system is compelled to allow for possibilities of choices that must never actually take place since they would disintegrate the system, and the function of the unwritten rules rules is precisely to prevent the actualization of these choices formally allowed by the system. One can see how unwritten rules are correlative to, the obverse of, the empty symbolic gesture and/or the forced choice: unwritten rules prevent the subject from effectively accepting what is offered in the empty gesture, from taking the choice literally and choosing the impossible, that the choice of which destroys the system. In the Soviet Union of the

1930s and 1940s, to take the most extreme example, it was not only prohibited to criticize Stalin, it was perhaps even more prohibited to enounce publicly this prohibition, i.e., to state that one is prohibited to criticize Stalin—the system *needed* to maintain the *appearance* that one is allowed to criticize Stalin, i.e., that the absence of this criticism (and the fact that there is no opposition party or movement, that the Party got 99.99% of the votes at elections) simply demonstrates that Stalin is effectively the best and (almost) always right. In Hegelese, this appearance qua appearance was essential.

This dialectical tension between the vulnerability and invulnerability of the System also enables us to denounce the ultimate racist and/or sexist trick, that of "two birds in the bush instead of a bird in hand": when women demand simple equality, quasi-"feminists" often pretend to offer them "much more" (the role of the warm and wise "conscience of society," elevated above the vulgar everyday competition and struggle for domination . . .)—the only proper answer to this offer, of course, is "No, thanks! Better is the enemy of the Good! We do not want *more,* just equality!" Here, at least, the last lines in *Now Voyager* ("Why reach for the moon, when we can have the stars?") are wrong. It is homologous with the native American who wants to become integrated into the predominant "white" society, and a politically correct progressive liberal endeavors to convince him that he is thereby renouncing his very unique prerogative, the authentic native culture and tradition—no thanks, simple equality is enough, I also wouldn't mind my part of consumerist alienation! . . . A modest demand of the excluded group for the full participation at the society's universal rights is much more threatening for the system than the apparently much more "radical" rejection of the predominant "social values" and the assertion of the superiority of one's own culture. For a true feminist, Otto Weininger's assertion that, although women are "ontologically false," lacking the proper ethical stature, they should be acknowledged the same rights as men in public life, is infinitely more acceptable than the false elevation of women that makes them "too good" for the banality of men's rights.

In (the still Communist) Slovenia in the mid-1970s, there occurred a famous political incident known as "the affair of 25 delegates." The unfortunate 25 "delegates" (self-management newspeak for the members of the National Assembly) proposed a candidate for one of the two

Slovene members of the collective Yugoslav Presidency an additional name, on top of the two "official" candidates, so that the voters would have to choose two among the three; they broke absolutely no rule, their procedure followed all formal rules, even the person they proposed was an absolutely faithful Party apparatchik—the unbearable trauma for the Power was the simple fact that another name emerged *outside the established unwritten rules of choosing the candidates.* So, immediately after this "affair," a violent campaign took place in all public media against the unfortunate 25 "delegates," accused of "pseudodemocratic formalism," anti-Socialist activity, etc.—they were all forced to step down.[13]

## *VII*

This tension between socio-symbolic reality and its "unwritten" fantasmatic background is clearly discernible in one of the most painful and troubling scenes from David Lynch's *Wild at Heart.* In a lonely motel room, Willem Dafoe exerts a rude pressure on Laura Dern: he touches and squeezes her, invading the space of her intimacy and repeating in a threatening way "Say fuck me!," i.e., extorting from her a word that would signal her consent to a sexual act. The ugly, unpleasant scene drags itself on, and when, finally, the exhausted Laura Dern utters a barely audible "Fuck me!," Dafoe abruptly steps away, assumes a nice, friendly smile and cheerfully retorts: "No, thanks, I don't have time today; but on another occasion I would do it gladly . . ." He has attained what he really wanted: not the act itself, just her consent to it, her symbolic humiliation. What we have here is rape in fantasy which refuses its realization in reality and thus further humiliates its victim—the fantasy is forced out, aroused, and then abandoned, thrown upon the victim. That is to say, it is clear that Laura Dern is not simply disgusted by Dafoe's (Bobby Perou's) brutal intrusion into her intimacy: just prior to her "Fuck me!," the camera focuses on her right hand which she slowly

13. And, incidentally, the same goes also for Lacan's "return to Freud." There is nothing truly subversive in asserting that, beyond the discursive consciousness caught in its cobweb of representations, there is a vast domain of irrational drives; it is far more subversive to remain more "modest" and to claim that the very domain of discursive representations is in itself unconscious ("the unconscious is structured like a language"). As Lacan emphasized again and again, the true scandal of the Freudian unconscious does not reside in its irrationality, but in the fact that it is thoroughly "rational" . . .

spreads out—the sign of her acquiescence, the proof that he stirred up her fantasy.[14] The point is thus to read this scene in a Lévi-Straussian way, as an inversion of the standard scene of seduction (in which the gentle approach is followed by the brutal sexual act, after the woman, the target of the seducer's efforts, finally says "Yes!").

One of the most repulsive racist rituals from the American Old South was to force the African-American cornered by a white gang to commit the first gesture of insult; while the African-American was held tightly by his associates, a white racist thug shouted at him "Spit on me! Tell me I'm scum!," etc., in order to extort from him the "occasion" for a brutal beating or lynching—as if the white racist wanted to set up retroactively the proper dialogical context for his violent outburst. Here we encounter the *perversity* of the injurious word at its purest: the proper order of succession and implication is perverted; in a mocking imitation of the "normal" order I compel the victim to insult me voluntarily, i.e., to assume the discursive position of the offender and thereby to justify my violent outburst. It is easy to perceive the homology with the scene from *Wild at Heart:* the point of this repulsive racist ritual is not simply that white thugs compel the well-meaning humble Uncle Tom–ish African-American to offend them against his will—both parties are well aware that the besieged African-American does cultivate aggressive fantasies about his white oppressors, that he does consider them scum (in a quite justified way, considering the brutal oppression he and his race were exposed to), and their pressure serves to awaken these fantasies, so that, when the African-American finally spits on the white thug or tells him "You're scum!," he in a way lets go his defenses, his sense of survival, and displays his true desire, cost what it may . . . exactly like Laura Dern in *Wild at Heart* who, in saying "Fuck me!," yields not only to external pressure but also to her fantasmatic kernel of *jouissance.* In short, the poor African-American is beaten (probably killed) for his desire.

The traumatic impact of these two scenes thus relies on the gap between the subject's everyday symbolic universe and its fantasmatic

14. "How can such a repulsive figure like Bobby Perou stir up Laura Dern's fantasy? The figure of Perou is not simply repulsive: it is repulsive insofar as it embodies phallic vitality in all its power: as was pointed out, Perou's whole body evokes a gigantic phallus, with his head the head of a penis . . . Even his final moments bear witness to a kind of raw energy which ignores the threat of death: after the bank robbery goes wrong, he blows off his own head not in despair, but with a merry laughter . . ." (Michel Chion, *David Lynch* [1995]).

support. Let us approach this gap through another disturbing phenomenon. When attention is drawn to the fact that women often do fantasize about being handled brutally and raped, the standard answer to it is either that this is a male fantasy about women or that women do it insofar as they "internalized" the patriarchal libidinal economy and endorsed their victimization—the underlying idea being that the moment we recognize this fact of daydreaming about rape, we open the door to the male-chauvinist platitudes about how, in being raped, women only get what they secretly wanted—their shock and fear only express the fact that they were not honest enough to acknowledge this. To this commonplace, one should answer that (some) women effectively may daydream about being raped, but that this fact not only in no way legitimizes the actual rape—it makes it even more violent. Let us take two women, the first, liberated and assertive, active; the other, secretly daydreaming about being brutally handled by her partner, even raped. The crucial point is that, if both of them are raped, the rape will be much more traumatic for the second one, *on account of the very fact that it will realize in "external" social reality the "stuff of her dreams"*—why? (Perhaps a better way to put it would be to paraphrase yet again the immortal lines of Stalin: it is impossible to say which of the two rapes would be worse—they are *both worse,* i.e., real against one's attitude, of course, is in a way worse, since it violates our disposition, but, on the other hand, the very fact that rape was done in accordance with our secret disposition makes it even worse . . .) There is a gap that forever separates the fantasmatic kernel of the subject's being from the more "superficial" modes of his or her symbolic and/or imaginary identifications—it is never possible for me fully to assume (in the sense of symbolic integration) the fantasmatic kernel of my being: when I approach it too much, when I come too close to it, what occurs is the *aphanisis* of the subject: the subject loses his/her symbolic consistency, it disintegrates. And, perhaps, the forced actualization in social reality itself of the fantasmatic kernel of my being is the worst, most humiliating kind of violence, a violence that undermines the very base of my identity (of my "self-image").[15]

15. Another way to make the same point is to draw attention to the crucial fact that *men who actually perform rapes do not fantasize about raping women*—on the contrary, they fantasize about being gentle, about finding a loving partner; rape is rather a violent *passage à l'acte* emerging from their incapacity to find such a partner in real life.

*Chapter 4*

# The Vestal and the Fasces: Property and the Feminine in Law and Psychoanalysis

*Jeanne L. Schroeder*

The fasces was an axe attached to a bundle of sticks. It symbolized the majesty of Roman law. Consuls, emperors, and other high-ranking officials were escorted in public by *lictors* bearing the fasces as the visible representation of the state. Offenders could be mercifully flogged with one of the sticks or justly executed with the blade.[1]

The Vestals symbolized the sanctity of the Roman family. These priestesses of Vesta guarded the sacred hearth of Rome insuring the continuing warmth, intimacy, fertility, and order of the families of individual Romans. During their thirty years of service, the six Vestals were required to maintain the strictest chastity. But, unlike the virginity of Christian nuns, the Vestals' chastity was not considered a more perfect, spiritual form of life or a reproach to matrons. Their maidenhood was not exemplary, but extraordinary—a form of ritual purity. Through contrast, it emphasized maternity as the norm.[2] The Vestals dedicated themselves so that others could marry.[3] They were guardians of the family. They officiated at fertility rites. They guarded a ritual phallus that may have symbolized the ineffable goddess herself.

The Vestal did not dress as a maiden but wore the headdress of a Roman bride and the *stola,* or dress, of a Roman matron. The Vestal's

1. Mary Beard, "The Sexual Status of Vestal Virgins," 70 *J. Roman Stud.* 12, 17 (1980); Sarah B. Pomeroy, *Goddesses, Whores, Wives and Slaves: Women in Classical Antiquity* 213 (1975).

2. Peter Brown, *The Body and Society: Men, Women and Sexual Renunciation in Early Christianity* 8–9 (1988).

3. Upon the expiration of their official term, they could leave the temple and marry although, reportedly, few did so. Beard, *supra* note 1, at 21.

investiture ceremony—the *captio* or "capture"—was reminiscent of a Roman wedding. The state's high priest, the Pontifex Maximus, roughly seized the initiate from her father in a mock abduction in memory of the legendary rape of the Sabine women.[4]

Most mysteriously, upon their investiture these priestesses, who were paradoxically both symbolically raped virgins and unviolated wives, were also elevated to the legal status of men. The Vestals, alone of all women, were escorted by the fasces.[5]

The seeming paradox of the symbolization of the private accompanied by the symbolization of the public can be resolved in a Hegelian/Lacanian context. The public and the private serve complementary functions and mutually constitute each other. Both the law and the virgin served as the representation of the Other—the external object by which the Roman man was able to define himself as an acting subject.

Meanwhile, late-twentieth-century jurisprudence has been hard on the law of property. It has "discovered" that the unitary, possessory, and tangible nature of property, which supposedly seemed so self-evident to our ancestors, was merely an illusion.[6] A common modern formulation is that property, like the fasces, is merely a bundle of sticks.[7] Like a modern lictor, the property lawyer can use property in part or in whole to flog his case or execute his judgment.

But if unity, tangibility, and physical possession are merely illusions, they continue to haunt us with a ghostly persistence. Many scholars who state that they adopt a desegregated bundle-of-sticks analysis of property, as an alternative to the unitary, possessory, and tangible view, implicitly reinstate a unitary view of property that privileges physical possession of tangible objects.[8] The very imagery of the bundle

4. Beard, *supra* note 1, at 13–15; *see also* John Percy Vyvian Dacre Baldson, *Roman Women: Their History and Habits* 182–84 (1962).

5. Pomeroy, *supra* note 1, at 213; Baldson, *supra* note 4, at 238.

6. *See, e.g.*, Kenneth Vandeveld, "The New Property or the Nineteenth Century: The Development of the Modern Concept of Property," 29 *Buff. L. Rev.* 325 (1980).

7. The "bundle of sticks" metaphor is often associated with Wesley Newcomb Hohfeld, although he does not use this expression in his great work. Wesley Newcomb Hohfeld, *Fundamental Legal Conceptions as Applied in Judicial Reasoning* (W. Cook ed., 1919). The expression might be have been coined in Benjamin N. Cardozo, *The Paradoxes of Legal Science* (1928). *See* Thomas Ross, "Metaphor and Paradox," 23 *Ga. L. Rev.* 1053, 1055–63 (1989).

8. Jeanne L. Schroeder, "Chix Nix Bundle-O-Stix: A Feminist Critique of the Disaggregation of Property," 93 *Mich. L. Rev.* 239 (1994).

of sticks is itself a possessory and tangible metaphor. A stick is something that one can see and hold in one's hand. In addition, it is obvious that the stick and the bundle of sticks—the fasces—are archetypically phallic images.

The bundle-of-sticks analysis does not solve the metaphysical problems that these scholars purport to identify in the unitary, possessory, tangible concept of property. It merely postpones, and thereby replicates, the unitary theory and its problems. If property is merely a bundle of arbitrary sticks, this bundle consists of separate little sticks, each a separate unity with its own metaphysical problems.

This process of reinstating the unitary, possessory view of property, even while denying it, is typically done in one of two ways. The cruder approach is the adoption of an "ostensible ownership" theory. The proponents of this view assert the fact that when we see that a person has physical possession of a tangible thing, we presume that person also has the unfettered ownership in that thing. The non sequitur drawn from this empirical claim is that interests not reflected in physical possession of tangible objects are a "problem." Consequently, these interests must either be "explained" or voided. For example, property interests in intangible objects that are incapable of being either seen or physically held must be made to display these characteristics through metaphor. The nonpossessory title granted in hypothecation must be symbolically made possessory and visible through filing public notice of ownership.[9]

A second, more subtle reinstatement of unitary property theory purports to show that the old theories were naive, inept, or self-contradictory. It then concludes that various legal relationships are not "property" after all, or that the concept *property,* although once valid, is obsolete, or that "property" does not exist as a coherent legal category *precisely* because it lacks the characteristics identified in the old theory.

---

9. Probably the most vociferous champions of this approach are Douglas Baird and Thomas Jackson. *See* Douglas Baird and Thomas Jackson, "Possession and Ownership: An Examination of the Scope of Article 9," 35 *Stan. L. Rev.* 175 (1983). Baird and Jackson extrapolate from "traditional" hatred of secured lending an ostensible ownership problem with respect to all nonpossessory property interests. This is despite the fact that the law has traditionally recognized and enforced other types of nonpossessory interests such as leases and bailments. For an excellent critique of the ostensible ownership thesis see Charles Mooney, "The Mystery and Myth of 'Ostensible Ownership' and Article 9 Filing: A Critique of Proposals to Extend Filing Requirements to Leases," 39 *Ala. L. Rev.* 683 (1988).

That is, despite their claimed rejection, these authors do not successfully reconceptualize property. They implicitly continue to see the unitary, possessory, tangible conception of property as the only possible one.[10]

Why do phallic metaphors of physical possession, holding and seeing tangible objects, continue to dominate property discourse? In this essay, I will suggest that property serves a function in law parallel to the function of The Woman in the Lacanian psyche. They are both types of the "Phallus." Both property, according to Hegelian philosophy, and the Feminine, according to Lacanian psychoanalysis, are fictions that enable us to constitute ourselves as acting subjects.

The parallelism I am suggesting between Hegel and Lacan should surprise neither Hegelians nor Lacanians. Jacques Lacan often acknowledged Hegel's influence on his rewriting of Freud, although he frequently tried to distinguish himself from his intellectual forebear. But I would argue that Lacan's "science of desire" derived as much from Hegelian insights as it did from the Freudian theory of the unconscious.[11] Unlike the person hypothesized by classical liberal philosophy, and unlike the masculine stereotype of pop psychology,[12] the Hegelian and Lacanian subjects are not self-standing, autonomous individuals seeking to maximize their utility by owning and controlling things and people. Both Hegel and Lacan considered subjectivity to be a human creation—a hard-won achievement. The subject is not autonomous but is driven by an erotic desire to be recognized and desired by another person. Subjectivity can only be intersubjectivity.

The direct and conscious influence on Lacan, particularly in his early period, of Hegel's theory of desire as developed in *The Phenomenology of Spirit*[13] in general has been widely recognized.[14] I am making

10. E.g., Thomas Gray, "The Disintegration of Property," in *Nomos XXII, Property* (J. Roland Pennock and John W. Chapman eds., 1980); Charles Mooney, "Beyond Negotiability: A New Model for Transfer and Pledge of Interests in Securities Controlled by Intermediaries," 12 *Cardozo L. Rev.* 305 (1990); James Rogers, "Negotiability, Property, Identity," 12 *Cardozo L. Rev.* 471 (1990); Joseph Sax, "Some Thoughts on the Decline of Private Property," 58 *Wash. L. Rev. 481* (1983); Joseph Singer, "The Reliance Interest in Property," 40 *Stan. L. Rev.* 611 (1988); Vandeveld, *supra* note 6.

11. *See* Edward S. Casey and J. Melvin Woody, "Hegel, Heidegger, Lacan: The Dialectic of Desire," in *Interpreting Lacan: 6 Psychiatry and the Humanities* 75 (Joseph Smith and William Kerrigan eds., 1983).

12. Including the stereotype adopted by self-declared "different voice" or "cultural" feminists.

13. Georg W. F. Hegel, *The Phenomenology of Spirit* (A. V. Miller trans., 1977).

14. *See, e.g.*, Anthony Wilden, "Lacan and the Discourse of the Other," in Jacques

a slightly different point. I am arguing that Hegel continued throughout Lacan's life to exert an indirect and, perhaps, unconscious influence on his developing theory of feminine sexuality. I wish to emphasize the similarity between Lacan's account of the origin of law, language, and sexuality and Hegel's account of the origin of law, property, and contract in *The Philosophy of Right.*[15] But the interrelationship between Hegel and Lacan goes further. If Hegel was right that the totality of his dialectic is a logical necessity, and if Lacan was right that the application of Hegel's dialectic results in the Lacanian theory of the psychoanalytic subject, then one should be able to go back to Hegel and find the Lacanian subject already waiting there. If Lacan is a true son of Hegel, this can only be because Hegel's Minerva was already great with her Freudian child.

### *The Hegelian Story of Property*

Hegel introduced his theory of property in the first part of *The Philosophy of Right* in which he discusses the development of the legal person, abstract right, and law. Hegel's initial account of property, like his account of abstract right, civil society, and the state generally, purports to be an internal one. That is, Hegelians claim to explore the rationality of property within the rhetoric of property. This is opposed to external or utilitarian analyses that purport to examine the uses property law concepts serve.

To explain Hegel's theory of property, it may be useful, at this point, to consider briefly Hegel's approach to the individual. This discussion is, of course, out of order from a Hegelian standpoint because the complete individual does not yet exist at this stage of the dialectic.

---

Lacan, Speech And Language In Psychoanalysis 159 at 163, 284–93, 306 (A. Wilden trans., 1968); Casey and Woody, *supra* note 11, at 75; Wilfried Ver Eecke, "Hegel as Lacan's Source for Necessity in Psychoanalytic Theory", in *Interpreting Lacan: 6 Psychiatry and the Humanities* 113 (Joseph Smith and William Kerrigan eds., 1983); Jean-Luc Nancy and Phillippe Lacoue-Labarthe, *The Title of the Letter: A Reading of Lacan* 121–27 (François Raffoul and David Pettigrew trans., 1992).

Arguably, Lacan's work passed through several periods—an earlier expressly Hegelian period, and a structuralist period. *Slavoj Žižek, For They Know Not What They Do: Enjoyment as a Political Factor* 230–31 (1991). The fact that Lacan's thought developed over time does not mean that it should be divided into strict, exclusive periodization. Lacan never totally rejected his debt to Hegel, and, as I shall argue, Hegelian theory expressly or implicitly continued to influence Lacan's later work on feminine sexuality.

15. Georg W. F. Hegel, *Elements of the Philosophy of Right* (T. M. Knox trans., 1967).

Unlike liberalism, Hegelianism does not presuppose the existence of the subject in the sense of the autonomous individual.

From a Hegelian viewpoint, a philosopher presupposing autonomous individualism is equivalent to a magician sneaking the rabbit into the hat. Biographically, we are not born autonomous, but totally dependent on others for all of our needs. Consequently the private is as problematical as the public. Hegel argues that the individual and society are equally in need of explanation.

In the introduction to the first chapter of his *Science of Logic*,[16] Hegel discusses his goal of creating a philosophy without presuppositions. To put it simply, he concludes that it is impossible to *begin* a logical analysis without intentionally, if tentatively, adopting presuppositions. One needs an initial working hypothesis.

Hegel's starting place for the *Philosophy of Right* is the most abstract concept of selfhood which he calls "*absolutely free will*"—that which is an end in itself and is not the means to some other entity's end.[17]

The problem with the conceptualization of the self as absolutely free will is that it is empty, abstract, arbitrary, and negative[18]—it is by definition totally stripped of all distinguishing characteristics. It is also, by definition, subjective (in the sense of abstract, solipsistic, and impoverished) even as it claims to be universal. But real people are not abstract. They have content, have concrete existence, experience themselves positively, and interrelate with other people.

In order to resolve these contradictions the will needs to give itself a differentiating content by embodying or expressing itself somehow. It needs to "objectify" itself so that it can be recognized by other subjects and can recognize other people as subjects in their own right.

Property is the means by which the abstract subject objectifies itself. The self as abstract will claims to be essential reality, but the existence of external things, objects, and our dependence on external reality contradicts this. The self therefore needs to appropriate external objects—it must own property. The self becomes particularized, rather than abstract, through ownership.

Although free will and appropriation are only early moments in the development of the subject, this does not mean that free will and

16. Georg W. F. Hegel, *Hegel's Science of Logic* (A. V. Miller trans., 1989).

17. Hegel, *supra* note 15, at 37.

18. *Id.* at 27.

private property can disappear in later stages. Hegel's concept of sublation requires that each earlier logical moment and its negative be preserved in the next. As appropriation was necessary for the subject to objectify itself, to be an end for itself, private ownership must continue in some form.

Before we turn to how property leads to intersubjectivity and to contract, let us examine a little more closely what Hegel meant by objectivity and ownership. This is useful because some of the language used by Hegel (at least as translated into English), including references to "things," "objects," and "possession," has an unfortunate tendency to suggest the very phallic metaphor of property as the physical holding and seeing of tangible things that I am criticizing. Upon careful reading, however, it becomes clear that Hegel did not hold such unsophisticated concepts of property.

First, I wish to remind the reader of the ambiguity of the English word *property*. On the one hand, as Hohfeld explained, the legal term *property* refers to a legal interrelationship between at least two subjects with respect to an object.[19] On the other hand, we also use the word *property* to refer to the object that is the subject of the property relationship. That is, *property* is both the term for the system of ownership and exchange, as well as the name of the thing owned. In this essay, I use both meanings of the word *property*. When I refer to *property* as a type of Phallus, I am primarily referring to property as the object of desire, possession, and exchange. I am referring to this meaning when I compare property to the psychoanalytical concept of The Woman as the object of desire, possession, and exchange. When I refer to the legal system of ownership and exchange called property (or contract), the psychoanalytic parallel is the linguistic system of ownership and exchange called sexuality.

Second, although the word *object* in colloquial English often refers to physical things, in philosophical and psychoanalytical discourse the term *object* refers to anything that is external to the subject and (in the case of Hegel's theory) that does not itself have will. This definition of *object* is logically necessitated by Hegel's starting definition of the subject as free will. That is, the subject is initially the will in the sense of being one's own end—not the means to the end of another. External things that themselves have will (i.e., other human beings) cannot be objects of property. This is because appropriation is the infusion of the

19. *See* Hohfeld, *supra* note 7, at 65.

will of a subject into an object.[20] External things that do not have their own ends, but are merely the means to the ends of another, can properly serve as objects. Objects lack the subject's capacity of self-transcendence They are not ends in themselves and, therefore, offer no moral resistance to their appropriation. They can only be means to the ends of a will, and therefore appropriation of property by a will is legitimate.

Tangible things are, obviously, merely a small subset of the objects that are eligible to be property. Since the concept of the object is defined in terms of what is not (i.e., the subject), anything that "can be conceived as immediately different from free personality"[21] can be a "thing," including my desk, apartment, bank accounts, and stock portfolio, as well as my talents and ideas.[22]

Consequently, Alan Brudner argues (correctly in my opinion) that the view expressed in much modern jurisprudence that the dematerialization of property is a recent invention inconsistent with, and subversive of, classic property theory is simply wrong.[23] It is wrong on a jurisprudential basis, given the work of Hegel and others, not to mention the long history of nontangible forms of property recognized by the common law, such as incorporeal heriditaments.[24]

### The Elements of Property

Hegel identifies three essential elements of property: possession, use, and alienation. These are not three separate "rights" arbitrarily tied together like a bundle of sticks. Although these are the same three elements commonly identified by liberal theory, unlike liberals, Hegel

---

20. Slavery is wrong precisely because it is a system by which human beings are treated as the means to another's ends. Animals do not have "will" as that term is used in the Hegelian system. They are, therefore, proper objects of property. Hegel, *supra* note 15, at 48.

21. Peter Benson, "Abstract Right and the Possibility of A Nondistributive Conception of Contract: Hegel and Contemporary Contract Theory," 10 *Cardozo L. Rev.* 1077, 1164 (1989).

22. Hegel, *supra* note 15, at 40.

23. Alan Brudner, "The Unity of Property Law," 4 *Can. J. of L. and Juris.* 3, 20 n.5 (1991).

24. *Id.* "All the same, Hegel stretched the notion of property in other contexts in much the same way that theorists of the 'new property' do." Alan Ryan, "Hegel on Work, Ownership and Citizenship," at 178, 179, in *The State and Civil Society: Studies in Hegel's Political Philosophy* (Z. Pelczynski ed., 1984).

does not presuppose the existence of these rights.[25] Rather he analyzes them from an internalist position to determine how these rights function.

For an interest to be "property" in its richest sense, it must contain all three elements. This does not mean, of course, that all interests either contain complete manifestations of all three elements or lack all three completely. Some property interests are more adequate and complete than others.

The most "rudimentary" element of property is possession. By referring to possession, Hegel did not, however, adopt the phallic metaphor and refer to physical, sensuous holding. Indeed this necessarily follows from Hegel's realization that the "objects" of property are not necessarily, or even archetypically, tangible.

> Owing to the qualitative differences between natural objects, mastery and occupancy of these has an infinite variety of meanings and involves a restriction and contingency that is just as infinite.[26]

Nor, by "rudimentary," did he imply that the concept of property originated historically in the physical possession of tangibles and expanded to include other interests by analogy and metaphor. As we have just seen, property originates in the internal necessity of the will. Consequently, possession is defined as the will's taking mastery over something so that the will is embodied in it. "Possession is man's physical and anthropological capacity to appropriate externality for human purposes."[27]

This means that sensuous holding is merely one form of possession. It is the most determinate form and, consequently, the least complete form.[28] This is because the will's mastery over the object is depen-

25. This, of course, is the misinterpretation of Hegel by Radin who sees Hegel as another liberal philosopher. Margaret Jane Radin, "Property and Personhood," 34 *Stan. L. Rev.* 957 (1982).

26. Hegel, *supra* note 15, at 45.

27. Seyla Benhabib, "Obligation, Contract and Exchange: On the Significance of Hegel's Abstract Right," in *The State and Civil Society, supra* note 24, at 159.

28. Ever since "critical" legal scholars announced that the law was "indeterminate," there has been a tendency to associate determinacy with "good" and indeterminacy as "bad." Indeed, the slogan "law is indeterminate" is intended as a critique. In Hegel, determinacy is a descriptive, not a normative, term. Some things are more determinative, but this means that they are more contingent and less universal. Other things are more universal, but they are then less determinative.

dent upon contingency. Sensuous possession is not, therefore, total dominion. The mastery of any individual will over an object through physical possession can be defeated by any stranger who wrests it away.

Consequently, Hegel identified at least two other, and more complete, ways of taking "possession" of an object: forming it and marking it.[29] Forming the object is superior to physical holding because

> [t]o impose a form on a thing is the mode of taking possession most in conformity with the Idea to this extent, that it implies a union of subject and object, although it varies endlessly with the qualitative character of the objects and the variety of subjective aims.[30]

What is more,

> [t]o take possession by marking a thing is of all sorts of taking possession the most complete, since the mark is implicitly at work to some extent in the other sorts too. When I grasp a thing or form it, this also means . . . that I mark it, and mark it for others, in order to exclude them and show that I have put my will into the thing. The notion of the mark . . . is that the thing does not count as the thing which it is but as what it is supposed to signify.[31]

If marking is the most complete form of possession it is, consequently, the most indeterminate.[32] There is, therefore, a considerable role to be played by positive law (whether by statute, custom, or whatever) in specifying what modes of marking will be considered legally cognizable in any specific society.

The next element of property is use—or what I would prefer to call the "enjoyment"—of property.

> The use of the thing is my need being externally realized through the change, destruction, and consumption of the thing. The thing

29. Hegel, *supra* note 15, at 46.

30. Hegel, *supra* note 15, at 47.

31. *Id.* at 239.

32. *Id.* at 49 (as opposed to holding which is the most sensually determinate yet the least complete).

> thereby stands revealed as naturally self-less and so fulfills its destiny.[33]

What constitutes "use" or enjoyment will depend on the actual object. It might be physical manipulation, as in driving one's car, or collection of a debt, or whatever.

These first two elements standing alone are insufficient to constitute property to Hegel precisely because he conceives of property as a way that the will objectifies itself as an end in itself. Both possession and use are self-contradictory in that the subject is dependent on the object. The object, therefore, remains independent of the will, rather than its embodiment. The very act of mastering the object makes one simultaneously mastered by the object.

What is more, if property is seen as flowing from the insatiable desire of the individual will to objectify itself by appropriating objects, then the properties of different individual wills at this level are mutually inconsistent. This is because the competing appetites of different wills cannot be fulfilled simultaneously.

This contradiction is mediated by the third element of property recognized by Hegel—alienation:

> The reason I can alienate my property is that it is mine only in so far as I put my will into it. Hence I may abandon (*derelinquere*) as a *res nullius* anything that I have or yield it to the will of another and so into his possession . . .[34]

Alienation enables the will to reassert its mastery over an object through indifference. But alienation contains its own internal contradiction: The will can no longer objectify itself in the object because it no longer owns it. And so, alienation risks defeating its very purpose—the initial driving desire of the will for objectification.

### Adding the Third Term

By abandoning property the will has not yet resolved the contradiction between its supposed mastery over an object and its dependence on the

33. *Id.* at 49.
34. *Id.* at 52.

object. Abandonment is one way of demonstrating the nothingness of the object. But mere abandonment cannot be enough. If the subject merely abandons an object, he destroys his objective confirmation. Such objective confirmation can only come from the recognition of the act by a equal acting subject—both subjectivity and objectivity must become intersubjectivity.[35]

One possible alternative to the contradictory form of alienation through abandonment is alienation by gift. Gift is more adequate than abandonment because it more explicitly recognizes the third term. Gift, to Hegel, is a form of contract because there are

> two contracting parties . . . one of them has the negative moment—the alienation of a thing—and the other the positive moment—the appropriation of the thing.[36]

Although more complete, this too ultimately proves to be inadequate to the tasks of mediating between the subject and the other, and of satisfying the human desire for recognition. By receiving a gift, the donee recognizes the donor's objectification in the property as well as the donor's independence from the contingency of the particular object given. However, in gift, the donee herself is treated as the end of the donor. The donee may recognize the donor, but the donor does not yet relate to the donee as a legal person. Remember, for Hegel, to be a will is to be one's own end. The donee, however, is seen only as a means to the donor's end, rather than a will in her own right.

The step beyond gift is exchange. As in gift, the other recognizes my objectification in the object I give to her, as well as my independence from the specific object. But now, I simultaneously recognize the other's will for acquisition. I recognize her objectification in the object she gives me in exchange, as well as her independence in that specific object. That is, I no longer see the other merely as a means to my end. I recognize her as a legal person who is an end in herself. And vice versa. Consequently, through exchange, I recognize the other as a person whose recognition counts. Pursuant to the Hegelian doctrine of the identity of identity and difference, it is only at the moment when I and the other are joined in the unity of common will that we can recognize each other as unique individuals.

And so we see that property simultaneously leads to the creation

35. *Id.*
36. *Id.*

of both the person creating the contract and the contract. The object of property in this stage of development is the external object of desire, which is exchanged between subjects. This does more than merely enable persons to recognize each other as acting subjects. Rather, this mutual recognition is precisely what makes us into subjects with the capacity of acting and contracting.

### *The Lacanian Story of the Feminine*

I will now show that the Phallic[37] Woman in the psychoanalytic-linguistic theory of Lacan serves a parallel function to that of property in Hegel's *Philosophy of Right*. At first blush, Hegel and Lacan seem to adopt different starting places for their analysis. As we have seen, Hegel tried to derive logically a philosophy without presuppositions even as he realized that one must tentatively adopt a working presupposition in order to start the logical process. He chose to start with the Kantian construct—the most universal and thereby abstract conception of the individual—in order to derive the development of the complex, concrete experience of actual human beings. Hegel's description of the development of the subject and the society purports to be logical, not literally temporal in the psychological or historical sense. The logical necessity of the theory is retroactive, not prospective.

Lacan explored the development of the psychoanalytical subject. One might initially assume that his starting place and ending place would seem to have been given as a biographical and empirical matter—we all start out as babies and we end up as adults. This makes the theory sound like a temporal, biographical account based on the observation that babies are speechless but learn to speak as children. The autonomous individual of liberalism would have no place in Lacan because, if for no other reason, if he did exist, he would have no need of a psychiatrist's couch. On further reflection, however, it becomes apparent that Lacan's theory, like Hegel's, is not inductively derived from the observation of children and does not necessarily purport to be an accurate description of human biography. Rather, as Lacan insists, his theory is a fiction—a story retroactively written through abduction and dialectical logic to explain a Hegelian conception of the person.

The gender types described by Lacan are at least facially consistent with many contemporary gender stereotypes—many of which are

37. I will try to use the terms "Phallus" and "Phallic" (with a capital "P") to refer to the psychoanalytical concept, and the terms "phallus and "phallic" (i.e., with a small "p"] to refer to anatomical metaphors.

highly misogynist. I would hope that feminists do not dismiss his theories out of hand because of this. I and many other feminists find his account not merely provocative, but evocative. In reading Lacanian theory, however, one needs to keep several things in mind.

First and foremost, Lacan's theory does not "explain" patriarchy in a scientific or causative sense. Rather, it presupposes patriarchal family.[38] Lacan's method was that of abduction. The Hegelian-Lacanian dialectic method (which characterizes the symbolic order, generally) is retroactive—time runs backward.[39] Consequently, Charles Sanders Peirce argued that abduction was better termed "retroduction."[40]

Abduction is the logical process by which we try to imagine possible explanations of initially surprising phenomena. That is, Lacan did not observe infants acquiring language and deduce that conventional gender roles would inevitably develop. Rather, he observed the existence of the patriarchal family and tried to imagine a satisfying story that might make their existence seem understandable. This means that Lacan purports neither to show how patriarchy originally came into being as a historical matter nor to argue that patriarchy is inevitable. At most, it suggests the structures through which Western patriarchy, once in place, reproduces itself.

Consequently, on the one hand, the theory holds out to feminists at least a theoretical possibility of change—a rewriting of gender roles. On the other hand, Lacan's retroactive account of patriarchy as a self-reproducing system takes seriously the crushing "reality" of the fiction of gender roles as lived.

Leading from this, Lacan was not arguing that empirical women *are* these misogynist stereotypes, that anatomy is destiny or that patriarchy is inevitable or "natural." To the contrary, he was attempting to explore how (misogynist and patriarchal) gender identifications arise. Male superiority is not empirically true but a fantasy, yet it is a fantasy in which we live our lives. Lacan was trying to show how and why this situation arises.

---

38. As Lacan noted: "Judging from experience [the function of woman as the symbolic object of exchange among men] can only happen within an androcentric and patriarchal framework, even when the structure is secondarily caught up in matrilineal ancestries." Jacques Lacan, *The Seminar of Jacques Lacan, Book II: The Ego in Freud's Theory and in the Technique of Psychoanalysis 1954–1955* 272 (J.-A. Miller ed., S. Tomaselli trans., 1988).

39. Žižek, *supra* note 14, at 201–2.

40. Jeanne L. Schroeder, "Abduction From the Seraglio, Feminist Methodologies and the Logic of Imagination," 70 *Tex. L. Rev.* 179 (1991).

One of Lacan's contributions to Freudian psychoanalytic theory is precisely that he moved it further away from the anatomical and natural.

Thus, Lacan reinterpreted the Freudian concept of "penis envy" into a purely linguistic concept of "castration."[41] As Jane Gallop put it, Lacan rewrote Freudian penis envy as a nostalgia for an imagined lost state of wholeness, contrasted with a fear of deprivation. The former is associated with the feminine and the latter with the masculine.[42] In other words, the Oedipus theory is reinterpreted in terms of the Hegelian desire for mutual recognition of subjects.

Lacan argues that sexuality is linguistic. This means that when he speaks about "men" and "women" he is not speaking literally about empirically anatomical male and female human beings. He is, rather, referring to the "masculine" and the "feminine" as psychoanalytical, or linguistic, positions that human beings must take up to become speaking creatures. These positions are only generally associated with the biological sexes. That is:

> For Lacan, men and women are only ever in language ('Men and women are signifiers bound to the common usage of language' . . .) All speaking beings must line themselves up on one side or the other of this division, but anyone can cross over and inscribe themselves on the opposite side from that to which they are anatomically destined.[43]

This does not deny that biological sex might be fundamentally important to our identity as subjects. If gender is a lie, it is a lie that we *live.* We must adopt a sex in order to become adult subjects. As we shall see, the theory holds that identification of these psychological categories with biological analogues is practically inevitable in our society, even if it is erroneous. Anatomy is not irrelevant.

## The Real, the Imaginary, and the Symbolic

Lacan locates three orders of experience. He retroactively imagines the infant passing successively through these orders, but as he passes into

41. Lacan, *supra* note 37, at 272.

42. Jane Gallop, *Reading Lacan* 146–57 (1985).

43. Jacqueline Rose, "Introduction II," in *Jacques Lacan And The Ecole Freudienne, Feminine Sexuality* 49 (J. Mitchell and J. Rose eds., 1983).

the next order he never leaves the previous order. This reflects the Hegelian dialectic in which an unsublated trace always remains after each stage.

The initial order is the Real—the object world; which for present purposes may be considered (somewhat inadequately) the physical and anatomical.[44] Next is the Imaginary: which is now suppressed in the unconscious. Finally, there is the Symbolic—the order of consciousness: law, language, and sexuality. The categories of longing that correspond to these three orders are "Need," "Demand," and "Desire," respectively.

It should now start to become more clear what I meant when I said that the Lacanian psychoanalytical subject is a fiction. The subject is not "real" because it is not physical. It is not merely imaginary, because the subject speaks and is therefore not only in the unconscious. The subject is a creation of the Symbolic order of language. But we humans exist in the physical and the unconscious as well as the conscious, although we may not have direct conscious access to the first two orders. Consciousness and subjectivity can, therefore, never be adequate to their end of describing and understanding the psyche.

In the first stage, the infant exists only in the Real, the physical, biological order of Need. It does not yet have awareness or consciousness, let alone language, because these belong in the orders of the Imaginary and Symbolic. Most specifically, it has no awareness of the separation of itself and the rest of the world. At this point the infant experiences itself and its mother as one. Or more precisely, it has no sense of itself as a self, and no sense of its mother as a person.

Need is always full. Because Need is physical, the infant experiences his Needs as either fulfilled or not. Even this statement is somewhat misleading, because to realize one is experiencing something is already to become conscious of one's existence and therefore one's separation from the world.

And so, of course, the infant cannot stay positioned in the Real but begins to enter the Imaginary in the next, or mirror, stage. In the mirror stage the infant first becomes aware of its own body and its mother as something other than its body. Or rather the discovery of the body and

44. This identification of the Real with the anatomical is convenient, but perhaps misleading. Since we do not have direct access to the Real, we can only retroactively abduct its existence. The Real might better be described as the unknown which limits us. It is not, therefore, just the body, but the impossible, the gods and death.

its mother, the beginnings of awareness of self and the outside world, are one and the same. The realization that Mother is Other—radical alterity—is the start of the infant's realization that it is a self. It not only has Needs, it now recognizes that it lacks—it Demands of (M)other.[45]

Demand is not yet conscious language. It is the call to the Other.[46] The infant is not yet a subject, and to say the same thing, it does not yet recognize Mother as another subject. She is just Other. Infant and other are merely negatives, oppositions. It is not an individual, it is not-Mother. But if the unconscious is beneath language, it is structured like a language. Consequently, Lacan calls the unconscious "the discourse of the Other."[47]

The mirror stage is consequently both a stage of great gain—the experience of self—and of incalculable loss and violence. In the imaginary the infant retroactively imagines that it was once one with Mother. Or at least, that is how it imagines that it remembers the experience. Now they are separate.

The infant can and does Demand because it is aware that it wants something, and that there is someone else who has something that it does not have. Unlike Need, Demand is not full. "Ask yourselves what the call represents in the field of speech. Well, it's the possibility of refusal."[48] This will be imagined as castration, a concept that will become more clear when we get to the discussion of the oedipal stage.

The infant desperately wants and Demands to reexperience union with the lost Mother. This is a terrible, violent, and frightening Demand. If it and Mother are one again, then they are no longer two. One must disappear. The new infantile self is terrified that it is the infant who will disappear. After all, it is Mother who is all powerful, who has been the source of fulfillment of its Needs, and who is now the object of its Demands. But if Mother disappears, it will no longer have

45. Note that the term "Mother" means the person initially recognized by the infant as the other, rather than his female parent. Consequently, it is sometimes written as "(m)other" by English speaking Lacanians. In patriarchal family structure this person is also usually the child's mother in the usual sense, or a person socially recognized as a mother surrogate (i.e., nanny, nurse, guardian, widower, or whatever), hence the choice of terminology. The fact that the other, as second term, is identified with (m)other in our society (and because, as we shall see, the third term will be identified with father) will determine the positions of sexuality.

46. Jacques Lacan, *The Seminar of Jacques Lacan: Book I Freud's Papers on Technique 1953–1954*, at 84 (J. Miller ed., J. Forrester 1988).

47. *Id.* at 85.

48. *Id.* at 87.

a mirror. If the infant has no mirror in which to see itself, will the infant disappear?

This violent hypothesis is reaffirmed in daily oral experience. I love what I eat, and I eat what I love. What I eat disappears. What I love disappears. I love Mother.[49] The experience of the mirror stage is the joy of self reflection and the terror of eat or be eaten.[50]

As in the first stages of Hegelian property, we have an ostensibly binary system. This binary system is unstable and looks ahead toward, and presupposes, its own overthrow. The self in the Imaginary is contradictory in the same way as property before exchange—the infant is both now separate from and dependent on the defining Other. This can only be resolved by the addition of a third term and exchange.

### Adding the Third Term

In the oedipal stage the infant becomes aware of the third term necessary for subjectivity—Father. The child is at the threshold of the Symbolic, and the father is a symbolic father, sometimes referred to as "the Name-of-the-Father."

Once a third term is introduced, Mother is no longer merely the child's mirror—its negation. Nor is Father. This allows the infant[51] to start to experience himself as an individual rather than merely not-Mother. The infant realizes that he is not Mother's entire life. He has a rival; she Desires Father. He now realizes that Mother is not the all powerful self-sufficient, totally Other. If she was, she wouldn't Desire. If she Desires Father, Father must be greater than she, he must have whatever object she Desires. The psychological term for this object of

49. My thanks goes to my colleague Arthur Jacobson for his account of the exploits of his son Benjamin Petruck Jacobson who was going through his mirror stage during my research for this article.

The consuming orality of the mirror stage is cleverly depicted by Maurice Sendak in his illustrations to Peter and Iona Opie's collection of classic children's rhymes. Peter Opie and Iona Opie, *I Saw Esau* (1992). The first line of the familiar doggerel, "I one my mother" shows a sweet looking baby nursing at his mother's breast. The illustrations progress with each line so that the mother has been totally consumed by the greedily smiling infant who, as the pun implies, "eight" his mother.

50. Clement points out that Lacan's theory comes largely from his study of certain insane women murderers. Those who do not successfully leave the mirror stage can be violently insane, attempting literally to destroy other people they identify as their mirror image. See Catherine Clement, *The Lives and Legends of Jacques Lacan* 76 (A. Goldhammer trans., 1983).

51. I use the masculine pronoun generally in discussing the child's acquisition of subjectivity because it presupposes the masculine point of view.

Desire is the "Phallus." The Phallus is one of the Names-of-the-Father; that is, it is the universal signifier of subjectivity. He now sees his mother as desiring the Phallus and, therefore, as castrated.[52]

But he still wants the lost union with the Mother that he imagined he remembered in the Imaginary. He is becoming a subject who, as a Hegelian subject, Desires.

For the conscious subject Desire is the Symbolic experiential counterpart of Need and Demand in the Real and Imaginary. Like Demand, and unlike Need, Desire is always incomplete. And so, the child now Desires that Mother Desire him. First he wants to be the Phallus. But he also wants to be a subject recognized as a subject, not an object. He wants to have the Phallus, so that he can offer it to Mother so she will return his Desire. He concludes that Father must have the Phallus, which is why Mother Desires him. The irony is that the infant only turns to the Father as a means of obtaining the Mother, but the price the Father imposes for his services is permanent loss of the Mother—castration.

In order to learn what the Phallus is, the child wants to learn what the Name-of-the-Father is in order to determine what it has that (m)other lacks yet Desires. As discussed below, the Phallus thus becomes the signifier of subjectivity. But the subject did not exist until it recognized the Phallus as signifier. That is, Phallus is a signifier without a signified—the subject is nothing, a zero that exists only because it is signified. Signification—that is, the Symbolic order of language—brings the fiction of subjectivity into being by the trick of making zero count as one.[53]

The child retroactively supposes that the Name-of-the-Father imposes law—the incest taboo upon the child. Mother is Father's object of Desire; the child may not have her. It is Father who castrates the child by forever separating him from his Phallus. It is even more complex than this. The Symbolic (i.e., law as prohibition, language, and sexuality) is necessary for Desire to be created and to function. That is, Desire is that which cannot be filled. The law, which separates the subject from its object of Desire, makes Desire possible. Language itself is the barrier that separates us from the Imaginary and the Real. And so we see, identical with Hegel, the moment of the creation of law is the moment of creation of the subject: subjectivity and law are mutually constituted.

For the son, the origin of law and the creation of subjectivity and intersubjectivity is also, as in Hegel, a result of exchange. For the male

52. Jacques Lacan, "The Meaning of the Phallus," in *Feminine Sexuality, supra* note 44, at 76.

53. Žižek, *supra* note 14, at 50.

child, this is seen as the father who threatens to take away his penis. The incest taboo is the origin of law, language, and culture. It is this repression that makes us into human beings.[54] If the son submits to the Law-of-the-Father, the Name-of-the-Father will recompense him by allowing him to adopt the father's name and marry another woman. As in Hegel, the son sees himself and his Father as being mutually constituted as subjects through the exchange of the object of Desire. Each recognizes the other as a subject objectified through objects of Desire, yet not dependent on any specific object of Desire. Through this symbolic exchange of the Phallic Woman, the community of subjects is created, just as the actual exchange of Phallic property constitutes abstract right, the first stage in the eventual development of the community of the state.

Of course, a typical initial reaction to this theory is that this story seems less satisfactory for girls than for boys.

> For her, the oedipus complex involves no rewards, no authority, no compensation for her abandonment of the mother; rather, it entails her acceptance of her subordination. It involves the "discovery" that what the boy has been threatened with—castration—has already taken place in the girl. He believes that she and the mother are castrated. In her "recognition" of her narcissistic inadequacy, the girl abandons the mother as a love-object, and focuses her libidinal drives on the father now recognized as "properly" phallic. The girl has quickly learned that she does not have the phallus, nor the power it signifies. She comes to accept, not without resistance, her socially designated role as subordinate to the possessor of the phallus, and through her acceptance, she comes to occupy the passive, dependent position expected of women in patriarchy.[55]

The girl experiences a nostalgic longing for subjectivity and community she is denied insofar as she is positioned as a "woman." The Desire to *have* the Phallus is forever thwarted because the Symbolic names the Phallus as that which is possessed and exchanged only between those positioned as "men." Insofar as she is recognized as a "woman" she is

54. Casey and Woody, *supra* note 11, at 85.
55. Elizabeth Grosz, *Jacques Lacan: A Feminist Introduction* 69 (1989).

a person without a Phallus—she is castrated. This is the rewriting of penis envy.

But perhaps the girl's situation only seems less satisfactory than the boy's at first blush. Castration is the universal initiation rite of subjectivity. The apparent exchange between those who are positioned as "men" cannot be truly satisfactory, because it is not Real. It is a lie. Desire can never be satisfied. The son exchanges something it does not have (access to the Mother) for something that does not exist (the Phallus, access to The Woman) in order to achieve something with no content (subjectivity).

## Woman Does Not Exist

Perhaps the most notorious and most misunderstood catchphrase associated with Lacan is "Woman does not exist."[56] We can now explore what this means.

Remember, during the mirror stage, the infant experienced the tragedy of separation from (m)other and Demanded that she come back. Now he sees himself as a separate subject and Desires Mother. Mother is the object of his Desire. Mother is his Phallus, the Phallic Mother.

The mirror stage was experienced as the separation from Mother. This is now "remembered" in the Imaginary (which still exists in the repressed form of the unconscious) as the loss of the Phallic Mother. The Phallic Mother as the feminine represents the dream of an unmediated relationship with the other. This utopian relationship is imagined by the subject to have existed in the Real, and is now forever lost in the Imaginary.

The unconscious always remains infantile, crying for Mother.[57] "Woman, as a result is identified by her lack of the phallus. She is difference *from* the phallus."[58] Even, as she also "is" the Phallus—but the Phallus that is always Desired and never obtained. The Feminine is therefore projected as "lack." Woman does not exist—she is imaginary.

Because of the conflation of gender and sex, the female child insofar as she takes on the position of "woman" tends to identify with her

---

56. Drucilla Cornell, *Beyond Accommodation: Ethical Feminism, Deconstruction And The Law* 39 (1991).

57. Grosz, *supra* note 57, at 83.

58. Cornell, *supra* note 58, at 38.

mother, as the castrated self. She can never fully join the community of castrating Fathers because she, and they, conflate her lack of the penis with the inability to have the Phallus. She, therefore, can only aspire to be the Phallus, to be the object of Desire for men.

Consequently, the quote about Woman ascribed to Lacan can be misleading. Indeed, it is a misquote. The more accurate translation is:

> The Woman does not exist. [T]he woman can only be written with *The* crossed through. There is no such thing as *The* woman, where the definite article stands for the universal. There is no such thing as *The* woman since of her essence—having already risked the term, why think twice about it?—of her essence, is not all.[59]

As I have already emphasized, the fact that there are fictional, delusional, lying aspects of our psyches does not imply that we can choose not to believe them. We experience ourselves as our lies, and we live our lies. We cannot leave the lies of the Symbolic without giving up the language that is created in the Symbolic. We cannot de-repress the repressed Imaginary without becoming babbling infants. Repression is not a mental disease. We need language and repression to function and speak. Lacan believes he is telling truth about lies, because lies are the only truth we are capable of.

What is more, as we have seen, the community of subjects is constituted through the symbolic exchange of the Phallus between Father and son. Unfortunately for those of us who are positioned as women, the Phallic object of Desire that is identified with the Feminine is conflated, not only with the phallic male organ, but with actual women. For this linguistic system to work, those who position themselves as men (which tends to be those who are also biologically male) must objectify women. The feminist cliché that men treat women as sex objects takes on new meaning in Lacan. The theory gives essential significance to empirically familiar phenomena. Many men identify themselves with, and through, social groups that are characterized primarily through their exclusion of woman—fraternities, private "business clubs," the priesthood, and until very recently, the military, academia, and government. In order to experience themselves as subjects, men

59. Jacques Lacan, "God and the Jouissance of The Woman. A Love Letter," in *Feminine Sexuality, supra* note 44, 137 at 144.

need to seek to experience women as objects. We continue to try to lead our lives this way even though it doesn't and can't work.

Lacan particularly notes that the institution of patriarchal marriage requires the exchange of women as objects. Giving women property rights, therefore, threatens the very structure of our society. This is because Lacan, as a good Hegelian, agrees that allowing a woman to own and exchange property with subjects must lead to the recognition of her as a subject. If she becomes a subject, she can no longer serve her function as object. And so Lacanian feminists would agree with the rhetoric of the American religious right—feminine emancipation is a threat to traditional family values.

I have argued elsewhere that both American cultural, and MacKinnonesque radical, feminist jurisprudes are implicitly and immanently conservative in that they accept and reinstate rather than effectively critique the masculinist status quo. This is because they accept the traditional American stereotype of masculinity and femininity, although they disagree as to what the response to these stereotypes should be (i.e., cultural feminists celebrate the feminine stereotype, while radical feminists denigrate it and encourage women to adopt behavior more similar to the masculine stereotype).[60] That is, both groups tend to accept the characterization (associated with Carol Gilligan)[61] that men tend to be more separate, individualistic, and concerned with right and justice. This liberal ideal is treated as an empirically accurate description of men. Women, who in this view are the negative of men, are declared to be (either essentially or as a result of social conditioning) more relational and communitarian, concerned with needs and care.[62]

Lacanian theory is potentially more radical in that Lacan first reverses this order. The Lacanian account turns the cultural feminists' story "on its head."[63] It is the masculine that is the key to community. The masculine subject is not individualistic, because the subject is an

60. *See* Jeanne L. Schroeder, "Feminism Historicized: Medieval Misogynist Stereotypes in Contemporary Feminist Jurisprudence," 75 *Iowa L. Rev.* 1135 (1990); Schroeder, *supra* note 41.

61. *See* Carol Gilligan, *In a Different Voice: A Psychological Theory of Women's Development* (1982).

62. See Robin West, "Jurisprudence and Gender," 55 *U. Chi. L. Rev.* 1 (1988). Cornell has criticized cultural feminists such as West as confusing sociology (how people act in social groups) and psychology. Cornell, *supra* note 58, at 50–51.

63. Drucilla Cornell, "The Doubly-Prized World: Myth Allegory and the Feminine," 75 *Cornell L. Rev.* 644, 664 (1990).

intersubjective linguistic concept totally dependent on the exchange of Phalluses with other men.

> Although both genders are cut off from the repressed Mother, and, theoretically, have access to the position of the other, only men, to the degree they become traditional, heterosexual men, are fundamentally 'connected' to one another in the order of the symbolic. Without this connection, there would be no ground for masculine identity.[64]

Women, insofar as they are the feminine, are isolated from community. It is only by taking on the masculine role of subjectivity that they have access to community. "Put simply, to enter into the masculine world, women must take up the masculine position."[65] "The Lacanian story also demonstrates that women, as well as men, are masculine in so far as they enter the symbolic."[66]

The radicalism resides in the fact that this is not a mere reversal in the sense of a mirror image that would just reflect back upon the status quo. Rather, it is a subtle warping and re-valorization of the status quo. The Lacanian community of castrating Fathers is not that of warmth and fulfillment imagined by cultural feminists. It is based on repression, castration, and law.[67] It is not, therefore, surprising that men often engage in aggressive attempts at individuality in order to achieve a separation from community that they cannot achieve. Similarly, as Julia Kristeva argues, many women engage in clinging and seemingly relational behavior in a desperate attempt to have relations and achieve the closeness of community that is always denied them.[68]

### *The Phallic Woman and Property*

The Phallic Mother, like property, constitutes the subject through signification. My analogy is still, however, incomplete. I have shown that our masculine subject lies to himself and says that he *possesses* the

---

64. *Id.* at 664.
65. Drucilla Cornell, *The Philosophy of the Limit* 175 (1992).
66. Cornell, *supra* note 64, at 672.
67. *Id.* at at 664.
68. Julia Kristeva, *The Kristeva Reader* 201 (T. Moi et al. trans., 1986).

Phallic Woman. He seeks self-recognition through the fiction that he engages in the *alienation and exchange* of the Phallic Woman with other male subjects through submission to the incest taboo and initiation into the Symbolic. But, Hegel argued, there are three necessary elements of a full property necessary for the formation of a subject. It is not enough to possess and alienate the desired object of property. One must also have the ability to *enjoy* the object. Our split masculine subject cannot achieve his Desire and *enjoy* the Phallic Woman. We have seen that, by definition, language is the bar to enjoyment that makes Desire possible. But that does not mean that enjoyment cannot occur. The psyche is not merely the illusory subject of consciousness. Not everyone is always positioned as masculine speaking subjects trapped in the Symbolic.

### The Silent Jouissance of Women

As the conscious world of the Symbolic is linguistic, in a curious way, women can never "speak" in a feminine voice. They must always become or mime the masculine in order to speak. That is, language is Phallic in that the Phallus is the universal signifier of the speaking subject. In order to speak, one must take the position of the one who has the Phallus. To have the Phallus is to be symbolically masculine.

Of course, in the schema, the "Feminine" still exists in the unspeakable order of the real, but the moment we realize we are forming ideas and we try to speak, we are back in the Symbolic, and the Feminine is lost. In the spoken world in which we live, it is as though Woman does not exist. But it only seems so. The feminine still exists in the slippage of meaning in language.

Slippage always occurs. "[T]he sliding of the signified under the signifier, which is always active in discourse (its action, let us note, is unconscious) is the function of the dream."[69] And yet "the efficacy of the unconscious does not cease in the waking state."[70] It is in this slippage that we glimpse the Real. Access to the Real cannot come directly through words, but through that which is beyond words, what Lacan

69. Jacques Lacan, *Ecrits: A Selection* 160 (A. Sheridan trans., 1977).
70. *Id.* at 163.

calls the *jouissance*[71] or *enjoyment* of and by the Woman. But we only glimpse her; the Feminine remains "Euridyce twice lost."[72]

### *An Abduction from the Seraglio*

I have referred to phallic metaphors of property as an "abduction." The process of abduction is as follows: I observe a surprising thing. I do not like to stay surprised. Consequently, I try to make up a story that, if it were true, would make the surprising thing no longer surprising, but a matter of course.

The abduction of property law reflects the experience of the masculine. The point of my analysis is not yet to suggest that Phallic metaphors in the jurisprudence of property are psychoanalytically inevitable in all cultures and under all circumstances. The goal of psychoanalysis is not the recognition of inexorable fate, but the furthering of human freedom through the increase of knowledge. Nor am I arguing in the alternative that the Phallic metaphor property is a delusional masculinist instrument of oppression. Indeed, Lacan's linguistic theory holds that metaphors and metonymy are always necessary elements of all language and, therefore, law.

I am merely suggesting reasons why this particular metaphor—the abductions that property is unitary and tangible and that possession must be physical and visible—might seem so "natural" and reassuring. Lacan explains how we tend to conflate the psychological concept of the Phallic Mother (the object of Desire) with the physical organ of the penis, to equate the Phallic with the phallic. In parallel, we might have a psychological tendency to conflate the parallel legal Phallic concept of property (as the object of Desire) with the phallic metaphors of holding and seeing. The psychological conflation can serve positive functions, such as the development of gender identity and the creation of lan-

71. There is no precise English cognate for the French word "*jouissance*" as used by Lacan. Literally, it refers to enjoyment or joyfulness generally. It includes the legal right of "enjoyment" of property, but is also a slang term for sexual orgasm specifically. Bice Benevenuto and Roger Kennedy, *The Works of Jacques Lacan: An Introduction* 179 (1986). Lacan's precise definition of the term can only be understood in context because it is defined to have no definition and to refer to that which cannot be expressed in words.

72. Jacques Lacan, *The Four Fundamental Concepts of Psycho-Analysis* 25 (J. Miller, ed. A. Sheridan trans., 1981) Lacan's metaphor also beautifully captures the retroactive nature of Hegelian and Lacanian dialectics. Hegel and Lacan, like Orpheus, are glancing backward. But, according to Lacan, the Feminine, like Euridyce, escapes our understanding. The second she is glimpsed, we enter the Symbolic and she is lost.

guage. But it can also cause tragedy in the form of mental illness, the oppression and rage of women and the despair of men. Similarly, I am suggesting that the parallel jurisprudential conflation might also both serve positive functions, as well as risking legal results that are not merely confusing, but unjust. This does not necessarily mean that we should abandon such metaphors, but that we be aware that we use them, so that we can consider whether it is the best alternative.

Lacan offers one explanation for the use of masculinist Phallic metaphors in the law. Another explanation might initially seem simpler. Until very recently, all lawyers were men. In this simplistic view, the empirical fact that some lawyers are now biological women should add a feminine "different" voice to the law.

The power of Lacanian theory to me lies in its insight that things are not so simple. It suggests that insofar as I am writing this and speaking to you I am also speaking in the masculine voice. Even "cultural feminists" speak in a masculine, rather than a "different," voice. They adopt a stereotype of femininity that is merely the negative of the archetype of masculinity. It essentializes what they believe is the empirical experience of women who are psychically positioned as the defining other of man. Consequently, the "feminine" of the cultural feminist is a mirror image reflecting back the masculine. It is Imaginary in the technical sense of the term.

Does this mean that legal abductions can only replicate the masculine? I have stated that Lacanian psychoanalysis does not explain the inevitability of patriarchy or the use of phallic metaphors to describe Phallic concepts such as property. However, in our society it is mandatory that we adopt a sexual identity with respect to having or being the Phallus to even be able to speak. Doesn't this show that, while patriarchy may not be natural or inevitable, it has a rapacious reproductive potency?

The inevitable masculinity of abduction seems apparent from its very terminology. As I have explained elsewhere,[73] the more common meaning of the English word "abduction" is not the logic of imagination, but kidnapping for sexual purposes. To be blunt, it means rape. Abduction was one of the ancient forms of marriage—indeed the form memorialized in the Vestal's initiation rite of *captio* (capture).

At first blush, this might suggest either the symbolic exchange of Woman posited by Lacan as the origin of the subject and law, or the actual abduction or exchange of women posited by Lévi-Strauss as the

73. Schroeder, *supra* note 41, at 115–17.

origin of culture. But at second look, the image is more ambiguous. The thinker does not rape his ideas, he is raped by them; he is ravished by his imagination, taken by a new thought. The imagery reflects the masculine vision of female sexual experience—silent, passive, and orgasmic. And so, at one moment, the theory of abduction is the masculine myth of the feminine joy of rape.

But it is more. The imagery of imagination as abduction is *precisely* the Lacanian concept of women's access to the Real through *jouissance.* Lacan said that the masculine subject is stuck in the Symbolic order of language and has no direct access to the Real. The terminology of abduction reflects the concept that in order to give birth to new ideas and to experience *jouissance,* "he" must take on the position of the feminine. That is, if we need to take up the position of the masculine to speak, we must take up the position of the feminine to enjoy.

### *Epilogue: Vesta, the Phallic Mother*

The Vestal was sexually ambiguous. She dressed as half bride, half wife. She was a consecrated virgin, married to the state, who insured fertility. She was a woman with the legal status of a man. The Vestal was considered capable of mediating between the human and the divine *precisely* because she was poised in transition between all permissible social roles—she was simultaneously maiden, wife, and man, sterile and fertile, virgin and phallic.[74]

Abduction is a mediation between the unspeakable order at the Real and the legal and linguistic order of the Symbolic. The imaginative thinker must, therefore, be ambiguously positioned between the permissible psychic roles of masculine speaker and feminine *jouissant.* "He" becomes an imaginative thinker only if "she" is captured by imagination. The initiate became a Vestal only through *captio.* Perhaps abduction is described in the language of sexual relations because it *is* a sexual relation. Is it marriage as well as rape?

The great goddess Vesta was the epitome of the Phallic Mother: she was simultaneously the most virginal and sterile of all Olympians, was addressed as Mother and granted fertility. Mythographers tell us that Vesta had no myths other than her identification as the oldest Olympian entitled to priority in reverence and sacrifice over all other

74. E.g., Pomeroy, *supra* note 1, at 210; Baldson, *supra* note 1, at 235.

gods.[75] Unlike the other classical gods, Vesta was rarely depicted. Instead, she was symbolized by her flame, the fire stick, and a ritual phallus. The myths of her priestesses were limited to accounts of their miraculous impregnation by a phallus that would appear within the flame that was the manifestation of the goddess.

But was Vesta, like the Lacanian Woman, really so beyond language that she could not even be spoken of? Our knowledge of Roman religion comes entirely from Roman men—Roman women did not write and Roman men did not know Roman women's rites. Roman women worshipped other mysterious silent goddesses. The Vestals officiated at the most important religious holiday in the Roman calendar: a festival that was so mysteriously feminine that no man, male animal, or even male image could be present; a festival in honor of a deity that was so powerfully feminine that men were not even told her name but referred to her only as the *Bona Dea*. But was she nameless to the women? Did they know the "good goddess" as Vesta, or by some other name? Was she really mythless or did the Vestals make their *enjoyment* eloquent and sing her exploits among the women?

And so let us remember that even though those of us who are positioned as women might speak in the masculine voice when we practice law, this position might also give us different access to the unconscious. Lacan wanted us to believe that this different access, *enjoyment*, is *necessarily* dumb. But is this because the Woman does not or cannot speak, or because the legal community of fathers will not listen or cannot hear? Perhaps she has screamed for so long that her voice is hoarse.

Lacan insisted that she was silent all along.[76] But he may have "cooked the books." Lacan declared that language is to be defined as

75. Robert Graves, *The Greek Myths* 74 (1955) (referring specifically to Hestia, the Greek goddess with whom Vesta was identified).

76. Lacan's image of *jouissance* is the great Counter-Reformation saint, Theresa of Avila. She sees God but swoons in mute ecstasy.

But it is Lacan, not Theresa or God, who says she is silent. Tellingly, Lacan's description is not based on studying Theresa herself, but Bernini's statue of her in the church of San Maria de Vittorio in Rome. This beautiful statue is a perfect reflection of the male image of the female experience—those exquisite marble lips seem about to quiver in orgasm, but she will never disturb you with female prattle.

Had Lacan tried to listen to the real Theresa, he would have heard plenty. Theresa did experience ecstasy—and eloquently described and analyzed it in great detail in her writings. She was one of the greatest theologians of mysticism. Indeed, because of her teachings she is considered by Catholics to be a Doctor of the Church—an authoritative teacher, and speaker, of doctrine.

masculine. If one accepts this, then the Feminine is *defined* as lack, the feminine voice is *defined* as no-voice. Our speech as women has been defined away and is no more speech than the barking of dogs.[77]

As feminists we must strive to rewrite the Feminine—or write her for the first time. We must emphasize that the myth of castration is *imaginary.* It is a myth both in the negative sense of delusion and in the affirmative sense of a story we tell to give meaning to our lives. Unmediated relations with others cannot be a forever lost and infantile state that we can only mourn *precisely* because this state never existed. We did not even become individuals with the potential for relationship until the moment of mediation. In Hegelian terms, to return to our unmediated state is to regress to the lonely abstraction of free will, and to stay at the level of simple mediated relationships identified by psychoanalytic theory is to remain at the inadequate, unsatisfactory, and "cold-hearted" level of abstract right. The feminine as unmediated relation is, therefore, a desire, a dream, and an inspiration. The feminine will never be *re*covered because she has not yet come into existence. She will be a creation, like the subject.

At this point perhaps all we can say is that abductions from the male position are not unique or inevitable. But will we ever be able to make our *jouissance* eloquent? Will there be a moment when the Vestal ceases to be fasces, virgin, matron, or man, and becomes The Woman?

---

I am not the only feminist who has called Lacan on this example. Jacqueline Rose, in her introduction to a book of essays by Lacan and his followers on feminine sexuality makes precisely the same point. Rose, *supra* note 44, at 51. I am not suggesting that the ineptness of one example necessarily disproves the core ideas of Lacan's theory of feminine *jouissance.* I do, however, find it suggestive.

77. Jeanne L. Schroeder, "Subject: Object," 47 *U. Miami L. Rev.* 1, 6–7 (1992).

*Chapter 5*

# Love Me, Love My Dog

*Renata Salecl*

Why is the dog such an attractive animal for human beings? From antiquity, there is the well-known case of the philosopher Diogenes, who actually found in the dog life the ultimate model for human life and had himself decided to live like a dog. Diogenes was thus barely dressed, lived in a barrel, and liked to masturbate in public, all to show his contempt for civilization and praise for nature. With his rude behavior, Diogenes liked to provoke his fellow man, in order to prove that they were too flimsy to compete with him. He thus boasted that no one dared to go hunting with such a distinguished dog as he.

Recently, the Western art world got a new dog-like human being in the persona of the Russian artist Oleg Kulik. He usually has a doghouse built in the gallery, where he then lives day and night being totally naked, behaving in a dog manner, walking like a dog, barking, etc. But Kulik's fame really began when at two art shows (in Zurich and in Stockholm) he started biting the visitors of the show. In both cases, the organizers of the shows called the police, who then enchained Kulik and took him to the police station for questioning. The shocked policemen first did not believe that Kulik was invited to the exhibition to act like a dog. But, when the story was confirmed from the side of the organizers of the show, Kulik was released, since it became unclear what offense he could be accused of.[1]

Before dealing with the problem of what it means to behave like a dog, let me point out that I personally do not see a great artistic practice

1. Kulik's imprisonment in Stockholm was a paradoxical event, since the organizers of the art show knew beforehand about Kulik's troubles with the police at the show in Zurich. However, they thought that was just part of the game. But when Kulik started biting visitors in Stockholm, the organizers were so shocked that they themselves called the police.

in Kulik's biting the visitors. The Kulik affair, however, can help us to deal with some theoretical issues that concern the divide between human beings and animals, which is for Jacques Derrida the last metaphysical divide not yet deconstructed.[2] But first let us see how Kulik's case undermined the naive belief in the idea of artistic dialogue and, second, how the whole dilemma of the East–West relationship was restated.

The Interpol exhibition in Stockholm was presented as an attempt to establish a dialogue and a new form of communication between artists coming from the East and from the West. If one does not understand communication only in terms of the Habermasian ideal speech situation, where the parties involved tolerantly exchange their ideas thus creating an ideal democratic universe, but one takes into account also some contemporary psychoanalytic and poststructuralist reasoning, then communication becomes much less ideal. We know from the theory of Foucault, as well as from Deleuze and Guattari, that communication, dialogue, and exchange of ideas are all means for various forms of power struggle. And the debates about the violence of language, about so-called hate speech, have clearly proven that a simple speech act can contain the most aggressive racist attack.[3] On the one hand, dialogue and communication can involve a great deal of violence. But, on the other hand, someone can easily understand violence and destruction as a way to communicate. Thus, if the organizers of Interpol want to have dialogue as the form of the exhibition, they should not be too surprised if some artists use violence and destruction as a mode of communication.

The paradox of the second dilemma was that Kulik was invited as a particularity—as a Russian dog. I am certain that if an American artist played a dog, he would be of much less interest to the international art scene than the Russian artist. We all know that the majority of people in today's Russia live a dog-like life. And the first association a Westerner has in regard to Kulik's performance is that he is representing this reality of contemporary Russia. Kulik-dog is therefore of interest for the Western art world because of the fact that he is the Russian "dog."

2. *See* Jacques Derrida, "'Eating Well,' or the Calculation of the Subject: An Interview with Jacques Derrida," in *Who Comes After the Subject* (Peter Connor and Jean-Luc Nancy eds., 1991).

3. *See* Renata Salecl, "See No Evil, Speak No Evil: Hate Speech and Human Rights," in *Radical Evil* (Joan Copjec ed., 1996).

The trauma of the West in regard to Russia in recent years is that the West regards Russia as a superpower, but only on condition that it does not act as one. And, in regard to Kulik's performance, it can be said that the East finds an aesthetic pleasure in observing the Russian "dog," but only on condition that he does not behave in a truly dog-like manner. When Kulik ceased to be the decorative art-object—the Eastern neighbor who represents the misery of the Russian dog-like life—and started to act in a way that surprised his admirers, he quickly became designated as the enemy. His performance (together with the performance of another Russian artist Alexander Brener, who at the Interpol show destroyed a work by Chinese-American artist Wenda Gu) was described as a "direct attack against art, democracy and the freedom of expression," and as a "classical model of imperialist behavior."[4] Here we encounter a similar deadlock as in the way multiculturalists tend to treat the other. The other has to be a passive, submissive victim-like other; but, when the other does not act in this way, he or she quickly becomes designated as imperialistic, fundamentalist, totalitarian, etc. (Remember how the Bosnians who ceased to play the role of victims and started to arm themselves quickly were named Islamic fundamentalists?)[5]

The paradox of Kulik's performance is that he does not want to expose his particularity of being a Russian artist, but tries to give an answer to the universal dilemma of the man–animal relationship, man's place in nature, etc. In the catalog of the recent Manifesta show in Rotterdam, where Kulik played Pavlov's dog, we get some answers to this dilemma in the form of the program of Kulik's art, written by his collaborator Mila Bredikhina.

The program very much resembles the theory of so-called deep ecology and its criticism of anthropocentrism. Kulik thus propagates a new agricultural revolution, which would bring new symbiosis between humans and animals; he wants to limit human population to a third of its present size in order to establish a new balance in the biosphere; but, especially, he wants to encourage studies of the psychology of animals, which would result in a new dialogue between animals and human beings. In this program, we also read that man should stop per-

4. *See Open letter to the art world, Siksi* 1 (1996).

5. For the analysis of the Western media's representation of the victims of the Bosnian war, see Renata Salecl, *The Spoils of Freedom: Psychoanalysis and Feminism After the Fall of Socialism* (1996).

ceiving animals, not as the non-anthropomorphic Other, but as his alter ego. However, this will only be possible when we question the entire logic of the organization of human society and especially the nature of democracy. For Kulik,

> True democracy can only be established on the politically inclusive idea of zoocentrism, (*i.e.*, man is but a part, rather than a measure of, our planet's biosphere). Zoocentrism integrates man as a subculture in the larger whole of a united culture of noosphere (derived from noos: the ability to smell, to feel).[6]

Since ideal democracy is not possible, one should recognize that actual democracy looks like a jungle, where some inhabitants take advantage of the fact that they are stronger or faster than others. Thus Kulik concludes:

> A jungle is in fact a more efficient society, devoid of the oversophistication that is currently stifling humanity. The main thing is that the jungle is the only place where the strong, the wise, and energetic can bring all their capabilities into play.[7]

However, Kulik's program also demands some improvements for the "democratic law of the jungle" which include "the further escalation of political inclusiveness, legal foundations of bioethics, universal suffrage, etc."[8]

The theoretical position of deep ecology is much more radical than traditional ecology or environmentalism. In its demand for the protection of nature, the latter still takes the human being as the center of the world. It therefore claims that nature has to be protected because it presents a vital environment for humans. Deep ecology opposes such a view, since in its perspective we need to give up on anthropocentrism totally in order to create a new form of society that would rely on a symbiosis of nature and human beings.

---

6. See the catalog of *Manifesta 1* (Biennial exhibition, Rotterdam, 1996).

7. *Id.*

8. *Id.* "This law is to become political reality when all the biological species of the planet enjoy equal political rights. The first step on this road has already been made: the Political Laboratory of Biosphere and the Party of the Animals [Kulik's party] have been successfully functioning in Russia for two years." *Id.*

Deep ecology has many troubling theoretical stands, but, for the purpose of my argument I will invoke only two—the problem of the Cartesian subject and rights. Deep ecology finds the main culprit for the lack of symbiosis between humans and animals in the notion of the Cartesian subject. Critics usually focus on Descartes's perception of animals as soul-less machines and on his devalorization of nature. However, deep ecologists make a mistake when they regard the Cartesian subject as the ultimate anthropocentric notion, when it is actually with the advent of Cartesianism and the Copernican revolution that was tied to it that the subject lost its rooting in nature as well as its central place in the universe. On the one hand, the subject became pure substanceless subjectivity, with no determined place in nature or culture, but, on the other hand, the subject also became one among many elements of the universe.

On the basis of this subject, the modern notion of rights was established. Although in the contemporary understanding of rights, nature and especially animals are getting more and more legal protection, it is clear that the human subject is still perceived as the dominant bearer of rights. In their fight for the equalization of the rights of humans and animals, deep ecologists rely on utilitarian theory and its claim that each being wants to maximize its happiness and avoid suffering. As Peter Singer says, "it is not in my interests to suffer. If I am suffering, I must be in a state that, insofar as its *intrinsic* properties are concerned, I would rather not be in . . . "[9] For deep ecologists animals are similar to human beings in this avoidance of suffering, which is why they need to be treated in the same way as humans.[10]

If psychoanalysis teaches anything, it is that human beings are not inclined to achieve happiness. On the contrary, they find special enjoyment in suffering. And the whole history of psychoanalysis is concerned with discovering the mechanisms that drive the subject on this path of self-destruction. The ecologists' insistence on the avoidance of

9. Peter Singer, "The Significance of Animal Suffering," in 13 *Behavior and Brain Sciences* 11 (1990).

10. Daniel C. Dennet points out the distinction between pain and suffering in animals and humans. He agrees with the ecologists' stand that animals feel pain, but not with the claim that the notion of suffering applies to animals in the same way as to humans: "Snakes (or parts of snakes!) may feel pain . . . but the evidence mounts that snakes lack the sort of over-arching, long-term organization that leaves room for significant suffering." Daniel C. Dennet, "Animal Consciousness: What Matters and Why," 3 *Social Research* 707 (1995).

suffering might be true for animals, for whom it can be said that they are driven by the instinct of self-preservation; however, for humans, it is the opposite—as beings of language they are essentially marked by a force of self-annihilation, i.e., the death drive.

Precisely because the human being is not anymore a natural being, he or she has lost the ability to instinctually avoid suffering; however, to say it with Kant: by ceasing to be a natural being, the human being has acquired freedom because of which he or she will also be able to feel sympathy with the suffering others—the animals, for example—and develop responsibility toward them. Thus: "We have seen men sacrifice their lives to protect whales . . . ; [while] the reverse is far less common."[11] It can also be said that a man biting an animal is treated as responsible for his behavior and might be punished for his violent act, while in the reverse case one cannot speak about responsibility. Here Kulik's claim that he is a dog who bites also opens up the question of responsibility.

When Kulik was taken to the police station in Stockholm, at some point he stopped playing the dog and started to give reasons for his act. He put some blame for his behavior on the visitors who treated him as a dog by teasing him, kicking him in the head, etc. Kulik also complained that the organizers had put him on a too long chain, which allowed him to trespass the warning sign "Dangerous dog!" It was crucial for Kulik-the-person not to take responsibility for the behavior of his other self, Kulik-the-dog. However, while at the police station, he also did not want to be treated like a dog—without any rights to explain his action.

In medieval Europe, animals were treated as responsible for their wrongdoings. There are well-known cases of the weevils who were put on trial because they invaded the vinyard, the leeches who were prosecuted for their invasion of the lake, and so on.[12] In court, animals were represented by counsel chosen for them, who usually defended their action by claiming that, as creatures of God, animals have the same rights to live in a certain environment or consume plants. There were many trials where the animals won the case, and as a result the municipality had to give them compensation in the form of a land where they could freely live without intruding into the lives of humans. As can be

11. Luc Ferry, *The New Ecological Order* 41 (1995).
12. *Id., see also* Jean Vartier, *Les procès d'animaux du Moyen Age à nos jours* (1970).

expected, the insects weren't too pleased with such a decision and thus rarely moved to the designated place.

From the position of deep ecology, the laws that protect the animals and nature in general are rejected because they treat the latter only as property of humans. And the new equalization of the right of animals and humans on which deep ecology insists should primarily change the status of animals as property, so that animals will not be protected because of the interests of humans but because of their own interests and inherent values.[13] One can easily get the impression here that before the emergence of capitalist society and its notion of property, animals were better treated by the law. But the paradox here is that the very idea of animal protection itself emerged only when the law started to regard them as property.[14] Thus it is only in the early nineteenth century that the anticruelty statutes became an essential part of Anglo-American law. These anticruelty laws first applied to domestic animals like cattle, and it took some time before pets like dogs and cats were perceived as property, too, and thus got legal protection. Since the dog is regarded as property, this also implies the responsibility of the owner: it is the owner who is prosecuted if his dog bites people.

I assume that Kulik would support the deep ecologists' claim that animals should not be treated as property: however, in practice, Kulik acts differently. Whenever Kulik is invited to a show, he insists that he cannot travel alone, but needs to be accompanied by his owner—his wife. Now, let's speculate that Kulik's offense would be tried in court, and that, at the same time, a judge would actually take him as a dog and not as a human being who is just playing a dog. Since we no longer follow the medieval law that puts animals themselves on trial, the only way for the law to deal with Kulik's offense is to put on trial his owner—his wife.

As for Kulik's attempt to create a new "united culture of noosphere," which would be grounded on "noos"—the ability to smell, or feel—one can only say that culture as such (in contrast to nature) was established at the moment when the human being ceased to rely on his smell.

13. For a detailed analysis of the ecologists' objection to the treatment of animals as property, see Gary L. Francione, *Animals, Property, and the Law* (1995). See also the well-known book by Tom Regan, *The Case for Animal Rights* (1983).

14. See Jerrold Tannenbaum, "Animals and the Law: Cruelty, Property, Rights . . . Or How the Law Makes Up in Common Sense What It Lacks in Metaphysics," *Social Research* 3 (1995).

Jacques Lacan points out that what prevents the dog from rising to the level of man is his strong ability to smell.[15] Through the sense of smell, the dog still has a direct relation to objects, while with man this ability has been lost. Here we can take into account Freud's thesis that in the history of humanity it was crucial when the human being stood up and stopped orienting himself primarily with the help of his smell, but instead with the help of his eyes. At that moment, excrement also became perceived as something that smells badly and as something by which one is disgusted. Freud especially points out that with young children, one does not yet find the disgust over excrement; on the contrary, excrement is perceived as part of the body. It is only socialization that introduces disgust over excrement: the child's anal eroticism has to undergo the phase of "organic repression" when the child is being formed into a social being.

Freud also says that "man scarcely finds the smell of *his own* excreta repulsive, but only that of other people. Thus a person who is not clean—who does not hide his excreta—is offending other people; he is showing no consideration for them."[16] We perceive such behavior as an abuse, and sometimes we say that such a dirty person is behaving like a dog. However, Freud concludes that

> It would be incomprehensible . . . that man should use the name of his most faithful friend in the animal world—the dog—as a term of abuse if that creature had not incurred his contempt through two characteristics: that it is an animal whose dominant sense is that of smell and one which has no horror of excrement, and that it is not ashamed of its sexual function.[17]

In contrast to the animal, the human being, by gaining his erect posture, has not only lost his ability to smell, but also the ability to copulate in an animal way. As is well-known from the history of psychoanalysis, the human being in the process of becoming a speaking subject undergoes symbolic castration which introduces a bar, a lack, because of which the subject will be forever deprived of the wholeness that animals still have. This will also prevent the subject finding sexual satisfaction in simple copulation. As Freud points out, with the erect pos-

15. See his unpublished seminar, *Identification* (1961–62).
16. Sigmund Freud, *Civilization and Its Discontents* 288–89 (1985).
17. *Id.*

ture, it is not only anal eroticism that falls victim to organic repression, but the whole of the subject's sexuality.

The animal therefore still has wholeness, as well as the ability to obtain sexual satisfaction, which the subject lost upon entrance into language. Animals and humans thus differ essentially because of language. Lacan deals with this difference in his seminar on identification, where his argument is that it is not only the subject who lives in language but also domestic animals; only their relationship toward language is different. To exemplify this point, Lacan takes the case of his own dog Justine, named after the Marquis de Sade's novel. By observing how this dog behaves toward her owner, Lacan, one can say that the dog speaks, communicates with him, shows her love and affection, even shows jealousy. The dog is therefore in language. But for Lacan it is crucial to point out that the dog has a very different approach to language than man. First, the dog speaks only when she needs to speak, because of some inner pressure or need. Only then does the dog establish a relationship toward the other, but this other is not the big Other in the meaning of the social symbolic order. So, the dog is in language, but she, however, does not relate to the chain of signifiers—the big Other.

Let us exemplify this point by taking into account the famous Pavlovian experiment.[18] As is well known Pavlov tried to show that a repetition of some act—feeding the dog at the sound of a bell—at some moment produces the effect, so that the very sound of a bell, without being accompanied with food, incites the dog to salivate, which otherwise happens only in reaction to food. The animal therefore develops a conditional reflex, which is no longer linked to some real stimulus (food), but to a purely symbolic one (the bell). Lacan's thesis is that Pavlov actually behaved as a structuralist *avant la lettre*, since his experiment confirms the function of the signifier and does not, as Pavlov thought mistakenly, simply give evidence about the functioning of the dog's brain. In Pavlov's view, the experiment was supposed to prove that with dogs the conditional reflex always exists, while Lacan points out that such a conclusion is purely ideological, since it masks the fact that it is only the signifier that incites this reflex.

Lacan further points out that the subject of Pavlov's experiment is

18. *See* Jacques Lacan, *The Four Fundamental Concepts of Psycho-Analysis* (1981); Jacques Lacan, *L'Acte psychanalytique* (1967–68) (unpublished seminar); Jacques Lacan, *L'Angoisse* (1962–63) (unpublished seminar).

not the dog, but actually Pavlov himself. The dog has no interest in the bell but only in the meat. The experiment also had no intention of introducing some change: to amend or to impair the condition of the dog. As such the experiment was of interest only to the experimenter Pavlov. It can even be said that the experiment proved the existence of none other than Pavlov, or as Lacan says, "there is no other subject here [in this experiment] than the subject of the experimenter."[19] What does this mean? The bell has a meaning only for Pavlov: it is the signifier which represents the subject of science (Pavlov) for another signifier—the production of saliva. The subject of the experiment was therefore all the time Pavlov: he was the agency of the experiment, and he was also the one who got satisfaction out of the knowledge that the experiment was supposed to establish.

Does not Kulik's Manifesta performance also simply demonstrate the existence of the experimenter? The paradox of Kulik is that he pretends to be Pavlov's dog, while in actuality his role is none other than Pavlov's. Kulik thus wants to be a dog, but ends up actually representing Pavlov, since here it is also Kulik himself who is the subject of the experiment. But this time he is the scientist who does not need the dog anymore to validate his theories—the best results are gained when the scientist becomes the dog himself. Kulik's performance in the final instance proves Lacan's point that the dog does not care about Pavlov's experiment—so why deal with the proper dog? Now the trouble with Kulik is that he tries to look and behave as much as possible like a real dog and does not recognize it is only a human being who can enjoy this game—that is why there are no dogs who come running to see his show.

If Kulik with his experiment cannot prove anything other than his own existence as the experimenter, what then is his enjoyment in the show, and also why is the public attracted to his performance? And continuing this line of thought, what is the enjoyment of the dog as such whom the artist tries to imitate?

For domestic animals it is crucial that they live in language, since we cannot say that a dog, for example, behaves in the same way when it lives in nature as when it lives in a house. Language introduces change in the dog; in the case of Pavlov's dog, it can even be said that language makes the dog neurotic. However, this neurosis is in no way

19. Lacan, *Fundamental Concepts, supra* note 18, at 228.

similar to the hysterization of the human being, which is essentially linked to the subject questioning the desire of the Other.[20] In Pavlov's experiment it is not the case that the dog becomes troubled with the desire of the experimenter. Dogs do not question the desire of the Other. And this is what distinguishes them from human beings. However, this nonquestioning of the desire of the other is also what makes dogs more lovable than humans.

Now, how come this happens? Why are we so much in love with our pets, that we even act against their well-being—for example, by dressing up dogs and cats? One possible explanation of this love is that humans see in these animals some lost freedom, wildness, animality, etc., that they do not have anymore. The animal would thus stand for the natural object, which is forever lost for the human being and which he or she still nostalgically mourns. Another explanation is that the animal presents for the human being an ideal other. It can even be said that the dog became man's best friend, because of the impossibility of man being man's best friend.

The fact that a domestic animal lives in language means that it has been trained, pacified in the way that suits humans. However, the fact that the animal nonetheless is not barred by language and is thus not marked by a constitutive lack also means that the animal is not submitted to the logic of desire. The lack that marks the speaking subject forever prevents the subject from finding satisfaction, from fulfilling his or her desire—the subject is thus endlessly perturbed with his or her own desire and with the desire of the Other.

The problem of the subject of desire can best be illustrated with the help of Kafka's famous story, "A Fasting Showman." The main character of this story gets immense pleasure from public fasting; his only complaint is that he is not allowed to fast longer than 40 days. When at some point people get bored with his fasting performances, the circus

---

20. For Lacan, our relationship in regard to the big Other, the symbolic order, is always marked by this hysterization. It can even be said that the subject as such is a hysteric for the simple reason that he or she is a speaking being. The main dilemma for the hysteric is: what does he or she represent for the Big Other, what kind of an object is he or she for the Big Other? That is why the hysteric endlessly searches for the Other that would provide the proper answer and thus end the uncertainty that the hysteric has in regard to her being. Through this question, the hysteric tries to overcome the constitutive lack that bars the subject and thereby tries to find confirmation for her identity. However, the subject never finds the satisfactory answer to his or her dilemma of bankruptcy, since the Other is also barred, marked by a constitutive lack.

becomes the only place where he can still perform, but even there he gets little attention. Totally forgotten by the public, he is finally able to fast as long as he wants. One day, the circus overseer decides to use the presumably empty cage of the fasting showman for some better purpose; however, when cleaning the cage, he discovers that the fasting showman is still half alive under the dirty straw. With his last strength, the fasting showman reveals his secret by saying that he shouldn't have been admired for his fasting since fasting was something he simply had to do. Or, better, he could not do anything else but fast. To the overseer's inquiries as to why not, the fasting showman responds, "speaking . . . right into the overseer's ear, so that no syllable might be lost, 'because I couldn't find any food I liked. If I had found any, believe me, I should have made no bones about it and stuffed myself like you or anyone else.'"[21]

With the revelation, the fasting showman gives us the perfect definition of what the logic of desire is all about. The subject who is masked by an essential lack never finds the object that would fill this lack: as in the fasting showman's case, there is no proper object (food, for example) to satisfy the subject. One way to deal with this dilemma is that the subject endlessly goes from one object to another, while always remaining unsatisfied. And the second option is that the subject, similarly to the fasting showman, gives up the search for the proper object and finds a special enjoyment precisely in this abstinence—for example, in fasting.

One finds an example of such a restraint in anorexia. Psychoanalysis understands anorexia as a form of hysteria, which primarily has to do with the subject's dilemma of her desire. This impasse of the subject's desire is essentially linked to the dilemma of the mother's desire. Lacan points out that with the anorexic one usually discovers that as a child she was nurtured with too much love, even to the point of being fed too much. In this case the child's refusal of food paradoxically has to be understood as the way the subject deals with her own desire in regard to the mother's love. The mother's love blocked the child's desire, thus for the child the rejection of this love in the form of the refusal of food is the only way to keep her desire in motion.

Psychoanalysis links anorexia with the hysteric's demand that her desire remain unsatisfied. This dissatisfaction is connected to the fact

21. Franz Kafka, "A Fasting Showman," in *Wedding Preparations in the Country and Other Stories* 173–4 (1978).

that the subject never finds the object that would fill the lack, thus in the final instance there is no way to escape the bar that marked the subject when she entered language. In the case of the anorexic, however, one finds a very peculiar way for the subject to deal with this lack. The anorexic would thus not be a subject who does not eat, but the subject who eats precisely this "nothing"—the lack itself. Similarly, the fasting showman fasts because he did not find the food that would satisfy his desire. The deadlock of his desire brings him to the point of self-destruction: until his very death he eats the "nothing" in order to keep his desire unsatisfied.

For both, the fasting showman and the anorexic, it is crucial that they need the big Other who observes their doing and whom they are trying to convince that they can go even further in their sacrifice. This need for recognition is what is essential for the hysteric. In Kafka's story, the fasting showman wants to be recognized by the Other even when he is dying, thus he tells his story in the overseer's ear so that nothing be lost.

At the end of Kafka's story we learn that the circus authority later put a young panther in the fasting showman's cage. In contrast to the fasting showman, the panther has no problem with his desire. Thus one would not expect the panther to find enjoyment in fasting. This is so because the panther "lacks nothing," not even freedom:

> [H]is noble body, furnished almost to bursting point with all that it needed, seemed to carry freedom around with it too; somewhere in his jaws it seemed to lurk; and the joy of life streamed with such ardent passion from his throat that for the onlookers it was not easy to stand the shock of it. But they braced themselves crowded round the cage, and did not want ever to move away.[22]

The fact that in the case of the panther no lack has been introduced by language gives him a mark of self-sufficiency, which makes him at the same time attractive and horrifying.

Kulik also tries to obtain this animal wholeness and self-sufficiency by playing a dog. It can be said that Kulik tries to realize in the flesh the desire of deep ecologists to return to the state of nature. Kulik thus hopes to rediscover in his dog-like body the lost object of desire in

22. *Id.* at 174.

order to attain wholeness that man lacks. However, Kulik cannot escape the burden of being a human subject. This is very much proven by the fact that he desperately needs the audience, the gallery, or in general the big Other. Kulik, like his predecessor Diogenes, finds enjoyment in posing as a dog only when being observed by others. Thus it might be harder for humans to learn self-sufficiency from the dogs than it is for dogs to learn language.

A man who behaves like a dog hopes to escape the big Other and find true enjoyment, the lost animality of human nature. However, here we can invoke Lacan's famous reversal of Dostoyevski's phrase, "If God doesn't exist, then everything is permitted," into "If God doesn't exist, then nothing at all is permitted any longer."[23] Thus the man who rejects the restraints of human rituals and behaves like a dog will not find the desired enjoyment, but even more prohibitions. For Lacan, only a saint with his asceticism might find enjoyment that is not linked to the big Other. But this also means that there are no gallery openings for the saint's performance.

---

23. Jacques Lacan, *The Seminars of Jacques Lacan, Book II: The Ego in Freud's Theory and in The Technique of Psychoanalysis 1954–1955* at 128 (Jacques-Alain Miller ed. and Sylvana Tomaselli trans., 1991).

*Chapter 6*

# The Identity of the Constitutional Subject

*Michel Rosenfeld*

[J]e pense où je ne suis pas, donc je suis où je ne pense pas.
Jacques Lacan

The identity of the constitutional subject is elusive and problematic as uncontroverted foundations are hard to come by in contemporary constitutional regimes. The notion of the constitutional subject is itself ambiguous because it is not clear whether it refers to those subject to the constitution, or to the makers of the constitution, or to the subject matter of the constitution. Moreover, to establish constitutional identity over time it is necessary to weave together the past of the framers, one's own present, and the future of unborn generations. The problem, however, is that the past as much as the future is uncertain and open to conflicting possibilities.

Ultimately, constitutional identity is problematic because, in addition to remaining opposed to, and distinct from, other relevant identities, such as national, ethnic, religious, or cultural identity, constitutional identity is inevitably forced to incorporate them partially to acquire a sufficiently determinate meaning. Accordingly, the key question becomes how constitutional identity can distance itself sufficiently from the relevant identities against which it needs to forge its own image while, at the same time, incorporating enough elements from these identities to remain viable within its own sociopolitical environment.

---

Jacques Lacan, *Écrits* 517 (1966) ("I think where I am not, therefore I am where I do not think") (my translation).

This initial glance into constitutional identity and the constitutional subject reveals that it is much easier to determine what they are not, rather than what they are. Building upon this insight, I explore the thesis that it is ultimately preferable and more accurate to regard the constitutional subject as an absence rather than a presence, with these two provisos: First, the absence of the constitutional subject does not negate its indispensability, thus necessitating its reconstruction; and, second, the constitutional subject always involves a lack because it is inherently incomplete, and hence always open to a necessary but impossible quest for completion. Accordingly, the constitutional subject is in constant need of reconstruction, but no such reconstruction can ever become definitive or complete.

The thesis that the identity of the constitutional subject originates in a lack or absence bears certain strong affinities with Freud's and Lacan's psychoanalytic theory of the subject and with Hegel's philosophical theory of the subject. I shall, accordingly, draw on certain insights developed by these theories to elaborate some of the key features of my thesis. In section I, I refer to these theories to determine the position of the constitutional subject and to justify the need for reconstruction. In section II, having concluded that the constitutional subject is the subject of constitutional discourse, I argue that the principal tools of reconstruction are negation, metaphor, and metonymy—the first being central to Hegel's philosophy, and all three to Freud's and Lacan's theories. Finally, in section III, based on the dialectics of reconstruction as elaborated in section II, I explore the potential and the limitations of the constitutional subject in its struggle to strike an equilibrium in an ever changing sociopolitical landscape.

## *I. The Position of the Constitutional Subject and the Need for Reconstruction*

### A. The Clash between Self and Other

The question of the subject arises out of the need to confront the other.[1] As retraced in Hegel's *Phenomenology,* the confrontation between self

1. *See* Georg W. F. Hegel, *Phenomenology of Spirit* ¶¶ 175–96, at 109–19 (Arnold V. Miller trans., Oxford University Press 1977) (5th ed. 1952); Lacan, *supra* unnumbered chapter opening note, at 655–56 (1966).

and other emerges out of the split between subject and object.[2] Animated by desire, the subject pursues objects, but these objects can only assuage desire momentarily, for once they are incorporated, desire inevitably turns its quest elsewhere. Eventually, the subject realizes that desire cannot be satisfied by objects. Rather, in order to perpetuate itself, it must turn to other subjects who can over time satisfy its desire. Hence, the desire of the subject prompts the self to seek out the other. Similarly, in the context of psychoanalytic theory, the subject seeks fulfillment in objects, but this is impossible, thus prompting a need for adjustment through a process of renunciation. In other words, the ego of psychoanalysis must forgo appropriation of forbidden objects, to aspire to recognition by the other (through internalization of the edicts of the superego).[3]

The foregoing accounts reveal the subject as lacking in at least two different senses. First, to the extent that the subject needs objects, the subject is characterized by a lack in the sense of being incomplete. Second, the as yet unrecognized (by an other) subject is a lack, in the sense of being nothing but the negation of its objects, i.e., its defining characteristic is the subject not being any of the objects of its desire. Accordingly, upon splitting from the object, the subject emerges as awareness of absence and incompleteness. In short, the question of the subject arises upon the subject in question experiencing the pain of absence and unfulfilled completeness.

Upon realizing that the road to fulfillment is not through objects of desire, the self of Hegel's *Phenomenology* turns to the other for recognition. The identity of the subject thus becomes predicated on recognition by others. But, as Hegel's celebrated account of struggle between the Lord and the Bondsman illustrates, shifting the focus from objects to other subjects does not, of itself, bring about reciprocal recognition among equals.[4] Instead, the Lord, having overcome the fear of death, opts to become the recognized self, whereas the Bondsman, constrained by his fear of death, agrees to assume the role of the recognizing self. Accordingly, the Bondsman gives up his own identity to save his life, while the Lord buttresses his self-identity by having the Bondsman execute his commands. Because of the working of the dialectic,

2. Hegel, *supra* note 1, ¶¶ 166–77, at 104–11.

3. *See* Sigmund Freud, *Civilization and its Discontents* 72–73 (James Strachey trans. and ed., W. W. Norton and Co. 1962) (1930)

4. *See* Hegel, *supra* note 1, ¶¶ 178–96, at 111–19.

however, the Bondsman's work for the Lord leads to a reversal of roles. Indeed, as a consequence of his reliance on the Bondsman's work to satisfy his needs, the Lord becomes dependent on the Bondsman, and the identity of the recognized self becomes subject to being shaped through the labors of the recognizing self. Conversely, through his labor, which he grasps as his own notwithstanding that it is being undertaken pursuant to the Lord's commands, the Bondsman gains a sense of his own identity and of his mastery over his products. In sum, although the Lord seeks to become master of his own identity and to enslave the Bondsman to secure a faithful reflection of his lordly self-image, in the end, in the terms of Jean Hyppolite, the slave becomes the master of the master, while the master becomes the slave of the slave.[5]

Hegel's insight that the self's attempt to root its identity as subject leads to subjection to the other is further elaborated by Lacan.[6] Pursuant to Lacan's analysis, the child's initial grasp of identity as subject involves a twofold process of alienation, or of subjection to the other.[7] Prompted by his failure to fully or successfully merge with the object of his desire, the child experiences himself as a lack and strives to fill this felt void by acquiring an identity as subject—an identity poised to counter the centrifugal movement of unchecked desire driven toward an infinite series of objects that resist satisfactory incorporation. To acquire an identity as a subject, however, the child must leave behind the world of objects and enter into the symbolic order of language. Only through the mediation of language can the child hope to assert his or her identity as a subject. But language and the rules that organize it into a system of communication are imposed on the child from the "outside." Accordingly, language alienates the child by making submission to a symbolic code imposed by others a prerequisite to acquiring his or her own identity as a subject.[8]

To the alienation produced by the necessary confrontation with language must be added, consistent with Lacan's account, yet another alienating experience along the child's path toward identity as a subject. Indeed, as the child struggles to get his or her bearings in the sym-

5. *See* 1 Jean Hyppolite, *Genèse et Structure de la Phénoménologie de l'Esprit de Hegel* 166 (1946).

6. For a discussion of Hegel's influence on Lacan, see Bertrand Ogilvie, *Lacan: La Formation du Concept de Sujet (1932–1949)*, at 30–31, 108–9 (3d ed. 1993).

7. *See* Lacan, *supra* unnumbered chapter opening note, at 839–40 ("alienation is the reality of the subject") (my translation).

8. *See id.* at 655.

bolic universe circumscribed by language, he or she first gains a sense of identity through recognition of his or her name. Because it is the parents who name their child, and because it is others who first address the child by his or her name, however, gaining identity by recognizing a name as one's own is alienating. In other words, the first articulable experience of one's identity as a subject is alienating, inasmuch as it consists in identifying oneself with a name chosen by another, and in acquiescing to being identified as a symbol in the discourse of the other.[9]

Although Hegel and Lacan present us with different narratives, their conclusions concerning initial attempts to establish the identity of the subject are remarkably similar. In both cases, the subject emerges in its own right as a consequence of a lack, and it requires mediation in its search for identity. In both cases, moreover, the subject's initial thrust toward identity proves alienating as it results in an unexpected subjection of the self to the other.

Based on the lack and alienation that emerge out of the self's encounter with the other, the constitutional subject finds itself in a position that requires it to forge its identity through the medium of a constitutional discourse, embedded in a common language, that binds together the multifaceted constitutional self with its multiple others. This constitutional discourse, moreover, must build upon a constitutional text that must be placed in its proper context, taking into account relevant normative and factual constraints. As text is dependent on context, and as the context is open-ended and subject to transformation over time, the constitutional subject must resort to constitutional discourse to invent and reinvent its identity. In other words, motivated by the urge to overcome its lack and its inherent incompleteness, the constitutional subject must avail itself of the tools of constitutional discourse to construct a coherent narrative in which it can locate a plausible self-identity.

### B. Construction and Reconstruction

Once it is admitted that the constitutional subject can only acquire an identity in the intersubjective realm circumscribed by constitutional discourse, it should become apparent that personifying the constitutional subject ought to be avoided. Neither the constitutional makers,

9. *See id.* at 298–300, 655.

nor the interpreters of the constitution, nor those who are subject to its prescriptions, are properly speaking the constitutional subject. They all form part of the constitutional subject and belong to it, but the constitutional subject as such can only be grasped through expressions of its self-identity in an intersubjective discourse linking all the human actors who were, are, and will be brought together by the same set of constitutional norms. The full expression of constitutional self-identity is only conceivable through an imaginary exercise involving an extreme compression of all times, and a simultaneous grasp of all possible interpretive variations, combined with an ability to distill it all into an authoritative and coherent narrative. Short of that, however, constitutional self-identity can only be articulated piecemeal by a partial subject who must construct it from disparate fragments that need to be projected into an uncertain past and future. Moreover, for such construction to escape being perceived as merely arbitrary, it must be supplemented by a reconstruction. As we will see, the construction affords but a glimpse of constitutional identity, and the function of the reconstruction is to transform that glimpse into a determinate image.

To understand the relationship between construction and reconstruction, one must bear in mind that constitutional self-identity revolves around the antinomy between the real and the ideal. The reality of the constitutional subject, as riddled by lack and incompleteness, is too impoverished to generate a viable self-identity capable of furnishing a coherent grounding for the constitutional order. Thus, for example, from the limited and fragmented perspective of the single constitutional judge, who at best has a partial and incomplete access to the empirical reality of the constitution makers and but the faintest insight into the reality of future generations, it seems all but impossible to develop a coherent picture of constitutional self-identity based exclusively on historically accessible and empirically verifiable data. Because of this inherent poverty of the real, it is necessary to have recourse to the ideal to frame an adequate conception of constitutional self-identity. Indeed, inasmuch as we cannot see, from our own limited historical vantage point, the constitutional self of which we are a part, we must strive to imagine it. To establish a viable constitutional self-identity, the real must be supplemented by the ideal, or, to put it in another way, facts must be enriched by *counterfactual imagination.* Consistent with this, construction and reconstruction are meant to erect bridges linking the real to the ideal, and facts to counterfactuals. However, because the ideal not only supplements the real but also contradicts it, construction and reconstruction, while necessary, are dangerous tools that must be properly used and adequately legitimated.

Construction and reconstruction to deal with antinomies between fact and norm, and between the real and the ideal, have a long and venerable lineage that includes the reconstructive theories of, among others, Hobbes, Rousseau, Kant, Rawls, and Habermas.[10] Moreover, reconstructive theory has been creatively applied in legal and constitutional interpretation by Dworkin.[11] Since an infinite variety of ideals are imaginable, the key to properly assessing the worth of a particular reconstructive theory lies in determining the logic and persuasiveness with which that theory matches the real and the ideal, or facts and the counterfactual imagination.[12] Furthermore, two different purposes are likely to inform reconstructive attempts at matching the real and the ideal. To the extent that the ideal is conceived as supplementing the real, reconstructive theory is oriented toward grounding a normative justification for the status quo.[13] On the other hand, insofar as the ideal is regarded as contradicting the real, reconstructive theory is primed to furnish a critique of existing institutions.

Construction and reconstruction represent two distinct moments in the ongoing quest to obtain a better grasp of the evolving and incomplete self-identity of the constitutional subject. Constitutional decision making always arises under conditions that preclude full determinacy, and it makes construction necessary. In fact, constitutional decision making involves construction to the extent that constitutional issues always require making choices between two or more plausible alternatives. Thus, for example, the 1973 decision by the United States Supreme Court in Roe v. Wade,[14] recognizing for the first time a constitutional right to abortion, certainly involved creative judicial construction. Indeed, neither the text of the Constitution nor previously articu-

---

10. *See* Michel Rosenfeld, "Law as Discourse: Bridging the Gap Between Democracy and Rights," 108 *Harv. L. Rev.* 1163 (1995).

11. *See* Ronald Dworkin, *Law's Empire* (1986).

12. For an excellent discussion of counterfactual imagination in the context of Habermas's work, see Michael Power, "Habermas and the Counterfactual Imagination," 17 *Cardozo L. Rev.* 1005 (1995).

13. Rawls's use of "reflective equilibrium" provides a good example of how reconstructive theory pursues this objective. *See* John Rawls, *A Theory of Justice* 20–21, 48–51 (1971); *see also* Power, *supra* note 12.

14. 410 U.S. 113 (1973).

lated Supreme Court jurisprudence could fairly be taken to *compel* or *preclude* the decision reached by the Court. Moreover, the act of judicial construction that resulted in the holding in Roe had an unmistakable and significant impact on the constitutional identity of the United States. On the one hand, given the nature of the religious, moral, and political debate concerning abortion, recognition of a constitutional right to abortion projects a noticeably different image of American constitutional identity than that which would have emerged had the Supreme Court refused to recognize such a right. On the other hand, given the bitter controversy that followed the Roe decision and the vigorous efforts over the years to have the Roe decision overturned, it is hardly an exaggeration to claim that it provoked a crisis in the constitutional identity of Americans.

Although Roe is exceptional because of the magnitude of its impact on the American constitutional identity, all significant constitutional decisions have some impact on constitutional identity and hence call for justification. Reconstruction affords the means to tackle the task of justification and makes possible cogent vindication or condemnation of the constructs associated with constitutional decision making. In other words, constitutional interpretation and elaboration introduce new elements that have a bearing on the makeup of constitutional identities. The task of reconstruction is to harmonize these new elements with previous existing ones; or, to the extent that the new elements disrupt relationships established among previously existing elements, to recombine all the elements involved into an intelligible and cogent picture. Such harmonization or recombination, however, cannot be achieved exclusively on the basis of the fragmentary reality that it confronts, and thus it calls for the exercise of our counterfactual imagination.

## *II. The Reconstructive Tools of Constitutional Discourse*

Constitutional discourse must articulate a self-identity by means of a counterfactual narrative that takes into account both the applicable constitutional text and the normative constraints flowing from constitutionalism. Such a narrative, moreover, must strive to bridge the gap that splits the constitutional subject into self and other, while, at the same time, furnishing sustenance to the constitutional subject by endowing it with a distinct identity. Whether constitutional discourse is used to justify or to criticize existing constitutional arrangements, it operates mainly by means of the same essential tools: negation, metaphor, and metonymy.

Negation, metaphor, and metonymy combine to select, discard, and organize pertinent elements with a view to producing a constitutional discourse in, and through which, the constitutional subject can ground its identity. Negation is crucial to the extent that the constitutional subject can only emerge as distinct, through exclusion and renunciation. Metaphor or condensation, on the other hand, which proceeds by stressing similarities at the expense of differences, plays a key unifying role, in producing partial identities around which constitutional identity can revolve.[15] Finally, metonymy or displacement, with its emphasis on contiguity and context, is essential to guard against the constitutional subject fixating on identities that remain so condensed and abstract as to gloss over the differences that must be taken into consideration if constitutional identity is genuinely to encompass both self and other. An accurate picture of how constitutional discourse can shape the identity of the constitutional subject through the work of negation, metaphor, and metonymy depends on a proper account of the interaction between the three. Indeed, it is through such interaction that constitutional discourse acquires determinate meaning. But before examining how negation, metaphor, and metonymy interact, it is necessary to look at each of them individually to get a better handle on their respective roles in shaping constitutional discourse.

### A. Negation

The role of negation in the process of establishing the identity of the constitutional subject is multifaceted, intricate, and complex. It involves, among other things, rejection, repudiation, repression, exclusion, and renunciation. These functions, moreover, may intertwine in various ways and simultaneously operate at different levels of reality.

15. *See* Michel Rosenfeld, "Modern Constitutionalism as Interplay Between Identity and Diversity: An Introduction," 14 *Cardozo L. Rev.* 497, 498 (1993) (national, regional, linguistic, religious, ethnic, political, and ideological identities are likely to figure in the determination of constitutional identity).

In view of this rich diversity, I can only briefly outline some of the most general aspects of the essential contribution of negation to the definition of constitutional self-identity.

In the broadest terms of Hegel's conception of the dialectic of the subject, negation provides the fundamental link between the initial stage in which the subject emerges as mere lack and the final stage in which the subject becomes substance, or, in other words, in which the subject becomes *for-itself* as it is *in-itself*.[16] Pursuant to Hegel's dialectic logic, the subject first acquires its own identity by negating that it is reducible to the objects of its desire. That initial identity of the subject, however, is purely negative and oppositional as it focuses upon what the subject is not, without revealing what it is. After having emerged as pure negation, the Hegelian subject enters into the next stage of its logical evolution in search of a positive identity. In the course of this search, the subject negates that it is merely the lack that emerged in the first stage, and it seeks a positive identification in the manifold diversity of its concrete manifestations. But as it embraces these manifestations, the subject loses sight of its unity and is thus unable to grasp its emerging positive identity as its own. Moreover, because of this inability, the subject becomes alienated from itself. In the third stage, the Hegelian subject, through a negation of the (second stage) negation, finally assumes its positive identity as its own, thus becoming for-itself what it is in-itself.

The path toward the establishment of the identity of the constitutional subject can be reconstructed as a three-stage process conforming to Hegel's dialectical logic of the subject. In the first stage, the constitutional subject's identity can be conceived as pure negation because the constitutional subject acquires a distinct identity by negating that it is (the same as) the preconstitutional subject, or a mere product of existing cultural, historical, ethnic, or religious identities. In other words, the constitutional subject first enters the scene by cutting loose from all those already constituted subjects found within the relevant spatiotemporal framework. Moreover, the constitutional subject arrives at this purely negative identity through: repudiation of the (prerevolutionary) past; rejection of traditional identities; repression of the urge to embrace a dominant, positive identity to the detriment of the plurality of (nonconstitutional) identities sought to be protected by constitution-

16. *See* Michel Rosenfeld, "Hegel and The Dialectics of Contract," 10 *Cardozo L. Rev.* 1199, 1208–9 and n.51 (1989).

alism; exclusion of any militantly antipluralistic tendency that would defeat constitutionalism; and renunciation of dreams of hegemony by those in a position to shape the destiny of the constitutional subject.

As pure negativity, the constitutional subject experiences itself as a lack and consequently strives to fill the void within itself by developing a positive identity. The search for a positive identity marks, moreover, the second stage in the logical development of the constitutional subject. But such positive identity only proves possible if recourse is had to the very identities discarded in the first stage of the constitutional subject's formation. Indeed, the objectives of constitutionalism cannot be pursued in a vacuum; they require establishing a viable institutional apparatus that must, of necessity, draw upon the history, traditions, and cultural patrimony of the relevant polity.

Recourse to identities discarded during the first stage does not signify, however, a return to the realm of the preconstitutional. Consistent with Hegelian logic, the dialectical transition from one stage to the next involves a process of *Aufhebung* or sublation, whereby what emerges in the first stage is at once preserved and transcended within the perspective of the second stage.[17] Applied to the constitutional subject, this means that the second stage is marked by a selective incorporation of discarded identities rather than by any wholesale return to preconstitutional identities. In other words, the traditions incorporated into the constitutional subject during the second stage are not pursued for their own sake. Instead, these traditions are only invoked inasmuch as they are capable of serving the interests of constitutionalism.

Analogously, as partial preconstitutional identities become incorporated into the constitutional subject during its second stage of logical development, they combine in novel ways and come to occupy different positions from those they occupied in the preconstitutional era. Imagine, for example, that a polity divided into several different regions along ethnic and religious lines decides to become a constitutional democracy and opts for a federal system of government. Under such a federal system, moreover, imagine that each ethnically and religiously homogeneous region was to be accorded equal representation in the upper chamber of the national legislature, but that representation

17. As Hegel states: "To transcend (*Aufheben*) has this double meaning, that it signifies to keep or to preserve and also to make to cease, to finish. . . . Thus, what is transcended is also preserved; it has only lost its immediacy and is not on that account annihilated." Georg W. Hegel, 2 *Science of Logic* 119–20 (W. H. Johnston and L. G. Struthers trans., George Allen and Unwin Ltd. 1966) (1812–16).

in the lower chamber was exclusively a function of the size of the population, with the consequence that more numerous ethnic groups would be likely to achieve greater representation than their less numerous counterparts. Finally, assume that the constitution in this new federal democracy divides the sovereign powers of the state between the national legislature and the respective legislatures of the various constituent states, based on a desire to institute a system of "checks and balances." Under these circumstances, the identity forged by the new federal democracy would be neither that projected by the national legislature, nor that put forth by the various state legislatures. Instead, the identity of the new federal democracy would seem bound to be grounded in the opposition between state and national legislatures. Furthermore, existing ethnic and religious identities would certainly figure in the identity of the new federal democracy, but they would do so in a significantly transformed way. Thus, points of convergence would more likely be stressed than points of divergence; some differences would probably be left out altogether through the implementation of "gag rules"; and some particular ethnic and religious identities would inevitably figure more prominently than others, either because of their spread over greater numbers, or for other reasons.

### B. Metaphor

If negation is crucial inasmuch as identity can only be conceived in terms of what one is not, metaphor is essential to the interplay between identity and difference that sustains the constitutional subject's quest for a positive self-identity. As a tool designed to establish similarities and equivalences, metaphor provides the discursive underpinning for the pole of identity in the dialectic between identity—in the sense of sameness—and difference. Through a process of combination and substitution, metaphor ferrets out similarities and equivalences to forge links of identity.

Metaphor is the discursive equivalent of Freud's concept of condensation. According to Freud, condensation is a psychic process whereby similarities are drawn together and emphasized, at the expense of differences. In the context of dream formation, for example, the image of a single face can serve as a representation of several different persons, by means of the work of condensation, which consists of drawing a composite picture that emphasizes common facial features and disregards or cancels out divergent ones.[18] Moreover, by combining and organizing complex and multifaceted elements in terms of similarities, condensation makes possible or sharpens our grasp of where genuine identities might be found. Condensation, however, can also perform a function of substitution, whereby an objectionable picture can be replaced by a composite substitute made up of similar but not identical features. Through substitution along a series of similar, though not identical, features, condensation opens a channel of expression for repressed material. As we shall see, moreover, the availability of an analogous channel of expression for the constitutional subject is important. It allows both for substitutions of identities incompatible with the constitutional order and for criticism of identities associated with the constitutional subject as mere stand-ins for identities that ought to be banished.

Through his concept of metaphor, Lacan systematizes Freud's notion of condensation in the context of linguistic theory. Building on Roman Jakobson's linguistic theory,[19] Lacan conceives of the metaphoric function as establishing relationships of similarity.[20] Meaning, moreover, is generated through interaction between the metaphoric function and the metonymic function. Metaphor contributes to the production of meaning by cementing relationships of similarity in reference to a code, or, in other words, by linking signs along a paradigmatic axis.[21]

In the realm of constitutional discourse, metaphor not only operates at the level of rhetoric, but also contributes in setting the cardinal reference points of the constitutional order. A particularly telling example is the American Supreme Court's handling of the claim that constitutional privacy ought to be extended to protect sexual relationships among consenting homosexual adults in Bowers v. Hardwick.[22]

18. *See* Sigmund Freud, *The Interpretation of Dreams* 327–28 (James Strachey trans. and ed., Avon Books 1965) (1900).

19. *See* Anthony Wilden, "Lacan and the Discourse of the Other," *in Jacques Lacan, The Language of the Self: The Function of Language in Psychoanalysis* 244–46 (Anthony Wilden trans., Dell Publishing Co. 1968) (1956).

20. *Id.*

21. *See* Roman Jakobson, *Child Language Aphasia and Phonological Universals* 70 (Allan Keiler trans., 1968).

22. 478 U.S. 186 (1986).

Against the background of its precedents extending constitutional privacy protection to consensual heterosexual sex among adults,[23] the Supreme Court, in a five–four decision, held that consensual homosexual sex among adults was not a protected constitutional privacy right. The Court's majority emphasized that homosexual sodomy had traditionally been forbidden and criminalized,[24] and a concurring opinion noted its condemnation under Judeo-Christian morals and ethical standards.[25] The dissenting justices, however, did not dwell on the treatment of homosexual sex in different cultures throughout history. Instead, they focused on similarities between heterosexuals and homosexuals, and through metaphorical thinking managed to depict them as being essentially similar. In the words of Justice Stevens,

> From the stand point of the individual, the homosexual and the heterosexual have the same interest in deciding how he will live his own life, and, more narrowly, how he will conduct himself in his personal and voluntary associations with his companions. State intrusion into the private conduct of either is equally burdensome.[26]

Thus, by moving away from the sexual practices involved, and from the historical, cultural, and religious mores concerning these practices, metaphorical reasoning leads to the abstract level where each individual is similar to every other individual, as possessing a need for intimate associations and as deserving privacy to freely pursue fulfillment of such a fundamental need. More generally, reaching higher levels of abstraction through metaphorical reasoning plays an important role in framing constitutional rights and in defining constitutional identity. As we shall see below, however, metaphorical ascent to the high levels of abstraction required to secure constitutional rights comes only at a heavy price.[27]

23. *See* Griswold v. Connecticut, 381 U.S. 479 (1965) (constitutional privacy rights bar state from prohibiting use of contraceptives by married couples); *see also* Eisenstadt v. Baird, 405 U.S. 438 (1972) (Griswold rights extend to nonmarried individuals).

24. 478 U.S. at 192–94.

25. 478 U.S. at 196–97 (Burger, C.J., concurring).

26. 478 U.S. at 218–19.

27. *See infra* text accompanying notes 62–68.

### C. Metonymy

In contrast to metaphor's pursuit of similarities in relation to a code, metonymy promotes relations of contiguity within a context.[28] As consideration of the dissent in Bowers v. Hardwick indicates, the metaphoric process tends to be acontextual, whereas the metonymic process represents the opposite tendency. Drawing again on Jakobson's linguistic theory, Lacan conceives of metonymy as the discursive embodiment of Freud's notion of displacement.[29] According to Freud, displacement makes expression of repressed thoughts possible by redirecting them in all of their emotive intensity toward a target that bears a relationship of contiguity to the would-be target rendered inaccessible by repression.[30] Thus, for example, if one's unconscious hatred of an uncle who uses a cane cannot find conscious expression because of repression, such hatred may be displaced toward canes, resulting in a conscious aversion to canes.

Elaborating on Freud's notion of displacement, Lacan envisages metonymy as symbolizing the flight of desire from object to object, as frustration stemming from the need to repress the original object of desire leads to the unsatisfactory pursuit of contiguous objects that might approximate without ever matching the original object. Thus, for Lacan, the metonymy of desire points to a lack of being, or in Hegelian language, to being-for-itself as a lack.[31]

As a meaning-endowing device, metonymy proceeds by establishing contextual relations along a syntagmatic axis.[32] Thus, to metaphor's paradigmatic axis, which can be regarded as a vertical axis, corresponds metonymy's syntagmatic axis, which can be viewed as horizontal.[33] Or to put it in another way, the opposition between metaphor and metonymy corresponds to the contrast between synchrony ("the axis of simultaneities") and diachrony ("the axis of successivities").[34]

The metonymic function, like its metaphoric counterpart, also

28. *See* Wilden, *supra* note 19, at 245–46.
29. *Id.* at 244.
30. *See* Freud, *supra* note 18, at 209–10.
31. *See* Wilden, *supra* note 19, at 242.
32. *See* Jakobson, *supra* note 22, at 70.
33. *See* Wilden, *supra* note 19, at 246.
34. *Id.*

plays an important role in legal rhetoric and in constitutional discourse. At the most profound level, Lacan's notion of the metonymy of desire is reflected in the constitutional subject's above-mentioned grasp of its identity as a lack.[35] Inasmuch as the constitutional subject's search for identity is analogous to the metonymy of desire, the constitutional subject cannot fully overcome the experience of itself as (at least in part) a lack. Indeed, the metonymy of desire is ultimately animated by the desire of desire[36] which can only be sustained so long as there remain objects of desire.[37] Similarly, the constitutional subject could only fully overcome its lack if it became fully determined, or in Hegelian terms, if it became for-itself what it is in-itself. Accordingly, the constitutional subject's lack is ultimately the unfulfilled desire for exhaustive determination. Such exhaustive determination, however, could only be realized as a consequence of full contextualization—that is, a synthesis of all past, present, and future instantiations of the place of the constitutional subject within the constitutional order. And that is, of course, impossible; not only because the future cannot be fully prophesied, but also because the past cannot be fully remembered.

In legal rhetoric, the metonymic function plays as important a role as the metaphoric function against which it is pitted. In the context of adversary proceedings, arguments stressing similarities are bound to be countered by arguments emphasizing differences. Legal arguments based on metonymy evoke differences by contextualizing, relying on relations of proximity to carve out a picture that reveals as many concrete details as possible. In common law jurisdictions, metonymic legal argument militates against the extension of precedent by contextualizing the relevant situations to the point that differences appear to far outweigh similarities. The rhetorical strategy of metonymic legal argument is to demonstrate that proposed analogies are *beside* the point. And taken to its logical extreme, metonymic legal argument would systematically undermine reliance on precedents, since upon being exhaustively contextualized every situation is ultimately unique.

The metonymic function also plays an important role in constitutional discourse since it figures in constitutional constructs and contributes to the definition of constitutional rights and constitutional

35. *Id.* at 242.

36. Through an infinite series of objects which do not bring it satisfaction, desire, in the last analysis, aims at itself.

37. Indeed, desire can only maintain a relation to itself through the mediation of not-yet-incorporated objects.

identity. The metonymic function pulls in the opposite direction of its metaphoric counterpart. At the level of constitutional arguments, metonymy leads to greater contextualization just as metaphor points to similarities. Moreover, as in metaphor, metonymy may be used to foster extension as well as constriction of constitutional rights, depending on the circumstances. Thus, for example, through metonymic contextualization, it becomes possible to surmount the color-blind hurdle in the pursuit of racial justice.[38] Against whites who seek to disadvantage African-Americans because of their race, the color-blind principle remains a barrier. But such a barrier need not be made into an impediment against redressing the lingering injuries stemming from racism.[39] Once the difference between healing the wounds of racism and further aggravating them is firmly in mind, rigid adherence to the principle of color blindness seems both unnecessary and undesirable.

The use of metonymic contextualization to limit constitutional rights, on the other hand, is vividly illustrated by the majority and concurring opinions in Bowers v. Hardwick.[40] As already mentioned, the Supreme Court's refusal to extend intimate association privacy rights to protect consensual homosexual sex was sought to be justified by traditional repudiation through criminalization of homosexual acts and by hostility toward homosexuality rooted in the Judeo-Christian religious tradition. To combat the metaphor of the autonomous individual left alone to decide about his or her intimate associations with full responsibility and dignity, the justices in the majority in Bowers chiefly resort to contextualization. Moreover, their metonymic contextualization is not confined to the circumstances surrounding the case,[41] but

38. *But see* Michel Rosenfeld, "Decoding *Richmond:* Affirmative Action and the Elusive Meaning of Constitutional Equality," 87 *Mich. L. Rev.* 1729, 1761–62 (1989) (contrasting acontextual "atomistic mode of interpretation" with contextual "ecological mode of interpretation").

39. It is interesting, in this connection, to note that one of the frequent arguments against race conscious policies designed to improve the plights of traditionally disadvantaged racial minorities is that once the color-blind barrier is lifted, even for a worthwhile purpose, there is no principled way to insure that racists will not take advantage of this development to better perpetuate their reprehensible aims. *See,* e.g., City of Richmond v. J. A. Croson Co., 488 U.S. 469 (1989). Underlying this line of argument may be a fear that left to their own devices people will be unable to properly contextualize issues regarding race.

40. 478 U.S. 186, 196 (1986).

41. In this connection, it is particularly noteworthy that the Court's majority departed from customary practice by interpreting the generally worded Georgia antisodomy statute applicable to heterosexuals as well as to homosexuals, exclusively in the context of its application to homosexuals. *See* Bowers, 478 U.S. at 190.

also encompasses the relationship between the case at hand and relevant precedents. In Griswold v. Connecticut,[42] the right of privacy was upheld in the context of the marital relationship. Through metonymic displacement, Griswold can be represented as a constitutional endorsement of the sanctity of the marital relationship[43] and thus sharply contrasted with Bowers, which concerns homosexuality contextualized as abhorrent under Judeo-Christian canons of morality. Eisenstadt v. Baird,[44] however, cannot be subsumed under the sanctity of the marital relationship, as it explicitly extends rights to sexual intimacy to nonmarried individuals. Accordingly, to distinguish Bowers from Eisenstadt requires metonymic contextualization along other lines. Through metonymic displacement, Eisenstadt can be portrayed as a case about heterosexual, that is, "normal," sex, which the Constitution protects among consenting adults. In contrast, by focusing on the long history of its criminalization, the majority in Bowers can present homosexual sex as "deviant" or "abnormal" and thus as distinguishable from the kind of sex afforded constitutional protection in Eisenstadt.

The metonymic function's contribution to the delimitation of constitutional rights becomes manifest in the implementation of such rights. In the abstract, everyone should enjoy the same equality or freedom-of-religion rights. In practice, however, such rights cannot be equally enjoyed unless they are properly tailored to the diverse needs and circumstances confronting their intended beneficiaries. To the extent that equality requires proportionality rather than mere similarity of treatment, it is necessary to contextualize and to take certain differences into account. Thus, for example, equality for women arguably involves more than being treated the same as men. Similarly, freedom to exercise one's religion requires contextualization since generally applicable laws may not have the same impact on different religious practices. A Sunday-closing law, for instance, is likely to be burdensome on sabbatarians inasmuch as it would force them to close their

42. 381 U.S. 479 (1965).

43. Further contextualization makes it ironic that Griswold could be viewed as promoting the "sanctity" of marriage, since Griswold affords married couples the constitutional right to use contraceptives—a right that is at odds with the "sanctity" of marriage as historically understood within much of the Judeo-Christian religious tradition. Metonymic contextualization, however, tends to be relative rather than absolute, and its precise limitations in a given case are likely to be determined by the aims and interests of its proponents.

44. 405 U.S. 438 (1972).

businesses for two days, whereas their competitors could close on only one day without violating their religious convictions.[45]

The metonymic process also contributes to the definition of the identity of the constitutional subject. Inasmuch as constitutionalism implies pluralism and heterogeneity, constitutional identity cannot be reduced to a mere relationship of similarity. Because constitutional identity must bridge a gap between self and other, it must incorporate differences through contextualization to avert subordination of some to others within the same constitutional regime. For example, in a multicultural or religiously pluralistic society, it is most unlikely that a positive identity that is neutral as between all cultural or religious groups could ever be achieved.[46] Accordingly, taking certain differences into account may lead to a more satisfactory constitutional identity than simply glossing over them.

Metonymic influence on constitutional identity may on some occasions involve more than mere contextualization and amount to downright displacement. When a partial identity is too powerful to be successfully suppressed, yet too divisive to be openly and fully acknowledged, its impact may be masked through a focus upon contiguous partial identities. The American constitutional experience with the relation between the state and religion—or at least a plausible interpretation of that experience—provides an example of metonymic displacement as a means to bridge the gap between constitutional identity and the forces animating constitutional practice. From a cursory look at the Religion Clauses of the First Amendment,[47] it would appear that the state should maintain a completely neutral stance toward religion. On the one hand, the state should do nothing to promote religion; on the

45. *But see* Braunfeld v. Brown, 366 U.S. 599 (1961) (Sunday closing law held not to violate Orthodox Jew's First Amendment right to freely exercise his religion).

46. *See,* e.g., Reynolds v. United States, 98 U.S. 145 (1878) (criminalization of bigamy upheld notwithstanding Mormon claim that polygamy was a religious duty); Department of Human Resources v. Smith, 494 U.S. 872 (1990) (sacramental use of peyote not exempted from criminal prohibition). In contrast ritual use of wine by Catholics and Jews was exempted from prohibition mandated by the Eighteenth Amendment. *See* Board of Educ. v. Grumet, 114 S. Ct. 2481 (1994) (Kennedy, J., concurring) (referring to Prohibition exemption for use of alcoholic beverages for sacramental purposes). For a more systematic argument that abstraction beyond differences is not neutral, see Rosenfeld, *supra* note 14, at 234–38.

47. The First Amendment provides in relevant part that "Congress shall make no law respecting an establishment of religion, or prohibiting the free exercise thereof." U.S. Const. amend. I. These two clauses are referred to respectively as the "Establishment Clause" and the "Free Exercise Clause."

other, it should do nothing that would interfere with its citizens' freedom to practice the religion of their choice. Accordingly, whereas Americans may be by and large a religious people, their *constitutional* identity would appear to be one of neutrality, fairness, and equanimity toward religion. Based on a consideration of relevant practices and the Supreme Court's jurisprudence regarding the Religion Clauses, however, it is certainly a plausible conclusion that American constitutional identity is at bottom predicated on endorsement of a particular religion—or more precisely, a particular brand of religion—to the detriment of other religions.

Although the Supreme Court's Religion Clauses jurisprudence has been subject to fluctuations, overall, and when taken in conjunction with prevalent institutional practices, it is arguably best understood as an endorsement of a moderate mainstream, mainly Christian, brand of religion. This endorsement, moreover, militates against, on the one hand, atheism, and on the other, more fundamentalist brands of Christianity; and against other religions removed altogether from the Judeo-Christian tradition, such as Native American religions.[48]

The most ubiquitous and powerful metaphor, in the Religion Clauses, is that of the "wall of separation" between church and state.[49] And the most controverted public debate concerning the Religion Clauses is whether this "wall" should guarantee complete separation between church and state, or whether it should be lowered to permit state aid to religion so long as the state refrains from officially endorsing any particular religion.[50] This debate, however, conceals the dominant constitutional identity that emerges from institutional practices and Supreme Court opinions on the Religion Clauses.

The official endorsement of mainstream religion is effectuated through several different practices and discursive processes, among which metonymy plays a limited but crucial role. Official endorsement of God against atheists is prevalent in institutional practices, such as the recitation of prayers by official chaplains at the opening of a legislative session;[51] or the printing of "In God We Trust" on official paper and

48. *See* Timothy L. Fort, "The Free Exercise Rights of Native Americans and the Prospects for a Conservative Jurisprudence Protecting the Rights of Minorities," 23 *N.M. L. Rev.* 187 (1993).

49. *See* Reynolds v. United States, 98 U.S. 145, 164 (1879) (citing Thomas Jefferson).

50. *See* Laurence H. Tribe, *American Constitutional Law* § 14–4, at 1166–68 (2d ed. 1988).

51. Marsh v. Chambers, 463 U.S. 783 (1983).

coin currency; or the statement by a Supreme Court justice, in the course of an Establishment Clause opinion, endorsing belief in a "Supreme Being."[52] At the doctrinal level, the Supreme Court has upheld a congressional statute exempting from combat conscientious objectors opposed to "war in any form" because of their "religious training and belief"—"belief" being defined as a "belief in a relation to a Supreme Being involving duties superior from those arising from any human relation, but [not including] essentially political, sociological or philosophical views or a merely personal moral code."[53] Taken together, these developments unmistakably point to a constitutional identity that is not neutral on questions of religion, but rather biased in favor of broad theistic views, at least as against atheistic or agnostic views.

The constitutional bias in favor of mainstream religion to the detriment of other religious practices emerges, on the other hand, from the Supreme Court's Free Exercise Clause jurisprudence. This bias is reflected in the Court's general tendency to refuse exemptions from generally applicable laws for practices, such as polygamy[54] or ritual use of peyote,[55] which are repugnant to mainstream religion or to the mores of the majority.

Finally, both the bias against atheists and that against nonmainstream religion underlie recent Supreme Court Establishment Clause jurisprudence, most notably the 1984 decision in Lynch v. Donnely.[56] In Lynch, the Court upheld a city's Christmas display that included a crèche, located at the heart of the shopping district, as not violative of the Establishment Clause. To reach this result, the Court had to overcome two doctrinal hurdles: it had to find that there was a secular purpose to the display of the crèche, and it had to conclude that the display did not amount to an official endorsement of religion by the city.[57] Since

52. Zorach v. Clauson, 343 U.S. 306, 313 (1952).

53. Section 6(j) of the Universal Military Training and Service Act of 1948, upheld though broadly interpreted in United States v. Seeger, 380 U.S. 163 (1965). Statutory reference to a "belief in a relation to a Supreme Being" was deleted in a 1967 amendment to 6(j). Nonetheless, the statute still precludes exempting an avowed atheist claiming an exemption on purely moral grounds. But see Justice Black's plurality opinion in Welsh v. United States, 398 U.S. 333 (1970), reading the relevant statutory language so broadly as to blur the distinction between religious and nonreligious ethical views.

54. *See* Reynolds v. United States, 98 U.S. 145 (1879).

55. *See* Department of Human Resources v. Smith, 494 U.S. 872 (1990).

56. 465 U.S. 668 (1984).

57. *Id.* at 679.

the crèche depicts the nativity scene, which is of profound religious significance to Christians but not to those who adhere to other faiths, such as Judaism, the hurdles confronting the Court's five–four majority seemed rather formidable. Nevertheless, through a combination of negation and metonymic displacement, the Court managed to decide that public display of the crèche amounted to neither a lack of secular purpose nor an official endorsement of (a particular) religion. As against atheists and advocates of rigid separation between church and state, the majority justices argued that display of the crèche did not endorse any particular religion any more than generally accepted practices, such as printing "In God We Trust" on coins.[58] As against both non-Christians and Christians for whom the crèche evokes strong religious convictions, the Court's majority trivialized the crèche, by stressing its display in the context of commercial and other national secular traditions now associated with the Christmas holiday.[59]

From the perspective of atheists or rigorous separationists, Lynch is an impermissible endorsement of religion. From the perspective of a profoundly committed Christian, on the other hand, Lynch represents a trivialization of religion and an ultimate surrender to secularism.[60] By nurturing the antagonism between these two entrenched positions, the Court's majority in Lynch manages to promote mainstream religion through a double displacement that may appear to be an effort to appease both sets of antagonists. Indeed, mainstream religion is contiguous to both separationists, on one side, and to those who are profoundly religious, on the other.

Accordingly, both the holding in Lynch and the American constitutional approach to the relation between state and religion can be metonymically portrayed as carving a nonreligiously motivated, and predominantly neutral, middle course between ardent secularists and profoundly committed adherents to religion; when, at bottom, they promote a particular brand of religion that is neither neutral nor heterogeneous. Consistent with this, metonymic displacement enables a

58. *See* Lynch v. Donnelly, 465 U.S. 668, 676 (1984).

59. In the words of Justice O'Connor, the "crèche is a traditional symbol of the holiday that is very commonly displayed along with purely secular symbols, as it was in Pawtucket." 465 U.S. at 692 (O'Connor, J., concurring).

60. An adherent to a non-Christian religion could either side with the separationist if he or she most fears state favoritism toward Christianity or with the profoundly committed Christian if his or her greatest concern is surrender to secularism and trivialization of religion.

constitutional identity shaped by mainstream religion to remain hidden behind a mask of fairness and neutrality toward religion(s).

### D. Reconstructive Constitutional Discourse and the Relation between Negation, Metaphor, and Metonymy

The preceding discussion of negation, metaphor, and metonymy reveals the complexity of the discursive processes associated with the reconstructive search for constitutional identity. This complexity is compounded when one considers the ways in which negation, metaphor, and metonymy operate while they interact. Indeed, such interaction not only modifies and delimits the ways in which these three discursive devices combine to project images of constitutional identity; it also shapes the elements slated to become building blocks in the (re)construction of constitutional identity.

It is beyond the scope of the present undertaking to attempt any comprehensive account of the intricate ways in which negation, metaphor, and metonymy actually combine in the course of the reconstructions of constitutional identity. Instead, I will concentrate on the most salient aspects of the interaction between the three previously mentioned devices in relation to the determination of constitutional identity as a whole, without special regard to how the individual elements involved are themselves derived. From such an overall standpoint, negation—particularly through determination, repression, and renunciation—assumes the principal role in carving out the identity of the constitutional subject, with metaphor and metonymy fulfilling the important task of providing content to the respective roles of identity and difference. Indeed, negation delimits the constitutional subject by mediating between identity and difference. But only through the work of metaphor and metonymy can identity and difference acquire determinate form. In other words, only metaphor and metonymy will reveal *which* identity—or, more precisely, identities—and *which* difference—or differences—ought to be mediated through negation to yield a plausible reconstruction of a suitable constitutional subject.

The function of metaphor and metonymy in delimiting constitutional identity must be understood in terms of the previously discussed overall role played by negation in the definition of the constitutional subject. By upsetting the status quo and uprooting settled meanings, negation creates a vacuum that must be filled through the pursuit of equivalent meanings along the paradigmatic axis, and contiguous meanings along the syntagmatic axis. The replacement of uprooted meanings, moreover, requires a concurrent journey along both these axes, as all meanings hinge on relations of similarity as well as on relations of contiguity. Thus, constitutional meaning and identity depend on establishing coordinates along the syntagmatic and paradigmatic axes. In order to understand how reconstruction of the constitutional subject's identity works, therefore, it is necessary to take a closer look at the relationship between metaphor and metonymy, and, in particular, at how interaction between the two results in securing determinate coordinates along the paradigmatic and syntagmatic axes.

As already mentioned, metaphor functions by setting relations with reference to a code, whereas metonymy does the same with reference to a context. Neither metaphor, standing alone, nor metonymy completely cut loose from any code can generate any coherent meaning. In other words, for meaning to be produced, the semantic path made up of metaphoric relations must intersect with its counterpart built on metonymic relations. Indeed, journeying along the metaphoric path can be analogized to attempting to ascertain the meaning by *exclusive* reference to a dictionary. Assuming no reference whatsoever to any context, reliance on the dictionary proves completely circular. Each term would have to be defined by other terms, with the original term sought to be defined eventually figuring in the definition, thus referring back to itself. On the other hand, should the syntagmatic relations along the metonymic path be considered completely separately from any paradigmatic relations, it would also be impossible to generate any coherent meaning as each term within a sequence would lead to the next term within the same sequence, without ever acquiring an identity of its own.[61] It would be as if one became familiar with a set sequence of words in a completely foreign language. After a while, upon reading the first word in the sequence, one would be able to recite the rest of the sequence in its proper order, but without thereby being in any better position to understand the meaning of the sequence.

Notwithstanding that meaning requires reference to both the

61. As noted by Jakobson, in aphasia leading to destruction of the capacity to establish relations along the paradigmatic axis, terms tend to become perceived exclusively in terms of their syntagmatic relations, thus making it impossible to name things. Roman Jakobson, *Essais de Linguistique Générale* 54 (1973).

metaphoric and the metonymic paths, particular utterances may rely on a preponderance of either metaphoric or metonymic relations.[62] Depending on differences in personality, culture, and style, metaphoric or metonymic processes may gain the upper hand.[63] Moreover, as already mentioned, in the realm of legal argumentation, tilts toward metaphoric or metonymic processes are to an important degree determined by stakes in the legal outcomes; with those wishing to extend application of an existing legal norm relying on metaphor, while those seeking to contain the spread of such norm appeal to metonymy.[64]

At the more global level of the formation and evolution of constitutional identities, metaphoric processes are intertwined with metonymic ones in an ongoing dialectic. At the highest level of abstraction, this dialectic confronts the challenge of projecting an identity lending support to the perception that the *same* constitution endures through the generations, stretching back to that of the constitution makers. At the more concrete level of particular constitutional rights, moreover, this dialectic strives to promote an equilibrium between the pole of identity and the contrary pole of difference. This is perhaps best illustrated by reference to constitutional rights to equality.

Viewed from a formal standpoint, constitutional equality requires properly accounting for relevant identities and relevant differences. Consistent with this, *ideal* constitutional equality would fully account for, and optimally integrate, all relevant identities and differences. Practically, however, the relevance of identities and differences will be contested. Moreover, this problem is compounded to the extent that identities and differences are not simply given, but rather constructed.[65] Finally, given the logic of the dialectic between identity and difference, both identity and difference can be invoked, depending on the circumstances, either to make equality rights more inclusive or more exclusive.

For example, against the background of African-American slavery,

62. *See id.* at 61.

63. *Id.* Jakobson points out that when children are given a name and asked for a verbal reaction, they invariably react in one of two ways: they either utter a verbal expression linked to the name in question by a relation of similarity, or else, by a relation of contiguity. *Id.* Thus, for example, confronted with the term "ice cream," a child may be more drawn toward metaphoric processes and answer "cake," or be inclined toward metonymic processes and respond "summer."

64. *See id.*

65. *See, e.g.*, Patricia A. Cain, "Feminist Legal Scholarship," 77 *Iowa L. Rev.* 19 (1991).

stress on the metaphoric process that leads to an identity beyond race seems bound to result in a more inclusive conception of constitutional equality.[66] By contrast, in a polity divided into a majority and a minority linguistic group, identity in disregard of linguistic differences, practically resulting in advantages for members of the linguistic majority, would lead to a relatively more exclusive conception of constitutional equality.[67] On the other hand, it is obvious that stress on metonymic process to highlight difference can serve the purposes of restricting the scope of constitutional equality. Thus, differences relating to gender have been used to deny women equality.[68] Less obvious, perhaps, is that emphasis on differences can also go hand in hand with efforts to expand the scope of equality rights. As examples, one can mention equal catering to the different needs of men and women, or of diverse linguistic groups.

Granted that developments along the metaphoric path must be correlated to those along the metonymic path, the question remains how trajectories along both these paths can be reined in so as to single out identities and differences best suited to reconcile the self and other *within* the constitutional subject. In other words, all the terms susceptible of substitution along the metaphoric path have the same exchange value, and the question is, what makes some of these terms have greater use value than others? For their part, all terms along the metonymic path relate to one another in terms of contiguity, and the question becomes, what determines the location of meaning-endowing pauses that render metonymic sequences intelligible? Or, put somewhat differently, what accounts for the punctuation that endows sequences of contiguous terms with determinate meaning?

The selection of particular identities and differences to figure in a given project of constitutional reconstruction is a function of the confluence of structural constraints imposed by the constitutional order, and of the sociocultural heritage of the relevant polity. These structural

66. Compare the majority opinion in Plessy v. Fergusson (racial apartheid held consistent with Equal Protection Clause of the Fourteenth Amendment) with Justice Harlan's dissenting opinion (consistent with the color-blind principle, racial apartheid should be deemed unconstitutional).

67. Thus, if all government business must be conducted in the majority language, equal opportunity to compete for government employment may in fact result in a disadvantage for speakers of the minority language.

68. *See,* e.g., Bradwell v. State, 83 U.S. 130 (1873) (state denial of right to practice law to women held constitutional and justified in terms of woman's role as wife and mother).

constraints account for the establishment of a plausible constitutional identity depending on the production of a meaningful narrative through negation, substitution (metaphor), and displacement (metonymy). The sociocultural heritage, on the other hand, furnishes the material that must be reshaped through negation, metaphor, and metonymy; in such a way as to promote both links to, and contrasts with, the preconstitutional and the extraconstitutional self.

To understand how negation, metaphor, and metonymy combine to reshape materials drawn from the sociocultural heritage of the polity into a constitutional identity, it is necessary to first briefly consider the role of constitutional law in a democratic legal order. Even in a democracy, law looms as an alienating intrusion of the other upon the self. Law is by and large experienced as coercive, and submission to its edicts can be likened to bowing to the constraints devised by the superego.[69] Notwithstanding a law's democratic enactment, and one's support of such enactment, that law's application imposes external constraints on all those who come within its sweep.[70] Inasmuch as constitutional law is *law,* moreover, it is also constraining and alienating. Inasmuch, however, as *constitutional* law can be invoked to counter or set aside coercive democratically enacted laws, it also contributes to self-affirmation and to emancipation.[71]

In the last analysis, both the self whose self-affirmation and emancipation are promoted by constitutional law, and the other who pursues self-affirmation through majority-backed legislation are meant to be included in the constitutional subject. Accordingly, besides being constraining qua law, the constitution is at once constraining and emancipatory: it constrains all those who come within its sweep as members of the legislating sovereign; and it contributes to the emancipation of the

69. *See* Lacan, *supra* unnumbered chapter opening note, at 130.

70. Even if one agrees with Rousseau that each member of a democratic polity is at once an integral part of the sovereign who enacts laws conforming to the general will and an individual who is obligated to obey such laws, *see* Rousseau, *supra* note 15, at 16–18, there still seems to be an insurmountable split between these two roles that makes the obligation to obey the law both constraining and alienating, *see* Rosenfeld, *supra* note 16, at 868. Indeed, in Rousseau's own famous words, "whoever refuses to obey the general will shall be compelled to it by the whole body: this in fact only forces him to be free." Rousseau, *supra* note 15, at 18. Needless to say, legislative minorities subjected to laws that they have opposed are even more clearly subjected to onerous external impositions.

71. The most obvious example of the emancipatory potential of constitutional law is furnished by the protection of fundamental rights. Thus, freedom of expression protects against submission to majority views.

members of the very same group, to the extent that they become obligated to abide by the dictates of duly enacted laws. Consistent with this, moreover, negation, metaphor, and metonymy must combine to reshape materials issued from the sociocultural heritage of the relevant polity so as to construct a constitutional identity at once suited to the constraining and to the emancipatory role of constitutional law.

### *III. Potential and Limitations*

That the identity of the constitutional subject always involves a lack is at once reassuring and worrisome. It is reassuring, in that there is always room for further improvement and greater perfection. It is worrisome, however, not only because what is open-ended and forever incomplete is likely to provoke anxiety, but also because efforts to perfect a (necessarily) less than fully elaborated constitutional identity may result in a setback rather than in any improvement. Although Hegel's dialectical logic has proved persuasive in examining the vicissitudes of constitutional reconstructive dynamics, his confidence in the necessity of progress no longer rings true.[72] But even if we take this into proper account, and notwithstanding the danger of losing ground, the constitutional subject cannot stand still, much less remain fixated on the originary myth surrounding the generation of constitution makers. Stunting the evolution of constitutional identity is bound to lead to pathologies, as the obsolete constitutional constructs of yesteryear become more likely to yield repression rather than to enhance possibilities of emancipation.

The evolving identity of the constitutional subject relies on invention and reinvention of tradition. This does not mean, however, that constitutional identity can be crafted at will, or that it is bound to remain arbitrary. *Which* elements of preconstitutional tradition may figure in the reconstruction of constitutional identity, and *how* they may become integrated with new or transformed elements to make up a plausible neotradition, is subject to determinate structural, functional, and cultural constraints. These constraints rarely, if ever, compel any

72. *See* Charles Taylor, *Hegel* 537–38, 547, 551 (1975) (Hegel's actual synthesis has become obsolete and his belief in the complete overlap of reason and reality seems highly implausible today). *But see* Slavoj Žižek, *The Sublime Object of Ideology* 6 (1989) ("far from being a story of [the] progressive overcoming [of antagonism], dialectics is for Hegel a systematic notation of the failure of all such attempts").

single outcome, but they significantly curtail the number of available options. Indeed, inevitable competing pressures call for the work of overdetermination, which, in turn, results in a great narrowing of the semantic choices along the interstices of negation, metaphor, and metonymy.

Within these constraints, the identity of the constitutional subject can never become settled, for there is no way to overcome the split between self and other. As gauged from the vantage point of the constitutional subject, moreover, this split is both internal and external. On the one hand, it is internal inasmuch as the constitutional polity is necessarily pluralistic in nature. Such polity may be atomistically pluralistic, with each individual pitted against all others, or made up of a plurality of distinct groups, or both. In any event, the constitutional polity is bound to be internally split, which accounts for its yearning to become enveloped in a commonly shared constitutional identity. On the other hand, the split between self and other is external to the extent that a polity as a whole distinguishes itself from other polities. Furthermore, the external other can play a significant role in shaping the national and constitutional identity of a polity. Thus, not only is national identity likely to be shaped, at least in part, by the rejection of foreign identities, but also constitutional identity may be partially determined by negative incorporation of constitutional norms prevailing in another polity.[73] Consistent with this distinction, the self should seek reconciliation with internal others and adopt an inclusionary approach toward them. In contrast, it seems permissible for the self to keep external others at a distance and even, in some cases, adopt an exclusionary attitude toward them.[74]

73. By "negative incorporation" of another country's constitutional norm, I refer to the situation in which country A specifically rejects, after careful consideration, a constitutional norm previously adopted in country B. *See* Gary J. Jacobsohn, *Apple of Gold: Constitutionalism in Israel and the United States* 12 (1993).

74. There is a tendency to regard exclusionary attitudes as being reprehensible. Upon careful consideration, however, whether a policy of exclusion is to be lauded or condemned depends on the circumstances involved and on who is being excluded. Thus, exclusion of Nazis or racists from a political organization would seem laudable in most all cases. Similarly, it seems commendable to seek implantation of a constitutional identity that contrasts with that of a neighboring country that has become prey to an oppressive regime. Moreover, even when the excluded alternative is not inherently undesirable or reprehensible, an exclusionary approach may nonetheless be justifiable. For instance, in choosing between an inclusionary policy making adults responsible for the welfare of all children and an exclusionary policy making parents liable for the well-being of their own children, it is certainly defensible to argue that the exclusionary alternative is prefer-

The divide between internal and external others, however, does not by any means always track national boundaries. This is undoubtedly due, in part, to the emergence of transnational constitutional or quasi-constitutional norms since the end of World War II.[75] But it is also due, at least as significantly, to the external other often dwelling *within* the polity. Thus, for instance, African-American slaves must be considered as constituting an external other in the context of American constitutional identity, prior to the Civil War. Moreover, as both the internal and the external other can readily move across national boundaries, what is important is above all the generic differences between the two, and the dialectic that links them to one another in the pursuit of constitutional identity.

Focusing upon the broad outlines of the dialectic between internal and external other sheds useful light on the potential and limitations of the constitutional subject in its quest to strike an equilibrium between self and other. Under the best possible conditions, the division between internal and external other rests on a legitimate basis that is morally defensible. Under such conditions, moreover, the constitutional subject should treat the internal other in an inclusionary manner, while dealing with the external other in an exclusionary way. Finally, inclusionary treatment can revolve either around identities or around differences. In the first of these cases, the self includes the internal other on the basis of commonly shared identities—in the sense of similarities—which must be stressed above all differences, thus requiring both self and other to exercise self-censorship and curb that which sets them apart. In the second case, inclusion encompasses recognition and acceptance of differences, which means not merely tolerance of diversity but rather positive encouragement of the pursuit of difference, with a view to maximizing both the self's and the internal other's potential for flourishing in an atmosphere of mutual care and respect. Accordingly, all else remaining equal, inclusionary treatment of the internal other honoring differences is preferable.[76]

able in view of the natural bond that exists between parent and child. Accordingly, a greater number of children may well be better off if left to the care of their own parents rather than to that of the adult population at large.

75. *See* Louis Henkin, "A New Birth of Constitutionalism: Genetic Influences and Genetic Defects," 14 *Cardozo L. Rev.* 533, 537 (1993).

76. An example of a situation in which stress on difference would seem less desirable than stress on identity would be where, under pressure from an aggressive external other, the internal other is in danger of becoming transformed into yet another external

Even under the best possible conditions, however, full reconciliation between self and internal other is bound to remain out of reach. This means that the identity of the constitutional subject can never be wholly representative of, or equally satisfactory to, all those who come within its sweep. Thus, even in the most multicultural and pluralistic of constitutional polities, not all cultures or religions could be equally accommodated. This is because it is impossible to ascend to a neutral position equidistant to all the differences vying for inclusion within the constitutional subject.

Consistent with these observations, the best equilibrium between self and other that the constitutional subject could hope to achieve is one in which as many differences as possible are accommodated in the inclusionary gesture toward the internal other. The ideal of integrating all differences, though unreachable, serves a useful critical purpose as a counterfactual meant to remind us that all constitutional identities fall short and are in constant need of further perfection and completion. Exclusive reliance on this ideal, however, is inadequate when it comes to criticizing a reconstruction of constitutional identity from the standpoint of a preferable, yet attainable alternative. When a constitutional identity falls short of such an alternative, it is that alternative which must provide the counterfactual baseline for critical assessment. Moreover, the availability of such alternatives depends on the possibility, within the constraints imposed by constitutionalism, for the self to further accommodate the differences of the internal other without compromising the core elements or the integrity of its conception of the good, as mediated by the fundamental requirements of constitutionalism. Further mutual adjustment is often possible, as conceptions of the good and value preferences are not static, but rather susceptible of transformation in ways that may promote greater overall emancipation without calling for increased overall repression.[77]

The thrust toward greater inclusiveness and greater accommodation of differences, however, is fraught with risks. As the realm of the internal other expands beyond the boundaries of the nation-state, the self may well become more uncertain and more insecure about its iden-

---

other. Under such circumstances, stress upon differences may exacerbate the danger whereas stress on identities might minimize it.

77. *See* Jürgen Habermas, *Communication and the Evolution of Society* 90 (Thomas McCarthy trans., Beacon Press 1979) (1976) (arguing that needs are not fixed, but rather susceptible of dialogical transformation).

tity. And the more one's positive identity appears under assault, the more tempting it may seem to regain control through exclusion.[78] To prevent that, the counterfactual imagination must rise to the challenge and provide the critical tools necessary to undermine the implantation of unnecessarily repressive constitutional identities.

78. Paradoxically, as the realm of the internal other extends farther, the external realm may well move ever closer to home and become perceived as a growing threat within the polity. When this happens, exclusionary identity tends to replace the pursuit of inclusiveness and openness to difference. Taken to its logical extreme, this tendency would be destructive of constitutionalism and of the constitutional subject as the exclusionary self would secure its identity through subordination and oppression of those whom it could cast as being different. But even far short of that, the tendency toward exclusionary identity may rob the constitutional subject of much of its emancipatory potential.

*Chapter 7*

# The Other Dimension of Law

*Pierre Legendre*

Translated by Yifat Hachamovitch

What kind of a questioning would make it possible for psychoanalysis to become theoretically useful for jurists? How could such a questioning have an effect on the practice of law? In the same measure, is it theoretically plausible for psychoanalysts, attached as they are to their own casuistry, to interrogate the law? What must be recognized from the start, if this questioning is to be more than superficial, is that the intellectual and social dogmas of today are obstacles to the liberty of thought [*esprit*].

We do not yet comprehend what an anthropological reconsideration [*démarche*] of law means for the Occident. The juridical phenomenon has not yet made itself felt as that very thing the Romans, inventors of our normative logic, designated by the formula "*to institute life.*" We do not understand that what lies at the heart of ultramodern culture is only ever law; that this quintessentially European notion entails a kind of atomic bond, whose disintegration carries alongside it the risk of collapsing the symbolic for those generations yet to come. My reference to these smallest of bonds, these atoms, is a metaphoric gesture, meant to emphasize, to emblematize, the radicality of the juridical question, to make us see that life is *originarily* affected by law. From the very start, then, we must consider something not so simple to consider: the idea of law depends on the idea that our societies make themselves out of their own notion of life.

What stops thought from thinking about the relation between law and psychoanalysis is usually repressed or sidestepped [*écarté*] in the schools. Let us consider, then, some of these problems before we begin our questioning.

1. The first problem of recognition lies in conceiving of a juridical system that constitutes itself as the discourse of Reason. This construction of Reason is a phenomenon of cultures, and in the case of the Occident, a *representation of choice* presides over this construction. The elaboration of normative structures in the Middle Ages followed from this *choice of a representation,* setting the stage for the *Revolution of the Interpreter* of the twelfth and thirteenth centuries. One cannot overemphasize the significance of this first Revolution of the Occident, which sets off the second life of Roman law. It comes in response first of all not to socioeconomic exigencies, but to a mythological and religious captivation, which founds the human *relation to law.* We forget that it is Roman law, duplicated by the pontifical invention of canon law, that served as the institutional *habitus* of Latin Christendom, itself the inventor of the scholastic concept of the state. We do not see that it has become the logical armature of our normative systems. In misrecognizing this, we lose sight of a major element of such logical armature: its repression of any dissonant system of interpretation, most acutely instanced in the extreme form of its repression of the Torah and of the Talmudic mode of reasoning, judged contrary to Reason by the Christianized Roman law tradition honored by the school of Bologna.[1] The anthropological construction of Reason would not only lay down the groundwork of *what is called modernity* by appealing to the concept of a "state," the guarantor of the institution of life through the Romano-Christian scaffolding of the Law of Persons, but it would represent this principal Guarantor of Law as a part of the stagecraft of the principle of Reason. What is this notion of stagecraft? Essentially, it is the cultural elaboration of images on which Reason is founded, images which conserve the institution of life—in classical anthropological terms, the *Muttertum* and the *Vatertum.* How was it that the Occident came to elaborate its founding images, its script for Reason, by way of choosing Romano-canonic law as its *historical representation,* as against the Torah? The recognition of

1. The principal *event* of the twelfth century is the Renaissance of Roman Law. The *Corpus Iuris Civilis* diffuses a mode of reasoning that is thereupon opposed to Judaic interpretation, presented by *Novels* 146 of the Emperor Justinian (533) as *insensible* [*insensée*]. For my comments on this text, see Pierre Legendre, "Die Juden interpretieren verrückt. Gutachen zu einem klassischen Text" [The Jews are Interpreting Crazily: Evaluation of a Classic Text], 43 *Psyche: Zeitschrift für Psychoanalyse und ihre Anwendungen* 20 (1989) (Anton Schütz trans.).

the prevalence of this representation would remove one of law's major obstacles in coming to terms with psychoanalysis.

2. A reflection on law and psychoanalysis will inevitably meet with what remains a permanent problem for psychoanalysis: the relation between the subject and language must be understood by grasping the institutional workings of language on the whole of a culture. What Freud sketched out in the notions of Totem and Taboo is the textual horizon [*portée langagière*] of the juridical montage. The tradition that followed upon the Revolution of the Interpreter, in very much the same way as the one issuing from the Torah, was obsessed first of all with the question of speech and with the relation of discourse to the subject. But we mistakenly misrecognize the technical part of the instrumentation of a system of norms, the fact that the law was managed [*aménagé*] from the very start, as an *exercise of power over language.* What sort of power is at issue here, and how do states, whether their laws be codified or customary, come to be considered as the *logical titularies* of a founding power through the workings of the juridical system that they themselves control? One scholarly work, leading to the publication of a series on the theme,[2] has discovered what the continental system of laws, such as it was constructed and transmitted by the jurists of medieval scholasticism (by the Romano-canonic system, laicized much later on), defined as the sovereign political attribute: *the power to say what constitutes the relation of signification between a word* [*verbum*] *and a thing* [*res*]. This power expresses itself in modern states in the form of legislation and by way of jurisprudence, through which each state institutes the foundation of interpretation. It is an unhappy fact that the social sciences and their annexes can build barracks for the intellect, militarize thinking, but cannot even conceive of the existence of this power and how it sets itself up at the heart of Euro-American culture, an essential anthropological function at play everywhere and at all times. Misunderstanding, for the many reasons I have evoked in my work, the structural,[3] that is to say, logical character, of the sovereign power to divide words and things, they also misunderstand why this

2. The work in question is a study of an originally theological work that had been inserted into a collection of decretals of Pope Gregory IX (1234), a collection of great significance for the formation of the European *Customary Law* [*Ius Commune*]. This text, inserted into Book 5, Title 40 (*de verborum significatione*), chapter 6, was made the object of the expertise of several historians of scholasticism, whose joint efforts in my Laboratory will be published under the title *The Power to Divide Words and Things.*

3. The French *structural* has been rendered as carpentered or carpentry below. *Trans.*

power finds itself, in contemporary societies, transferred de facto to the sciences and why, as a consequence, the play of law is entirely mixed up, thrown into confusion. How is it possible, given these conditions, for a questioning of law to take account of the Freudian discovery and what follows from it, a discovery inseparable from the general problematic of language, this institution of the animal that speaks?

3. It is when we take the trouble to study the montages of normativity from this perspective that the problem of the law's epistemological foundation makes itself felt, that is to say, the problem of representing the question of tragedy, the ancient discourse of destiny summoning Oedipus: *why are there laws?* This structural question subtends every cultural representation of logic, of causality, of *what is called in the Occident a law,* and that would want to be somehow outside the law. Where are we if not in an age of industrial scientific propaganda that has taken on the vigorous religiosity of an old myth, a propaganda that, in spreading the word that science is the *true source of precepts,* is thereby exercising a de facto sovereign power to divide words and things? Is the normative system of the state and its laws no longer anything more than a sort of formalism inherited from history? One theoretical way out of addressing the practical consequences of our ideal representations—the method of a theory wrapped up in seduction—evokes the autopoiesis of the law, its auto-referential mechanism. But this method falls into an impasse, because, too inspired by sociology, it can only be indifferent to the anthropological stakes of the law. The discourse on autopoiesis does not grasp the subjective horizon of the images of causality within the domain of norms, nor does it understand that the law is engaged to construct the principle of Reason and to translate it into social practices. This said, only to show what obstacles meet us in thinking the question of tragedy: "*why laws?*"—in a manner that is sensitive to the Freudian discovery—a question our ultramodern societies cannot avoid in elaborating their juridical montages. We meet this obstacle of a sociological conception of society, unsuited to the radical problems posed to contemporary jurists. It is therefore a matter of sidestepping these conceptions, of taking a firm stand that the notion of society must be revised, if we are to grasp the stakes of Reason at play in normative montages and in juridical practices. Society must first of all be considered in its function as a register that brings into relief [*relèver*] the atomic bond of the law: the logic of Interdiction for the subject. In other words, society is a function for the subject. This perhaps

can serve as a leeway for a thought that plays on new questions in its problematization of the relation between the field of psychoanalysis and that of law.

Society must be understood as a function for the subject. It is time then to discuss the meaning of this formulation in order to mark the meeting place of law and psychoanalysis as the place where the language of Interdiction is reproduced. It is this reproduction that binds a living space for the human being.

It is necessary for us to recover the reasoning from which classical notions of law started out, to discover for ourselves what the Roman jurists might have had in mind when they claimed to be reasoning about foundations by means of philosophy itself, not the fantasm [*la philosophie vraie, non simulée*].[4] What did they mean by this? According to the formula of Ulpian himself, author of the celebrated text: "he who carries all the burdens of the law must first learn to recognize where the name of the law comes from."[5] The *approach* (Ulpian uses the Latin verb *adfectare*) to philosophy itself, not a fantasm, proceeds from this primordial position of questioning: to learn to recognize from where the name of law descends. On this basis, which served as the platform [*socle*] from which the revolution of the interpreters in the Occident set out, we can proceed step by step in an interrogation of the concept of society as a function for the subject.

It is of note that the Roman position of a base—to learn to recognize from where the name of the law descends—indicates which way we must go. The reflection on foundations presents itself as a road from the very beginning, and this beginning is a word, the word *law* [*ius*]. The jurist is invited to study the descendance of the name; it is this matter of the name that comes to designate an entire ensemble of juridical tasks. Let us consider for a moment what it is proposed that we question, let us ask what this means, this idea of interrogating the name of the law [*nomen iuris*], of seeing the way it descends, from a properly genealogical perspective. Is it not merely a distraction for a civilization of science to attend to this type of discourse?

4. "[V]eram nisi fallor [if I am not mistaken] philosophiam, non simulatam affectantes." Dig. 1.1.1.1 (Ulpian, Institutionum 1), *reprinted in* 1 *The Digest of Justinian* 1 (Theodor Mommsen and Paul Krueger eds., Alan Watson trans., 1985).

5. "Iuri operam daturum prius nosse oportet, unde nomen iuris descendat." *Id.* at 1.1.1.introduction.

Such a descendance of words is not a mere servitude of rhetoric, made possible by etymology, or, as was the case with the medieval scholastics, by a usage propped up by parental metaphors. When the jurisconsult Ulpian declares that calling of the law originates from the word *justice* (the word *iustitia* containing the word *ius*), he is not indulging in semantic jugglery; he is staging or dramatizing *the logic of the origin,* that logic without which the law could not have developed its multiple effects.

We are faced then with a very delicate problem: to understand that the law, if it is a social construction, does not limit itself to translating and reflecting relations between or among individuals or groups, nor again relations of interaction, such as are found in nature, economics, and the like. It is a matter of understanding that the social is reduced to discourse, to an assemblage of words, a textual order, organized to speak to any subject. At this level of abstraction, the industrial, commercial, demographic development of the state, of the social, does not really matter; what matters is how, in accord with which discursive practices, this particular society sets itself up as a scene of speech, and appeals to a subject. What this supposes is a theatrical construction, a setting for the *why are there laws?*, and, consequently, a fiction of origin. It is in light of this that the continental jurists, commenting on Ulpian's text, would repeat again and again that justice was at the origin of law and was the seat of its well-founded logic. Thus it came about that the classical authors—this was the case in the seventeenth century of the well-known G. B. de Luca—titled their synthetic theses on law by evoking the theater: de Luca calls his work *The Theater of Truth and of Justice.*[6] We shall try to draw out this description.

In reestablishing the social as a phenomenon of discourse and of a speech addressed to any subject, we are unshelling the essential genealogical sense of such discourse, the logical core of the referential function. If it appears that in the domain of law, as the Roman law reference to the word *justice* would indicate, the order of texts could only make sense by referring back to the signifier of its cause (the term *iustitia*), it is not because the word *justice* (its current equivalent would be *democracy*) draws its force from some magical power. Rather, it can effectively represent the "cause" because it locks into the institutional scene, more precisely the *order of places of discourse* that organizes the

6. Giovanni Battista de Luca, *Theatrum Veritatis et Iustitiae (Apud Henricum Rommerskirchen 1706)* (n.p.).

social, for the society of third-century Rome. But this accession to the institutional scene is not a characteristic reserved for a classical organization; it is a logical concept, viable still, because it is justified by a genealogical structure, coextensive with every culture. True philosophy, as opposed to the fantasm, may now be defined as the effort, remade indefinitely, to accede to the logic of reference.

Now is the time to reconsider why it is that a reference, a function or functionary that refers, may be called genealogical. What is it that establishes the connection between law and socially constructed speech? It is a matter of situating the law in the order of places of discourse. I will say simply this, translating what knowledge the continental tradition had of this logical order into familiar terminology: *the space of the law was thought to be asymmetrical to the space recognized in the causal signified,* more generally, to the space recognized in the discourse of Reference, in the textual place of foundations. It is for this reason that metaphors of descent and generation (justice engendering law) are laid out in a symbolic show: to register the sense of the dissymmetry. Where is this symbolization today? It is when we situate the law as a structured place [*place structurale*] that we begin to get a vague sense of what might prompt an appeal to psychoanalysis. It is the Aristotelian notion, banalized by jurists, of the relation of power and speech: man is called the political animal because he is endowed with speech.[7] Psychoanalysis makes it possible for us to grasp the problematic of this relation, in showing that the subject entering language is met by the institution of separation, a separation from things, from beings and from self by his words. The representation of power, for the subject, is inscribed in this confrontation. We shall try to specify.

What psychoanalysis designates by general formulas such as *the original* or *the law of the Father* is nothing other than an original separation that inaugurates subjective life (in the sense of a separation of the infant from the maternal entity), as subject to the law of differentiation through speech. Now separation supposes an aside [*écart*], a representation of emptiness, the integration, both by society and by the subject, of the category of negativity. It is in light of a textual arrangement of spacing necessary for the life of a representation, for the reproduction of the animal that speaks, that the function of reference may be appre-

7. A celebrated passage of Aristotle, explicating that man alone of all the animals speaks and that therefore he alone may be called the political animal. Aristotle, *Politics* (bk.I, sec.2, l.9), *in The Complete Works of Aristotle* 1988 (Jonathan Barnes ed., 1984).

hended as a logical function of society. Such a function has as its task to put into play, in the unconscious representations of the subject, the power to institute separation by words. *We are concerned with the essence of the symbolic function.*

It follows from this remark that it is a matter of a genealogical power, that is to say, of an office or a duty to refer, bound to an original or to the law of the father, thus a structural function, set up in every human living space through diverse cultural inventions that organize symbolic life. In no way should this problematic be confounded with the history of those conceptions called patriarchal, in contrast to matriarchal ones, relating to progenitive systems, still less with the history of the struggle of the sexes. It is rather a problematic of the power to refer that is the condition of the subject's entry into language.

That should set us off understanding how the structural place of the law presents itself. Being essentially text [*langagière*], a juridical construction cannot not be concerned with the power to refer so defined. One can envisage the law as the workshop [*mise en oeuvre*] of the institution of splitting, the juridical practices as interpreting the original or law of the Father; a system constructed in such a way that it proffers itself to the subject as a system of messages addressed only to him. If one follows this chain of logic, it is easy to understand how the law articulates its relation to the discourse of foundations, that is, its relation to the speaking place of the social Third. We are entering now into a hermeneutics of the normative foundations of the subject.

When I evoke in my work the notion of hermeneutics, I mean the assemblage of discursive machinery that sets the scene up as theater, that is, the ritual procedures and the emblematic figurations, the *modern Hermes,* society itself as normative speech addressing the subject. It is a matter of instituting the Third of language and of making it produce normative effects. We shall see in a moment that it is a matter of organizing a vast social system of interpretations that fix law's singular rightful place within the transmission of what psychoanalysis, following classical anthropology, designates by the contemporarily obscure term, *Interdiction.*

What then is the *mise en scène* of the Third of language or of the social Hermes, that we ought to treat as a category necessary to the workings of law? Returning to Roman law, Ulpian tells us that jurists, because they cultivate justice, can be called for this reason *priests* [*sacer-*

*dotes*].[8] In other words, as the root of this term indicates, justice is inscribed in the *space of the sacred.* To translate this idea of a space reserved for what is sacred into the usage of a secularized culture: every society notifies the subject of a separate dimension in the form of a discourse of the undisclosed, of what is, for the subject himself, inaccessible. This means: the subject is not everything, he must integrate this lack (not being everything) in a representation; he is met by a limit, as the very condition of his symbolic life. Let us reiterate: the intervention of the Third of language is nothing other than the institution that separates the subject from the fantasm of being whole. In the same way as classical religions would develop institutional procedures calculated to notify the subject of his status of *being separated*—separated from things and separated from the fantasm of being whole, by marks inflicted on his body (for example circumcision), the industrial *montage* must resolve the same question: how to reinvent indefinitely the function of the separator Third, how to dramatize the category of negativity, necessary for the subject's entry into humanity.

These summary directions[9] slowly uncork [*débouchent*] the problematic of Interdiction. In a nonoccidental vocabulary that is nonetheless familiar because of anthropology, and then a psychoanalysis now in style, the equivalent of the *Interdiction* would be the *Taboo,* which is itself a reference to the concept of the *Totem.* This translation brings us back to the correspondences between a mythical or religious conception of the world, where the normativity of savage thought reigns, and our rational, historical and industrial, conception of the state and of law. Now, structurally, with regard to the logic of separation, these systems are strictly equivalent: a society carpenters with its speech the fiction of *Hermes,* inventor of speech; that is to say, carrier of the normative message of foundations, whatever its cultural form; it organizes a space, which the Romans called "sacred," that is to say, undisclosed or inaccessible to the subject, where in the equivalent of a movie a spectacle is offered to his view, in order to tell him of the intrigue of origins, the cause of his being and the law of his being, declaring itself the narrative conductor [*récit porteur*] of instituting and instituted representations. It is the necessity of this discourse that psychoanalysis unveils

8. "Cuius merito quis nos sacerdotes appellet: iustitiam namque colimus . . . ." Dig. 1.1.1.1 (Ulpian, Institutionum 1), *reprinted in 1 The Digest of Justinian, supra* note 5, at 1.

9. I have developed these problems in particular in Pierre Legendre, *Leçons VI: Les Enfants du Texte. Étude sur la fonction parentale des États* 25–31, 73 (1992).

and incites us to recognize in its complexity, and that defines the state as anthropologically significant: the state is the sacred place of the Totem, wherever it takes hold, whatever its constitutional form may be, the religious or mythical space of the discourse called upon to *guarantee the foundations* without which the law would remain unthinkable. From this perspective the specific place of law appears clearly as being that of the normative effects of this discourse of foundations, whose interpretations the law claims to guarantee.

Thus dependent on the discourse of foundations, on the *mise en scène* of the Third that separates, the law decisively appears to us as an integral part of the order of texts that, in traditional Western European societies, assumes the function of translating the Interdiction for the animal that speaks, introducing man to the institutional dimension of the limit. In any culture, it is not enough to produce human flesh; it is still necessary to institute it for it to live, for life to reproduce. To institute the subject is to institute life. Because it is bound to the problematic of language, the juridical system is, originarily [*dans son principe*], burdened by the idea of genealogy. One might say that it is by virtue of this *symbolic instrument* that industrial societies, insofar as they also submit to universal necessity, *infantilize the subject indefinitely.* If the conservation of human space occurs by way of the conservation of the subject, this means that the law, as an occidental version of normative logic, refers to the order of life. It is at this specific point, as I noted previously, that the contact between the fields of law and of psychoanalysis was made. Now it is a matter of measuring the practical consequences.

But before beginning a reflection that would try to clarify the practices of jurists as well as those of psychoanalysts, it should not be superfluous to take, if I might say it thus, a panoramic view of the law, this general effect of legislative and jurisprudential rules that irrigate, through their interpretations, the most diverse domains of modern life. When we evoke *the other dimension of the law,* on which we have yet to elaborate, is it a matter of indifference whether it is a vast mass or whether it is only a few pieces? We must be more precise.

The next step consists of discovering what I have called *an atomic bond of law.* The areas of specialization that cover up the general notion of law are not appealed to by their title to witness what takes place in this next step. Revenue law [*droit fiscal*] and land law [*droit de immobilier*] do not have the same calling for the problematic of the Interdiction as the law of persons, articulated directly through the oedipal question, or likewise the law of obligations, contracts, promoter of the concepts of credit, faith, belief, and of debt, as essential to the functioning of genealogical justice, or still yet the law of trusts, of goods and of successions, inheritances, so important in the practices of transmission. Still, one cannot exclude one particular juridical domain, in an effort at clarification. I have had the opportunity to show how everything turns on this notion, as juridical as it is economic, of the convertibility of currencies, in order to grasp the unsuspecting character of free planetary exchange:[10] money is a symbolization of the Third, one of its theatrical figures in society; an ultramodern economy and the juridical arm of the contract tend to alter radically the image of the Third in humanity, by projecting normative systems and their founding discourses in a universe of marketplaces, where currencies are themselves subject to the law of simultaneity. Now then, through money, another version of the original that separates, that is to say, of the Totem or of the law of the Father, that is implicated in the scenario of the marketplace. Are we witnessing the market waging a war to exterminate all foundational discourses? Could the convertibility of all currencies be, so to speak, its most visible and exacerbated form? Psychoanalysis can teach us about the conservation of the subject that has thus far remained the anthropological reserve of institutional montages. A generalized Economism and Managerialism is in the process of impairing the symbolic capital of humanity. This works to remove from the domain of thought the question attached to the reproduction of the animal that speaks: the problem of rendering the discourse of the Interdiction habitable by each human being. A return to the bond of the law will map out in detail what such an interrogation implies. We shall thus try to define this bond.

This is not too difficult, in my view. It is enough to account for the elements that constitute the primary material of man: *biology, the social, the unconscious.* This is what confronts the law, as the occidental version of a normative logic of the living—of *life endowed with speech.* By the expression *bond of law* I mean therefore the part of the juridical system that binds these elements, in order to institute the subject. Without apprehending the aspect of materiality with which the practices of law

10. I have already evoked this question of convertibility of normative systems in *Leçons VI. Les Enfants du Texte, supra* note 10, at 272.

are concerned, it is not possible to understand this matter of bonding. But how is it possible to situate materiality itself in order to study it from the perspective of the institutional montages necessary to subjective life?

If one should want to reflect incidentally on the question of a Third not directly accessible to us in the manner of a scientifically observable phenomenon, one would first have to consider what science, by its very method and objective, has overturned: the category of the tragic, in the sense of the oedipal drama, an object of study central to psychoanalysis, thus a notion oriented toward a domain where the most essential kind of questioning takes root and bears a consequence. The domain of the oedipal tragedy that served as Freud's guide made visible the unconscious foundation of symbolic life: *incest with the mother and the murder of the father.* These unconscious stakes of representation of the subject can be apprehended in a privileged manner in *sexual casuistry,* such as has actually developed in occidental culture, in that interesting field of transsexualism. I will start off with a case judged in America during the course of the 1980s, worthy of being considered as a *textbook case,* because it puts into focus the oedipal tragedy with which the jurists are preoccupied, as interpreters of the symbolic structures of the montages.

The case, decided in Canada, is the following.[11] It concerned an adolescent boy who lived from an early age with his divorced mother, who was his guardian. Since the deposition of the father's parental authority was obtained by the mother, the infant carried her name. Soon, the judgment says, the mother, by means of surgery, "had taken on the appearance of the masculine sex"[12] and was granted a change of name. Having thus modified his civil status, the mother introduced an appeal to adopt the infant as a father, in order to give him a birth certificate that conformed to the new identity of his parent. The child had consented to this adoption. Sustained by the conclusions of expert psychiatrists familiar with the proceeding, the tribunal approved the appeal. One argument rendered in the judgment is worth noting: "according to the infant himself, as corroborated by a social worker, for the infant, his mother has died; he is in mourning."[13]

11. Judgment of March 31, 1988, Droit de la Famille—480, [1988] Recueil de Jurisprudence du Québec [R.J.Q.] 1138.

12. "[L]ui donnet maintenant l'apparence du sexe masculin." *Id.* at 1139.

13. "Selon l'enfant lui-même, corroberé en cela par le travailleur social, pour l'enfant, sa mère est morte; il en a fait son deuil." *Id.* at 1140.

Recognition by law of a change of sex has just received the support of the European Court of Human Rights.[14] Without weighing all the consequences attached to this recognition as to the status of persons or its theoretical implications for the question of the fate of the bisexual elements discovered by psychoanalysis in each subject, the dissenting judges did not hesitate to state their specific objections,[15] insufficient as they were at the level of principle. The political notoriety of the new doctrine on transsexualism (its reattachment to the rights of man) exposes the extent of the problem, specifically on the anthropological grounds of a bond between the unconscious, the biological, and the social in the representation of the subject's sex: has occidental culture given up thinking about the structure of the Interdiction and, consequently, given up on introducing the subject to the institution of the limit? What will the foreseeable effects be of such a renunciation with regard to generations yet to come, thus withdrawn from the symbolic law, hitherto considered by humanity as the support of the life of the species?

One such mode of interrogation postulates that the montages of the Third who founds and of the law should be reattached to a wider questioning, making apparent what in my *Lessons* I have designated by the following formula, inspired by the material of interpretation at our disposal by virtue of psychoanalysis: *the symbolic determinism of the speaking animal.* This means that the question of sex does not refer only to a biological given, but to a complex textual construction, called, for this reason, symbolic, and whose disturbance or deviation, whether social, or by virtue of familial pathology, produces devastating effects on subjective representation. Symbolic determinism signifies, in the case of the Canadian decision, *a death scene, not physical, but symbolic,* of the young boy, deprived of the institution of the representation of the parental couple—in Freudian terms, cut off from *the original scene* [*la scène primitive*], out of which each subject, boy or girl, constructs his relation to sexuality on the basis of an unconscious representation, that

14. *See* B. v. France, 232 Eur. Ct. H.R. (ser. A) (1992).

15. One of the dissenting judges, manifestly ignorant of the relevant case law [*jurisprudence*], emphasized the most pertinent objection in the following form: in an action by a natural child for the right to search for his father, since after his birth the man who had engendered him will have been operated on for a change of sex and will have obtained rectification from the civil state, this infant will claim that a woman be recognized as his father. *Id.* at 62.

is to say, by elaborating his relation to images of the mother and the father, images instituted by law and by culture. When one ascribes them to the unconscious foundations of subjective life, the successive demands of the mother in the Canadian case—demands endorsed by the judges—make sense: this woman, entering maternity biologically and claiming paternity as well, does not *subjectively* recognize any limit or order of places of discourse; in oedipal terms, this ex-mother becomes a new father, set off unconsciously against his son: here again we only ever have the fundamental fantasms—incest with the mother and murder of the father. Thus the fact that these fundamental fantasms, instead of being juggled and played out humanly in the name of an inaccessible norm instituting a separation from the representation of being whole, finds itself played to the limit, overturning the anthropological function of law. This fact gives the sentence of adoption the sense of a coalition of the tribunal and the mother, a coalition whose symbolic stake is the infant, but which in fact is conducted, managed, orchestrated against the very principle [*principe*] of a limit, that is to say, against the juridically instituted montages of the Totem and the Taboo in occidental culture. In accord with this jurisprudential hypothesis, the law has become the discourse of destruction of the symbolic life of the child. Is this then what new ultramodern culture wants to attack: the montages of Interdiction, necessary for reproduction in a space of speech? Certainly not. But the gravity of what is at work here, unsuspected by biomedical technology, by the positivist propaganda of science, by the invitations of the surgical marketplace, and by our democratic ideals themselves, should inform a critique that owns up to these matters, that is to say, a critique concerned with the problem of the foundation which is devoid of religiosity or reactionary stupidity. At what intellectual cost is this possible?

To respond: at the price of thought, an effort of thought that takes account of the atomic bond of law by way of a general reflection on humanity's elaboration of genealogical structures. In the Occident, we do not have a choice. The secularization of our societies and the prevalence of scientific reasoning in our methods of interrogating life make us discontented with vague discussions of the ethics of modern liberty, but in order to grasp the articulation between the institutional dimension and subjective autonomy, we must take up the question of symbolic determinism, which is also the indelible question of Interdiction. The contribution of psychoanalysis may be outlined, yet it is difficult to integrate, because of this notion of the unconscious that seems to contradict the whole idea of knowledge. How is it possible to understand a human subject, of whatever sex, that is to say, *the child of one sex and of the other sex,* in accord with the saying received in Europe through Roman law (*filius utriusque sexus*), in the grip of unconscious representations of incest and of murder, in the oedipal sense of these two terms, and how is it possible to translate this into a mode of knowledge assimilable as a theory outside of the psychoanalytic field proper? A reworking is essential because the progress of the sciences of life is turned against life, and the normativity that serves as the guarantor of symbolic life is dynamited from within by an erroneous vision that excludes from its field the order of causality discovered by Freud.

In order to overcome the inherent difficulties of the kind of questioning that is wanting, particularly so as to come to distinguish clearly between the distinct levels at which the sciences—experimental or positive—and psychoanalysis are located, and in the same step to understand all at once that the principle of Reason in the genealogical construction of the subject does not coincide with scientific Reason, and that the law is a masterpiece of the social scaffolding of reason, jurists dispose of a trump, their knowledge of the state, guarantor of the civil rights of persons and thus of rules for human reproduction. The power of the state, *in a civilization of civil law,* is the historic relay of religious power; it exercises the essential anthropological function traditionally put in the hands of religions, namely, the power to divide words and things. It is this power that authorizes it to preside over a casuistry of sex as the Third who separates, the social Hermes, inventor of normative categories for the two sexes and guarantor of interpretations, in other words, the *genealogical Third guarantor of filiations.* A work that followed the development of a Canadian criminal case[16] marked my interest in relating the problematic of the Interdiction and its juridical translations to the history of religious interpretations, in the first instance those figuring in the commentaries on the celebrated *Aqedah* in the rabbinical tradition. From a theoretical perspective, one can say that the binding [*ligature*] of Isaac by his father Abraham is a prototypical metaphor and constitutes the best introduction—considering the inexhaustibility of classical thought—to the problematic of normative struc-

16. An attempt perpetrated in the vicinity of the National Assembly of Quebec, and that ended in three deaths. I have given an account of this case in Pierre Legendre, *Leçons VIII. Le Crime du Caporal Lortie. Traité sur le Père* (1989).

ture for jurists today; this structure is finally nothing other than the work of *the genealogical binding* of the subject. One can grasp there the very basis of the question of the Interdiction: the question of staging the sacrificial stake of the reproduction of a subject (what psychoanalysis designates by the expression *symbolic castration*) and of translating into normative terms the imperative of the limit. On this basis, I have shown in the course of my *Lessons* the importance, in European culture, of juridical inventions transmitted by Christianity across this sacrificial terrain and particularly of the devices generated by the classical law of penitence.[17]

*The other dimension of law* is therefore that dimension that, by taking into account the biological and social elements of subjectivity, forces us to consider the function of the institution as a bond, which integrates the elements of subjectivity, the subject and its unconscious representations. What follows is a change of perspective on the role of the sciences in law, on the notion of society as such, and on the concept of the person itself. Psychoanalysis is a knowledge of the subject and comes to modify the occidental idea of how we conjure ourselves from the power to institute and from its relation to the question *"what is life?"*

From the perspective opened up through this reflection, what is being rethought is not only the foundation of law and its anthropological design, but psychoanalysis itself. The juridical tradition, such as it has been reorganized since the Middle Ages, starting with the Revolution of the interpreter (of which my works have, elsewhere, shown the numerous philosophical implications), bears exquisite indications of the *mise en scène* of the Totem and the modern practices that produce normative effects, those that Freud designated by a term borrowed from ethnology, the Taboo. We can recognize this huge problematic in the scholastic conceptions developed by the Romano-canonic tradition around the theme of the Father, more specifically *the image of the substance of the father* [*paternae imago substantiae*], which is equivalent to the totemic principle in European civilization, which was defined in this construction in anticipation of the advent of the industrial system. What then is this substance of the father in terms of the logic of the symbolic, for psychoanalysis? It is a matter of who founds, for every sub-

17. What has become of penitential power in the era of secularized states? It is possible to understand this from the notion of the *jurisdiction of the subject. See Leçons VI. Les Enfants du Texte, supra* note 10, at 370.

ject, the entrance into speech, the separation from his own narcissistic image, the socialization of the drives that binds the unconscious representations of incest and murder. The image of the substance of the father, inscribed in the principle of the juridical montages, has the sense of instituting the representation of pure alterity, giving consistency to the founding discourse by representing the Other as a concept, in order to spread the effects of the Interdiction, that is to say, juridically organized effects. In spite of the important clarifications of the problematic of the Other brought to France by Lacan, Lacan himself was not prepared to work out all the essential implications for the study of the principle of alterity. Psychoanalysts continue in general to ignore the dimension of institutionality, so important for the clinical practice of psychoanalysis, as I have tried to show in my many refrains these past years, notably on the occasion of casuistic works carried out by the Laboratory that I have founded.[18]

A difficulty thus persists in forcing the admission of the inevitable relation between the field of law and that of psychoanalysis. In light of the questions that I have raised, we still live in the wake of a Cartesian vision of man "master and possessor of nature," a vision that returns us to certitude, to the concept of the *subject of certitude,* to the Cartesian *cogito.* In spite of the decay [*caducité*] of such a position, what may be thought remains an institutional matter, still bound to a subject of discourse which is posited as disconnected from juridical normativity, in the collective representation of what is called thinking. Taking up again the formula of a commentary on Descartes, I would say that the Cartesian subject, to which in fact we remain attached, is an *insular subject,* who ends by thinking himself master and possessor of himself whom he believes to be a being of nature, that is to say, who thinks of himself as removed from any chastening [*continent*]—from the chastening of the Interdiction and the institution in general. Under these conditions, relating psychoanalysis and law is a difficult enterprise. It provokes skepticism, at the same time that the intense distress of new generations would seem to force, to push us there, above all because that rapport opens up such a huge horizon of thought.

It seems to me that a reflection on the juridical phenomenon and its relation to the Freudian discovery—a discovery insufficiently understood at all the different levels of this palimpsest that is ultramodern

18. European Laboratory for the Study of Filiation.

culture—ought to be recast on a scale adapted to the historical failures lived out in the contemporary Occident, and recast in a persuasive fashion. My work is comparable to the disturbance introduced by Cubism in painting at the beginning of our century. Cubism was a revolution of thought, in the sense that it accomplished an undoing [*defaite*] of the object. It conquered the belief in the imperialism of appearances, as the standard for painting the hidden face of the object. That was, at the time, considered to be a violation of logic, but it was followed by a renewal of thought in painting. Thus, I work in my studio in France, so as to effect, in our field, such an undoing of the object, messenger of a thought on the horizon [*hauteur*] of our era.

*Chapter 8*

# Sons of the Writ, Sons of Wrath: Pierre Legendre's Critique of Rational Law-Giving

*Anton Schütz*

By nature we have been sons of wrath, according to a thoroughly explored passage of Pauline theology.[1] I should like to put this text to a test. My purpose in this essay is to view the work of a twentieth-century Sorbonne professor of law through the lens of this Pauline text. Clearly, such a procedure assumes some sort of extraordinary similarity of preoccupation as between these two thinkers. It assumes that the semantic components, *filius* and *ira,* and the question of their relationship are equally crucial to both figures: to the fervent apostle and epistolographer who happened to have served as an appointed persecutor of Christians before being blinded by a voice from heaven and—despite two millennia—the law professor who happens to be at the same time a practicing psychoanalyst. The first thesis of this essay is therefore that the problem of being *filii irae,* or sons of wrath, is common both to Paul of Tarsus and to Pierre Legendre. This status as children of wrath is their common problem, the problem they share, as adversaries always share the problem to which they give opposed solutions. The thesis, in other words, is that Legendre, like Paul, is both dependent on and subject to the grand European theme of a mankind composed of *sons of wrath.*

In section I, I give some biographical data, remarks on style and a basic, if fragmentary, introduction to the link that Legendre establishes between the psychoanalytic *discovery* of the unconscious and legal his-

1. "[E]ramus natura filii irae." *Ephesians* 2:3.

tory, conceived as a history of *reference* to the unconscious. In section II, I try to place Legendre's work in the context of the mainstream of contemporary critical legal work. In section III, I reconstruct the antinomic relation between the teaching of the Apostle Paul and Legendre. Finally, in section IV, I outline the relationship between Legendre's notions of origin and filiation, and Freud's concept of the original scene.

## *I*

First of all, let us make the necessary introductions. Who is Pierre Legendre? Take an expert on postcolonial politics in French-speaking Africa, who directed a United Nations program before leaving it with *éclat*—since then denouncing the complicity of French and other international development strategies in the technocratic exploitation of the Third World. Take a scholar of extraordinary erudition in matters of medieval law, both canon and Roman, a specialist in the history of textual transmission, to whom numerous manuscripts owe their discovery and their identification.[2] Take a psychoanalyst who shared a close intellectual exchange and personal relationship with Jacques Lacan through the decisive years of classical Lacanian theory formation, and yet who has no link with Lacan's followers and posthumous pupils.[3] Add to this the fact that Legendre is not a former student of the *École Normale Supérieure,* one of Napoléon's "*Grandes Écoles,*" unlike Foucault, Bourdieu, and many others. Add the fact that he fails—for this and other reasons—to appear as a typical representative of what, at least at a distance, seems to be *the* "Parisian intellectual scene" and that, by more global standards, he also fails to display some of the essential characteristics of a pure, maybe even of a "real," legal academic. This double failure, you might suggest, cannot be thought of as being a felony in itself. What, however, if you learn that the subject, besides his many titles to academic exterritoriality, teaches Law at the Sorbonne and holds offices in other high-ranking institutions closely linked to the French national identity? What if, furthermore, you learn of a teaching devoted not so much to discovering law's truth in relation to the con-

2. Six of those contributions are assembled in the first part of the volume, Pierre Legendre, *Ecrits juridiques du Moyen Age occidental* (1988).

3. *See* Pierre Legendre, "La Phalla-cieuse: Le roman du feminin dans le Texte occidental," in Armando Verdiglione, *La Jouissance et la loi* 9–31 (1976).

duct of human affairs, but rather to the truth about law? In more precise terms, Legendre's is a truth owed to the most disparate and arcane of sources: It is a truth that comes from obscure glossators, from the law on transsexualism, elaborated in epochs never taught about in regular law courses; a truth that is instanced in the *Magic Flute*, in the paintings of Ernst, Dalí, and Magritte, and a truth owed to the thoroughly and classically unlawful, legal-order-subverting discipline of psychoanalysis. Yet psychoanalysis, in Legendre's view, is merely an "accident in the history of thought."[4] Now ask whether or not this teaching constitutes an abuse of public funds of goodwill. Whatever the answer, you won't be alone.

In fact, Legendre not only teaches Public Law at the Sorbonne, he is also the author of what is considered to be the indispensable manual of modern French administrative history for students of Law.[5] Administrative law, the Sorbonne, Africa, opposition to neocolonialism, Freud and Lacan, medieval legal manuscripts: how can the conditions of the copossibility of these diverging data be determined?

As an initial hypothesis, it might be suggested that Legendre, right from the beginning of his academic *and* of his psychoanalytic career, found himself in a situation equally as improbable as rare: the situation, neither of the insider nor of the outsider, but rather of what would be an insider *en rupture de ban*, an outlawed insider. It is the position of one who, rather than suspending his judgment in all spheres but one, lays claim to a range of competence that exceeds what, technically speaking, is his professional competence or specialism. It is the position of one who has escaped, or pretends to have escaped, from specialization or "professional reduction." It is the position of one who is an insider, but an insider in the archetypically "dangerous" position—an insider with more than one set of corporate ethics and with no exclusive subjection to anyone. In what has been Legendre's position,

4. *See* Pierre Legendre, *Leçons V: Un accident de la pensée: la psychanalyse* (forthcoming).

5. Pierre Legendre, *L'Administration, du XVIII$^e$ siècle à nos jours* (1969). An augmented new edition of this study has been published as Pierre Legendre, *Trésor historique de l'Etat en France: L'Administration classique* (1992). For anyone interested in what Legendre calls the "capital Administration" (*l'Administration majuscule*), but suffering from a specific linguistic weakness in French, let it be noted that there exists an Italian translation of *L'Administration*, under the title Pierre Legendre, *Stato e Società in Francia: Dallo Stato paterno allo Stato-Providenza: storia del amministrazione dal 1750 ai nostri giorni* (1978).

right from his beginnings, we can therefore recognize the classic sulphur of institutional dissidence—the position of the "former member," of the apostate who has left both the legal academy and the psychoanalytic establishment. In short, notwithstanding the limits of both of his professional appointments, he remains true to the transdisciplinary scope of the subject of human subjectivity. As a law professor, no less than as an analyst, Legendre has indeed successfully refused to abnegate his claim to judgment.

To conclude this initial hypothesis: it seems that Legendre owes his exceptional role as an observer of institutional facts to personal experience. His experience has been acquired "on site," far from Paris, and appears to be equally exceptional among academic lawyers and psychoanalysts. There is a relation between Legendre as a legal academic and as a psychoanalyst to what he was able to witness during his African years, that can appropriately be described as one of overdetermination. This experience, however, concerns not so much a positive apprenticeship in some remaining fragments of "African culture," but rather a perception of the way in which the Western model of humanity, and of postcolonial politics, could be observed in action, a model that, deaf to the contact with Otherness, consists of pursuing the export of Western economic and, particularly, institutional models. It is an experience of the ever-extending boundaries of what Legendre would later term *Western Humanity.* The Northern and, in particular, the Western world's African performance is, from Legendre's viewpoint, the rigorous and undeniable proof of what occidental inventions—social, organizational, ideological, technological, and scientific—are about. It is the proof that they are tantamount to an enterprise, unavowed and unavowable, unconscious and concealed (in particular, by utilitarian "reason-finding"), for conquering the world, for despoiling non-Western subjectivities, for deprecating the other extant institutional models of humanity, and for replacing them with the best-performing, output-oriented, rationalized and ever-rationalizing Western model itself. In short, there is, at the very beginning of Legendre's psychoanalytic and legal reflections, an experience of the kind you never succeed in overcoming: the testimony of a witness of the Western model of humanity in action—an experience, indeed, of the traumatic kind. It is also a gladly and consciously endorsed one. Unhesitatingly, Legendre, when asked about his "background," prefers to present himself as a disciple less of Lacan than of another close relation, Hampate Bâ, the illustrious sage and politician some of whose sayings—like: "A dying old man, in my country, is a library ablaze"—have eventually become classical references among Africanists.

In the academic sphere, Legendre first attracted attention with his doctoral thesis on legal history. He took as his subject the then largely unexplored question of the bonds that link the legal order of the medieval Church to the heritage of classical Roman law as codified by Justinian. These bonds were interpreted as unambiguously expressive of a one-way dependency. Legendre, who at this time was just preparing his doctorate, defined the relationship of Roman law to the legislation of the Church neither genealogically, by referring to questions of influence and origin, nor agonistically, by referring to the evolutionary "victory" of one legal corpus or tradition over others, nor by reference to the scenario of an "absorption" due to quantitative superiority. Rather he defined them in blunt terms taken from the semantics of sexual possession, or *jouissance,* namely as "penetration." This mode of expression appeared far off academic limits.[6] If one looks more closely at the totality of Legendre's work, one finds however that the reference to penetration is only the first in a series of shocking predicates attached to venerable institutions.[7]

On a general level, what distinguishes Legendre's ambition of vocalizing the sources of a millennium of commentaries on European institutions from current mainstream academic textual exegesis is the frontal directness of his interpretations: specifically, in the candor of understanding and association, and in the extraordinary humor required to dare to use—while dealing with matters buried in legal archives—a direct and always either sensuously appealing or sensuously aggressive,[8] sometimes hyperbolic, sometimes ultraexplicit, style of formulation. For example, consider the following titles: *The Beloved*

6. *See* Pierre Legendre, *La pénétration du droit romain dans le droit canonique classique* (1964).

7. Note however that, at other times, Legendre understands thoughtlessness as a necessary and, thus, irreproachable ingredient of the functioning of legal institutions at large. Other authors, facing legal problems in a less subjective and, at the same time, in a more "apologetic" manner, talk about law's redundancy, as about a necessary and fruitful technical device. Where Legendre doubts the reality of anything like legal thoughts, or thinking lawyers, functionalists suspend this question and prefer to speak of the steady work of "a stream of reassurances." *See* Martin Shapiro, "Toward a Theory of Stare Decisis," 1 *J. Legal Stud.* 125, 132 (1972); Niklas Luhmann, *Das Recht der Gesellschaft* 370–71 (1993).

*Censor: An Essay on Dogmatic Order;*[9] *The Joy of Power: A Treatise on Patriotic Bureaucracy;*[10] *The Passion To Be Another, Study for Dancing;*[11] *Poetic Phrases Run Astray from the Text: Lessons on Industrial Communication;*[12] *Truth's Empire: An Introduction to the Dogmatic Space of Industrialism;*[13] *The Priceless Object of Transmission: A Study of the Genealogical Principle in the Occident;*[14] *God's Political Desire: Study on the Scaffold of the State and of the Law;*[15] and *Caporal Lortie's Crime: A Treatise on The Father.*[16]

These title-phrases are expressive of at least two parallel preoccupations. On the one hand, there emerges a systematic tendency in favor of intrinsically antirrhetical, tension-laden, oxymoronic expressions. One might have in mind an electrotechnical device, which short-circuits the poles of conscious and unconscious that divide the human subject, thus producing an explosive spark. Power and *jouissance* are thereby fused in a single title-phrase, as are censorship and love, patriotism and bureaucracy, poetry and "industrial communication," and, at another level, truth and dogmatics, God and Desire, Law/State and "Scaffold": a cruel type of enlightenment. Creating a whole new "Theatre of Cruelty"—a legal theatre of legal cruelty, obtained by bending the official language of the law to its other end, to the language of its silenced subject. As long as they remain silent, the silent subject's law and law's language constantly work on each other. However, the tech-

8. See, for example, the repeated reference to the task of a "sensuous apprehension of thought," in an expression attributed to T. S. Eliot. Pierre Legendre, *Leçons II: L'Empire de la Vérité: Introduction aux espaces dogmatiques industriels* (1983).

9. Pierre Legendre, *L'amour du censeur: Essai sur l'ordre dogmatique* (1974).

10. Pierre Legendre, *Jouir du pouvoir: Traité sur la bureaucratie patriote* (1976).

11. Pierre Legendre, *La Passion d'être un autre: Étude pour la danse* (1978).

12. Pierre Legendre, *Paroles Poetiques échappées du texte: Leçons sur la communication industrielle* (1982).

13. Legendre, *Leçons II, supra* note 8.

14. Pierre Legendre, *Leçons IV: L'inestimable objet de la transmission: Étude sur le principe généalogique en Occident* 51 (1985).

15. Pierre Legendre, *Leçons VII: Le désir politique de Dieu: Étude sur les montages de l'État et du Droit* 70, 186 (1988).

16. Pierre Legendre, *Leçons VIII: Le crime du caporal Lortie: Traité sur le Père* 21, 136 (1989). In order to complete the list of the *Leçons,* add to it: Pierre Legendre, *Leçons IV, suite: Le dossier occidental de la parenté* (1988); Pierre Legendre, *Leçons IV, suite 2, Filiation: Fondement généalogique de la psychanalyse* (1990); and Pierre Legendre, *Leçons VI: Les enfants du texte: Étude sur la fonction parentale des États* (1992). *See* Pierre Legendre, *Leçons III: Dieu au miroir: Etude sur l'institution des images* (1994).

nique of short-circuiting intimate and unconscious subjective values with the unremitting "master-voice" of the law is remarkable also from another point of view, namely by its kinship to a particular tradition and practice of supervision: spiritual *direction-de-conscience,* or the intimate care of the subject's relationship to itself. One of the foremost strategies of a director of conscience, as of his heirs, the personal adviser, and the business consultant, is the exigency that the "blame" must be put on the subject, on the subjected individual or the subjected enterprise. There is no hope of change without this indispensable move that endows the self with responsibility. Making the subject understand its own contributions to what it is suffering from is the only possible way out. Thus, the subject is told that it is the self that fosters its own censor, and that benefits from its own ever-unrequited love (*The Beloved Censor*); it is told that power, if corrupting, also leads ceaselessly to *jouissance* (*The Joy of Power*); it is told that passion, far from being the individual's last and unalienable property, lies always and already in the hand of institutions that use it for their own ends—ends devoid of the slightest "functional" relationship to the passionate individual (*The Passion to be Another*); that the discourse of those indifference-fraught institutions—the legal, administrative, and political—is nonetheless interwoven by elements of unwitting subjectivity, an often almost artistic meaningfulness (*Poetic Phrases Run Astray from the Text*); it is told that modern or "ultra-modern"[17] society, while pretending to be utilitarian, value-free, maximization-oriented, science-referred, that is, *industrial,* in its forms of social and subjective reproduction, nevertheless bears within itself an irreducible core of ritual and myth, the very absolutist adhesions that anthropologists tend to see only in *other* cultures (*Truth's Empire*); the subject is told further that rationality, secularization, and disenchantment have not been able to kill off "the monumental question of the structure" where, by *structure,* reference is made to the institutional artifices of parenthood, and particularly paternity (*The Priceless Object of Transmission*); that the fundamentalism of *ratio scripta*—written Reason, in short Roman legal culture—still endows the West with its answer to "the question no society can do without: Why laws?" (*God's Political Desire*); and finally, that murder can be understood as the ultimate act of someone seeking words, that is "real" words, words that will hold good (*Caporal Lortie's Crime*).

17. *See* Legendre, *Leçons VI, supra* note 16.

## *II*

But, on the other hand, what is immediately expressed in these titles is the author's own passion for the task of finding ultimate words, limit words, powerful enough to change the real. The specific *real* that ought to be changed is that of the ongoing destruction of human subjectivity through the science-induced elimination of the *capital Reference.* By *capital Reference* Legendre refers to the pivotal text of a particular symbolic order, and to the ultimate (factually and historically existent) source of signification that credits a particular institutional system with its coherence.[18] His titles show Legendre himself as being the first witness to this idea, namely as a subject ceaselessly referring to the *Référence.* What is expressed through the heavy wording of these titles is the desire to *occupy* the symbolic, the need to render homage to the foremost symbolic power position, the will to "say the words," to name what has to be named. Ultimately, the heavy words should force the silent violence of speechless normalization to avow itself and, in so doing, to destroy itself. The technique is not new. Of great things, as Nietzsche wrote in his notebook, one should not speak, or else speak greatly. Legendre, indeed, chooses "great," heavy signifiers rather than "innocent," transparent signifiers lacking quality. He projects factually decisive or "influential" signifieds. He chooses great, heavy signifiers, rather than any that would be recommended by analytic finesse or that would bear any obvious or direct relationship to their signifieds. It is consistent with this signifier-centered textual strategy that words able to signify are preferred to words able to explain—not a common preference among academic law teachers but, by Legendre, a deliberate and important one, given that he considers what is generally called *explanation* as merely some kind of side-effect of a suspect, questionable, and ambiguous enterprise. The author of the phrase "the more we can explain, the more we are innocent" views legal argumentation as an enterprise based on extorting consent in return for reasons. Consciously or not, avowedly or not, but in any case guided by what is recognizable as a genuine instance of lawyer's instinct, he follows in this respect the ascendancy that rhetoric exerted, since time immemorial, over the legal practitioner. For Legendre, arguments are measured by their weight rather than by their epistemological credentials or propo-

18. *See* Legendre, *Leçons IV, supra* note 16.

sitional consistency. That is to say, arguments are measured by their anticipated or proven effects, by the influence they attain if exposed to an audience (their public). This professor of public law deliberately challenges the academic order of discourse by systematically preferring the efficacy of power-laden formulas to their abstract proposition—or truth-content. He systematically opts in favor of "the obscure object of desire"—to quote a title of Buñuel, one of Legendre's favorite film directors—and against the inert and unappealing subjectivity that wittingly or unwittingly marks the object of scientific knowledge.[19]

This heretical attitude—an aspect of what Legendre conversationally would call his personal "*style barbaroïde*"—amounts roughly to a proposition like: words count more than thoughts, at least (though far from only) in the legal domain. What is original about this predilection for rhetoric—a predilection widely shared today among legal academics—is the fact that, in the genealogy of Legendre's work, and quite contrary to what might be expected, there is no trace of any inspiration gained through Nietzsche, and almost nothing of Heidegger. Legendre's rehabilitation of the signifier, his vindication of *le symbolique* to the profit of the history of legal institutions, is not undertaken in the name of freely suspended general ideas, however apt, and is not an application of philosophical truths to legal affairs, whatever their value or overriding interest. Legendre's inspiration is an immediate result of work done on the materials of the institutional archive. It is through the legal and religious archives that Legendre has come to terms with the inspiration, generated by the Lacanian interpretation of the Freudian hypothesis, that the unconscious is structured like a language.[20] Legendre's style is, thus, rhetoric-bound not for philosophical reasons and, maybe, not for any "reasons" at all: it is simply expressive of what constitutes, according to him, the only available identity of law and the only reality accessible to law. This reality lies within the subject and is

19. The idea that scientific knowledge fails to provide an effectively convincing subjective reason to *acquire* it, is probably one of the few basic continuities with the views of Jacques Lacan, see *Séminaire XX: Encore* (1975), with its now classical opposition against Aristotle's conception of a knowledge acquisition founded anthropologically, in some pulsional device, and against the derived, up to now widely university-official, ideology of a human craving for knowledge (*Wißtrieb*).

20. On the relationship of legal and psychoanalytical concerns, and on their common derivation from the notion of "dogmatics," see in particular the programmatic last chapter: "La fonction dogmatique et son unique dictionnaire," in Legendre, *L'amour du censeur, supra* note 9.

therefore open to its psychoanalytic *traversée.* The sole ambition of Legendre's "*barbaroïde*" style is, thus, to confront lawyers, and whoever else asks questions concerning or involving law, with the unexpected, but incomparably intense, psychoanalytic weight or undercurrent from which legal matters cannot be detached or abstracted. According to a twelfth-century text quoted in *L'Empire de la Vérité,* even the aforementioned weighty use of condensing formulas as titles becomes understandable as a device for polarizing attention, and for directing it toward the knot that binds the human subject to legal prescription.[21] One may add that it is precisely its legal autochthony that confers upon Legendre's work, whatever its marks of strangeness and idiosyncrasy, its monumental importance; unlike deconstruction, it does not apply a concept signed by philosophy. Consistent with certain recent psychoanalytic writings, but in opposition to academic legal writing at large, Legendre's books are about *the* Law. They refer concretely, sometimes mimetically, to the unequal and disquieting choreography of what Lacan, in one of his most ambiguous titles, termed the "*insistence of the letter in the unconscious.*"[22] They recognize, in an unending series of philological *trouvailles,* the mark of the letter's insistence in the letter of the Law.

The embeddedness of the legal phrase in the universe of rhetoric has in recent jurisprudence come to be more generally accepted among scholars.[23] This "embeddedness"—if that is not too weak a term—may be observed *in actu* in the titles of Legendre's work. It has been noted, however, that the efficiency of legal discourse is not just a matter of successfully inhabiting the procedures listed by the history of oratorical know-how,[24] and this, too, holds true in Legendre's case. Indeed, Legendre seems to have chosen a position firmly and equidistantly established at the junction of two impossibilities. He shares, as we have seen, the practitioner's preference for effective words, rather than the

21. Knots or, more precisely, nooses of law, according to Rogerius, "The Quaestiones super Institutis," *in Studies in the Glossators of The Roman Law* 133 (Hermann U. Kantorowicz and W. W. Buckland eds., 1938). For the text "*laqueis iuris innodata,*" *see* Legendre, *Leçons II, supra* note 8, at 135.

22. Despite the rendering of French *instance* by English *instance.*

23. *See* Theodor Vieweg, *Topik und Jurisprudenz* (1954); Costas Douzinas et al., *Postmodern Jurisprudence: The Law of Text in the Texts of Law* (1991).

24. See Peter Goodrich, "We Orators," 53 *Mod. L. Rev.* 546–63 (1990), about the reindoctrination of living law students with the "classical"—lawful, pretendedly "natural," in short, acceptable—rhetorics.

current theorist's ambition to achieve intelligible thoughts. Yet, at the same time, his ambition for justice goes well beyond the level of the exigencies facing either the practitioner, the conventional legal philosopher, or the theorist. This opens up another, deeper, perplexity between the alarming prospect of a humanity fascinated by words *and unable to face that fact*—thus "loving its censors" unwittingly (which means ferociously)—and the worrying tendency that would replace this type of verbally fascinated humanity with an order of wordless self-regulation, where censor and love, truth and passion, Otherness and desire, are equally absent; where there is no longer any question of transgression or prescription, and where the subject is deprived of any institutional support or *habitus.* Indeed, this "alarm" and this "anxiety" are both present in Legendre's work, even if the emphasis shifts progressively from the first to the second. The attitude of *alarm* corresponds to the energy and audacity of the earlier books, whereas, what seems predominant in the later work—essentially the *Leçons*—is an *anxiety* about the maintenance of the conditions of humanity.

Identifying Legendre as the exponent of a certain kind of enlightenment, that of making things understood through signification rather than through explanation, emphasizes the psychoanalytic dimension of his work. From a more literary angle, this question of "enlightenment" might be seen as a matter of style. In reality, Legendre's predilection for, or openness to, the lure of plerophoric formulations and "thinking through words," his inclination to symbolic plenitude—fullness of expression—is inseparable from the content of his writing, namely, legal history. Yet, on the other hand, this content itself appears as an example of what was termed, within the antique classification of genres, the *protreptic* style of writing, the aim of which was to persuade the reader to subscribe to a particular discipline, to commit himself to its study. Legendre's protreptical efforts are deployed in favor of the study of the legal history of the premodern, especially that of medieval Europe, whose largely handwritten and as yet largely unpublished records would, if appropriately used and understood, offer an incomparable stock of concrete and historically "legitimized" instructions regarding the efficiency of the symbolic order in its specifically Western development. According to Legendre, a systematic acknowledgement of the work of the medieval glossators is an indispensable antidote to the utilitarian misunderstanding and self-misunderstanding of law as a means of implementing political strategy. It is the obvious, yet largely ignored, defense against the conception of legal order as an infinitely malleable technology at the disposal of voluntaristic policymakers. It offers an outside to an empire of law, understood as the use of law as an arsenal of will-enforcement, an observing position situated beyond the *rationalité managériale* of the power-holding managers of the human flock.[25] Indeed, according to Legendre, medieval legal commentary is in some fashion the occidental way to the *civilization of power,* this term being understood in the sense it has been given by Norbert Elias[26] as ongoing process (but without accepting Elias's historical assessment, which focuses on postmedieval evolutions) and not as a directionally oriented process that would have some "starting point." The lawyers of the incipient academic legal culture of twelfth-century Europe—the exponents of the "revolution of the interpreter"[27]—have, according to Legendre, contributed more than modernity at large to this process of civilizing power.

According to Legendre, this history of the civilization of power is one to which the history of legal thought is intimately related, also from another point of view: essentially, legal institutions must be understood as being in charge of "instituting life."[28] This implies that law has to be considered a very special kind of *social fact;* it takes the form of a permanent collective effort to safeguard the decisive and indispensable, if "hidden," subjective conditions of social life: an effort of resistance, not against the violation of legal prescription as such,[29] but against the—mostly politically motivated—antilegal campaigns which show up repeatedly in European history. Taking as their pretext law's notorious

25. *See* Pierre Legendre, "Les juifs se livrent à des interprétations insensées: Expertise d'un texte," *in La psychoanalyse est-elle une histoire juive?* 93–113 (D. J. Rossial and A. Rossial eds., 1981).

26. Norbert Elias, *The Civilizing Process: The History of Manners* (Edmund Jephcott trans., 1978).

27. *See* Legendre, *Leçons VII, supra* note 15, at 105–14. The "revolution of the interpreter" is an answer, of course, to Harold Berman's "Papal revolution," to which it is the exact contemporary.

28. *See* Legendre, *Leçons IV, supra* note 16, at 349.

29. The Roman idea according to which a legal prescription vitally needs an efficient safeguard against possible violations—since its "violation" would be indistinguishable from its abolishment—has been reformed, if not replaced, ever since the content of legal prescriptions became a matter of politics, deliberation, and decision making. *See* Yan Thomas, "De la 'sanction' et de la 'sainteté' des lois à Rome: Remarques sur l'institution juridique de l'inviolabilité," 18 *Droits: Revue française de théorie juridique* 135–51 (1993); Anton Schütz, "L'immaculée conception de l'interprète et l'émergence du système juridique," *Droits* 24 (1994).

foundational weakness, they propose a new, superior, and more perfect way of instituting society. This aspiration to a new kind of societal order is a historical phenomenon. It may be described as *postlegality.* Two possibilities have proved to have a particular momentum: the faith-inspired aspiration to a new, postlegal, religious conception of the individual, as first exemplified by Paul, and the recent, social science–inspired aspiration to replace law's logic of normative insistence with the logic of learning and adaptation.[30] In Legendre's view, the relationship between these two programs of establishing postlegal conditions is one of profound continuity—even if those interested would probably reach a divergent or opposite conclusion. The common feature lies in the fact that both religious faith and scientific truth offer a type of "ruling" that can, in one perspective, do more and better than the law's ruling, namely, enforce a kind of submission that not only prohibits, but factually prevents transgression,[31] or at least promises to do so. From the point of view of obedience, the advantages of such nonlegal or postlegal rulings are obvious. Obedience would be based on more effective, less litigious, less conflict-generating, and hence also more "economical" foundations than those that support respect for fragile (transgressable) legal prescriptions. Factual impossibilities exclude transgressions, whereas legal prescriptions, interdictions, sayings, and writs in general cannot exclude anything. As distinct from factual impossibility, the Law is "human," in the precise sense that results from the fact that it is *in words:* Legendre defines man as the eloquent beast, *l'animal parlant.*

The efficacy of law, however, rests in the hands of its addressees. Being incapable of preventing transgression, the Law can do no more than authorize ways of reacting. In particular, the advantage of governing the human herd through the introduction of factual impossibilities, rather than through the means offered by law, would lie in bypassing exposure to contradiction and inconsistency, thereby avoiding the deep, indeed incurable, wounds inflicted on the body of the power-holding instance. Further, the problematic relation of statutes to judgments does not arise.[32] Outside the spheres of Law and Reference, one

30. *See* Jean Carbonnier, *Flexible droit: Pour une sociologie du droit sans rigueur* (7th ed. 1992).

31. *See* Legendre, *Leçons IV, supra* note 16, at 252.

32. For the Relationship of "impossible" and "forbidden," see Slavoj Žižek, *For They Know Not What They Do: Enjoyment as a Political Factor* (1990).

is dealing with a kind of power excluding the very possibility that its decrees might be transgressed; one is dealing with an omnipotence that resists human freedom or disobedience—what psychoanalysts of the Lacanian school term simply the "Real."[33] The Real, according to this conception, is the all-powerful sovereign—but its power is of an unusable and ineffective kind: it is a power that no subject can ever possess. Such scientific disciplines, however, as theology and technology are poised on the brink of a constant temptation to merge mimetically into the Real, gradually taking over and exerting its power. It is this theo-technological power, which is incontrovertible, speechless, and simply "effective," as opposed to the human or legal type of power, which is controvertible, talkative, and largely ineffective, that Legendre visualizes as utter barbarity, a human branch of cattle-breeding, or the butcher's way of approaching humanity. Technique and science are thus understood, contra Habermas, as much more than mere "ideology." They are considered against a very different background—that of the classical imagery of false majesty, the image of the unavowable inhuman power that constantly threatens to overpower human power, a power conceived as legally founded, nonperverted, speechbound, and, thus, open to opposition as much as to contradiction.

These are also the grounds of Legendre's opposition to the illusion of *neutrality* that accompanies a preoccupation with method and, in particular, the scientific and yet also theological criterion of "evidence." In a legal context, scientific proofs, explanations, and demonstrations officially serve a single and invariable goal: they support and reinforce the fragile instance of the prescribing word. By doing so, however, science, when operating as a legal reference, bypasses the law and tends to replace it, by turning rational procedures to the task of putting something incontrovertible, alias scientific truth, *in place* of the legal word. The legal citadel, besieged by critique and weakened by a chronic crisis of legitimacy, appeals to the army of science to lift the siege. Clearly, such helpful maneuvers, when successful, modify the statute of the helped one; law will hitherto have to "speak in the name of science," or rather leave the question of the name in which it speaks open—and thus avoid the "subject." Now, from a Freudian point of view, it is obvious that such a situation is likely to be extremely productive as to returns of the repressed, and one of Legendre's books is expressly

33. *Id.*

devoted to these returns. In *Poetic Phrases Run Astray from the Text: Lessons on Industrial Communication,* Legendre presents his collection of legal notions, formulations, and phrases unwittingly witnessing and avowing that which the law, by scientific standards, is bound to marginalize: the subjective nature of the legal word and its efficacy—Freudian "slips," as it were, but in the discourse of institutions, not of individuals.[34]

The idea of opposing legally founded and "officially" professed power to scientifically based power is a feature Legendre's work shares with others. One thinks, naturally, first of the authors of the Frankfurt School, twenty or thirty years ago. On the other hand, Legendre's blunt deconstruction of the law's necessarily "thoughtless" functioning, his denunciation of the legal order as an empty ritual, a pure pretention, and an incurably *"délirant"* derivation from the standard of a pure arbitrariness, would seem to draw it close to the more recent program of Critical Legal Studies. Yet what distinguishes his views from either is the unflinching homage to the endlessly obligatory instance of the Text; the capital Reference generates subjectivity, and that is seen as moderating or civilizing arbitrariness—as absorbing, as it were, power, and establishing, by doing so, the conditions of a humane life. Reading Legendre promises to create problems for the standard adept of the critical tradition(s) in at least one point: that legal problems cannot be resolved otherwise than by legal means.[35] Rather than aspiring to some exogenous simplifying solution or deliverance from a legal order understood as locus of the "Injustice of the Great-All" (to express this widespread critical feeling in Lautréamont's competent words), Legendre chooses to address himself to lawyers. He surmises that, if thoughtlessness is a necessary and irremovable attribute of the subject referring to the couple law/unconscious, this by no means excludes legal professionals, nor singles them out as particularly inapt to learn

34. *See* Legendre, *Paroles Poétiques, supra* note 12.

35. A thesis by which Legendre seems, if unwittingly, to share the Luhmannian idea of social agencies as autonomous and "self-substituting." According to this theory, a deficient legal solution must be replaced by a solution less deficient, but no less legal. This does not, of course, exclude the *possibility* that legal problems be treated by other, in particular military, economical, or political, and even scientific, means. History abounds with examples on this point. Rather, Luhmann's idea is of conceiving modern society as having attained a level and an importance of society-internal differentiation that makes any de-differentiation, any reuniting of functionally diverse jobs in one hand or decision-making agency, appear as a costly and disadvantageous outcome. *See* Niklas Luhmann, *Gesellschaft und andere selbst-substitutive Ordnungen, in* 3 *Soziologische Aufklärung* (1980).

about it. In reality, thanks to their notion of legal dogmatics, professional lawyers might well gain insight into this difficult relationship more easily than other people—they might more easily access what Legendre dubs "Inhuman Sciences." In other words, Legendre—in spite of what his impressive rhetoric might suggest—does not share in the habit of dragging the legal order before the tribunal of universal conscience, of civic or public opinion. If, as I would like to advocate, Legendre's work is to be understood as an enterprise of legal enlightenment, it is not an enlightenment of the "direct" kind, where the light, illuminating/eliminating darkness, is content to take the place of darknesses. It is an enlightenment of the "after" kind rather than of the "instead" kind, an enlightenment less oriented toward the replacement of existing structures than toward the coexistence of structures with time—time yet to come. Legendre shares this approach with psychoanalysis, deconstruction, and second-order observation—postmodern enterprises equally devoid of the hope of eliminating what they are illuminating, that is, respectively, the repressed unconscious of the analyzed person,[36] the effects of presence on the deconstructed text,[37] and the observation of the observed observer.[38]

As can be observed in any of these three cases, the postmodern transition from the "instead" to the "after" species of enlightenment implies a shift in the public. From the indefinite, generic addressee *mankind,* it melts down to *those concerned,* a set of persons sharing, for reasons tautologically given—what is called "their" reasons—a specific type of interest. As for Legendre, he addresses himself to "lawyers" or, at least, to people dealing with the legal sphere. This is also the point where Legendre too pulls out from the line of what Foucault defined as the distinctive feature of the "classical intellectual." From Voltaire to Sartre, the classical intellectual's characteristic gesture is that of proclaiming, of publishing and bringing to knowledge, a disagreement, a complaint or *gravamen,* generally one concerned with a case of abuse of power. The postclassical intellectual, aware of the fact that attention is the most precious, the most searched-for and, thus, the least available

36. According to Lacan's late works, psychoanalysis no longer aspires to eliminate the symptom. *See* Žižek, *supra* note 33.

37. Jacques Derrida, *Of Grammatology* (Gayatri C. Spivak trans., 1974).

38. Heinz von Foerster, *Observing Systems* (2d ed. 1984).

resource,[39] aims at a carefully selected target group. Legendre finds himself in a situation where the great idea of European political history, that of curing the observable deficiencies of the legal system by appeal to justice or some other metalegal instance—that is, the idea of presenting cases that the specialist tribunals could not adequately resolve to the spontaneous verdict of civil society—had become no more than an abstract ideal, an idea without application. In this new situation, professional decision making, however inadequate, cannot be replaced by public conscience. Remaining temptations make one think of Lacan's famous title ". . . or Worse."[40] Or, if one prefers, of a revised Dantean maxim: "you who enter in the Hell of Law, leave behind you any hope of redemption through an outside redeemer." Legendre—who is a keen observer of his public—addresses himself, as he says, to an "instructed" public, a public more and more composed of categories: judges, social workers, child therapists, and less and less of individuals.

Legendre's conception of the symbolic, his claim that the interplay of legal text, legal interpreters, and legal dogmatics is indispensable for the maintenance of the symbolic, might be considered, as also could certain facets of Lacan's theory, as an expression of political conservatism. One may even safely surmise (here again, in the absence of any explicit discussion) that not even the latest Habermas would agree with the outstanding importance Legendre attributes to the legal "writ," to Legendre's conception of "children of the Text." But the actual reason why Legendre's work—in the same way as Foucault's, in this respect—cannot be seen as consistent with most of the existing spectrum of critical theories, Frankfurt- or Harvard-based, lies in its distance from the optimistic imagery of communitarian consciousness of society, and in the resulting choice of its addressee, its public. It is this distance that makes his work incompatible with the classical conception of critical theory, and with the strategy of frontal enlightenment. Rather than having recourse to an ever-wider *forum justitiae,* he prefers to submit his observations of the legal order, its operations and effects, to the very people participating in this order, operating these operations, and contributing to these effects.

39. *See* Niklas Luhmann, *A Sociological Theory of Law* (Martin Albrow ed., Elizabeth King and Martin Albrow trans., 1985).

40. Jacques Lacan, " . . . ou pire" (Séminaire 17) (forthcoming).

## *III*

If the question of being sons of wrath can be considered as being common, and commonly central, to Paul and to Legendre, it is, with reference to Legendre, nevertheless obvious that *wrath* neither stands for the doctrine of humanity originating in sin, nor for the assertion of the evil substance of flesh, nor for the relationship to the day of the last judgment (*dies irae*). Rather, in order to specify the impact of *wrath* on human existence, to define what is at stake in a proposal to abolish or replace it, the crucial reference is not theological, but rather it is decidedly mundane. It is the relationship of parenthood: parenthood because it is the most uncompromising no-choice-relationship that can be imagined. This particular feature of excluding any rational (or other) choice is the precise reason why Paul referred to parenthood. Conversion, as proposed by Paul, is essentially change of kinship (*filiation*), conversion to another paternity. The strategy of Paul's argument is as simple as it is effective. It asks for only one thing to be accepted: that your substance—today, one would say, your social identity—is, specifically and exclusively, a function of whom you are *child* to. Identity, in other words, is a function of origin, and human subjectivity, an attribute of kinship.[41]

One might reply, thinking of racism or of sociobiology, of ethnic warfare or segregationism, that this is precisely what one does not want to grant—neither to Paul, nor to Legendre, nor to anybody else. But this argument is misleading—misleading, paradoxically, not so much in relation to Paul, whose already "antiracist" aim is to dismiss origins and to erase difference of filiation by means of the construction of a unifying divine paternity, but most certainly in relation to Legendre. Legendre challenges this proposal, because he sees the problem of subjectivity as a problem bound to one subject's personal symbolic commitment and, therefore, vigorously denies that the battle against racism and neotribalism can be won by refusing to take this commitment into account. In fact, there are not two, but at least three points of view involved. Conceiving "origin" as a kind of *measure,* either from a political perspective, with regard to what is shared among co-originary individuals, or from a scientific perspective, concerning what can be known, through its origin, about somebody's qualities or aptitudes, is

41. *See* Legendre, *Leçons IV, supra* note 16.

one thing. Proclaiming, as Paul does, that origin is a difference that does not *make* a difference, vindicating—in conformity with a whole strand of contemporary opinion, composed of unwitting Paulinists—and promoting the idea that origin has *to be treated* as indifferent in order to *become* indifferent through a self-fulfilling ruse, through the establishment of conditions that prevent the question of origins being of any consequence, is another thing. In the face of the traditional opposition of racism and antiracism, conceiving "origin" as a human self's unalterable source of specificity, as its capital "*Référence*" and as its base element in the institutional "scaffold of subjectivity," as does Legendre,[42] amounts to a third distinct conception. This third conception should not be confused with either of the other two, nor with antiracism, Pauline or current, and even less with racism. Why should this confusion be so tempting? The answer might lie in the fact that what is at stake in Legendre's institutional reading of original *différence* is not only racism or antiracism, but rather what is at issue is a whole conception of man, the typically Western "realistic mentality." This mentality is built on an ignorance of the symbolic order. But the symbolic order takes revenge for being ignored. Its revenge is that of forcing those that ignore it to establish the conditions in which their ignorance itself is, so to speak, symbolically correct. It is not difficult to define such conditions. The fact is that ignorance, to be correct, must in its turn be ignored. In order to be justifiably ignorant, to innocently enjoy one's "realism," one is obliged to silence and to wipe out the least sign or trace of the symbolic order, as "meaningful matter in the wrong place," to erase the instance and the insistence of the symbolic. It is clear that this collusion (functionally speaking: this mutual augmentation) of ignorance and correctness will be challenged by any word about the symbolic order. Any such proposition will open a wound in the order of things.

As against racism, origin and filiation can neither be shared, nor serve as a measure. As against antiracism, they cannot be successfully ignored either, for it is a *principe de différenciation.* Yet, if your identity depends on your filiation, then to be a *son of wrath* obviously describes an unbearable, unlivable, and disqualifying condition. In fact, Paul's phrase appears to be paradoxical—at least if it is not meant to be an

42. *See* Pierre Legendre, *Les maîtres de la Loi: Etude sur la fonction dogmatique en régime industriel, in* 38 *Annales: Économies-Sociétés-Civilisations,* 507 (1983), *reprinted in Écrits juridiques du Moyen Age occidental* 507, 527 (1988).

insult. If you happen to be a son to "wrath," and if your filiation is the one thing you cannot change, then what rationally is the use of my stating this inescapable fact? What is the point of thematizing an incurable handicap? If, on the other hand, what I intend is to suggest some action to you, why should I make reference to what is the only subject that remains insensible to your action, that is, to your filiation? Indeed, Paul's paradoxical statement makes sense only if granted with the thoroughly fictional credit that, in contradiction to what is commonly true about matters of origin in general and of filiation in particular, there *is* a possibility of choosing, of changing. Another, more desirable, filial relation does exist and is available. Look at *me,* says Paul, who—using the first person of the past tense—offers himself as an example: *eramus filii irae,* we *used to be* sons of wrath. Thus, in fact, the whole question is introduced in view of an already tested alternative, in view of a well-checked exit from the natural-human condition, out of the childship to "wrath." Paul's message is a missionary's message. It reads: We—Christ-confessing humanity—have already been emancipated, by way of God's child-loving child-sacrifice, from the fatal, the "natural" filiation, the filiation to wrath. Now, what about *you*?

That the untenable condition of filiation-to-wrath is limited, in Paul's setting, to *natural* man, to the yet unconverted, is the decisive argument—as well as, certainly, a powerful one from the point of view of conversion. Christian subjectivity, according to Ephesians 2:3 has been emancipated from its filiation to "wrath"—while Hebrews 7:3 emancipates Christian priesthood from filiation altogether, stating that God's priest is not only "fatherless" and "motherless," but even "without genealogy" (*agenealogetos*). What gives these texts their interest—a thoroughly extratheological, concrete, and *public* interest—is, once more, their close connection with subjects common to psychoanalysis and law.

While viewing institutions from the viewpoint of their history is, at least since Max Weber, a generally acknowledged and often repeated enterprise, Legendre offers the opposite project, namely a view of historical development from the perspective—in the coding and the "wording"—of institutions. Instead of the central concept of a *ratio* in linear, cumulative, or exponential, but in any case, constant progress, the leading idea here is the concept of the "offices" or instances of western powerholding. The interinstitutional "office" is defined through the internal hermeneutics and practices of institutions, or through their internal history. Legendre, indeed, conceives the history of power in the West as an internal history of Western power-holding institutions, a succession of symbols and intransigent references to emblems such as the Empire, Roman and trans-Roman, *Regnum Anglicum,* the Papacy, and a few more.[43] Through two millennia, power, or more exactly sovereignty—power as civilized and controlled through the regulative program of responsibility, through *ratio* and *officium*—has been administered in the name of such emblematic formulas. What Legendre offers is exactly this: a conception of the office of a global rationalization, accompanied by a historical account of the bimillenary pretension of Western Christianity to this "office."

Promoting rationalization is not a cost-free undertaking. It is accompanied both by a historical account of the history of reason and by a juridico-religious account of its justification. In particular, it cannot, logically, do without dispossessing genealogy of its ascendancy over the construction of human identity. This work of narrowing the role of filiation has been a decisive and powerful instrument of Western universalism.

Neither is the question of universalism limited to religion. Equality, social justice, and the other goals of an "open society" depend on conceptions of their universality and are far too well established, too habituated and ingrained, to be exposed successfully to a purely philosophical challenge or to nothing more than ethical or historical criticism. The expansiveness of the universalist pretension to credit and legitimacy cannot be left, in Legendre's account, to any single discipline. The point is as follows: Western *universalism* is, and will ever be, *western* universalism, an instrumentalized universalism, subservient to particularism, to the Western pretention of worldwide leadership, be it based on Empire, Papacy, on an order of international relations, on deterritorialized scientific knowledge, or on international management. It will invariably be a universalism signed with a *particular* signature—a part of the historical game of *western* rationality and a consequent strategy in favor of the worldwide expansion of one—the Western, rationalizing, scientific, pragmatic, or managerial—system of institutions, at the cost of all the other existing and historically possible institutional systems.

43. For a detailed and commented list of the legal and, in particular, canonical phrases upholding these pretentions, see *id.;* Žižek, *supra* note 33.

But Legendre takes these seemingly geopolitical perspectives to be just the outermost contours and consequences of what is taking place close to us, of what is taking place, indeed, with us and within us. This "other scene" secretly corresponding, secretly communicating with the scene of planetary politics, this "black market" or *tripot*[44] supplementing the official and avowed management of power through authorized power-holders, is located by Legendre in the specific way Western humanity arranges its relationship with the question of subjectivity. The idea to which Legendre here returns is the common notion that there might be such a thing as a Western paradigm of the relation between power, legitimacy, symbolic order, and the governance of subjectivity, of a specifically Western subjectivity.

This idea is neither new nor original—in fact, it is a widely shared, if frequently unconscious, assumption of social analysis. No perspective can any longer be either Western or non-Western, so that, whether Eurocentric or anti-Eurocentric, any answer to the question of the specific character of Western subjectivity is bound to invoke a trail of ideological suspicions. Legendre, however, does not content himself with generalities. Throughout its history, Legendre contends, Western humanity, far beyond a few profoundly—that is to say, subjectively—insignificant successes in the domain of rational problem solving, has committed a crime of mythological rather than merely anthropological dimensions. It has intervened in the relation between political power based upon enforcement and a power founded in an unconscious, and therefore ungovernable, adhesion. This interference has led Western government to alter the lived quality, the *symbolia,* of subjectivity and its institutional life. Succumbing constantly, deliberately, innocently to the lure of contingent profit, Western science and technology have established their utilitarian manner of a global administration of humanity. "The more we can explain, the more innocent we are"[45]—the more efficient, also, in our science of farming the human livestock (*administration bétaillère, science bétaillère*). The microprocessing of the subject on a scientific basis leads to a general conception of humanity as

44. *See* Pierre Legendre, *Les juifs se livrent à des interprétations insensées: Expertise d'un texte,* in La psychoanalyse est-elle une histoire juive? 93 (1981).

45. This often repeated and commented-on phrase comes from Pierre Legendre's *Conférences,* held at the *Ecole Pratique des Hautes Etudes, Section des Sciences Religieuses* during the 1970s and 1980s.

defined by classes of substitution and by aptitudes for producing measurable results.

The essential feature of this accusation, according to Legendre, is that there is a secret knot tying together these two apparently independently observable facts: namely, the society-wide universalization of Western rationality at a planetary level, and the cross-disciplinary program of losing or loosening the genealogical construction of identity at the level of the subject. Both of these phenomena are historical, not "anthropological," and both are coeval with the occidental *Sonderweg*. On the other hand, unlike more technical kinds of innovation, neither of the two tendencies can be seen as the achievement of any particular period. They are not even referable to the *longue durée* of contemporary French historiography; such a concept has proven to be an appropriate framework for the evolution of mentalities, life-styles, experiences, or other fields of emerging historical novelty. The Western campaign of worldwide rationalization and the fading away of filiation is—this is, in any case, the point made by Legendre—internal to the whole historical bloc of Western evolution. We are dealing not with "historical facts," but with the immemorial, with the transhistorical identity of institutions. The primary aspect of such identity is not historical contingency, but rather its institutional framework or structure. The unequal development of reason (*ratio*) and filiation is not a phenomenon ultimately reducible to "modernity" or to "Christianity" or any other singular category. And indeed, as to Western Christianity, both decisive political factors, namely Western rationalization and the breakdown of Western forms of filiation, bear the hallmark of one seminal programmatic thinker: Paul.

If you are addressing people with a particular message, and if your message is that human filiation does not make a difference, it is not surprising that you create a sect with a remarkable proselytizing zeal. This holds true in religion as well as in science. For Pauline Christianity, anybody who has decided to "abandon his father and his mother"—who has decided, in other words, to refuse to take his genealogy into the account of his identity—promotes an ethic of individual choice, a social utopia of self-disposition, and even a principle of preference for contract over status.

Following Legendre, this "New Individual" of Western, Pauline Christianity distinguishes itself by a clause stipulating a universal condition, "If I Want to," between the Institution and itself. The customer is king. The individual is officially and institutionally granted the dream of being autonomous and self-dependent.

The dream is purchased, however, at the price of a giant sellout of individuality, and of individual difference.

## *IV*

In Legendre's perspective, a foundationless and filiationless, purely decisionistic model of humanity, designed by occidental Christian rationalism and realized by modernity as a society of *social mobility* and of *total inclusion*, presents itself as a huge demilitarized, factory-like counterpart of the Foreign Legion. This world is seen as an aggregate of people whose past is considered *tabula rasa* in order to make them more easily governable, manageable, and substitutable in the hands of universal reason: breeding hands, managing and butchering hands, hands objectifying, dealing, weighing, measuring, hands ceaselessly switching on and switching off. The rationalized individual is an output-oriented being. His conception of filiation is what Legendre calls the butchers' or the cattle-breeders', or simply a conception of meat (*viande*). The price of mobility is the surrender of subjectivity. What remain are de-subjectivized humans, "meat parcels"—to borrow one more expression from Brecht, demonstrating again their unexpected communality. Clearly, under such conditions, whether the legitimacy of this kind of management is to be provided theologically, or technologically, is neither a practical, nor even the primary question.

What makes the text from Ephesians such a telling and crucial *interpretamentum* for Pierre Legendre's critique of rational law-giving is the choice of *wrath* as a referent for *parenthood*. If "wrath" is interpreted as that which is inaccessible to rational procedures, *filii irae* must be understood, not as some purposive (and thus controlled) *action*, but as an *aperçu* of the obvious, yet in many ways problematic, fact that human existence involves some ultimately unaccountable *happening:* an encounter, a contingency, an event. Conceiving of humanity as composed of "children of wrath" is equivalent to conceiving human filiation as bound to sexuality. That human existence involves "wrath" might be the Pauline way of expressing the central proposition of psychoanalysis: the assertion of what Freud was to call the *original scene*.

Both the reference to wrath and the reference to the *Urszene* hold that sexuality is a universal feature of human existence and not just the solution to the mechanism of human reproduction. Both draw attention to the unconditional subjection of all human beings to their filiation or, in other words, to the ungovernability of origin. Thus one could read each of the two by reference to the other, or could treat them as being equivalent. Nevertheless there are certain limitations. If sexuality is conceived as "wrath" the emphasis is on the male participant in the encounter, who fails to master himself. What is called *wrath* is, indeed, just a failure, and a failure that is ceaselessly castigated by the philosophers and spiritual directors of pre-Christian as well as Christian antiquity. It is the failure to act as sovereign self, to be master of one's deeds, to control what, at any moment, is becoming substantive, manifest, and real through oneself. *Wrath* signifies the loss, at least momentarily, of self-control, self-command, self-possession. Nonetheless, *wrath* denotes only an inner emotion, or, at most, an individual transgression, while *original scene* denotes something of a very different quality, a theatrical representation.

Against this antique and neotestamentary notion of *wrath,* the interaction referred to by the modern concept of *original scene* is marked by a *double* ungovernability. On the one hand, it is a token of failed mastership, but, on the other hand, it is more than that: it is wrath, but wrath *grown to the status of the event.* It is wrath because the original scene involves individuals whose self-government gives way, momentarily, to the *orgè* of orgasm. If this result is wished for or follows an unsuccessful attempt to "resist temptation," if it is obtained by those subjected to love or censure, if it is placed, in Foucault's words, in the sphere of the "*ars erotica*" or the "*scientia sexualis,*" it is a different matter. If transgression means the violation of a rule, it does not make a difference in the relation of "wrath" or that of the "original scene." The difference is first numerical; the setting of the original scene involves a whole interaction rather than a single protagonist, and implies more than just *one* "wrath." But secondly, there is a whole new dimension of drama and history. Conceiving of this interaction as a "scene" implies something more, something very different from "wrath." A "scene" does not refer merely to an aggregate of behaviors, or simply to a cast, a list of dramatis personae. By coining the concept of the original scene, Freud *moved* the attribution of the happening from the actor(s) to the events. He ventured to "tell the dancers from the dance," or rather the dance from the dancers, the scene from the participants that "play" it. He is not concerned with the problem of attribution, nor with individual actions. He is concerned with a "case" and its historical and casuistic reconstruction. As long as you have actors, you either have control, responsibility, rationality and its duties, etc., or you have *loss* of control, guilty *abandonment* of responsibility, rationality, duty, due mastery of one's self, and so on. The question of attribution can be answered either way, and that is what "wrath" is about. But the original scene is additionally and specifically ungovernable by reason of its being an *event*. An event happens—*if* it does—and nothing more can be said or analyzed at its expense. An event precludes its attribution to actors, for events have neither an "author" nor a "master." It is the event that enslaves its actors, subjecting them to its unpredictable course.

Lawyers, of course, will not find this very helpful. For obvious reasons, deeply anchored in the kind of service they offer, lawyers must be, to some extent, blind to "events." They must cut "events" into actions, the imputable contributions of actors. But imputation to actors demands the magisterial fiction of mastery, the claim that there is a controlling conscience, individual, "collective," or divine in every actual happening. One could conclude that juridical logic faces particular difficulties in relation to the original scene and utilizes psychoanalytic insights for the critical study of law. At any rate, *contingere* is etymologically linked with touch and *contingency* is what the original scene is about: a contingent happening, complicated by the fact that it is, at the same time, an inchoate happening, a happening that—appearing, as it necessarily does, in retrospective—has ended up becoming causal, life-giving, the terminus a quo of a biography, and more specifically, the *terminus ad quem* of a psychoanalysis.

The origin of a human being involves the overruling of all rule-giving, all rule-following, all "mastering" behavior. For Legendre the psychoanalyst, the theatrical quality of the original scene and the breakdown of self-command in *wrath* are both indispensable interpretative devices in relation to human subjectivity and constitute, at the same time, a sweeping refutation of functional, scientific, or "consumer-oriented" accounts of sexuality. In Legendre's view, there is only one social fact of importance, sexuality; which is seen less as a question of a pragmatics of the body, appearing in historically variable forms, but as an *indicium* that human beings are *not created:* humans are not produced, invented, explored, or assembled according to instructions or rules.

Contrary to cattle, corn, factories, or business interests, humans are neither bred nor harvested, neither built nor obtained, but *procreated*. Sexuality, in this view, does not appear as one's "own," but curiously, as the sexuality of one's parents. The ungovernability of "wrath," the enhanced ungovernability of the original scene, are signs that human subjectivity is possible, that humans are possible as talking subjects of the Other's talk. On this capital point Lacan's lesson is fully retained. Frankenstein, the Golem, or their contemporary offspring, are created, not procreated. They are the fruit of the operations of an absolute master, not the fruit of an event, of something that has taken place between two persons in "wrath." Created objects, including artificial intelligence, can turn out to be useful or destructive; what they cannot do is develop subjectivity.

This absence of subjectivity, however, is not limited to objects. Modern humanity seems to deny subjectivity to an ever-growing part of itself; in denouncing this trend Legendre's writings become a huge indictment of contemporary civilization. For subjectivity to appear there is need of reference, of text and institution; in short of an entire culture of parenthood and filiation. But deprived individuals who never obtain full subjectivity, and who are reduced, through society's guilt, to the status of "scrap" (*casse*), are produced methodically. Abolishing the structure of filiation amounts to the criminal act of "symbolic privation" which however is not as yet an indictable offense.

Human parenthood, placed in the context of the original scene, presupposes a particular kind of wrath, of *orgè*, of loss of command. We are confronted with a paradox. *Wrath*, the explicitly negative signifier, was invoked by Paul to signify and focus the religious longing for "another" filiation, fully controlled by conscience, free of any scene or "touching" (contingency), and bound to a unique Creator, an almighty and heavenly father rather than to procreating parents; it now returns dubbed and positively adopted, in the work of a post-Freudian psychoanalyst. In Legendre's view *wrath* is a counterprinciple that exalts individual emancipation through conversion and that presents itself as a special kind of regulatory idea with respect to the conditions of livable subjectivity—in a historical moment at which the effects of Paul's proposals are firmly restricted inside the religious subsystem of the West. Human reproduction involves "wrath"—and involves, therefore, limits to control, to command, to power, and to master; this is, from a certain point of view, Legendre's capital "lesson." Any conception of

Law that assumes a complete, self-conscious, transparent, undivided subject, must be considered as *infantile.*

Similarly with the institution, filiation, as the ungovernable, intractable and nonfunctional *donnée immédiate* (immediate gift), allows the human being *to speak in somebody's name* and, by this means, gives the ability *to speak.*[46] The givenness of filial relationships cannot be replaced by the dispositional character of object relationships. A strategy of substituting filiation to "wrath" for another, more appealing, more maneuverable, or simply more choice-opening paradigm, or a strategy that would, in the words of Ernst Cassirer, substitute *function* for *substance,* is bound to fail in matters of the origins of the individual human being. But, for Legendre and against a number of post-Freudian theorists, the immutable substance, this *immobile absolutum* is *not* sexuality—at least not "your" sexuality; it is other people's past sexual event. It is the fact that there is no escape from the sexual condition of your existence, and that means that there is no alternative to and no salvation from your parents' sexuality. Needless to say that, from these different premises, follows a different account of social and political existence and action, a different conception of man, of history, and of literacy—and this is different not only to Paul. If there is no escape from the Pauline "spell," affiliating mankind to sexuality and its "wrath," then individual action is always oriented toward the Other and cannot be reconstructed as a bundle of object relationships. Furthermore, if man originates in the act of the flesh, rationality, conceived as mastery over objects, must be considered as a fundamentally biased approach for the understanding of human affairs. For Legendre, parenthood is an irredeemable spell. Any attempt at emancipation from filiation is bound to fail, and the Text is the one, irremediable *donnée immédiate* in anybody's genealogy.

But how could these insights apply in relation to the actions of an individual? They concern, obviously, the human subjective *bearableness* of the conditions of modern society, their subjective minimal conditions. But what is bearable, for whom, and at what price? The strange tone of pessimism at this point, not to say of *Kulturkritik,* stems from the absence of any clear answer to these questions. Legendre's basic concern, however, is that of a matchless witness of a certain blindness, or thoughtlessness, shared by everybody, but particularly acute in lawyers, judges, administrators, and professors of law; a thoughtless-

46. *See* Legendre, *Leçons IV, supra* note 16.

ness as to the conventional legal worldview, as to the way lawyers conceive and practice law, and as to their internal relations.

But has Legendre, the most virulent critic of this type of thoughtlessness in contemporary France, had any effect on French legal life? His influence is not absent, but it is not all-pervasive either, to say the least.[47] It would be extreme to attribute this exclusively to personal idiosyncrasies. Past and present experience shows that, with a few exceptions, the legal system can survive without paying much attention to criticism; indeed, it can forgo all temptation to argue, justify, or refute the critics and turn instead to the day's business. This is explained by recent theories of the self-referential or autopoietic character of law. According to these theories, the legal system links its operations at any one time to the results of its immediately preceding operations, a view that may help us understand why the legal system, as well as other autopoietically closed entities, seems so spectacularly to succeed in repelling its powerful critics. Critical legal scholars are well aware of and even obsessed with the problem of immunity that the legal system enjoys against criticism. This planned indifference, which allows the legal system to coexist peacefully with every argument, however critical or damning, as long as it does not refer to or be situated within its internal procedures, turns out to be the paramount problem of academic legal criticism. The legal system, however, seems unconcerned: it is "doing fine" with or without the attention paid to it from the outside. In fact, this immunity from critique of the critic's object turns out to be more threatening to critical legal scholars, by forcing them into positions that may turn their movement into an autopoietically functioning entity. For any critical movement, this is not a promising future but a kind of soft death after which what survives is not a movement but a system.

This threat, of which Legendre's case in France is an exemplary instance, faces every critical project including that of the genealogy of the *Antirrhetic*.[48] The productive use of textual polemics presupposes

47. Surprisingly enough, the subject concerned seems not to share this perception. *See* "The Lost Temporality of Law: An interview with Pierre Legendre," 1 *Law and Critique* 3, 15 (Alain Pottage trans., 1990). However, the sharpest form of mutual ignorance is present between Legendre and the world of legal academics. Practical lawyers, judges, and officers, as well as social workers, are the foremost followers of Legendre's interventions.

48. *See* Peter Goodrich, "Antirrhesis: Polemical Structures of Common Law Thought," *in The Rhetorics of Law* (Austin Sarat and Thomas Kearns eds., 1989); Peter Goodrich, "The Continuance of the Antirrhetic," 4 *Cardozo Stud. L. and Literature* 207 (1992).

an extremely high degree of societal openness and a fully functioning and powerful public sphere. A strategy based on the *Antirrhetic* would be decisive, in other words, if an ongoing and fertile dialogue existed in Britain or America between, for instance, the proponents of alternative dispute resolution and the legal establishment. But such a dialogue or exchange is conspicuously absent. Under such conditions, even polemics fail to "irritate"—to "become a difference that makes a difference." The two "systems," that of the practitioner and that of the legal academic, are operating independently, without meeting or disturbing each other. Academic criticism is in constant danger of its dangerlessness, of becoming what is known in gymnastics as "isometric exercises": exercises that do not change anything. Thus the quest for *extant points of potential irritation,* the exploration of the limits of the reign of indifference and irrelevance, seems destined to become the next crucial critical legal theme. But for a society that places little emphasis on its own voices, its own thoughts, needs, conscience, doubts, and desires, the promise of critique and of a strategy like *Antirrhetics* looks forlorn.

*Chapter 9*

# Translating Legendre, or The Poetical Sermon of a Contemporary Jurist

*Peter Goodrich*

In deference to the occasion and to the theme of this colloquium I will not endeavor to provide any coherent, systematic, or sustained introduction to the work of the French jurist and psychoanalyst Pierre Legendre.[1] I will begin instead with a brief history of a dual absence, that of psychoanalysis from law and of the writing of Legendre from the curriculum of contemporary jurisprudence. My question initially will be that of what can be predicated of this absence. What does it mean that the legal institution and specifically those that Legendre terms the moralists and bureaucrats—the "indolent pedagogues" of the legal academy—act as if psychoanalysis did not exist and as if the texts of Freud and Lacan would soon disappear from circulation?[2] Specifically, I will recount the history of a particular failure to translate the work of Legendre into Anglophone jurisprudence and I will subsequently comment upon the politics of that censorship or repression and the threat that accompanies the promise of a properly "analytic" interpretation of law.

The story, as the saying goes, is stranger than fiction or, in more

1. I have endeavored to provide a sustained introduction to Legendre's work in, Peter Goodrich, *Languages of Law: From Logics of Memory to Nomadic Masks* 260–96 (1990). For critical commentaries on his work, see Alain Pottage, "The Paternity of Law," *in Politics, Postmodernity, and Critical Legal Studies: The Legality of the Contingent* (Costas Douzinas et al. eds., 1994); Yifat Hachamovitch, "One Law on the Other," 3 *Int'l. J. for Semiotics of Law.* 187 (1990); Alain Pottage, "Crime and Culture: The Relevance of the Psychoanalytical," 55 *Mod. L. Rev.* 421 (1992); *see also* Anton Schutz, "Pierre Legendre's Critique of Rational Law-Giving," in this volume.

2. Pierre Legendre, *Paroles Poétiques échappées du Texte* 12 (1982).

classical terms, is a matter of *fictio figura veritatis*—fiction in the figure of truth. It begins at a conference in 1988. The editor of an established and well-reputed sociolegal periodical was seeking to commission articles on "major theorists" who have "substantially influenced contemporary understanding of law and society."[3] I suggested a proleptic article on the French legal philosopher Pierre Legendre, who in terms of bulk publication, I argued, if not necessarily by reputation, was a major theorist. He was even then author of twelve books and by any accounting a significant figure within Parisian circles and the French speaking and Francophile jurisdictions.[4] (In brief, although the editor had never heard of Legendre, an article was commissioned, a word limit was agreed upon, and certain editorial dictates were communicated. Specifically, the article was to be accessible to students, it was to be written in a clear style with frequent practical examples, and it would ideally be the kind of article that would be "useful" to colleagues. Undaunted, I undertook the commission.)

Some months later I completed a draft of the article and forwarded it to the editor of the *Law Review.* Allowing for certain stylistic digressions and an expansive view of the word limitation, I was confident that the article provided an introduction to the work of a significant and prolific juristic thinker and, in that sense at least, fulfilled its commission. Upon receipt of the article, and here I rely upon a variety of corroborative accounts, the editor of this prestigious review panicked. Knowing that I was associated with disreputable currents within jurisprudence and, specifically, with critical legal studies, and with the founding of the British critical legal studies journal *Law and Critique,* he surmised that the article was quite likely an account of the work of a nonexistent jurist intended as satire and likely to bring his hitherto reputable journal into disrepute. He immediately embarked upon an inquiry into whether or not Legendre existed. The issue was not that of the content of this psychoanalytic interrogation of law, nor of its impact upon legal thought. It was an altogether more essential question, that of the being of Legendre, that of whether or not such an author could exist, whether or not so dark and continental a figure of thought could claim a reality. Eschewing anything so obvious as ringing the Univer-

3. *See* Hugh Collins, "Roberto Unger and the Critical Legal Studies Movement," 14 *J.L. and Soc'y* 387 n.* (1987).

4. Legendre is listed as an "eminent Lacanian" in Elizabeth Roudinesco, *Jacques Lacan and Co.: A History of Psychoanalysis in France, 1925–1985,* at 688 (1990).

sity of Paris or, indeed, international directory inquiries, he contacted the Quain Professor of Jurisprudence at the University of London for specialist advice on the ontological status of Pierre Legendre. The Quain Professor of Jurisprudence had no immediate answer to the problem and so promised to make further inquiries and then to report back.

The Quain Professor of Jurisprudence discussed the problem with a colleague at Lincoln College in the University of Oxford. They agreed that the name Legendre was suspicious—it sounded invented, legendary even—and that the easiest way to pursue the matter would be to see if the Bodleian Library in Oxford held any books by this author. The Oxford Fellow undertook to check the Bodleian catalog and some days later responded with news that was at best equivocal. There were no books by Legendre in the Bodleian and there were only three references to articles by him but these were in journals so obscure as not to be kept in the Bodleian Library. The conclusion must be that Legendre probably did not exist and this was the report returned to the commissioning editor of the *Law Review*. The Quain Professor of Jurisprudence also informed the publishing house, in which a book of mine was to appear in a series that he edited, that one chapter of the book was devoted to the work of a legal philosopher who in all probability did not exist.[5]

The journal editor forwarded a one-sentence letter of rejection of the article. Such was not the end of the story. Some months later when the Quain Professor of Jurisprudence and the editor were jointly teaching a summer course in Hong Kong, they forwarded the following postcard from the Orient (fig. 1). The picture was of an old Chinese man against a white background. The ideographic inscription to the side of the old man was added at the request of the editor and translates as "man with no shadow." On the reverse of the picture was the message "Legendre unearthed in H K—with someone thought to be Mensonge. In-depth interview projected."[6] It was signed in the name of both parties, Phil Thomas and William Twining. In short, Legendre still did not

5. My book was entitled *Languages of Law: From Logics of Memory to Nomadic Masks* (1990) and was to appear in the "Law in Context Series." The publisher's response was to raise the question of Legendre's existence. The publisher was satisfied by my bringing to a meeting a copy of Pierre Legendre, *L'Amour du Censeur. Essai sur L'Ordre Dogmatique* (1974).

6. The reference is to the satirical novel by Malcolm Bradbury, *Mensonge: Structuralism's Hidden Hero* (1987).

exist, his thought was to remain untranslated and the threat which he represented was left unexamined. Legendre, the leading French Lacanian jurist, was not ready for export, he was turned back at the border, kept out of the market. Other disciplines might allow the unfamiliar, the indecipherable, the bizarre or obscure, but lawyers had no need of such importations. Common lawyers in particular could be proud of their history and continued resistance to continental traditions with their sophistic or simply foreign ways. The common law will continue, as it always has, acting as if the insular tradition was somehow autonomous; as if the continent and the written law were both external and alien; as if the practice of interpretation would somehow be confused by theories of the text; as if the legal compulsion to repeat in the form of custom and precedent would somehow be rendered meaningless by the intrusion of psychoanalysis.

The figures of this negation are necessarily significant. The unconscious, as Freud observed early on, thinks in images.[7] The image of the old Chinese man, it can be argued, has multiple significances. The Orient is by tradition the most threatening or perilous of the forms of the alien; it is the most complete "other" to the occidental. Its age or antiquity is again a form of threat; not only does it represent the oldest of traditions of writing and of written law, it also represents an indecipherable and inscrutable code. The antiquity of oriental law further indicates a dangerous sophistication; another script or writing that in its very historicity and particularity is unsettling to the mythologies of the Anglo-American legal order. The old Chinese man represents an oracular truth, an opaque or indecipherable wisdom, an absolutely alien text beyond the tradition and compass of common law. Like psychoanalysis and like writing, the image of the Oriental man conjures the ignorance of the common law and of the unwritten tradition, and also signals the relative brevity of its historical form. The story suggests that Legendre and psychoanalysis are dangerous and undesirable figures; they represent the threat of an internal stranger or of a certain foreignness within. I will elaborate that threat in terms of one aspect of Legendre's project—his theory of law's textuality and, specifically, of a revolution in textual interpretation.

The most common anecdote of Legendre's teaching is that of his

7. Sigmund Freud, *The Interpretation of Dreams* 82 (James Strachey ed. and trans., 1971) ("Dreams, then, think predominantly in visual images . . . what are truly characteristic of dreams are only those elements of their content which behave like images . . .").

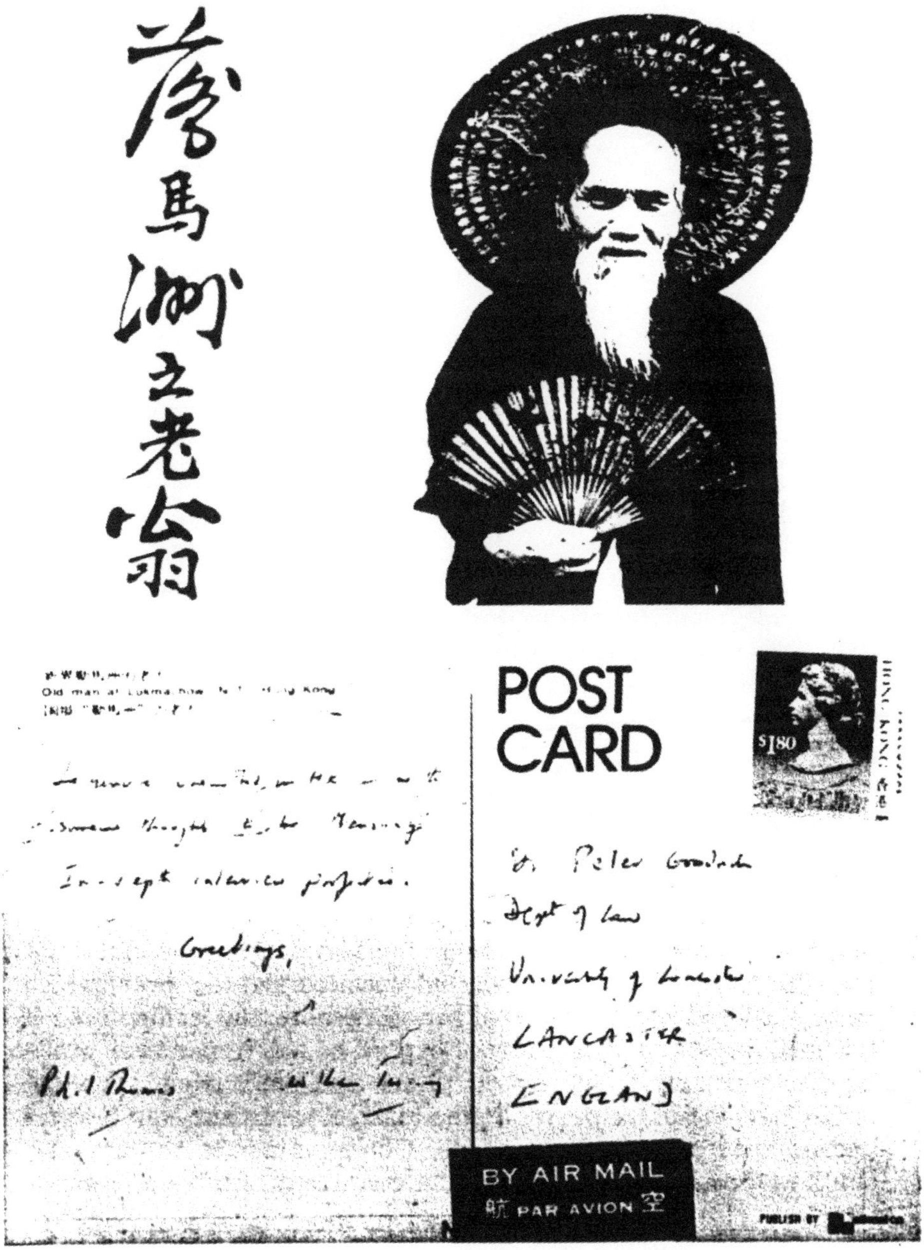


Fig. 1

appearing late at class and apologizing by saying "I had a wild night . . . amongst my texts." Love of the text and terror of the text are an essential theme in his historical reconstruction of the decay of dogmatic tradition or, more simply, of the death of the law. Certainly, to understand law is to understand writing and, specifically, the written reason, or *ratio scripta,* of the legal tradition. It is a question of returning to the text and of recounting "the war of texts."[8] It is a question of reading and rereading the materiality of law, the science of literality, of manuscripts and books that form a system, institution, and life to which Western culture still finds itself bound.[9] The radicality of Legendre's work does not, however, simply reside in a return to the foundational texts of the Western institution, namely the *Corpus Iuris Civilis* and its ecclesiastical equivalent the *Corpus Iuris Canonici.*[10] His work is radical and is also threatening in a deeper sense: it seeks to understand the reality, in Lacanian terms the trauma, of the institution. In returning to the roots of textual tradition Legendre, from his very earliest philological scholarship, has been concerned with listening to and reconstructing the "undesirable texts"; the failed or flawed or forgotten texts, the ambivalent, uncertain, and uncomprehended aspects of the textual tradition, its symbolism, images, and lost poetics.

The twelfth-century reception of Roman law established a highly specific, if complex, system of texts as law. The texts were a design for social life; they instituted life and established the legal subject as a child of the text.[11] While the Lacanian injunction to think of the unconscious as being like a language goes some way toward suggesting, both in style and in substance, the productive power of the text, Legendre goes

8. Pierre Legendre, *Leçons VII. Le désir politique de Dieu. Étude sur les montages de l'État et du Droit* 205–384 (1988) [hereinafter *Leçons VII*]: récits de la guerre des écrits: Casuistique du désir souverain dans la civilisation du droit civil.

9. On this theme, see particularly, Pierre Legendre, *Leçons II. L'empire de la vérité. Introduction aux espaces dogmaticques industriels* 131–87 (1983); *Leçons VII, supra* note 8; Pierre Legendre, *Leçons VI. Les enfants du texte. Étude sur la fonction parentale des États* 183–272 (1992).

10. On the relationship between the two great compilations, see Pierre Legendre, *Écrits juridiques du Moyen Age Occidental* (1988); Harold J. Berman, *Law and Revolution: The Formation of the Western Legal Tradition* (1983); Pierre Legendre, *La Pénétration du droit Romain dans le droit canonique classique de Gratien à Innocent IV* (1964).

11. The canonical maxim is that of a law that seeks to institute life (*instituere vitam*), a theme that was first elaborated in Pierre Legendre, *Jouir du pouvoir. Traité de la bureaucratie patriote* (1976).

further. The unconscious is a jurist and the soul a species of written law. The legal subject, the *persona,* the mask or image of the civilian tradition, is an unconscious body of Roman law. The law instituted life in a sense we no longer remember but have lengthily repressed. To recoup the meaning, the interior space, of that repression is both a historical and a biographical enterprise; a matter of social and subjective genealogies. What is, in individual terms, a question of slips, dreams, symptoms, and lapses, is in institutional terms, a matter of recollecting or of reconstructing the madness, delirium, and desire of political power, of subjective attachment to the institution. I will emphasize two aspects of this collective history of political love embedded in the tradition and theory of interpretation of the texts of law.

First, I will simply avert to the most standard of protocols of legal reading: it is not the letter but the spirit that determines the meaning of the law. The text is composed of dead letters (*litera mortua*);[12] the rule is no more than a "mute judge," a sleeping form,[13] requiring the interposition, *anima legis,* of jurist or judge. What is significant is not that the law is an unconscious text, a symptom, intensity, or spirit, but rather that the meaning of the law is internal to its living body, *viva vox iuris* or *lex loquens,* its image, interpreter, or legislator. In classical terms it is spelled out by reference to something beyond words: "to know the law is not to know the words of the law, but its force and power."[14] In a renaissance formulation we are similarly told that "no words, forms, niceties, or propriety of language is of any regard in the Civil Law, in comparison to truth, faithfulness and integrity. For *verba menti, non verbis servire debet;* words, are made as instruments to serve and express

12. This Pauline distinction can be found in Francis Bacon, *The Elements of the Common Lawes of England A 2 a* (London 1630): "[F]or if it be true that *silent leges inter arma,* it is also as true, that your majesty is in a double respect the life of our lawes: once, because without your authority they are but *litera mortua,* and again, because you are the life of our peace, without which lawes are put to silence . . ." *Id.*

13. See particularly Sir John Davies, "A Discourse of Law and Lawyers," *in* 2 *The Complete Works of John Davies of Hereford* 275–77 (Alexander B. Grosart ed., London, private circulation 1878) (1615). In a different context, see John Selden, *The Duello or Single Combat: From Antiquitie Derived into This Kingdom of England* 21–22 (London, I. Helme 1610). For commentary, see Donald Kelley, *The Human Measure: Social Thought in the Western Legal Tradition* 165–86 (1990).

14. Celsus libro XXVI digestorum. Scire leges non hoc est uerba earum tenere, sed uim ac potestatem Dig. 1.3.17 (Celsus), *reprinted in* 1 *The Digest of Justinian* (Alan Watson ed. and trans., University of Pennsylvania Press 1985).

the mind, and not to command it."[15] Truth, in other words, might be captured by writing, but it could only be discovered by an interpretation that went beyond the words and participated in the delirium of the text. In Sir Edward Coke's formulation: "in reading it is not the words but the truth which ought to be loved (*in lectione non verba sed veritas est amanda*)."[16] What is it that the jurist requires the reader to love, what passion or truth or spirit is referred to as being within the text but not of the text? What form of meaning can only be found in the soul or heard beside or beneath or beyond the text, *subauditio* or *subintellectio* as an intuition, image, discretion, or unconscious form?[17]

What the rule of interpretation recollects is not only the power of law but the subjectivity of the legal institution. The love, passion, or delirium of the text was precisely the life of the law, the spirit of the institution, the bonding of word to thing and of body to soul. At the level of the institution and of its representations of the legitimacy of sociality, legal thought has yet to come to terms with the art of writing as being historically and conceptually the quintessential legal art. The dream of a science of law was instituted as a species of poetics. The children of the text are not simply those that love writing or that inhabit texts and the protocols of their circulation. The twelfth-century revolution in interpretation—the reception of Roman and Canon law in the West—instituted the text as the image and form of the social and instituted also a tradition in which books were "devoured" and writing was attached to the flesh or held in the heart, archive, or breast of the sovereign: *omnia iura habet in scrinio pectoris sui.*[18] Again, however, this love of the text, this writing that devours and inscribes within, that is loved as truth and read in faith, is itself in need of interpretation. What kind of social subject was instituted by a law infinitely written and rewritten across fifty books of fragments of law? How could there be a legal culture without faith or without political love when the law itself was self-evidently too expansive, too extensive, and too vast to be known even after a lifetime of legal study? What other reason inhabited an institu-

15. Sir Robert Wiseman, *The Law of Laws or the Excellency of the Civil Law Above All Humane Laws Whatsoever* 70 (London, Royston 1664).

16. Sir Edward Coke, *Reports* Pt. III fol. C 7 b (London, Rivington, 1777 ed.) .

17. On the significance of *subauditio* and *subintellectio* see Ian Maclean, *Interpretation and Meaning in the Renaissance: The Case of Law* 166–75 (1992).

18. This maxim is lengthily worked through in *Leçons VII, supra* note 8, at 36. It is also discussed in *Paroles Poétiques, supra* note 2, at 91–108. *See also* Ernst Kantorowicz, *The King's Two Bodies* (1958).

tion whose texts were too fragmentary and contradictory to be systemized, too laden with symbols and glosses to be understood, too archaic and arcane to be of any practical relevance to the dominions that received these holy books of law?

Legendre suggests, perhaps uniquely, that a reinterpretation and recuperation of the revolution in interpretation will return jurisprudence to a living text, a speaking law. He offers no definite prognosis of the fate of such a jurisprudential poetics save to reiterate its necessity and to mark the lines of its resistance to contemporary positivisations of law. He evokes a tradition, established at the very birth of the reception of Roman law, that of peripatetic scholarship, of excluded figures and solitary teachers, of "undesirable texts," of passionate and delirious texts, of discourses that waver in reflection of a life that is over soon and not without its share of contingencies and uncertainties.[19] He offers the "danger" of poetry as the only possible mechanism for comprehending or, equally and just as productively, for failing to understand, the love and the power of the text, the obscure notion of a life lived in, or more properly as a commentary upon, the text. There is no legal subject without an obedient soul, no letter of the law without the *anima legis* of its interpreter, no text without its bearer, no exterior court without its predicate in an interior judgment or court of conscience. The stake of the reception was nothing less than the combination of two laws and two courts, those of spirit and of sense, body and soul, but also spiritual and temporal, an external and internal species of law.

Were I in turn to evoke a historical image of Legendre's massive and "immodest" project it would be to turn to the second feature of the radicality of his thought, namely that it seeks to recollect and release the originary resistances, the poetics and the play, the mixing of genres and of styles that the earliest satires of the reception threw in the face of the glossatorial tradition. The tradition of written law, of scripture and text as well as of scriveners, chirographers and tablers of rolls and fines, always had its internal critics, its oracles, seers, madmen, artists, and poets who would not submit to the mere authority of texts or who dissented from the dogma of their repetitions. I will offer one example, that of a twelfth-century text that was for a long time unattributed and of uncertain authenticity: the *Sermo de legibus* or "poetical sermon on

19. *Paroles Poétiques, supra* note 2, at 227 ("I have chosen to live my life in the company not of intellectuals, but of poets and of all those whose discourse wavers (*tous ceux dont le discours vacille*)").

the laws." In 1943, Herman Kantorowicz located the author of this work as the twelfth-century jurist Placentinus and published a definitive version compiled from the various surviving manuscripts.[20]

For Placentinus, law was writing and writing was a woman, or a woman was writing. The *Sermo de legibus,* an address to commencing law students, is an attempt in verse to spell out the conditions and, specifically, the interior space of law. At one level one might say that law binds through indetermination, through the image and through rhetoric and its uses of the *ars praedicandi.* The law for Placentinus can only be addressed initially through a forcible and emotional appeal to the spirit or what the medievals termed the "ghostly power" of divine rule.[21] The sermon is also a prayer, a song, an invocation of divinity or *rerum divinarum* and, as such, the study and interpretation of law necessarily addressed an interior space or *foro interiori.* The subject of law was first conscience—*insitum cordibus nostris*—and its practice was the practice of virtue while its science was that of ethics or of the *Ethica vetus.*[22] The images that Placentinus chooses to represent this ethics or ancient virtue are those of *aurora* and most specifically of *Jurisprudentia*—a goddess, a woman.[23] It is as a woman, as a virtue, and as justice that the poetical sermon can take the form of a satire that variously and vigorously castigates the inherited tradition, the *ager vetus* of Justinian's *Digest,* and the science of law or *legalis scienta* of the glossators, the sophists of the *literae* or dead letters of the text.

The dramatic form of the satire, a genre that combines vehemence, conceit, and polemic is entirely appropriate and historically exemplary of the critique of law. Placentinus writes against custom (*contra morem*) and against the ascetic and interminable character of legal study in the irreverent and fictive form of an encounter between our mistress ignorance (*domina Ignorantia*) and legal science (an old deformed, ugly, and disfigured woman).[24] Legal science dissembled the pedagogy of morals and of virtue while in truth it killed its subject with too much study, having first confused it with phantasms and disfigured it through pri-

20. Herman Kantorowicz, "The Poetical Sermon of a Medieval Jurist: Placentinus and His 'Sermo de Legibus,'" 2 *J. Warburg and Courtauld Inst.* 22 (1938).

21. On "ghostly powers" see Peter Goodrich, "Salem and Bizarre: A Short History of the Two Laws," 15 *Renaissance and Modern Studies* 1 (1994).

22. The reference is to Aristotle, *Nicomachean Ethics. See* Kantorowicz, *supra* note 20, at 34.

23. *Id.* at 26.

24. *Id.* at line 80.

vation. The science of legality, the scribal and sophistic observances of a glossatorial practice that merely relayed and repeated the authorities was dismissed not only as a stultifying science (*stulta scientia*) but further condemned as a murderous and self-nihilating undertaking:

> Dum corpus tuum afficis
> Tu te ipsam interficis
> Tu es homicida!
>
> [While you use your body in this way
> you are destroying yourself
> you are a murderer][25]

The glossatorial tradition offered affectation rather than authenticity: law was against life through being proprietary, jealous, and without desire. It offered tears, confusion, starvation, and a death within life: "*Tu morieris in vivendo/Atque vivis moriendo.*"[26]

The satirical poem or *prosimetrum* belonged, even if only through antithesis, loss, or repression, to the foundational discourses of law. It argued against the weary and desiccated texts of the exegetes with an image of vitality, youth, and creativity in the form of a woman and in the form of a savage and satirical ignorance—a pre-stoic cynicism. Here the scene of public life was the stage upon which to act out the great themes of the soul: fate, fortune, and desire as the laws of an interior prescience. The law thus always sought an interior attachment or juridical soul and Placentinus is remarkable only for the satirical and extreme version of the argument that he presents. It is that satire or cynicism which I intend to invoke as the flaw or failure through which the rewriting of the legal arts can take hold. It is that project to which Legendre's lessons can also be attached in the disparate figure of the immoralist, satirist, polemicist, poet, and interior peripatetic.

Returning to the postcard, I am inclined to draw a close parallel between the tradition represented by Placentinus and that founded in the *Laboratoire Européen pour l'étude de la filiation* by Pierre Legendre. Bearing in mind a biography that I am not prepared to relay, save in

25. *Id.* at lines 104–06 (my translation). *Interficio* also has the meaning of cutting up, of dissecting into small pieces, of cutting up with law's pedantry, sophistry, or "chop-logic." *Id.* at line 80.

26. *Id.* lines 99–100 [You are dying in the midst of life/and you live while deserving to die] (my translation).

observing that Legendre's first specialism was twelfth-century law and the philology of the pre-Accursian reception,[27] I am minded in even the briefest of terms to note the following. The *Sermo de legibus* is a vituperative medley of prose and verse and is a genre that, through the Palestinian Menippos of Gadara, probably came in the third century B.C. from the Orient. It is certainly taken up by Placentinus in the taunting and cynically hedonistic spirit of an internal Orient, a conscience at odds with its place and its peers. Let us go further. While Placentinus was popular as a teacher, he was vilified by the other doctors of law. His peripatetic lifestyle indeed began, we are told, when he ridiculed another Bolognese doctor, Henricus de Bayla, "and this man, who was at the same time a powerful knight, made a nocturnal assault on Placentinus, who fled in terror."[28] He taught law, so to speak, while on the run from its doctors, casuists, and other assiduous savants. He was not afraid to warn of the death of the law or of the decay of tradition while equally flouting its laws and mixing its genres.

Legendre too seeks the poetic right to interior freedom or to what Lacan termed that ignorance which puts knowledge to work. More than that, Legendre's style is most directly that of the cynic and satirist whose work is gauged to offend the university and to mock the "sophisticated imbecility"[29] of his academic colleagues. His work is addressed not to the academy but to its students, to those not yet seized in the ascetic, yet nonetheless delirious, apprenticeship to the science of law. The space of legal science is a space of silence, of rules, and not of speech: "the institution confines within a linguistic prison (*prison langagière*), a mystic prison which we ignore as such . . . convinced that poetry, mad or delirious words have no place there, in the space we call power."[30] The poetical sermon of the contemporary jurist expresses an interior difference and is designed to align writing—the art of the lawyer—with the gentle incomprehension of those whose discourse has the poetic strength to waver, to give up its certainties, its pretention, to science and engage instead in the hedonistic theater of interpreta-

27. *See* Pierre Legendre, "Recherches sur les Commentaires Pré-Accursiens," 33 *Revue d'Histoire du Droit* 354 (1965); Pierre Legendre, "Fragment d'un manuscrit perdu de la Summa Institutionum de Placentin," 33 *Revue historique de droit francais et étranger* 436 (1956). Both are collected in Pierre Legendre, *Ecrits juridiques du Moyen Age occidental* (1988).

28. Kantorowicz, *supra* note 20, at 25.

29. *Paroles Poétiques, supra* note 2, at 12.

30. *Id.* at 58–59.

tion. So too his colleagues have complained of his immoralistic teachings and have attempted to silence them. His popularity certainly does not lie in the constituency of the doctors of the civil law, nor is it likely that they would see a juridical face in the satirical mirror of his prose. In other words, it is not only common lawyers who are fearful to admit the existence of a psychoanalytic interpretation of law and of the exposition of our love of the censor.

No matter, however, that Legendre has lived before, even if his contemporary existence is subject to question. No matter that his precursor represented, not least etymologically (the name deriving from a Latin *placenta*), a nascent art of legal poetics. The issue is a broader one. While some are keen to label Legendre's enterprise as nostalgic, pessimistic, and obsessive, the stronger interpretation would trace the undecidability, the indefinition or fluidity of his poetical sermon to the originary flaw in writing itself. Legendre professes and practices a love of the text and that love costs him dearly. It still has to be asked, however, what threat this affection and this writing represent. At one level it could be said that the poetical sermon threatens by evidencing the identity of law and writing, of surface and substance in the same text. In another sense it displays the historicity of law and threatens through indicating the contingency of the norm. The more expansive point, however, is that Legendre's work traces the great absence within contemporary legal science. It is the absence of interpretation in its most technical and most poetic sense.

The poetical sermon of the contemporary jurist makes no effort to persuade and is quite indifferent to communication. It is satirical in style, it is figurative and in many respects hedonistic, but it rests, as does all writing, upon a sense of the history and fate of its genre. Legendre's work has endlessly belabored the history of legal interpretation. It has done so by way of tracing the fate of the two laws: spiritual and secular, external and internal. One law is enfolded in the other, and neither can be understood alone. The history of *utrumque ius* is also a history of the negation of the spiritual power, its denial and incorporation within the temporal law. Legendre's concern is to recollect the spiritual power of law and the discourses that expressed and contained that power in a written form: "The lesson of Baldus was again the following: the great lucubrations of power, which is to say those which make the body walk with the soul, those which move the unconscious to death, can only be expressed poetically, because power is organized around images and fictions. . . ."[31] It is the poetic art of law alone that can mobilize an *amor fati* long lost to a positivistic tradition of law in a soulless modernity. It is the history of the two laws that gives its peculiar force to Legendre's work, suggesting, as it does, not only the mystic body of the state but also the essential correlation of exterior and interior courts. *Amor fati,* to which theme Legendre increasingly returns, translates as a coming to terms with the unconscious, and this, in turn, suggests the prescient ability to think for oneself and so to live, if not poetically, at least with a certain degree of art.

The poetical sermon of a contemporary jurist suggests, in the genre of satire and in the hedonistic style of *amor fati,* a certain resistance, or more properly, interruption to the laws of writing. That interruption or interposition is poetic only in the sense that it demands a right to thought. In seeking an image to capture that right, I can think of nothing better than a variation on a well-worn theme: the parable of the countryman before the law. In a seventeenth-century treatise defending the Catholic Church against the Protestant charge of idolatry, the cleric Thomas Godden tells the story of a peasant before the law:

> a gentleman at Court passing through the Guard Chamber, saw a countryman there engaged in dispute with three or four of the yeomen. The clown, it seems, would have gone into the Presence covered. They pulled him back, and told him when he went into that room, he must pull off his hat. He asked for whom or what, for he saw no thing but a chair and a canopy. They told him it was the King's Chair of State, and he must do it to the chair out of respect for the king.[32]

In the description of the ensuing debate the countryman is concerned with the question of whether or not "any worship at all were due the chair or no?"[33] His argument being that if any worship was due to the chair, it was either the same or distinct from that owed to the king. If it was the same, then regal worship would be given to something beside the king, which would be treason. If distinct, then the chair itself would be worshiped with regal honor for itself and not relatively, "which were

31. *Id.* at 212.

32. Thomas Godden, *Catholickes no Idolaters or a full Refutation of Dr. Stillingfleet's Unjust Charge of Idolatry Against the Church of Rome* 179 (London 1672).

33. *Id.*

for a man to submit himself to a piece of wood."[34] Godden's argument against his adversary, the Anglican ecclesiastic Stillingfleet, is that the attitude of the peasant is absurd; a relative honor can be given to the Chair of State because it is possible to distinguish a "proportionate reverence" that is given to the graven image or chair: *honor est in honorante* [honor resides in the mind that gives it]. That proportionate honor owed to a relative presence represents the transmission of power, both its internality but also its objectivity, its transference from visible to invisible, from word to spirit, *litera* to *anima, verbum* to *veritas.*

The mystical presence of the Crown in the unoccupied Chair of State, as also the presence of law in the Court, is the signature of a hidden power, unconscious, or fate that Godden's countryman has poetically failed to perceive. The stake of legality, as also of the discourses that frame it, those of fate, nature, or necessity, is that of the transmission of power from person to person and from place to place by invisible means. Power is unseen, it can only be imagined through the surfaces upon which it is inscribed.[35] The image, symbol, or rite represents the stake of law and enacts, again in a parable, in allegory or image, the institution of legal writing as the lawful institution of life. The tradition of legal writing begins with the narrative of the decalogue or ten commandments. They inscribe the law through and across the destruction of an idol. The text takes the place of the image, the text becomes the image, it incorporates or embodies an image displaced from statuary to text. The peasant in resisting that law perhaps recognized the idol or plurality within the architecture of power, the image that remains in the text, the unconscious or poetic possibility of writing. The history of the image within secular doctrine is the history of the repression of plurality—it is that of the theater of the icon, of the semblance, simulacrum or unity of law's presence. It is significant then to recollect the satirical critique of law made by the youthful and feminine figure of *Ignorantia.* Law, *Legalis scientia,* had become old, disfigured, ugly, and deformed. It was a murderous discipline, a logic that cut into pieces and killed. In terms of the story with which these remarks began, it is salutory to recollect that law still kills; in terms of that anecdote it is psychoanalysis that was killed—that was denied an existence or representative—by the ascetic, austere, and unconscionable word of law.

34. *Id.*

35. *Leçons VII, supra* note 9, at 65 ("Consciousness occurs each time there is a surface such that it can produce what is called an image. That is a materialist definition.").

*Chapter 10*

# Rethinking the Beyond of the Real

*Drucilla Cornell*

It is commonplace to note that Sigmund Freud "discovered" another reality. This reality is the reality of the psychic life. The meaning of its unconscious underpinnings surfaces in the other world of dreams and in the slips of the tongue that indicate a beyond to the day-to-day life given to us by conventions of our form of life. Certainly, Freud always returns us to the *Jenseits*, the other side, the beyond of the unconscious, which leaves its traces and marks on so-called real objects, but which, on the other hand, can never be simplistically identified with them.

In recent times there may have been no more fierce and persistent a thinker of the analytic significance of the *Jenseits* in Freud than Jacques Lacan. It is this problematic in Freud that is frequently ignored by many analysts precisely because it appears as poetic, mythological, or worse yet, a product of old-fashioned irrational mysticism. More specifically, for the Lacan of his later seminars, his "return to Freud" involved the attempt to rethink the beyond to the pleasure principle, what Lacan himself called the Real.[1] To my mind, Lacan's lasting contribution lies precisely in his insistence on the relationship between psychoanalysis and the problematic of the beyond, *Jenseits*, the other side of the *Unheimlich*. Furthermore, Lacan, in characteristically provocative fashion, connects this problematic not only with the Real

1. Throughout this text I will rely on one of the later seminars of Lacan both because of its focus on the relationship between the pleasure principle and the Real and because this relationship is crucial for how Lacan understands the connection between the conditions for the establishment of moral law and order and correspondingly his own version of the ethics of psychoanalysis. *See generally* Jacques Lacan, *The Seminar of Jacques Lacan: Book VII, The Ethics of Psychoanalysis, 1959–1960* (Jacques-Alain Miller ed. and Denis Porter trans., 1992) [hereinafter Lacan, *Book VII*].

(which for him is the absolute Other to the web of significance given by the symbolic order), but also with the rethinking of the Kantian analysis of the transcendental conditions of morality and of the moral will. For Lacan, the very project of psychoanalysis should be understood as a preliminary to moral action. Thus, for him, ethics is not a side issue for analysts in the practice of their profession. Instead, psychoanalysis must be understood as a moral practice in the very specific sense that I will both discuss and critique in the course of this paper.

I want, then, to give this project of rethinking the relationship between radical alterity, what Lacan refers to as the Real, the limit of the symbolic, and what I call the ethical relationship, its due. Of course, the very use of the phrase "ethical relationship," which I borrow from Emmanuel Lévinas, signals my central disagreement with Lacan and his concern with an explanation of how the moral law is established. In Lévinas, my responsibility to the Other demands that I guard her alterity against her appropriation by any system of cognition including a system of morality when it is established as moral law. As we will see, both Lacan and Lévinas argue, if for very different reasons, that the ontological elaboration of the Sovereign Good attempted by classical ethics is philosophically unjustifiable, and even *unethical*. This rejection turns Lacan to his "Freudian" rereading of the inevitability of the imposition of the moral law because of the very impossibility of there being a Law of law in the sense of an actualized sovereign Good.

The purpose of this essay is to return to the problematic of the *Jenseits,* through a challenge to Lacan's understanding of the Real, as the Real in turn establishes the moral law through its very foreclosure by the symbolic order that sloughs it off through the necessary erection of the barrier that guards the world of meaning and sense. Lacanians frequently attest to the failure of "poststructuralists" to adequately grapple with the Real. I put "poststructuralism" in quotation marks because to my mind it is a code word that overwrites important philosophical disputes. Is Lévinas's "Jewish humanism" adequately described as "poststructuralism"? Indeed, the damage done to even grasping what, and perhaps more aptly who, is at stake in the debate over how to heed the radical alterity of the Real is itself a warning against facile stereotyping of subtle and important theoretical differences. Indeed, once we have revisited the dispute between the "poststructuralists"—and the target here is primarily Jacques Derrida—and their detractors, the table can and should be turned on the Lacanians. It will be my contention that Derrida continuously grapples with the Real *as radical alterity*. His deconstruction of metaphysics including his engagement with Martin Heidegger after "the turn" has at its heart the "matter" of the Real.[2] Ironically, Derrida's own deconstruction of Lacan shows that Lacan does not fully apprehend the otherness of the Real as "truly" beyond the symbolic.[3] We will return to that deconstruction shortly and its relationship to Lévinas's philosophy of alterity. My own purpose is not simply to set the record straight on Derrida and the matter of the Real. My emphasis will be on the relationship between the radical alterity of the Real and the ethical relationship, as opposed to Lacan's attempt to found the moral law through the other of the Real.

### *What is Lacking in Lacan*

#### The Real, the Pleasure Principle, and the Feminine Other

In this section, I will argue that *ultimately* Lacan can only grasp the meaning of the Real by ironically signifying it as the imaginary feminine Other, the repressed maternal "Thing." At least in Lacan's system, the Real cannot be known except as what is not there, *apart* from reality. But as *a part* of the symbolic reality, the lack in the Real is represented as the Thing. This is a paradox set up by Lacan's analysis of the Real. My argument is that he cannot resolve it. In other words, in his own terms, he cannot give the Real the difference from the Imaginary and the Symbolic that he himself attests marks the Real as an unreachable beyond. If the Real is unimaginable and unknowable, why is what is not *there*, signified for us as "no-thing" but a *lack?* Lacan continuously struggles to provide a satisfactory answer to that question. He answers it by linking the pleasure principle and the resulting inevitability of sublimation to the paradoxical representation of the Thing as "Nothing," and then defines Nothing as emptiness.

> This Thing is accessible in very elementary examples, which are almost of the type of the classic philosophical demonstration,

2. *See, e.g.*, Jacques Derrida, *Margins of Philosophy* 3–27 (Alan Bass trans., 1982).

3. *Id.; see also* Jacques Derrida, *Dissemination* 1–59 (Barbara Johnson trans., 1981) [hereinafter Derrida, *Dissemination*]; Jacques Derrida, *The Post Card: From Socrates to Freud and Beyond* 413–96 (Alan Bass trans., 1982) [hereinafter Derrida, *The Post Card*].

> including a blackboard and a piece of chalk. I referred last time to the schematic example of the vase, so as to allow you to grasp where the Thing is situated in the relationship that places man in the mediating function between the real and the signifier. This Thing, all forms of which created by man belong to the sphere of sublimation, this Thing will always be represented by emptiness, precisely because it cannot be represented by anything else—or, more exactly, because it can only be represented by something else. But in every form of sublimation, emptiness is determinative.[4]

But how can emptiness be determinative unless "the Thing that suffers" in the Real is inescapably associated with the logic of castration? And what is it that causes this association if not the symbolic order that cannot give significance to the feminine as Other than the lack, the horrifying gaping hole? Lacan's theoretical apparatus is ultimately not up to answering these questions without presupposing the very act of determination that he must explain if the Real is not simply to be reduced to the meaning given by the symbolic and the images of the Woman produced by the physical fantasy of Woman. His reasoning turns on itself because it cannot explain the determination without denying the alterity of the Real, which is exactly the presupposition he is attempting to justify. But to see exactly why Lacan cannot let the Real truly be Other, be beyond to the symbolic order, we must review in greater depth his attempt to resolve the dilemma of how a purportedly unknowable Real is only and inevitably known as "Nothing."

As is well known, Lacan distinguishes the Imaginary, the Symbolic, and the Real. In his early seminars which presented his searing critique of ego psychology, his focus was primarily on the relationship between the Imaginary and the Symbolic, and the transition between the Little and the Big Other.[5] For Lacan, the Little Other is the ego itself. Through an act of identification with the other who mirrors it, the ego sees himself as the "a." The ego, in other words, imagines the Little Other as itself so as to believe that the ego is "him."

The Big Other in Lacan is the symbolic order. This Big Other marks us as the speaking beings we are fated to become. For Lacan what

4. Lacan, *Book VII, supra* note 1, at 129–30.

5. *See* Jacques Lacan, *The Seminars of Jacques Lacan, Book II: The Ego in Freud's Theory and in The Technique of Psychoanalysis 1954–1955* at 235–47 (Jacques-Alain Miller ed. and Sylvana Tomaselli trans., 1991) [hereinafter Lacan, *Book II*].

exists, our entire reality, is given to us by this symbolic order. But how and why are we mandated to subject ourselves to this Big Other? For Lacan the answer lies in the most basic desire: "to be," to become an existent. In the unique sense of temporality that Lacan gives to the human "being," we only are as we have already been spoken for. The symbolic order and only the symbolic order provides the process in which we come to be spoken for.[6]

Why do we invest in ourselves as speaking beings? Why do we endure the burden of the subjection imposed upon us by the symbolic and what exactly is the form of that subjection? How does it save us from engulfment by nonbeing? According to Lacan, the answer lies in his reinterpretation of the Oedipus complex. He assumes that we initially invest in the Big Other because of a primary narcissistic wound. For Lacan, the genesis of linguistic consciousness and with it the inscription into the Symbolic order occurs when the infant is forced to register that the Mother is separate from himself. She is not just "there" as the guarantor for his identity. The registration of the Mother's desire and separation from her are thus inseparable, and such registration is, of course, inevitable since mothers are also actual women. Simply put, there can be no desiring "Mommy" in the imaginary infant/Mother dyad. Therefore, it is fated to be broken up by the third, the one the mother desires. But does this third necessarily have to be the Father, or if not the actual Father, then what the Father symbolizes? An answer "true" to the Oedipus complex would have to be yes.

The primordial moment of separation from the Mother is literally life-threatening because of the absolute dependence of the infant on this Other. The terror of the threat that the Mother presents in her separateness initiates the struggle to overcome dependence of the need the infant has for her. The move from need to demand, "Give me," is in part the infant's expression of resistance to the vulnerability of his need.

This resistance will be against the Mother because it is her desire that is registered as robbing the infant of his security. Of course, this kind of absolute security is a fantasy. The condition of this fantasy is that the Mother not "be" sexed. Thus, it is inevitably associated with the pre-oedipal phase, the time before the registration of the significance of sexual difference. The fantasy of absolute security then rests on the corresponding fantasy that the Mother is whole in herself and thus

6. *Id.* at 308.

a "being" unscathed by the rending of desire. This fantasy figure on whom the infant is totally dependent in its need is the Phallic Mother. Once the fantasized mother/child dyad is shattered, the Phallic Mother "remains" in the imaginary as all-powerful and threatening in her power to both bestow and take away life.

One result of the entry of the infant into the oedipal phase, marked by the infant's awakening to the Mother's desire, is terror of the fantasized otherness of this imaginary all-powerful Mother. The terror of and yet the longing for a return to this imaginary Other, accounts for the repression of this figure into the unconscious. This terror can also potentially explain the drive to enter into the symbolic realm so as to seek the fulfillment of desire that can no longer be guaranteed by the fantasy of the Phallic Mother who is only "there" for the infant. The desire, simply put, is for the one Other who can always and forever guarantee the fulfillment of my desire. Registered as separate from the infant, and as therefore incomplete, she comes to be abjected for her lack which is inseparable in the unconscious from her failure "to be" the fantasy figure who can guarantee the fulfillment of the infant's desire.

But this primordial moment of separation is not only experienced through terror and the fear of loss, it is also the gaining of an identity separate from the Phallic Mother. The attempt to negotiate the ambivalence of a loss that is also the gaining of identity in turn demands an unconscious identification with the One who is at least imagined to be able to bring the mother back because He is the site of her desire. The narcissistically wounded infant thus turns toward the Imaginary Father because the Imaginary Father is who "Mommy" desires. But what is it that singles out the Imaginary Father? What makes him so special? What is it, in other words, that Daddy has that Mommy desires, that symbolizes what "Mommy" wants? The simple answer is the penis, but Lacanians would never put it so simply.

The identification with the imaginary Father is inseparable from the projection of the power to control the Mother, to literally give her a name and in that sense guarantee that she, and correspondingly the infant, is spoken for. This Big Other that keeps the Mother as "his" in the specific sense of stamping her with his name is imagined as the guarantor of identity that is established, but only precariously so, through the loss of the fantasized Mother/child dyad. The terror is that he who is not spoken for slips through the cracks of social life into figurative nonexistence. With the crumbling of the fantasy that the Mother is phallic, with the recognition of separateness, comes the desire to turn to the third to guarantee the infant's identity since he can no longer count on the Mother to secure his being through unity with her.

Thus, it is the name of the Father and the symbolic register of his potency that is the basis for the identification with him and not the simple "fact" that he has the penis. On my interpretation, there would be no necessary basis for the identification of the phallus with the penis, and therefore, there would be no reason for the phallus to be appropriated to the side of the masculine. In other words, there would be no biological, or even representational, basis for the identification of the penis with the phallus. It would just be a matter of a reading, even if that reading would be so automatic that it would appear as inevitable.

As we have already discussed, what cannot be expressed for Lacan does not exist. Hence, for Lacan, Woman does not exist. Ultimately, Woman as the castrated Other "is" only as the symptom of "man," the inevitable return of the truth that he is inevitably marked as the "lack-in-having." "Man" endures this symbolic castration "to be" at all in the sense of having his identity as a speaking being secured by the Name of the Father against the ever-threatening, if Imaginary, Other. Ironically, woman is denied this very guarantee that secures "man." What then would be her investment in this symbolic? Needless to say we will return to this question.

But then it is to Woman that Lacan is always returning, as he would have to, since there is no way to escape her as his symptom at least as long as he is a "man." Indeed, Lacan seems to be fated to revisit the question of why we must always return to Woman. Is it because Woman is the repressed imaginary figure that will forever be "out there" as the unknowable object of desire, precisely because of the inevitability of her repression, if "man" is to exist and secure his existence through entry into the symbolic order? Or is the return to Woman a signal of a more fundamental lack, a "hole" in reality itself that is represented by Woman through the process of substitution? For me, if there is "a turn" in Lacan it involves the shift in emphasis from the repressed imaginary Woman, to Woman as the signifier of the cut—often indicated for Lacan by metaphors of the vulva[7]—which signifies in turn what is missing in the reality given to us by the symbolic.

7. Lacan, *Book VII*, *supra* note 1, at 168–69.

## The Significance of *das Ding* in Lacan's Reading of Freud

From the beginning, Lacan's answers to these questions revolved around his reading and rereading of Freud's own writing on *das Ding* and the functioning of the pleasure principle. This rereading can only be understood against "the dialectic of desire"[8] Lacan staged, and more specifically against the transcendental position Lacan attributes to the phallus as "the privileged signifier of that mark in which the part of the logos is joined with the advent of desire."[9] Against this background we can now return to the paradox of why the unknowable Real is represented for Lacan as the cut that marks what is missing: the Woman's "sex." We can also understand why the Real must always remain beyond, given our subjection to the pleasure principle. And yet this Real will operate to forever reestablish the moral law.

According to Lacan, the true pleasure principle as it functions in Freud is the dominance of the signifier.[10] We have already seen that what marks us as human is the symbolic order. Consciousness and the drive to symbolization are, under Lacan's view, inseparable and uniquely "human."[11]

This symbolic order that defines us as human in the sense of speaking beings is what separates animals from "man," for Lacan. Consciousness must come to terms with the outside world so as to meet the most basic needs. The need to control the outside cannot be separated from the attempt to see to it that the object returns to us as that which will always be *there*. That something that is there prior to us, and yet demanding our engagement with it, is what drives us into the world of signification. Significance gives us the world of our reality, but since that reality is marked by our intervention it cannot give us "the thing in itself." Here, Lacan is just repeating the Kantian insight that knowledge both gives us our world of experience and keeps us from reaching beyond it to what is just "there." The thing is lost as soon as we give it significance. But what is added is the psychoanalytic insight into what

8. *Id.* at 134.

9. Jacques Lacan, *Feminine Sexuality* 82 (Juliet Mitchell and Jacqueline Rose eds., Jacqueline Rose trans., 1982).

10. Lacan, *Book VII, supra* note 1, at 134.

11. *Id.* at 45, 52.

motivates us to keep up the search for the lost object and the inevitability of our continuing it.[12]

The desire to control, to find the object again, is connected not only to the desire to recover the original lost object but to stabilize reality so as to guarantee satisfaction. It is the pleasure principle that sets up the conditions of the search not in the least through this effort at stabilization.[13]

Since the drive for consistency stems from the pleasure principle, what is sought is not an actual object that corresponds to the representation but a world that allows the subject to minimize displeasure. Truth, in the sense of correspondence, is beside the point. This explanation of the motivation to represent explains the everyday experience we've all had of the futility of trying to convince someone to change their viewpoint with "evidence" that purportedly flies in the face of their organization of their world. Instead of change, such an attempt leads to a defensive reaction and even deeper commitment to the world as the subject represents it.

## The Law of the Hole

It is the connection drawn between Kant and Freud that provides Lacan with his unique understanding of the beyond of the Real and the Thing that suffers in it. But we can only understand the relationship between the Real as the ground of law and the foreclosure of Woman if we return to Lacan's dialectic of desire resting as it does on the abjection of the Phallic Mother and the resulting turn toward the One who in fantasy has the phallus. Even if we agree with Lacan, and I do, that *das Ding* is "something that on the level of the unconscious only a representation can represent,"[14] why would that representation mimic the characteristics of the creature stamped by the masculine symbolic as the castrated Other? Why, in other words, in all our sublimations would lack or emptiness be determinative?

To begin our discussion, we should remember that the Thing in Lacan is not simply identical with the Real. The Thing is that which "suffers in the Real from the signifier," suffers in the sense that "it" is

12. *Id.* at 52.
13. *Id.*
14. *Id.* at 71.

fated to be subjected to representations that cannot be faithful to it. The use of the word "suffers" clearly has ethical overtones, and not surprisingly, since for Lacan there is an inevitable connection between his emphasis on the Thing as an unconscious object and his insistence that psychoanalysis is inevitably an ethical practice. It is the "nature" of the Thing to be posited as exterior and precisely because of this positing to suffer as the ground upon which man must stand in order to be "man."

It is only through the trauma of the suffering of the Thing that we run up against the Real. The Real, in other words, has operational force precisely because of the trauma that "is" the Thing. Put in terms that reinforce the circularity of Lacan's argument, the Thing is the trauma mandated by the impossibility of inscription faithful to the Thing. Through this failure of symbolization, the lack of correspondence, we are brought up against the barrier of the Real. How do we know the Real is there? We only know the Real through the barrier that enforces a "re-turn." We are always forced by the Real to go back to the trauma that is the Thing we cannot escape. If the Real is at all, it is only there for us as trauma—a trauma inseparable from our enforced entry into the symbolic. It is only if we grasp the Real *as trauma* that we can understand how it is that the Real enforces a return so that "it" is always found again. This return that is enforced through the trauma of the Thing explains why Lacan can argue that "[t]he real, I have told you, is that which is always in the same place."[15] Only if we connect the Thing with the trauma of lack introduced by the symbolic can we understand Lacan's statement that there is nothing lacking in the Real. More forcefully put, there can be nothing lacking in the Real because the Real for Lacan is what remains beyond the scar left by inscription into the symbolic. As Lacan explicitly argues, "the fashioning of the signifier and the introduction of a gap or a hole in the real is identical."[16] To differentiate, to cut, is the very process by which something is there, because something exists only as it is given significance. What is not cut is by definition fullness in itself. But then it is not there for us. With "men" comes the inevitability of cutting through the Real with the signifier.

The Thing in itself results from the cut that necessarily posits it as the beyond to knowledge and yet what spurs us to have knowledge at all. But it is also to the Thing to which our desire for return attaches precisely because the way in which the pleasure principle functions so as

15. *Id.* at 70.
16. *Id.* at 121.

to foreclose the very Thing we seek. Thus, the drive to know is inseparable from the drive to cut—which is in turn inseparable from our enforced entry into the symbolic—a symbolic that grounds itself only through the cut from the Other, the Phallic Mother.

On this analysis the unconscious connection between Woman and the Thing is the result of an unconscious identification. If the Thing is what is cut out by man's knowledge of it and if Woman must be cut out from the symbolic for there to be knowledge at all, then through unconscious identification Woman comes to be imagined as the representation of the cut that can function to represent, the Thing that by definition can only be known through its substitutions. For Lacan this explains why Woman can be placed in the position of an original domain of creation, ex nihilo. For one unfamiliar with how the masculine symbolic functions as a bar to the symbolization of the reproductive power of the feminine "sex," this association would not be a surprise given that it was a while in human history before the male role in reproduction was given its "due." Women could thus continue to be unconsciously identified as those who give birth out of "no where." But to imagine Woman in this way is still to imagine her and signify her power, and that it is precisely what cannot be done if the phallus comes to be identified as the sole symbol of reproductive power. It is only because Woman through substitution stands in for the Thing that Lacan can explain to his own satisfaction "the incredible idea" that man places in "this beyond a creature such as woman."[17]

## How Freud Turns the Foundation of the Moral Law on Its Head

For Lacan, the Real grounds moral action because we are fated to "bang our heads against the wall."[18] The Real is the barrier that guarantees the Thing as the beyond to the pleasure principle. For Lacan, ethics was historically grounded in the search for what always returns to the same place. This search is primordially attached to ethics because ethics involves the establishment of order. According to Lacan, these structures allow for the arising of human culture, a culture based on speech and on the ability of man to turn himself into the sign of the creator of significance. As we have already discussed, this reproduction of man as

17. *Id.* at 214.
18. *Id.* at 70.

a speaking being is inseparable from the pleasure principle. The pleasure principle is what drives us into the search for the impossible object. For Lacan, it was Kant's world-historical insight to make of ethics itself an impossible object, a pure and simple object, at the same time that ethics is also an application of a universal maxim.

The categorical imperative demands that we be able to universalize the basis of our moral action. The words "be able" are crucial here because they point us toward the problem of moral motivation. For Kant, the possibility of moral action and of a free moral will can be explained because of the divide he draws between the phenomenal and the noumenal worlds. Lacan is certainly right that Kant strove to maintain "man's" moral freedom against the deterministic world view of Newtonian physics.[19] It is only if we understand that experience itself is founded in the divide between the noumenal and the phenomenal world that we can explain why free moral action remains possible in spite of the Newtonian revolution.

Lacan's argument is that psychoanalysis makes a crucial contribution to Kant's insight by explaining why we are forced to turn ethics into an impossible object, one that is forever sought but never achieved. The Freudian answer for Lacan turns on the way the functioning of the pleasure principle operates so as to foreclose the object of *jouissance.* It is this foreclosure that makes the moral law possible because it separates the law absolutely from the Good. The antinomic structure between law and desire that is the very basis of Kantian ethics, then, can be traced back to the functioning of the pleasure principle.

The ultimate law organizes our inaccessibility to the ultimate object of *jouissance,* the Thing. It is this law that we cannot transgress precisely because we are destined to be castrated from that ultimate object. Thus, ironically, the purportedly greatest transgressor of the moral laws that govern sexuality, the Marquis de Sade, is for Lacan a "true" Kantian. Sade always returns us to the law that forecloses our *jouissance.* This cut, this barrier to happiness, is what we are continuously returned to in Sade. For Lacan, no one more forcefully demonstrated the antinomic structure of law and desire than did Sade in his so-called antimorality.

> In brief, Kant is of the same opinion as Sade. For in order to reach *das Ding* absolutely, to open the flood gates of desire, what does

19. *Id.* at 76.

> Sade show us on the horizon? In essence, pain. The other's pain as well as the pain of the subject himself, for on occasions they are simply one and the same thing. To the degree that it involves forcing an access to the Thing, the outer extremity of pleasure is unbearable to us. It is this that explains the absurd or, to use a popular expression, maniacal side of Sade that strikes us in his fictional constructions.[20]

It is also not a coincidence that Lacan chooses an author whose attention to antimorality is inspired by a call to sexual transgression. For Lacan, if we look at any moral code we will be returned either directly or indirectly to questions of sexuality and the lack around which the law organizes itself. But the attention to sexuality is also inevitable at the secondary level of actual law and codes because "men" become signs themselves only by entering the symbolic that has as its basis the enforced regulation of sexual difference, or more precisely its lack. "Men" become "men" against the feminine object. They show that they are "men" through the regulation of this object that in turn, as we have seen, takes on significance as a substitution for the Thing. Thus, when men regulate women and their relations to this object they are always expressing in different forms the fundamental foreclosure which is the basis for the law itself.

Indeed, Lacan gives an analysis of several of the Ten Commandments to prove his point that any moral code will be built around the fundamental law of the unconscious, the foreclosure of the Thing and with it our enforced entry into the symbolic. For Lacan, the Second Commandment succinctly summarizes this law.

> It is nevertheless the case that the Second Commandment, the one that formally excludes not only every cult, but also every image, every representation of what is in heaven, on earth, or in the void, seems to me to show that what is involved is in a very special relationship to human feeling as a whole. In a nutshell, the elimination of the function of the imaginary presents itself to my mind, and, I think, to yours, as the principle of the relation to the symbolic, in the meaning we give that term here; that is to say, to speech. Its principle condition is there.[21]

20. *Id.* at 80.
21. *Id.* at 81.

But it is in his discussion of the commandment that addresses itself to the property of one's neighbor that Lacan most directly spells out his understanding of Woman, the Thing, and the Law. The commandment reads as follows: "Thou shalt not covet thy neighbor's house, thou shalt not covet thy neighbor's wife, neither his man servant, nor his maid servant, neither his ox, nor his ass, nor anything that belongs to thy neighbor."[22] Lacan's focus is on the part of the commandment that forbids the coveting of the neighbor's wife. The covetousness that is forbidden is "not addressed to anything that I might desire but to a thing that is my neighbor's Thing."[23] This is why this commandment is the most basic commandment for Lacan. It expresses the distance we must keep from the Thing given expression as the neighbor's wife. The Thing grasped for is, by definition, always over "there" with the neighbor and so we must leave it. Yet precisely because it is "over there," we *must* desire it. Desire flares up precisely because of the law that marks the Thing as Other and, therefore, as what is most desirable. But if we were to have "it," we would not be "men"—speaking beings. The commandment thus expresses for Lacan the condition in which we become "men"; that condition must be *established* distant from the Thing. Yet because it is absolutely forbidden, it is the only "Thing" truly worth having. The law enforces our desire for it precisely as it enforces its otherness.

> It is to the extent that the commandment in question preserves the distance from the Thing as founded by speech itself that it assumes its value. . . .
>
> Is the Law the Thing? Certainly not. Yet I can only know the Thing by means of the Law. In effect, I would not have had the idea to covet it if the Law hadn't said: "Thou shalt not covet it." But the Thing finds a way by producing in me all kinds of covetousness thanks to the commandment, for without the Law the Thing is dead. Even without the Law, I was once alive. But when the commandment appeared, the Thing flared up, returned once again, I met my death. And for me, the commandment that was supposed to lead to life turned out to lead to death, for the Thing found a

22. *Id.* at 82.
23. *Id.* at 83.

way and thanks to the commandment seduced me; through it I came to desire death.[24]

Lacan is deliberately mimicking the famous speech of St. Paul, in which Paul is speaking of the evil Thing called sexual intercourse, that which was supposed to lead to life and instead led to death. This bad experience seemingly led Paul to equate the quest for eternal life with celibacy. Sin results from the seduction by the Thing in the guise of Woman who seduces us through the fantasy that we can have her again. Keep the women out and you have a chance "to be."

The use of Paul to summarize Lacanianism can help us understand how Lacan understands the fundamental ethical message of psychoanalysis. That lesson is that there can be no sovereign Good. The dominance of the signifier forever cuts us off from the Good.[25] But for Lacan, psychoanalysis tells us why and how we are cut off from the good by the Oedipus complex.

### Psychoanalysis as Moral Practice

This foundation of the moral law gives us the battlefield of our experience built as it is around a fundamental lack, the hole that is always at the center of desire. Given the foundation of the moral law, we cannot help but be forever returned to the "impossible" sexual relationship, because Woman cannot take the form of the signifier except as emptiness. Very simply put, no "man" can have a "relationship" to this "nothing." Man cannot not "relate" to what is beyond the pleasure principle, although he is fated to encounter "it" precisely as what cannot be known. His "existence" as a speaking being, which, as we have seen, is for Lacan the only kind of existence that "man" can have, depends on his cut from the Thing, the object of *jouissance.* Thus, those who attempt to thrust Her in man's face threaten him with the loss of sanity. The temptation is always there, precisely because she is what we are cut from, and yet the barrier *must* be maintained. Who better to tell us about the power of that temptation than Paul. That *must* is the moral law imposed by the name of the Father, which is why Lacan argues that

24. *Id.*
25. *Id.* at 70.

psychoanalysis is inherently moral. Psychoanalysis illuminates the moral law and how we must exist if we are to be "men."

But on Lacan's own analysis of Freud, "men" are given to be "men" only by being damaged, damaged by their very castration. Thus, according to Lacan, the question of the impossible sexual relation and how one lives with "it" as impossible has always been at the center of ethics. For Lacan, courtly love and its poets present us with a profound ethical code precisely in the sense that this practice was an attempt to regulate the "damage" of inevitable castration so as to live with the absolute otherness of the Thing. On this complex understanding of the battlefield of men's moral experience, psychoanalysis has a crucial role to play precisely because it must—again in the sense of a command—if it to be true to itself—and more particularly to its founder—return ethics to the hole that is at the center of moral life: the lack of love and of the sexual relation.

> Freud said somewhere that he could have described his doctrine as an erotics, but, he went on, "I didn't do it, because that would have involved giving ground relative to words, and he who gives ground relative to words also gives ground relative to things. I thus spoke of the theory of sexuality."
>
> It's true: Freud placed in the forefront of ethical inquiry the simple relationship between man and woman. Strangely enough, things haven't been able to move beyond that point. The question of *das Ding* is still attached to whatever is open, lacking, or gaping at the center of our desire. I would say—you will forgive the play on words—that we need to know what we can do to transform this dam-age into our "dame" in the archaic French sense, our lady.[26]

### Lacan's Infidelity to the Beyond of the Real

Lacanian analysis is driven, then, by the drive to transform this "damage," this "damn age," which given the analysis would have to involve a transformation. But isn't there something contradictory in Lacan's suggestion of what must be accomplished in the transformation? On Lacan's own analysis, this transformation cannot truly be accomplished precisely because of the effects of the sublimation demanded by

26. *Id.* at 84.

the project itself. Didn't the poets of courtly love try to overcome this damage precisely by turning that horrific "yucky" Thing into "Our Lady"? Didn't Paul's church? Isn't "Our Lady" just the other side of the "damage"; an other side that is always indicated in the Thing that cannot be reached?

Leaving aside for a moment how undesirable a feminist might find it to be transformed into any "body's" lady, we would still have to ask whether or not this attempt at regulation is doomed to failure by its own terms. And was it not Lacan that taught us that lesson? Is our damage the only thing that remains after the analysis? What remains for us to do if we are to escape this law imposed on us as it is—at least according to Lacan—if we are to be "men"?

The debate between the poststructuralists and the feminists, as I now want to recast it, turns around the question of what *remains* to be done if we do not think that our "damn age" can be transformed by turning our "damage" into "Our Lady." Lacan always reminds us that we cannot think at all beyond the conditions imposed by the law of the Real. But is the battlefield of experience he so profoundly analyzes truly our fate? Or is there a beyond that operates precisely as the remainder of the limit of our experience? Must the Real ground the law, or does it forever operate to disintegrate its basis? But before turning to the different configuration of the Real, the law of the symbolic, and impossibility—which I will spin out to give us another answer to the question of what remains to be done—we need to address why Lacan necessarily fails on his own terms to faithfully address the Real.

For Lacan it is only the symbolic that scars the Real as lack. It is this symbolic that in turn signifies the Woman as the castrated Other. Even if this connection is an unconscious identification between the Thing and Woman based on a primordial lack that marks "man's" desire, the very significance given to the lack cannot be separated from the symbolic. The Real *appears* in Lacan; it is given form. It is the appearance of the Real, its identification with its representation as lack, that Lacan analyzes. Lacan's infidelity to his own argument lies here: he takes the appearance of the Real *mandated* by this drive to representation as the Real. But on the terms of his own argument, there would be no basis for knowing what the Real in "it-self" mandated.

Kant never thought that the Real mandated any law in and of itself. It was the conditions of knowledge that gave us the laws of thought. The transcendental conditions of experience account for the possibility of objectivity and the laws that purportedly establish our world as shared. We know these laws through a transcendental deduction. But we do not know anything directly about the Real in itself. Simply put, Kant is consistent to the terms of his own argument; he tells us only about the transcendental conditions that are the laws that establish our experience as shared, not about the Real or what the Real mandates.

The structure of Lacan's argument and his very rhetoric is, as we have seen, Kantian. On this reading, Lacan is arguing about how the symbolic operates as law to give us the reality of our sexual difference, which in turn is read back into the Real itself because of the functioning of the pleasure principle. That would be the law that could account for why emptiness is determinative of all our sublimations. But that would be an account of the law of the symbolic that inscribes the Real as lack, not an account of what the Real mandates.

To know why man is driven to imagine the invisible in a particular way is exactly that—an explanation about why "man" is driven to imagine "it" in that way. Without an explanation of the unconscious identification between Woman and lack through the elimination of the feminine imaginary, there is no analytical basis for this identification. The analytic basis for Lacan is how the Oedipus complex operates through the Name of the Father to foreclose the symbolization of the mother, and through her lineage, the significance of feminine sexual difference. Before we turn to whether or not his foreclosure is guaranteed by the symbolic, we have to focus on the contradiction in his own thought that Lacan leaves us with at least in terms of his claim to give a status beyond the symbolic to the Real. If we cannot imagine the Real in itself, then we cannot imagine "it." What we have is an explanation of why "men" imagine it in the way they do. Lacanian analysis on this reading would give us an explanation of why for "men" emptiness is determinative of all their sublimations. Appearance can be justifiably equated with what is "there" as imagined.

Thus, what *remains* after Lacan is his very project of rethinking what *remains* beyond the symbolic, and with it, the question of whether the symbolic is guaranteed by its own law to endlessly reestablish itself as a system. Given that the Lacanian law of the symbolic is inseparable from the foreclosure of Woman, to answer these questions we will once again find ourselves returned to Woman and to the name of the Other, Woman.

### *The Poststructuralist Release of the Real*

#### The Deconstruction of the Status of the Phallus

As we have seen, for Lacan the symbolic is guaranteed against the feminine Thing that threatens man's very existence as a speaking being, by the establishment of the phallus as the transcendental signifier. This transcendental signifier cannot be known in and of itself; "it" can only be known through its displacement. For Derrida, in Lacan's seminar on Edgar Allan Poe's story *The Purloined Letter,* the story is used to demonstrate the decisive orientation that the subject receives from the itinerary of a signifier. It is the itinerary of the signifier that allows us to reconfirm the status of the phallus since we cannot know it directly. It is the truth of the itinerary that is the economy of the fiction, in this case Poe's story. Thus, Derrida interprets Lacan's statement that "truth inhabits fiction."

> "Truth inhabits fiction" cannot be understood in the somewhat perverse sense of a fiction more powerful than the truth which inhabits it, the truth that fiction inscribes within itself. In truth, the truth inhabits fiction as the master of the house, as the law of the house, as the economy of fiction. The truth executes the economy of fiction, directs, organizes, and makes possible fiction: "It is that truth, let us note, which makes the very existence of fiction possible."[27]

I have addressed elsewhere and in some detail why Derrida's interpretation of Lacan's statement cannot be used as the proof of his aestheticization of the Real itself by turning all forms of analysis into fiction in the sense of literature.[28] Ironically, Derrida's interpretation is "true" to Lacan's insight that "man" is the creature of fictions in the more general sense that his reality is given by a symbolic order. This reality is inevitably encoded in a chain of significance inseparable from metaphoric substitution and metonymic deferral. Who better understood that than Lacan! Yes, there is a dispute between Derrida and

27. Derrida, *The Post Card, supra* note 5, at 426.

28. Drucilla Cornell, *Beyond Accommodation: Ethical Feminism, Deconstruction and the Law* 79–118 (1991).

Lacan about the status of literature and the way it is used as "proof" of psychoanalytic insight, but the underlying disagreement behind that dispute is over how the itinerary of the signifier is established as truth. How is the itinerary of the signifier guaranteed so that the letter necessarily will return to its proper place? How can we *know in advance* that the letter will always return to its place? Indeed, how did Lacan come to give the letter the significance he gives to it as the truth of the itinerary of the signifier that points back to the phallus as the transcendental signifier?

The Lacanian answer is that the phallus as the transcendental signifier is always in its place by definition, and thus the truth of the Being of nonbeing will always be unveiled as a Woman. In terms of my own argument in the previous section, the Thing is that to which man is always returned and that Thing can only be figured as a hole. But the key word here, as I discussed, is figured. That the Thing must be figured is exactly what Derrida argues is the basis for the deconstruction of Lacan's truth claim about inevitable destination that allows us to know in advance the itinerary of the signifier. For Lacan, as we have seen, it does not shake his claim to truth that the Thing must be figured because that figure will *necessarily* be Woman. There can be no other figure. That is the law of foreclosure of the resymbolization of the feminine within sexual difference that I described earlier. It is solely on the basis of a guarantee that the figure of nonbeing has to be Woman, and she will remain the *only* object of substitution and displacement for the truth of the Real that Lacan's claims about how truth inhabits fiction can stand. Why is this the case? Because it is a fiction, in the sense of representation, that Woman "is" the Thing. We "see" woman this way because she is designated a priori as the castrated Other, as the site of the lack of the penis.

Not only is Woman the substitution of the hole, this hole can be known and indeed described, so that the entire itinerary of the subject is organized around it. Without this knowledge of the contours of the hole, there could be no accurate description of the economy of desire that could be analyzed as a regulated circulation that will necessarily replace the letter in its proper place.

> *The proper place, first of all.* The letter has a place of emission and of destination. This is not a subject, but a hole, the lack on the basis of which the subject is constituted. The contour of this hole is deter-

> minable, and it magnetizes the entire itinerary of the detour which leads from hole to hole, from the hole to itself, and which therefore has a *circular* form. In question is indeed a regulated *circulation* which organizes a return from the detour toward the hole.[29]

As we saw in the last section, even if the "later" Lacan reverses the order of how Woman comes to represent the lack in the Real—the Real is not imagined as lack because of the abjection of the Mother; instead Woman is the substitution for the always-already-there hole in the Real, the Thing—her form as a signifier still turns on an unconscious identification of Woman as emptiness, as ex nihilo. As I also argued, this unconscious identification cannot, in the end, be separated from a particular trajectory of repression that is inseparable from the foreclosure of sexual difference in the symbolic order. It is this foreclosure and the unconscious identification that designates Woman as lack that purportedly allows us to know the contours of the hole. This foreclosure is the law, but how is this law guaranteed? Without the law we cannot even know what the proper place of the letter is, let alone that it will return there.

When Lacan says that the letter has no proper meaning of its own, as Woman has no meaning in herself, he is still counting on another meaning by which he can know that—know that the letter has no meaning of its own. To know that Woman has no proper meaning in her self is to know her as the sign of Truth, if not as Woman. How can Lacan count on this meaning?

This knowledge can only be guaranteed by a transcendental semantics that, as I previously argued, has to be transcendental in the strong sense that it can analyze exactly how the cut in reality will take place. Knowing just how the Real will be cut is what gives us knowledge of the contours of the hole. If we didn't know how the Real would necessarily be cut, we wouldn't know why the letter would be put into circulation in the first place. The place of woman, of the hole that is Woman, as "it" is always designated as what is missing in its place, is also the lack that is never missing from it.

> This is where the signifier (its inadequation with the signified) gets underway, this is the site of the signifier, the letter. But this is also

29. Derrida, *The Post Card, supra* note 5, at 437.

> where the trial begins, the promise of reappropriation, of return, of readequation: "the search for and restitution of the object". . . . The singular *unity* of the letter is the site of the contract of the truth with itself. This is why the letter comes back to, amounts to [*revient à*] woman (at least in the extent to which she wishes to save the pact and, therefore, that which is the King's, the phallus that is in her guardianship); this is why, as Lacan says elsewhere, the letter amounts to, comes back to Being [*la lettre revient à l'être*], that is to the nothing that would be opening itself as the hole between woman's legs. Such is the proper place in which the letter is found, where its meaning is found, where the minister believes it to be in the shadows and where it is, in its very hiding place, the most exposed.[30]

### The "Place" of the Phallus

Thus, this place that is not "there" in reality is not "there" because it is a transcendental "place" deduced from a reading of a particular path of repression, which always leads back to the object we set out to find: the Thing. It is also important to remember that for Lacan, it is the impossibility that is the Real that keeps the Thing in its place. We will return to that conceptualization of the Real shortly. For now, we need to understand that Derrida's deconstruction of Lacan's concept of destination is itself put into circulation by Lacan's insight into how Woman's "place" as veiled/unveiled of castration gets the signifier under way.

The destination of the letter is only guaranteed if the status of the phallus is that of the transcendental signifier, and this status too, can be clearly established. Lacan himself always insists on the materiality of the signifier, even if he never gives any explanation of why this is the case. Derrida has argued that the letter, as the letter, can only return to its place if it is indivisible, if it is *one*.[31] This very idea of oneness can only be guaranteed by a transcendental semantics that stamps the phallus as an ideal object. Only as an ideal object can the phallus be one, the barrier that guarantees the circular logic of castration. Thus, before we even get to Derrida's own rethinking of the beyond of the Real, his deconstruction of Lacan shows, in its first movement, that the phallus can only operate to guarantee the law of the foreclosure of Woman if it

30. *Id.* at 439.
31. *Id.* at 441.

is justified as an ideal object. To give this status to the phallus negates Lacan's insistence on the materiality of the signifier. A signifier marked by materiality can always be fragmented, and this fragmentation would open up alternative trajectories for the letter itself. Thus, the law of the hole can only be established through a system of meaning guaranteed by an ideal object in Husserl's sense. It is his necessary commitment to ideality that opens up Lacan's phallic logic to Derrida's deconstruction.

But there is a more general philosophical point that Derrida makes. The phallus as a transcendental signifier cannot escape the deconstruction of the divide between *Sinn* and *Bedeutung*, a division that must be maintained in any transcendental semantics. A transcendental signifier must be true to its own form. Since we cannot know it directly but only in its expression and representations, it cannot achieve that purity. The project of purifying the concept of form gets bogged down by the very productivity of language in which it must be carried out and explained. It would only be possible to achieve the goal of a transcendental semantics if expression and representation did nothing more than transport a constituted sense to the exterior, and by so doing merely reissue a noematic sense by providing access to conceptual form. This is why Derrida states "Form 'Is'—its Ellipsis."[32] The phallus can only be maintained in its position if it can escape the ellipsis inevitably associated with linguistic expression and representation. But how could "it" and "it" alone be uniquely salvaged from the fate of the transcendental signifier? Lacan's only answer has to be an appeal to the ideality of meaning in the *unity of speech.* Derrida argues:

> We are always led back, from stage to stage, to the contract of contracts which guarantees the unity of the signifier with the signified through all the "*points de capiton*," thanks to the "presence" . . . of the *same* signifier (the phallus), of the "signifier of signifiers" beneath all the effects of the signified. This transcendental signifier is therefore also the signified of all signifieds, and this is what finds itself sheltered within the indivisibility of the (graphic or oral) letter.[33]

But what guarantees the unity of speech—or more precisely in Lacanian terms—the unity of the symbolic order? The answer, of

32. Derrida, *supra* note 2, at 169.
33. Derrida, *The Post Card, supra* note 5, at 465.

course, is the phallus. And what guarantees the phallus? The unity of speech. As we have seen, it is the itinerary of the letter's destination that supposedly allows us to trace our way back to the status the phallus must have for this logic to be maintained. The reasoning, as Derrida demonstrates, is circular. A circular logic does not and cannot fit with the rigor of a transcendental deduction.

### Lacan's Fallback Position

There would seem to be a fallback position for Lacan that would attempt to explain why it is that the phallus continues to be reinstated in the position of the lack for both "sexes," but in such a way as to guarantee that Woman will remain in her proper place—as the representation of the hole. That position would rely on the circularity of the argument itself to guarantee that the "effects," as well as the establishment of the law of the Father and with it the appropriation of the phallus to the side of the masculine, would forever reinstate the "cause," the phallus as the "signifier of all signifiers." This is the retroactive performativity that Slavoj Žižek attributes to Lacan, and which would free Lacan's argument from the need to rely on a transcendental deduction. In accordance with Lacan's argument about the role of the pleasure principle in the drive toward significance itself, the lost object would be produced by the search for it. The *cause* of the object then would be the search itself, which is why the effects of the search could become the cause. Žižek describes the paradox of retroactive performativity as follows: "First we have the paradox of a signifier which is part of the representation of reality (filling out a void, a hole in it). Then we have an inverse paradox of an object which must be included in the signifying texture."[34]

But this solution does not salvage Lacan's logic for the following reason. Even if we accepted the idea that the effects produced the object to be sought, which then became the cause of the effects through the process of the search itself, we would still have to ask why that object takes the form it does, why it is one particular search and only one possible object as the "result." In Lacan's words, we would still have to know why it is that "in every form of sublimation, emptiness is determinative."[35] Why, in other words, is it a particular signifier that fills out

34. Slavoj Žižek, *The Sublime Object of Ideology* 161 (1980).
35. Lacan, *Book VII, supra* note 1, at 130.

the hole in reality? The point of the seminar on *The Purloined Letter,* and of Lacan's teaching generally, is that it will be Woman that figures castration and will stand in for the Thing that is sought. But we can only know that this substitution will take place, and, therefore, that the letter will be put into a regulated circulation, if the phallus is already in the position of the transcendental signifier so as to guarantee the unity of speech and the foreclosure of Woman.

The response that desire produces an "object a" does not answer the question because the question addresses the inevitability of the *form* of the object that will be produced. The question does not address whether there will be an "object a," a residue that will be produced by desire. Any "Derridean," and dare I say "poststructuralist" feminist, would be more than happy to agree with that proposition. We need to have a specific answer as to how the feminine object gets marked as it is for Lacan as "the letter," and how it circulates in a regulated manner. Of course, Žižek's answer following Lacan is that it is the Real that guarantees the designation and the destination of the letter. But this Real as an inevitable trauma, for Žižek, "must be constructed afterward so that we can account for the distortions of the symbolic structure."[36] A Real defined in this manner, as I argued in the last section, is deduced from the symbolic. As such, it fails to adequately address the Real, and as a result turns us back to why the "distortions in the symbolic" are structured in a particular fashion.

Thus, even if we give Lacan his fallback position, we are still returned to the question of how the establishment of the phallus can be firmly established and the structures of its effects sedimented as reality. Even if the argument were presented that the citation of the phallus in the unconscious will determine how the "sighting" of the Mother's difference will be viewed—this is the interpretation I would give to Lacan's description of the circuit as a machine—this would still be a reading based on a past reading. Such past readings, as any good lawyer knows, can always be undone. Thus, there is an irony in the very idea of retroactive performativity. It is precisely the inevitability that language will "perform" on objects that makes it impossible to guarantee the distinction between *Sinn* and *Bedeutung* and with it the closed circuit that will always return the "effects" to their "cause," as Žižek suggests.

---

36. Žižek, *supra* note 34, at 162.

The very temporality of the Lacanian symbolic depends on the phallus already being in place as the transcendental signifier. But it is precisely that position that cannot be maintained because of the very conditions in which an ideal object must be "presented." As Derrida shows us, the very idea of a conceptually generalizable form gives way to the fragmentation of its expression. The phallus as a purportedly indivisible, and thus ideal, object cannot be spared this contamination. As a result, there can be no security against this fragmentation and with it the possibility of a multiplicity of meanings given to the phallus, Woman, and sexual difference.

As a fragmented object, the phallus is returned to the chain of meaning and, more specifically, of metonymic displacement and deferral. If the ultimate meaning is deferred then we will never be able to know for sure the pathway by which the "object a" is constructed, and, therefore, we will not be able to determine the destination by retroactively giving the "effects" a "cause." In place of the ideal ever-rigid phallus, there is only the dissemination of its meaning that overruns the neatly contoured "hole."

The only guarantee against the dissemination of meaning of the phallus, and with it the law of the hole, is the obedience of Woman—or in the case of *The Purloined Letter*—the Queen to the law. As Derrida reminds us:

> The letter—[the] place of the signifier—is found in the place where Dupin and the psychoanalyst expect to find it: on the immense body of a woman, between the "legs" of the fireplace. Such is its proper place, the terminus of its circular itinerary. It is returned to the sender, who is not the signer of the note, but the place where it began to *detach* itself from its possessor or feminine legatee. The Queen, seeking to reappropriate for herself that which, by virtue of the pact which subjects her to the King, i.e. by virtue of the Law, guaranteed her the disposition of a phallus of which she would otherwise be deprived, of which she has taken the risk of depriving herself, that she has taken the risk of dividing, that is, of multiplying—the Queen, then, undertakes to reform, to reclose the circle of the restricted economy, the circulatory pact.[37]

37. Derrida, *The Post Card*, *supra* note 5, at 440.

On this reading, the circuit is a "pact" that depends on Woman. And what guarantees her compliance? Her compliance to the law is only the result of her fear of being detached from the only position in which she could dispose of the phallus—the position of the King's wife. The risk she takes if she does not comply is of that position. But what makes this the only position by which she can dispose of the phallus? The answer is, the system in which Woman can only be as lack. If that system cannot be guaranteed—if there are other positions in which Woman can dispose of the phallus—then there would not be the same risk of noncompliance with the law. Queens could start to reinterpret what it means to be queens.[38] If the whole edifice turns on Woman's compliance with the law so as to secure the pact, then the true foes of Lacanism are the feminists and deconstructionists. But they are foes only because they undermine the law, not because they deny the Real.

To summarize, if the symbolic cannot be secured against the slippage of the signifier, then we cannot replace knowledge of the Real with knowledge of the law of the cut established by the barrier of the phallus. As a result, the distortions of the symbolic cannot be read back into a definition of the Real, so that the Real becomes the impossibility of escaping those distortions. In other words, the distortions of the symbolic cannot be read as the inevitable trauma of castration. For Lacan, this trauma is our destiny. That is the ultimate meaning of truth in Lacan: "man" is destined to be "man," and thus, castrated. Derrida's deconstruction of Lacan's transcendental semantics shows us that truth cannot hold up as the law that establishes the unity of the symbolic. Derrida himself succinctly summarizes his difference with Lacan. "The difference which interests me here is that—a formula to be understood as one will—the lack does not have its place in dissemination."[39]

## The Neographism of "Différance"

The above quote could be interpreted to prove the "truth" of the criticism that Derrida denies the Real. On this reading of "dissemination," there is nothing Other to this endless process by which meaning slips

38. For an excellent analysis of why queens taking themselves seriously as "queens" would disrupt the law of gender hierarchy, *see generally* Judith Butler, *Gender Trouble* (1990).

39. Derrida, *The Post Card, supra* note 5, at 441.

away from itself in the sliding of the signifier. By returning everything that "is" to the field of the signifier, Derrida purportedly denies the beyond of the Real. But for Derrida, on the contrary, the dissemination of the order of the symbolic is mandated by the attempt to be "just" to the alterity of that which remains Other to all conceptual systems. "Deconstruction is justice" in precisely this sense; deconstruction gets underway as an address to the Other that proceeds through the promise of fidelity to the remains.[40] As we have seen in Derrida's deconstruction of Lacan, what slips away from itself in the effort to maintain the phallus in the position of the transcendental signifier is the ultimate meaning of the logic of castration. Dissemination disperses the unity of speech that is the symbolic order. It is the ordering of the Real through the logic of castration that is deconstructed. What is left after that deconstruction is precisely what is left over, beyond any symbolic system. For Derrida as well, the limit of all symbolic systems is that to which we are always returned as the impossibility of the full inscription of the otherness of what Lacan calls the Real.

But this "Real," this Being, operates against the attempts of man to ensnare alterity and secure himself against it. It is not just the nonidentity of what matters with its current designations that calls for the deconstruction of identity logic thinking, but it is also the very conditions of presentation of what comes to be that defers any static definition of the Real. The Real, or in the Heideggerian terminology adopted by Derrida, Being as it is presented, as beings, as objects, is Other to these forms. This is Heidegger's distinction between the ontic and the ontological. But Derrida radicalizes the very idea of the *es gibt* through the introduction of temporalization. It is, then, not just the difference between Being and beings that keeps Being other to reality. The very presentation of being in time introduces a fundamental multiplicity and complexity that displaces any lingering stasis inherent in a notion of a beyond that "is," even as it disappears in what "is."

For Derrida we encounter the Real through the operational force of *différance.* This "Real," however, as a *force* has none of the traditional properties associated with the Real defined as it has been in Western metaphysics, including in Lacan, as a substance, subject only to limited divisibility. Derrida's own understanding of the operational force of *dif-*

40. I have figured Derrida as the ultimate chiffonnier to bring into focus the ethical relation that is promised to the remains by deconstruction. Drucilla Cornell, *The Philosophy of the Limit* 62–90 (1992).

*férance* has in common with quantum mechanics the displacement of the traditional pictorial representation of cause and effect precisely as it introduces temporalization into the very constitution of the Real. As we will see, the challenge to Lacan by Derrideans is not that there is no Real, but that the Lacanian notion of the Real is too limited.

The debate, then, between Derrida and Lacan is how to adequately address the Real and how one "knows" its operational force including the effects of sublimation. Once the debate is redefined in this manner, we can reexamine its ethical significance.

Before we return to the ethical, we need to examine the disordering, ordering "principle" that disrupts any conception of the Law of law including that introduced by Lacan's phallo-logocentrism. Derrida heeds this disordering, ordering "principle" as *différance,* which is not a principle in any strong philosophical sense. For Derrida, by definition, one cannot know the Real by conceptualizing it because what would be known would only be the concept, not the Real. Thus, he insists that *différance,* at least in the traditional philosophical sense, is "literally neither a word nor a concept."[41] If there could be a concept in the strong sense of the underlying principle of reality, it would reintroduce a notion of the Law of law.

For Derrida, the Law of law that could establish the law of limited divisibility is undermined by the inherent temporalization of Being. Being, what is, only presents itself in intervals. Derrida explains:

> An interval must separate the present from what it is not in order for the present to be itself, but this interval that constitutes it as present must, by the same token, divide the present in and of itself, thereby also dividing, along with the present, everything that is thought on the basis of the present, that is, in our metaphysical language, every being, and singularly substance or the subject.[42]

### The Deconstruction of the Traditional Representation of Cause and Effect

*Différance* cannot be separated from the becoming time of space and the becoming space of time. This becoming space of time and the becoming time of space is always already under way, as soon as anything "is."

41. Derrida, *supra* note 2, at 3.
42. *Id.* at 13.

Thus, there cannot be an adequate pictorial representation of a "before" this presentation of what is, because what "is" is already, always temporalized. The idea of temporalization undermines the pictorial representation of an empty space as "nothing" in which something comes to be in that space that is already "there." As a result, the traditional notion of the separation of time and space is philosophically undermined, and with them the idea of a "prior" nothing. As is only too evident, Lacan's metaphors of the "Nothing" as the Other, indeed even as the origin, clearly partake of an older world view in which there is a "there" of "nothing" before the symbolic world of things. It is that Nothing which remains Real to Lacan which is precisely why we know "it" as Woman.

But if Being is always already in intervals, and thus temporalized, there can be no absolute past that was just there "before," even as Nothing. Such past would not be presentable because as things are presented they are always, already in time, or more precisely things only are through time.

> In constituting itself, in dividing itself dynamically, this interval is what might be called *spacing,* the becoming-space of time or the becoming-time of space (*temporization*). And it is this constitution of the present, as an "originary" and irreducibly nonsimple (and therefore, *stricto sensu* nonoriginary) synthesis of marks, or traces of retentions and protentions (to reproduce analogically and provisionally a phenomenological and transcendental language that soon will reveal itself to be inadequate), that I propose to call archi-writing, archi-trace, or *différance.* Which (is) (simultaneously) spacing (and) temporization.[43]

This "simultaneity," which denies in any simple sense a past and present, motivated me to use the phrase "through time" rather than "in time." The phrase "in time" still indicates an object there "before" that then enters time and, indeed, implicates the whole structure of scientific investigation. It is precisely this "before" and "after," and with it a sense of deterministic relationship, that is inherent in the traditional pictorial representation of cause and effect.

But is *différance* as "the non-full, non-simple, structured and differentiating origin of differences"[44] itself just another conception of the

43. *Id.*
44. *Id.* at 11.

Law of law as an originary causality that causes things to be in a certain way, or, more precisely, gives us another law of limited divisibility? My own interpretation of *différance* would answer that question as follows. *Différance* is not a Law of law in the strong sense of an original causality, because the line between the "before" and "after," active and passive, cannot be maintained. A differentiating origin of differences cannot be known as an origin that is "there." What is always already differentiated, and in a web of relationships that is constitutive of the things themselves, undermines the traditional notion of an original law of causality. For example, we cannot know in any rigid sense, then, how and why the law of the ontic/ontological is maintained. Objects are not caused to be differentiated by *something other* so that we can know exactly how they will be differentiated. They are differentiated in and through a web of relationships in which what was the cause and what was the effect can be read differently because "nothing" can be taken out of the knot of reality and put absolutely in the prior position of the cause. As a result, there would not be a neat line that could distinguish cause and effect because what was there would be the relationality of what Derrida calls the sheaf. For Derrida, the word *sheaf* seems to mark more appropriately that the "assemblage to be proposed has the complex structure of a weaving, an interlacing which permits the different threads and different lines of meaning—or of force—to go off again in different directions, just as it is always ready to tie itself up with others."[45]

This idea of a sheaf of differentiations which are knotted and reknotted, but not in accordance with any prior law, goes beyond the idea of limited divisibility and introduces multiplicity and complexity into the very heart of the Real itself. Once one has introduced the idea of multiplicity and complexity into the very heart of the Real, there can be no way to predict absolutely, according to the Law of law, how things will next be cut. In Derrida's language there will be "retentional traces and protentional openings"[46] rather than any simple pictorial representation of cause and effect. Any strong notion of determinism depends on that picture. *A* causes *B* as the effect. Such deterministic reasoning assumes that there exists an *A* that can be designated as separate from the sheaf. Given the complexity and multiplicity of the figure of the sheaf we cannot reassure ourselves, if there are those of us

45. *Id.* at 3.
46. *Id.* at 21.

who would find it reassuring, by appealing to the inevitability of any order. The Real cannot, as Lacan would like to maintain, be "there" as the inevitability of order. Instead, as Derrida reminds us: "Not only is there no kingdom of *différance*, but *différance* instigates the subversion of every kingdom. Which makes it obviously threatening and infallibly dreaded by everything within us that desires a kingdom, the past or future presence of a kingdom."[47]

## Lacan's Outmoded Physics

In my interpretation of Lacan, it is the symbolic that reigns and effectively establishes the kingdom of reality in spite of what we do. This explains why a disgruntled feminist can scream out, "The King has no clothes!" and it won't matter because all the "men" will still see him dressed as the King no matter what he is actually wearing or not wearing. But Lacan would reject this idea that it is the symbolic that reigns as a self-perpetuating system. For the "later" Lacan, as we have seen, the Real is the ultimate guarantee of the kingdom. Derrida's sheaf of *différance* clearly challenges the idea that Lacan's notion of the Real can serve as that guarantee or, indeed, that the Real can be conceived as a "hard kernel," or the barrier that paradoxically is "no-thing." As I have already argued, Lacan's Real is irreducibly stamped by the symbolic and envisioned through the masculine imaginary. But, as I have suggested, it is also based on the world view of classical physics and with it the notion of a determining cause. Indeed, Lacan goes so far as to give us a psychoanalytic explanation of physics itself. But which "physics" is it that he is analyzing? For Lacan, the very study of physics is an expression of the foreclosure of the Thing.

> In the same way that in art there is a *Verdrängung*, a repression of the Thing, and in religion there is probably a *Verschiebung* or displacement, it is strictly speaking *Verwerfung* or foreclosure, that is involved in the discourse of science. The discourse of science repudiates the presence of the Thing insofar as from the scientific point of view the ideal of absolute knowledge is glimpsed, that is, a reality that posits the Thing while it pays no attention to it. As everyone knows, this point of view has proved philosophically and historically to be a failure.

47. *Id.* at 22.

> The discourse of science is determined by this *Verwerfung*, and, in the light of my formula that what is foreclosed in the symbolic reappears in the Real, this is probably why it leads to a situation in which, at the end of physics, it is something as enigmatic as the Thing that is glimpsed.[48]

But how exactly at the end of physics has science run up against the enigmatic Thing? According to Lacan, the answer lies in the content of what physics studies. And what exactly is that content? Physics studies matter, what remains, and the structuralization of reality through the fundamental laws that are unchangeable and give us sound predictions. In a more specific sense, the *Verwerfung* upon which physics is purportedly based explains why physics is determined by an obsession with what returns.

> Thus that first demand that made us explore the structuralization of the real down through history in order to produce a supremely efficient and supremely deceptive science, that first demand is the demand of *das Ding*—it seeks whatever is repeated, whatever returns, and guarantees that it will always return, to the same place—and it has driven us to the extreme position in which we find ourselves, a position where we can cast doubt on all places, and where nothing in that reality which we have learned to disrupt so admirably responds to the call for the security of a return.[49]

Lacan gives himself away in this quote, as he states that "nothing in . . . reality . . . responds to . . . the security of the return."[50] Physics, in other words, tries to create a structuralization of reality that is "untrue" to what can be found there. But is it physics or Lacanian analysis that seeks what always returns to the same place?—in which case it would be Lacanian analysis and not physics that is determined by the *Verwerfung*.

Indeed, modern physics has demanded nothing less from us than that we expand our conception of reality. Its most radical practitioners have added the demand that we give up the very idea of a "Law of law" that could ultimately explain the structuralization of the universe

48. Lacan, *Book VII*, *supra* note 1, at 131.
49. *Id* at 75.
50. *Id.*

and the very idea of a law of limited divisibility. Obviously, anything like a thoroughgoing discussion of the role modern physics, particularly quantum mechanics and quantum cosmology, has played and will continue to play in forcing us to rethink reality is beyond the scope of this essay. But at least it needs to be noted that the "fantastic" reality presented to us at the quantum level is precisely one that displaces the Lacanian notion of the "Real" as a "hard kernel" out there and with it the pictorial representation of cause and effect. Far from this physics giving us the Real as an absolute barrier, it gives us instead a "participatory universe" forced by attention to the quantum. The famous example of how the participant observer[51] shapes the reality she studies is the beam splitter experiment.[52] More important for our purposes here is how the delayed choice experiment shows us that the already "past" history of a photon can be changed by the decision whether to put in or take out the final half-silvered mirror at the last picosecond. The conclusion obviously is that the "past" can be changed at least in this specific sense. In this way the participant observer plays a crucial role of bringing about what happens and indeed changes history.

For Niels Bohr this inclusion of the measurement device and the experimental arrangement meant that the very idea of a given objective

---

51. I am borrowing this phrase from John Wheeler. *See* John Wheeler, *Law Without Law* (unpublished manuscript, on file with the author).

52. Wheeler succinctly describes the beam splitter experiment as follows:

> Of all the idealized experiments taken up by the two friends [Bohr and Einstein] in their effort to win agreement, none is simpler than the beam splitter of figure 4. With the final half-silvered mirror in place the photodetector at the lower level goes click-click as the successive photons arrive but the adjacent counter registers nothing. This is evidence of the interference between beams 4a and 4b; or, in photon language evidence that each arriving light quantum has arrived by both routes, A and B. In such experiments Einstein originally argued, it is unreasonable, for the single photon to travel simultaneously two routes. Remove the half silvered mirror as at the lower left, and one will find that the one counter goes off, to the other. Thus, the photon has traveled only one route. It travels both routes, but it travels only one route. What nonsense! How obvious it is that quantum theory is inconsistent.
>
> Bohr emphasized that there is no inconsistency. We are dealing with two different experiments. The one with the half silvered mirror removed in place provides evidence that the photon traveled both routes. But it is impossible to do both experiments at once. One can observe one feature of nature or the other complementary feature of nature but not both features simultaneously. What we choose to measure has an irretrievable consequence for what we will find.

*Id.* at 182–83.

reality had to be challenged. To express that challenge, Bohr developed his own definition of a phenomenon. "No elementary phenomenon is a phenomenon until it is a registered (observed) phenomenon."[53] It is only through an irreversible act of amplification that the phenomenon's history can become settled. This settlement, of course, in turn demands communication and accord by the scientific community. Thus, a phenomenon is nothing more or less than the "comprehension of effects observed under given experimental conditions."[54] As a result, the cause of these phenomena is complex, since it must include as full as possible an account of the experimental conditions. Not only is it complex, it involves a novel form of complementarity since the measuring device and the experimental conditions "are" the phenomenon. In classical physics, the interaction between the measuring instruments could be ignored. It is precisely because they could be ignored that it was possible to have the pictorial representation of cause and effect that characterized classical physics. Complementarity does not deny *any* explanation of causal sequence, but Bohr's idea of complementarity does reject determinism. Nor is there or can there be one Law of law of limited divisibility.[55]

John Wheeler has beautifully described the "quantum universe": "Individual events. Events beyond law. Events so numerous and so uncoordinated that flaunting freedom from formula, they yet fabricate form."[56] This "quantum universe" is very close to the one given to us by *différance*, a universe of "protentional openings" and "retentional closings."[57]

The Real as we have seen is the inevitability of an irruption that signals the incompleteness of the symbolic. It is, of course, a paradox that the Real is marked by an inevitable "accident."[58] The laws of physics are thus accordingly marked by the repression of the inevitabil-

53. *Id.* at 184 (quoting Niels Bohr).

54. Niels Bohr, *The Causality Problem in Atomic Physics* 24 (1982).

55. It is important to note that even if there is no Law of law of limited divisibility, that did not mean for Bohr that there was absolutely unlimited divisibility precisely because of the "creation" of phenomenon through "irreversible amplification." *See id.*

56. Wheeler, *supra* note 52, at 204.

57. Derrida, *supra* note 2, at 21.

58. For an excellent discussion of how Lacan philosophically grapples with causality and how his conception of causality is inseparable from the symbolic foreclosure of Woman, see Emanuela Bianchi, *Causation, Justice, and Feminist Politics, Lecture at the New School for Social Research* (June 1, 1993) (unpublished lecture, on file with author).

ity of this accident which is why Lacan believes that he has reversed the traditional notion of cause and effect. The ultimate cause is the gap known only through its irruption of the automaton of the pleasure principle. The gap Woman represents will always be there as the *causa noumenon.* This is still a cause of a cause of sorts and one that marks its effects as inevitable even if produced through Žižek's retroactive performativity. Thus, in spite of his claim to displace the traditional notion of causality, Lacan remains caught up in its pictorial representation with the addition of a strong sense of determinism.

Thus, ironically, for all of Lacan's claims to the contrary that the Real is beyond the pleasure principle, "it" should instead be grasped as its ultimate expression, at least as the pleasure principle is understood by Lacan. There is, then, no beyond to the automaton—at least not for Lacan—and this determined universe is at odds with modern physics. This is precisely why I said earlier that Lacanian analysis rather than physics ultimately may be based on a fundamental *Verwerfung,* the repression of Woman. This could easily explain why Woman is everywhere in Lacan, including in the Heavens. We "women" can be grateful to him for that. Lacanian analysis always returns to Woman. But we are once again returned to the question of how do we know if she will always be "there" in her proper place?

### Derrida's "Beyond" to the Pleasure Principle: "Cinders There Are"

It is precisely that Derrida "knows" that he cannot know the truth of Woman, that allows him to theoretically *open up* the possibility of a "Real" *beyond* the automaton of the Lacanian pleasure principle. That opening that cannot be closed is inseparable from the Real, if a Real is given to us by *différance.* The difference between an opening and a gap is that one cannot know what awaits on the other side of an opening, what "is" over there. In other words, "man" cannot know the contours of the opening or into what he will fall. This suspicion of Lacan's truth is inseparable from Derrida's profound awareness of how the unity of the masculine symbolic has marked the tradition of Western metaphysics. Thus, Derrida is in earnest when he questions whether or not one can even think the *es gibt,* "before" sexual difference, since the form of being has been inseparable from the metaphors of Woman. In his insistence that Western metaphysics is phallo-logocentric the question of woman is elevated to a philosophical status in a very traditional sense. We need to know how and why these metaphors of Woman have shaped the very conditions of knowledge and our most basic experience of what is. Thus, the deconstruction of phallo-logocentrism also always returns us to Woman, and more importantly to the limit of her meaning as imposed by a masculine symbolic. It is precisely this emphasis on the limit of the meaning of Woman that has been misunderstood in Derrida as one more attempt to put her in the place of the mysterious, unknowable Other. But it is only if we dislocate the meaning imposed upon Woman that we can even begin to recapture a feminine image. This, however, is my project.[59] For Derrida, the question of Woman is irradicably associated with the question of how to adequately address the "real" alterity of the Other, an alterity that is by definition beyond the masculine symbolic. But both projects depend on the disruption of the economy of desire described by Lacan.

Let me turn then to the question of how, for Derrida, there can be a beyond to the automaton of the pleasure principle, particularly as this automaton guarantees that emptiness will be determinative of all of our sublimations. The first step is to rethink the law of the pleasure principle. To do so we are once again returned to the operational force of *différance* and more specifically to the way the deferral of *différance* disrupts the specific itinerary of the destination of desire given to us by Lacan. For Derrida, as we have seen, objects—all objects—are constituted through a temporalization that disrupts the very idea of a "past," even one that is only there as the automatism of repetition. It is the deferral of the ultimate meaning of any of the principles, since they can only be understood through *différance,* that keeps Freud's work from being turned into the ultimate theoretical justification of a restricted economy of desire. The detour Derrida ascribes to *différance* could be the detour of the more traditional understanding of what the pleasure principle demands. Do we have to save ourselves only by cutting ourselves off from our pleasure? Is the choice between calculated pleasure and death? For Derrida, the alternative to the pleasure principle with its restricted economy is only death, if we already accept that we are fated to be in that economy. The *either/or,* in other words, is created by the way in which the pleasure principle and the reality principle are read together in traditional readings of Freud, including even Lacan's,

59. *See* Cornell, *supra* note 28, at 79–118.

rather than read through their difference from one another, so as to leave open the possibility of a risk of oneself to the other that would not just be an unconscious investment in absolute loss. Indeed, the very idea that advance calculation is safe depends on the idea that there is a reality just there that will ultimately ensure a payoff for the expenditure of energy. The *either/or* of presence or absence is displaced by the operational force of *différance.*

> For the economic character of *différance* in no way implies that the deferred presence can always be found again, that we have here only an investment that provisionally and calculatedly delays the perception of its profit or the profit of its perception. Contrary to the metaphysical, dialectical, "Hegelian" interpretation of the economic movement of *différance,* we must conceive of a play in which whoever loses wins, and in which one loses and wins on every turn. If the displaced presentation remains definitively and implacably postponed, it is not that a certain present remains absent or hidden. Rather, *différance* maintains our relationship with that which we necessarily misconstrue, and which exceeds the alternative of presence and absence.[60]

For Derrida the unconscious should be understood as exemplary of the excess of the dichotomy of either present or absent. It is other to consciousness, neither there as lost nor as found. Thus, in Derrida, unlike in Lacan, there is no such "thing" as an absolutely lost object that can be known in its very loss. Psychoanalysis proceeds down the path of after-effects, which are "the traces of 'unconscious' traces."[61] It is precisely the deferral that leaves only after-effects that disrupts the very idea of the retroactive reconstruction of the unconscious *cause* as "the Thing" that is lost. The irony is that in Lacan's attempt to know the unconscious Thing, even as what is lacking, he once again reinstates an identity between the unconscious and a present entity.

60. *Id.* at 20.
61. *Id.* at 21.

*Chapter 11*

# For the Love of Lacan

*Jacques Derrida*

Translated by Peggy Kamuf[1]

### *1. The Future Anterior in the Conditional*

What wouldn't Lacan have said!
What will he not have said!

This is an exclamation rather than a question: I am trying out my voice, looking for the right tone as in an experiment prior to beginning this idiomatic conjunction of negation, disavowal, the conditional, and the future anterior. My hypothesis: these grammars play either successively or simultaneously a role of screen and mirror in the modalities of the *with* [avec]. As well as in the modalities of the *since* [depuis] that will have determined Lacan's relation to the philosophers—to certain philosophers. These brief observations on temporal modalities will all be marked by the incidence of Stephen Melville's observation on "narration," thus on history, on the "temporal shifts," and also on the possibility of a *Kehre,* a "turning point" in Lacan following the *Ecrits,* that is, and more precisely, since 1966–67.

What will Lacan not have said! What wouldn't he have said!

What was it with Lacan *with* the philosophers? To approach this question, it would be necessary to shed light not only on what "with" can mean in this case, but on what Lacan said, did not say, will have or will not have said, caused to be said, or let be said—in the future ante-

1. Reprinted from "Pour l'amour de Lacan," trans. Peggy Kamuf, from Jacques Derrida, *Resistances: De La Psychanalyse,* trans. Peggy Kamuf (forthcoming), with the permission of the publishers, Stanford University Press. No part of this translation may be reproduced in any manner without the written permission of Stanford University Press.

rior or in the conditional. To deal with this enigma of the future anterior and the conditional, which is what I will be particularly interested in today, is to deal with the problem of archivization, of what remains or does not remain. It is an old, familiar problem. During this century, however, the birth of psychoanalysis, in *conjunction* with the advent of new techniques of archivation or telecommunication, has consolidated the apparatus of certain paradoxes with which, in my view at least, conventional history, the way in which history or histories are written or told, has not yet systematically come to terms. It is quite simply the concept of history that is no doubt at stake. The effects of these paradoxes, which could be termed techno-psychoanalytical (since they concern, *conjointly* and by the same token, what psychoanalysis can tell us about inscription, erasure, blanks, the non-said, memory storage, *and* new techniques of archivization—this one, for example—look at all the tape recorders that are in this room) do not concern exclusively Lacan, of course. But the example of Lacan offers certain singular aspects that merit the attention of anyone interested in these questions.

One problem with colloquia, in any case a problem I find hard to bear, is that no one goes into details. Instead of treating "things themselves" (ah, things themselves!) with as keen an eye as possible, we must, for lack of time and because our voice is swept along by swelling, choruslike rhythms, make do without the minutiae of the letter—that is, those microscopic or micrological displacements where I incorrigibly persist in hoping things get decided—at a given moment. But the given moment is never given. That this given moment be given is just what is never given in advance, and here we have arrived, too soon of course, well in advance, at the question of destination.

Owing to this macroscopia or macrologic of the colloquium, movements of "external" strategy—if one can put it that way and if there were a purely external strategy, which I do not believe—tend to prevail in the main. What thus tends to prevail are theses, positions, position-takings, positionings. I've never much liked these things, and theses are what I've rarely stopped to consider, which is not only a question of taste. It is nothing less than the question of philosophy, of what is accorded there to the *thesis*, to *positionality.*

In a reading of *Beyond the Pleasure Principle,* which is not just any book by Freud and, as you know, not just any book by Freud for Lacan, I attempted (in "To Speculate—on 'Freud'") to indicate in what way

Freud advanced only by suspending, without any possibility of stopping, all those theses at which his successors or heirs, his readers in general, would have liked to see him stop. That reading was also an interpretation of what links speculation on the name, the proper name, or family names to science, particularly to the theory and the institution of psychoanalysis. It goes without saying that my reading also concerned, explicitly (provided that certain code or program of translation was available), the question of Lacan's name, the problems of legacy, of science and institution, and the aporias of archivization in which that name is involved.

I will thus attempt to resist once more the impulse toward or expectation of position-taking. To those who are waiting for me to take a position so they can reach a decision [*arrêter leur jugement*], I say: "lots of luck."

So as not to become lost in the quantity and difficulty of the problems that would have to be addressed, so as not to keep you here too long, so as not to reopen all the texts, which are after all available to and in principle legible by whoever wants to look at them, I will take as my rule discussion (since this is the time for discussion) and first of all the discussion as it has been initiated by René Major and Stephen Melville in what they have just said here. But it goes without saying that, following my remarks, it will be up to you to propose, if you wish, another space for this discussion.

René Major cited the incipit of Lacan's seminar of November 16, 1976, which begins with "Were you able to read the poster? [*Avez-vous su lire l'affiche*?]" and which speaks of the *insuccès,* the nonsuccess ("l'Insuque-sait" or the "Unknown-known"). I translate this in my own manner (which is perhaps already no longer very Lacanian) as "l'insuccès qui échoue *à* arriver," "the nonsuccess that fails *to* arrive"; which is to say, the failure that fails—because it arrives, because it succeeds, that fails *to* succeed (the syntax of "to" displacing itself here surreptitiously, but very necessarily, and I have often played on this, in order to pass from one grammar to another: "I fail to arrive" meaning at the same time "I do not arrive," "I do not arrive at arriving" *and* I fail or I do not arrive *because* I arrive, I do not arrive *at* arriving, *once, because, since* I arrive—here it is the event that speaks, it is of the event, the arrival, the coming, and the "come" that I am speaking). Speaking, then, of the "insuccès" as what does not succeed in arriving, precisely *by* arriving, by the fact of arriving, because it arrives, Major cites Lacan's seminar dated November 16, 1976: "The single stroke [*le trait unaire*] interests us because, as Freud points out, it does not necessarily have to do with a loved one."[2] And Major is quite right to add: "I hasten to add that it is not always those who love you who render you the greatest service."

I would be dead if I didn't believe he was right on this point. I would be dead and, if I have understood correctly, this would not be without some secondary benefit, at least for my name; but I preferred to let things wait.

And if I were to say now: "You see, I think that we loved each other very much, Lacan and I," I am almost certain that many of you here would not stand for it. Many would not stand for it, which explains a lot of things. Many would stand for it, and not because it surprised them, not at all; I even wonder if this idea is not strangely familiar to them. Not because of surprise, then, but because it is a thing that ought not to have happened and above all that cannot be said without presumptuousness, especially by a sole speaker who says "we" all alone after the death of the other. Thus the Thing should not be said and especially not repeated; and yet, if I repeated "we loved each other very much, Lacan and I, each as he will have pleased, each in his way or each in our way," would that constitute a revelation, a confession, or a denunciation? Let everyone take it "as he may please."

This "as he may please" is a quotation from Lacan, from a quasi-private phrase between Lacan and myself, in which "he" is me. I will return to this shortly.

As for being shocked to hear someone say "we" when speaking all alone after the death of the other, there is not reason for it. This is also one of the most common phenomena of what I have called *destinerrance.* It inflicts an internal drift on the destination of the letter, from which it may never return, but to which we will have to return.

"We" is a modality of the *with,* of the being-with or the doing-with: *avoc, apud hoc,* at the home of [*chez*] the other, as guest or parasite. "We" is always said by a sole person. It is always a sole person who has the gall to say "we psychoanalysts," "we philosophers," "with you psychoanalysts," "with us philosophers," or still more seriously, "we psychoanalysts with the philosophers" or "with us philosophers." "Avec" (with) also means "chez" (at the home of; *apud, avuec, avoc, apud hoc,* cat-

2. Jacques Lacan, *The Four Fundamental Concepts of Psychoanalysis,* cited in Major, "Depuis Lacan," *supra* note 1, at 387.

egory of the guest or the intruder, of the host or the parasite, therefore, who always takes advantage as soon as he says "we").

This logico-grammatical modality seems interesting because, among other things, it is always me who says "we"; it is always an "I" who utters "we," supposing thereby in effect, in the asymmetrical structure of the utterance, the other to be absent, dead, or in any case incompetent, or even arriving too late to object.

The one signs for the other.

The asymmetry is even more violent if we're talking about a reflexive, reciprocal, or specular "we." Who will ever have the right to say: "We love each other"? But is there any other origin of love, any other amorous performative than this presumptuousness? If there is some "we" in being-with, it is because there is always one who speaks all alone in the name of the other, from the other; there is always one of them who lives more, lives longer. I will not hasten to call this one the "subject." When we are with someone, we know *without delay* that one of us will survive the other. So he already does and will be able or will have to speak on his own. And one can immediately draw the consequences from this. This happens every day. Even when we are singing the "Marseillaise" or joining in a chorus, what remains the exception and does not commit us very much is a self that can say "we," for example, "we love each other."

What is getting archived!

That is not a question. It is once again an exclamation, with a somewhat suspended exclamation point because it is always difficult to know if it is getting archived, what is getting archived, how it is getting archived—the trace that arrives only to efface itself only by effacing itself, beyond the alternative of presence and absence. It is not merely difficult to know this; it is strictly impossible and no doubt not because there is always more to be known but because it is not of the order of knowledge.

This is never a sufficient reason not to seek to know, as an *Aufklärer*—to know that it is getting archived, within what limits, and how, according to what detoured, surprising, or over determined paths. Earlier, René Major made an allusion first to an "underground" history in the trajectory of Lacan's discourse itself and then to a "question in question" that, I quote, "has a history, concerns texts, several texts, which are neither limited to an identifiable circle nor delimited by a geographic area, and this despite the fact that—even if and especially if—it does not take the advertised form of an academic and institutional program. The question of the question is more vast and stems from procedures of translation and theoretico-practical issues that join up at the borders (of several disciplines) that they destabilize."[3]

Yes, I believe that this is true in general and more particularly for what is in question under the title "Lacan with the Philosophers." The modalities of the "with" here call for a history and a type of historical interpretation that would have to be extremely careful and slow, bringing to bear great micrological refinement; they call for a constant attention to the paradoxes of archivization, to what psychoanalysis (which would not be just the theme or the object of this history but its interpretation) can tell us about these paradoxes of archivization, about its blanks, the efficacy of its details or its nonappearance, its capitalizing reserve or—but here we perhaps step beyond psychoanalysis—about the radical destruction of the archive, in ashes, without the repression and the putting in reserve or on guard that would operate in repression through a mere topical displacement. An equally keen attention is required with regard to what may be problematic in psychoanalytic discourse, for example Lacan's, as concerns, precisely, archivization, the guard or reserve, the economy of repression as guard, inscription, effacement, the destructibility of the letter or the name. A history that could measure up to these formidable difficulties, capable of taking them into account in its own historical discourse, ought to come as an addition to other readings of the archive, whether conventional or not and more classically symptomatic, without in the least disqualifying them since they are just as indispensable or at least inevitable. This is not about to happen soon.

Before proposing, in response to what has just been said, a modest, partial, and preliminary contribution to such a history, I will explain in a few words why and in what spirit I accepted the invitation so graciously extended by my friends at the Collège International de Philosophie, René Major and Patrick Guyomard—who, I believe, first had the fine idea of this great plural and international colloquium. If I said "yes," it is certainly not because I think I had something more or irreplaceable to say on these matters; the discussion of what I ventured almost twenty years ago around these questions would demand a microscopic examination for which neither you nor I have the time or

3. Major, "Depuis Lacan," *supra* note 1, at 387.

the patience; as I've already said, such an examination is, moreover, ill-suited to the rhythm and setting of a large colloquium. No, if I was happy to accept the invitation—and if I did so almost two years ago, even before I knew who would be speaking there and what would be said, in particular what Major would say, or even what would be the title of his talk since it never occurred to me to ask him—it is because this colloquium (besides the considerable and necessary work that can go on here on subjects that have been too often avoided up to now, especially within the analytic milieu, including the milieu around Lacan) also constitutes an international homage to Lacan. And it is to this event, to this justly deserved and spectacular homage to Lacan, that I was happy to be asked to associate myself. Not only but also because, in our time—and I mean the time of culture and especially Parisian culture—I find there is a political significance in this homage. I consider it an act of cultural resistance to pay homage publicly to a difficult form of thought, discourse, or writing, one that does not submit easily to normalization by the media, by academics, or by publishers, one that rebels against the restoration currently underway, against the philosophical or theoretical neoconformism in general (let us not even mention literature) that flattens and levels everything around us. In the attempt to make one forget what the Lacan era was, along with the future and the promise of his thought, thereby erasing the *name* of Lacan. As you know there are countless ways to do this, sometimes very paradoxical ways; in his lifetime, Lacan underwent the experience dubbed "excommunication." It can happen that some of those who claim to draw on Lacan's name, and not just his legacy, are not the least active or the least effective in this operation. Here once again the logic of the "service rendered" is highly tricky, and censorship, suturing, and orthodoxic defensive moves do not in the least exclude—on the contrary—the facade of cultural eclecticism. Whether one is talking about philosophy, psychoanalysis, or theory in general, what the flat-footed restoration underway attempts to recover, disavow, or censor is the fact that nothing of that which managed to transform the space of thought in the last decades would have been possible without some coming to terms *with* Lacan, without the Lacanian provocation, however one receives it or discusses it—and, I will add, without some coming to terms *with* Lacan in his coming to terms *with* the philosophers.

With the philosophers rather than with philosophy: I have always been seduced by the dramatization in which Lacan broke with the commentary or the historiography in use by many professional philosophers either when they give a more or less competent account of philosophers' lives or when they reconstitute the structure of systems. Instead, he staged the singular desire *of the* philosopher and thereby contributed considerably to opening the space for a sort of new philosophical culture. In which we are situated, despite the efforts to make us forget it so as to turn back the clock. The being-with or the coming-to-terms-with the philosophers attained a refinement, a scope, an unexpected illumination of the "searchlight effect" [*"coup de phare"*] of which there are few other examples either in the community of professional philosophers or in that of psychoanalysts. And therefore rarely to this degree will a frequenting of philosophers, a being-with philosophers have—and I say this in the sense of the greatest favor or fervor—*merited discussion,* merited that one discuss *with* Lacan the manner in which he will have managed his relations *with* the philosophers. Lacan's refinement and competence, his philosophical originality, have no precedent in the tradition of psychoanalysis. The return to a Freud-philosopher would have been from this point of view a regression or a weakness. Later on I will say a brief word about the paradoxical and perverse paradoxes that flow from the fact that Lacan is so much more aware as a philosopher than Freud, so much more a philosopher than Freud!

Having thus accepted with pleasure the invitation to participate in this reflection, this discussion, and this homage, I did not think I ought to take offense or become discouraged, as others might legitimately have done, and as some perhaps wished I would do when they put forward the pretext of a rule according to which only the dead could be spoken about here and therefore if one insisted on speaking of me, one could do so only under the condition that I play dead, even before the fact, and that I be given a helping hand when the occasion arose.[4] That is (it was enough just to think of it) to make me disappear nominally as a live person—because I am alive—to make me disappear *for* life. So I thought I should not let myself get offended or discouraged, *bon vivant* that I still am,[5] by the lamentable and indecent incident of the barring of my proper name from the program billing [*affichage*], of the veto exercised against those remains of a proper name that may be an adjec-

4. On this condition, I refer the reader to the Annexes (Correspondence and Post-Scriptum) published in *Lacan avec les philosophes, supra* note 1, at 420 ff.

5. The expression *bon vivant,* said of someone who enjoys life or who lives a high life, says literally: good living person.—*Tr.*

tive or attribute. I am referring to that "acting out" to which Major alluded a moment ago and whose essentials he in fact summarized. Although I was indeed shocked, as were many, by the symptomatic and compulsive violence of that acting out, I was not surprised by what it symptomized, for I have had a lot of practice analyzing this symptom for almost a quarter of a century. Therefore, to save some time, I will not add anything more for the moment—because I find all this increasingly tedious and because, let's say, "I know only too well." There is, finally, another reason: even if one sets aside the sinister political memory we have of the history that, in France and especially in eastern France, has been written, so to speak, not in ink but in the effacement of the name, even, then, if one sets aside this political memory, the most important of what there is to say on this subject has been said, by none other than Freud and by Lacan—who knew what he was talking about. And, if I may be allowed this self-reference, elsewhere, in several books including one of the names of Freud and Lacan, I have already sufficiently formalized readability under erasure and the logic of the event as graphematic event—notably as event of the proper name in which the little devil arrives only to erase itself/by erasing itself—to be spared having to add anything here for the moment. It is advisable out of modesty at least to follow such a course since in this case it seems to be a matter of my so-called proper name or of what may remain of it in an epithet. That said, if any among you wish me to do so, I will not insist on silencing what I think of all this, but only at the end, after we're done, as a post-scriptum, in parentheses, or "off the record" as one says in English.

"Off the record" means not recorded, outside the archive. We are thus brought back to the difficult question of the record, history, and the archive. Is there an "outside-the-archive"? Impossible, but the impossible is deconstruction's affair.

At bottom, beneath the question that I will call once again the remaining [*restance*] of the archive—which does anything but *remain* in the sense of the permanent subsistence of a presence—beneath this question of the deference or the destinerrance of the archive, there could take shape, at least for the time of a session, the silhouette of everything that, in my view, deserves to be discussed, since we are here to discuss or to continue discussions. By this I mean the silhouette of what seemed to me to deserve discussion not *with* Lacan *in general* and certainly not in the name of philosophy *in general* (on the subject, in the name, or from the point of view of which I have never spoken, no more than of antiphilosophy, as a consequence, which has always seemed to me the thing least deserving of interest in the world). Thus, not *with* Lacan *in general*—who for me does not exist, and I never speak of a philosopher or a corpus in general as if it were a matter of homogeneous body: I did not do so for Lacan any more than for any other. The discussion was begun rather with a forceful, relatively coherent, and stabilized configuration of a discourse at the time of the collection and binding of the *Ecrits,* in other words, in 1966.

The binding of the *Ecrits* is what holds them together and provides them with the most solid systematic structure, the most formalized constructure, as formalized as possible. Now, if there is one text that stands more than any other in this position and at this post of binder, it is indeed the "Seminar on 'The Purloined Letter.'" As you know, the "Seminar on 'The Purloined Letter'" is given a privilege, which is Lacan's word; I quote Lacan: "the privilege of opening the sequence [the sequence of the *Ecrits*] despite its diachrony."[6] In other words, the *Ecrits* collect and bind together all the texts out of which it is composed in the chronological order (according to the "diachrony") of their prior publication, with the exception, precisely, of the "Seminar on 'The Purloined Letter,'" which, by coming at the beginning, is thereby given the "privilege" (Lacan's term) of figuring the synchronic configuration of the set and thus *binding* the whole together. It is for this reason that it seemed to me legitimate to take a privileged interest in this privilege. If I am using the word *binding* here, the binding that holds together at the moment of reading and rereading, it is because on one of the two sole occasions in my life on which I met Lacan and spoke briefly *with* him, he himself spoke to me of binding and of the binding of the *Ecrits.* I am not telling these stories for the sake of the amusement or distraction of anecdotes, but because what we are supposed to be talking about here is the encounter, *tukhè,* contingency—or not—and what binds, if you will, the signature of the event to the theorem.

I only met Lacan twice and crossed paths with him a third time, long after, at a cocktail party. I don't know if that means we were

6. Jacques Lacan, "Seminar on 'The Purloined Letter,'" in *The Purloined Poe: Lacan, Derrida, and Psychoanalytic Reading* 28 (Jeffrey Mehlman trans., John P. Muller and William J. Richardson eds., 1988). ["Seminar" is not included in the selection of the *Ecrits* edited and translated by Alan Sheridan (1977). According to Sheridan, this selection was approved by Lacan himself. —*Trans.*]

together, one *with* the other, but in any case these two encounters did not take place at the home of (*apud*) one or the other but at a third party's, and in the first place, at the first meeting, abroad, in 1966 in the United States where both of us had been for the first time exported. (I say "exported" on purpose and in fact it is a quotation; perhaps you know that behind the pseudonyms deemed to be transparent by the newspapers, the recognizable character from a very bad novel [when I say bad, I mean in the "literary" sense and not only the "moral" sense], who first of all complains about not being translated abroad, who complains with a bitterness that seems to permeate the very paper itself, this character said quite recently, in a single breath, that Lacan and I, Lacan *with* me, alias Lauzun *with* Saïda for those in the know, were both of us "adulterated products fit for exportation." To find myself in the same export container with Lacan would have been rather to my taste, but this was not bearable for everyone or to everyone's taste since a journalist who shuttles back and forth between the editorial board of Gallimard and *Le Nouvel Observateur* attempted to separate me *from* [d'avec] Lacan by saying that, for the author of this disconcerting novel, it was only Derrida—for he used my name, not that of the fictional character, not ever Saïd, Sida, or Saïda—who, this time in the singular, through an adulterated quotation, becomes an "adulterated product fit for exportation." I alone, no longer *with* Lacan as the author or the character of the fable wanted it, but without Lacan, me all alone now, "adulterated product" in the export container, me all alone in my box, deported, exported abroad, and, why not, forbidden to frequent certain places, forbidden a resident's permit, me all alone, isolated, insulated by the decree of a cultural traffic cop. This is one of the things that are happening in France today, in the higher spheres of culture and politics that I spoke of at the outset.)[7]

So, to start over, when I met Lacan in Baltimore for the first time, in 1966, and we were introduced to each other by René Girard, his first words, uttered in a friendly sigh, were: "So we had to wait to come here, and abroad, in order to meet each other!: Here, I remark, perhaps because of the problem of destinerrance that is waiting for us and perhaps because of Baltimore's mortal name (Baltimore: dance or trance and terror), Baltimore the City of Poe, whose grave I looked for in vain during those days although I was able to visit his house on that occa-

7. [Derrida is referring here to the recently published novel by Julia Kristeva, *Les Samouraï* (1990). —*Trans.*]

sion (I went *chez* Poe in 1966), perhaps then because of this mortal name of Baltimore, I remark that the only two times we met and spoke briefly one *with* the other, it was a question of death between us and first of all from Lacan's mouth. In Baltimore, for example, he spoke to me of the way in which he thought he would be read, in particular by me, after his death.

At our second and last encounter, during a dinner offered by his in-laws, he insisted on publicly archiving in his own way, with regard to something I had told him, the disregard of the Other that I had supposely attempted "by playing dead." Elisabeth Roudinesco recounts very well this whole episode, which I reread this morning on page 418 of her monumental and classic *History of Psychoanalysis in France* (volume 2). Lacan's phrase speaks of a "father," and that's me, a father who "does not recognize . . . the way he himself disregarded the Other [big O] by playing dead."[8] I am still not sure I have fully understood the ventured interpretation in what was, we should not forget, a signed publication in *Scilicet* (where Lacan alone was authorized, by himself, to sign), but I have always wondered whether by making me out to be the father in this story, by naming me "the father," he was not taking aim at the son; I have always wondered whether he didn't mean to say the son, if he didn't want to play the son, to make me or himself into the son, to make of me the son who disregards the Other by playing dead, as he put it, or make himself into the son. As always, Lacan left me the greatest freedom of interpretation, and as always I would have taken it even if he had not left it to me, as it will have pleased me. He left me the greatest freedom to hear and to interpret because he added right after this: "To the father who said it to me, from here to hear me or not [*Au père qui me l'a dit d'ici m'entendre ou non*]. (This *didici* is magnificent; I hear it in Latin, as if in the dark of a *disco* this time, and not a ballroom, of a *disco* where the old professor cannot manage to give up [*n'arrive pas à renoncer*] the combined compulsion of the future anterior and didactics: *didici,* I will have told you, I will have taught you.) Lacan left me this freedom to interpret as I please on the flyleaf of the *Ecrits* when they were bound, because the inscription that accompanies it says: "to Jacques Derrida, this homage to take as he will." Message received: I have always, and again today, used this homage as it pleases me and as it pleases me to give it and give it back [*le rendre*].

8. Elisabeth Roudinesco, *Jacques Lacan and Co.: A History of Psychoanalysis in France, 1925–1985* 410–11 (Jeffrey Mehlman trans., 1990).

So, there was death between us; it was especially a question of death, I will say even *only* of the death of one of us, as it is *with* or *chez* all those who love each other. Or rather he spoke about it, he alone, since for my part, I never breathed a word about it. He spoke, alone, about our death, about his death that would not fail to arrive, and about the death or rather the dead one that, according to him, I was playing.

I am not forgetting the binding with which all of this is bound up. The thing is that the other worry Lacan confided to me in Baltimore concerned the binding of the *Ecrits,* which had not yet appeared although its publication was imminent. Lacan was worried and slightly annoyed, it seemed to me, with those at Le Seuil, his publishers, who had advised him to assemble everything in a single large volume of more than nine hundred pages. There was thus a risk that the binding would not be strong enough and would give way: "You'll see," he told me as he made a gesture with his hands, "it's not going to hold up." The republication in the two-volume paperback edition in 1970 will thus have reassured him and will have allowed him, in passing, not only to confirm the necessity of placing the "Seminar on 'The Purloined Letter'" at the "entry post" of the *Ecrits,* but also to fire off one of those future anteriors (antedates or antidotes) that will have been the privileged mode of all the declarations of love that he so often made to me, by mentioning (I dare not say by antedating), and I quote, "what I call literally the instance of the letter prior to any grammatology."[9]

(Prior to any grammatology: "Of Grammatology" was first the title of an article published some five years before Lacan's new introduction and—this is one of the numerous mistakes or mis-recognitions made by Lacan and so many others—it never proposed a grammatology, some positive science or discipline bearing that name;[10] on the contrary, both the article and later the book by the same title went to great lengths to demonstrate the impossibility, the conditions of impossibility, the absurdity in principle, of any science or any philosophy bearing the name grammatology. The book that treated *of grammatology* was anything but a grammatology.)

I link this and bind it once again to the binding of the great book. I go back then to this period (the end of the '60s, 1965, 1966–67) when the

9. Jacques Lacan, "Présentation," in *Ecrits* 11 (1966). [This new introduction is dated 1969 and was written for the paperback edition of the *Ecrits.* —*Trans.*]

10. Jacques Derrida, "De la grammatologie," *Critique* 16–42, 23–53 (December 1965, January 1966); *De la grammatologie* (1967).

*Ecrits* were being bound up under the sign of the "Seminar on 'The Purloined Letter.'" I would now like to venture a modest contribution to this history to come of the *being-with* of Lacan and the philosophers, a history which I am quite sure has never been written and which I am not sure ever can be written, even assuming it can be deciphered. What I will propose, then, are merely a few protocols to such a history, whether or not it is possible. And since I have already spoken too long, I will limit myself somewhat arbitrarily to *three protocols.* I am certain there is enough psychoanalysis and plenty of psychoanalysts here to prevent anyone from dismissing as self-indulgence or coquetry the fact that I will describe things not from an overview that looks down from above on this history, but necessarily from the place where I was and am still situated, inscribed, engaged, invested. A place that, I must say, will not have been very comfortable but also not a bad one for observation. I will schematize the three protocols according to several figures under the following headings:

1. *chiasmus*
2. *the future anterior of the after-the-fact* [l'après-coup]
3. *chiasmatic invagination of the borders—or the site of analysis.*

What happens to the *with between two* when there is chaismus, the after-the-fact of the future anterior, and chiasmatic invagination?

### 2. *First Protocol: Chiasmus*

Chiasmus was mentioned by Major. He spoke of the chiasmus between the trajectories of Freud and Lacan as regards science and philosophical speculation. I would like to give the example of another chaismus that occurs in France during the 1960s. At the point at which the "Seminar on 'The Purloined Letter'" proposes the broadest strategic formalization of the Lacanian discourse at the opening of the *Ecrits,* what is happening with the philosophers? Here we can no longer speak—assuming that we ever could—of philosophers *in general,* but of what happens to some of them, or of what happens to philosophy through some of them who are perhaps no longer simply philosophers, without all the same having anything against philosophy, which would be rather simplistic and scholastic. It so happened—and it happened to me—that at the moment at which a certain number of major or dominant philosophers, organized into what I proposed at the time to name phonocentrism and/or phallogocentrism, called for (so to speak, to go quickly) a deconstructive questioning (a questioning that was obviously, by definition, both philosophical and eccentric, ex-centering in relation to the philosophical as such, giving one to think the philosophical from a place that could no longer be simply philosophical nor counter-philosophical, within or outside philosophy), at this same moment, exactly at the same moment, it was possible to witness a theoretical binding of the Lacanian discourse that made the most strenuous, and powerfully spectacular, use of all the motifs that were in my view deconstructible, undergoing deconstruction. Even more serious in my opinion was the fact that it was a matter not only of the most deconstructible motifs of philosophy (phonocentrism, logocentrism, phallogocentrism, full speech as truth, the transcendentalism of the signifier, the circular return of reappropriation toward what is most proper about the proper place, whose borders are circumscribed by lack, and so forth, through a handling of philosophical reference whose form at least was in the best of cases elliptical and aphoristic, in the worst dogmatic, and I will come back to this in a moment); not only, then, was it a matter of the most deconstructible motifs but even of that which, crossing through and overflowing philosophy or onto-theology (I mean the Heideggerian discourse), seemed to me already—and this goes back to 1965—to in turn call for deconstructive questions. For Lacan at that time, as has frequently been mentioned here, referred habitually, in a frequent, decisive, self-confident, and sometimes incantatory way, to Heideggerian speech, to the *logos* interpreted by Heidegger, to the truth, which, moreover, was just as often taken in the sense of adequation as it was in the sense of veiling/unveiling. There is no point in recalling here once again that deconstruction, if there is any, is not a critique, still less a theoretical or speculative operation methodically carried out by someone; rather, if there is any deconstruction, it takes place (which I have said too often, and yet once again in *Psyché,* to dare to repeat it again) as experience of the impossible.

I attempted to show this in "Le Facteur de la vérité" and elsewhere; I would be unable to reconstitute all this here in so little time.

So here is the form of the chiasmus: I found myself at the time faced with a powerful philosophical, philosophizing reconstitution of psychoanalysis that articulated, assumed, and linked up, with the greatest consistency and consequence, all the motifs that elsewhere were offering themselves, although not without resistance, to something like a genealogico-deconstructive interpretation. At the same time, of course, it was not a matter of regretting, still less of opposing this philosophical restructuration of the psychoanalytic discourse or institutions, this philosophical and thus critical questioning. In also putting to work what is most vital in philosophy, linguistics, anthropology, in displacing and reformalizing them in turn in an original fashion, it was so much more interesting than what was then going about in a dogmatic slumber under the name of psychoanalysis. This chiasmus or, as Major put it, this criss-cross, was all the more paradoxical in that there was an impulse coming from psychoanalysis in general—and since Freud, whom I was trying as well to read in my own, not very Lacanian way, in "Freud and the Scene of Writing"—to deconstruct the privilege of presence, at least as consciousness and egological consciousness. In an apparently external but doubtless not fortuitous fashion, this impulse was converging with the necessity to deconstruct this privilege according to other paths, other questions, those with which I was involved elsewhere (reading of Husserl, Heidegger, the question of writing and literature, and so forth). With the result that the discourse that was at the same time the closest and the most deconstructible, the one that was most to be deconstructed was no doubt Lacan's. This was already signaled in *Of Grammatology* in 1965–66 with regard to the primacy of the signifier.

That is why, as I said in *Positions* in 1971, four years before publishing "Le Facteur de la vérité" (Major mentioned this a moment ago), my theoretical "coming-to-terms" *with* Lacan "consist[ed] in pursuing my own work according to its specific pathways and requirements, whether or not this work entertained a closer relationship with Lacan's along certain lines, and even—and I do not exclude it in the least—more than any other today."[11]

Was this not a way of saying that I loved and admired him a lot? And of paying homage to him, in a way that pleased me? It is in this same text that I said, with and without philosophy, *with* and *without* Lacan, "truth is necessary" [*il faut la vérité*].

So, since then? Since then, have we ever exited from this chiasmus? I do not believe we have. Given this chiasmus, which made Lacan's discourse too philosophical for me, too much at home *with the philosophers*—despite, of course, all sorts of disavowals on this subject—too

11. Jacques Derrida, *Positions* 111 note 44 (Alan Bass trans., 1981).

much at home with all those with whom I was in the process not of breaking, which makes no sense as I've said countless times, but of reconsidering all the contracts; a Lacanian discourse, then, too much at home with a Sartrian neo-existentialism (which has not been sufficiently discussed or whose remainders have not been sufficiently pointed out in Lacan's discourse right up to the *Ecrits,* where the discourse of alienation, authenticity, and so forth prevail), too much at home with Hegel/Kojève the "master" (and Hegel/Kojève is also Heidegger, for Kojève does not anthropologize only the phenomenology of spirit; he also Heideggerianizes it, as you know, which was very interesting—and there would be much to say about this, but I'm obliged to step up the pace here: Elisabeth Roudinesco gave us much to think about the other evening regarding this sequence). Given this chiasmus, which made of Lacan's discourse one that was too much at home with the philosophers and with Heidegger (and from 1965 on, my own reading of Heidegger was anything but "at home" there and explicitly raised questions that I have continued to elaborate constantly *since*), I myself could not be *with* Lacan the way a philosopher would be with a psychoanalyst. If I have lived *with* Lacan, if I have come to terms *with* him at my own rhythm, if I have discussed *with* him, this *being-with* has certainly not been that of a philosopher *with* a psychoanalyst. Anyway, if that had been the case, my place in this odd couple's *ménage* will certainly not have been that of the philosopher, and still less that of someone from the university or the academy, for which it seemed to me that Lacan always harbored, to my astonishment, an intense or even avid desire. His only excuse, as regards the university, is that he was not part of it. No doubt Lacan would have liked me to play this role of academic philosopher. But to take someone, me for example, to be an academic philosopher on the pretext that he gets paid for that by an institution, to identify him with or reduce him to that function on this pretext is above all not to read. This impulsive gesture, which is as self-interested as it is defensive, is more or less symmetrical—not altogether but more or less—with the gesture that would consist of taking an analyst for an analyst on the pretext that that is what he or she gets paid for: I have always avoided that gesture.

To say a little more about this chiasmus, all of whose textual and theoretical effects I cannot reconstitute (for that one would need years of minutely detailed and unflinching reading), I will take just one example. From the "Seminar on 'The Purloined Letter'" (thus from the

*Ecrits*), we'll take for example that which tightly adjoins and binds a certain number of motifs, which we'll limit arbitrarily to eight in order to suggest the standing institution of the infinite.

*1.* The motif of the proper and circular trajectory, of the reappropriating trajectory of the letter that returns to the circumscribable place of lack from which it had become detached, that letter about which Lacan says that "since it can be diverted, it must have a course *which is its own* [qui lui est propre]"[12] and a "straight path,"[13] obviously a circular straight path.

*2.* The motif of truth as adequation or readequation, in the circular return and the proper trajectory, of the origin to the end, of the place of detachment of the signifier to its place of reattachment—or as unveiling in, I quote, that "passion to unveil which has an object: truth,"[14] the analyst remaining "above all the master of truth,"[15] true speech [*la vraie parole*], authentic and authenticated by the other in sworn faith, being no longer speaking truly [*la parole vraie*][16] and this unveiling being the relay of adequation ("speech appears thus all the more truly speech when its truth is less grounded in what is called adequation to the thing").[17]

*3.* The motif of "present speech," "full speech" ("I might as well be categorical: in psychoanalytic anamnesis, it is not a question of reality, but of truth, because the effect of full speech is to reorder past contingencies by conferring on them the sense of necessities to come [thus, full speech and future anterior], such as they are constituted by the little freedom through which the subject makes them present");[18] "Analysis can have for its goal only the advent of a true speech [*la parole vraie*] and the realization by the subject of his history in relation to a future."[19]

*4.* The disqualification (whose spirit is also very Heideggerian in its relation to technics) of the "record," the "recording," and of the

12. "Seminar on 'The Purloined Letter,'" *supra* note 6, at 43 (French edition at 29) (emphasis added).

13. *Id.* at 50 (French edition at 38).

14. Lacan, "Propos sur la causalité psychique," in *Ecrits, supra* note 1, at 193.

15. Lacan, "The Function and Field of Speech and Language in Psychoanalysis," in *Ecrits, supra* note 1, at 98 (French edition at 313).

16. [The anterior placement of the adjective "vraie" suggests a more fundamental quality of the true-ness of speech than when it is in the posterior position. —*Trans.*]

17. Lacan, "Variantes de la cure-type," in *Ecrits, supra* note 1, at 351.

18. Lacan, "Function and Field of Speech," in *Ecrits, supra* note 1, at 48 (French edition at 256).

19. Id. at 88 (French edition at 302).

mechanical archive as "alienating": "But precisely because it comes to him through an alienated form, even a retransmission of his own recorded discourse, albeit from the mouth of his own doctor, cannot have the same effects as pyschoanalytic interlocution"[20]—which therefore must be direct, live, immediate, and so forth. Thus "full speech" that "is defined through its identity with that of which it speaks."[21] This point is very important for me—perhaps I'll return to it—because it links phono-logocentrism or phallogocentrism to the analytic situation without technical interposition, without an archiving apparatus of repetition, without essential iterability: a very old philosopheme, from Plato up to and including Heidegger.

5. The transcendental position of the phallus, "the privileged signifier of that mark in which the role of the logos is joined to the advent of desire,"[22] a transcendental position that is nothing other than the doctrine that links truth to castration and, I quote, to "the mother's lack of the penis in which the nature of the phallus is revealed."[23]

6. Phonocentrism, which was at the time militant ("A writing, like the dream itself, may be figurative, but like language it is always articulated symbolically, or even *phonematically* just like language, and in fact phonetically, from the moment it is readable."[24] As I pointed out in "Le Facteur de la vérité," this "fact has the value of *fact* only within the ethnocultural limits of so-called phonetic systems of writing, which moreover are never phonetic through and through—otherwise there would not even be a symbolic order. This explicit and massive phonocentrism will be contradicted by Lacan himself, as if it were nothing, as if it had always been so [future anterior of the after-the-fact], in 1972–73, not "before" but after "any grammatology," as I will show in a moment.)

7. The misrecognition of or the failure to take into account the literary structure of narration, the omission of the frame, of the play of signatures, and notably of its parergonal effect; I cannot reproduce the demonstration I gave in 1975 of this misrecognition, but it is not by

20. Id. at 49 (French edition at 258).

21. Lacan, "Réponse au commentaire de Jean Hyppolite sur la 'Verneinung' de Freud," in *Ecrits, supra* note 1, at 381.

22. Lacan, "The Signification of the Phallus," in *Ecrits, supra* note 1, at 877 (French edition at 692).

23. Lacan, "La science et la vérité," in *Ecrits, supra* note 1, at 87.

24. Lacan, "Situation de la psychanalyse et formation du psychanalyste en 1956, in *Ecrits*," *supra* note 1, at 470.

chance that the misrecognition, particularly in its treatment of the general narrator, resembles what Nicole Loraux and Philippe Lacoue-Labarthe talked about as a hasty collapse of the choir, the characters, and the spectators in the theater or in tragedy, producing thereby incalculable damage in the reading at the very moment it permits a certain formalizing calculation of pyschoanalytic hermeneutics.

*8.* A spiriting away of the effects of the double in Poe's story, effects which, as I believe I have also shown, ought to have blurred the borders between the imaginary and the symbolic, and thus the strictness of this tripartition to which, as you know, Lacan was also obliged to return much later.

These eight motifs—and no doubt other secondary ones that I don't have time to list—are strongly articulated among themselves; in fact they are indissociable and indispensable to the chief affirmation, which is fundamental moreover for both the destiny and the possibility of psychoanalysis, the chief affirmation *with* which it seemed urgent and strategically necessary to me to come to terms, namely, to quote the last words of the seminar: "Thus is it that what the 'purloined letter,' nay, the 'letter in sufferance,' means is that a letter always arrives at its destination."[25] Now, this conclusion was possible only insofar as the letter (which for Lacan is not the signifier, but the place of the signifier) is not divided. Lacan says that it "does not suffer partition": "Cut a letter into small pieces," he says, "and it remains the letter it is" (39). Consequently, what Lacan then calls the "materiality of the signifier" and that he deduces from an indivisibility that is nowhere to be found, always seemed and still seems to me to correspond to an "idealization" of the letter, to an ideal identity of the letter, which was a problem I had been working on elsewhere along other lines for quite some time. But—and I will limit myself to this one point in our context and given the time at our disposal—I could articulate this question and this objection (on which, as it could be shown, everything else depends: another logic of the event and of destination, another thinking of singularity, the dissemination of the unique beyond a logic of castration, and so forth), I could read, then, this surreptitious idealization, not to say this idealism of Lacan's, as Stephen Melville put it, only on the basis of a work that was already underway, in a deconstructive mode, with the philoso-

25. Lacan, "Seminar," *supra* note 1, at 53.

phers, and notably as concerns the constitution of idealities, of ideal objects in Husserl. Without pursuing this any further, suffice it to say that in order to read Lacan, to read him in a problematizing and nondogmatic fashion, it is also necessary to read, for example, Husserl and a few others, and to read them in a problematic or deconstructive way. There is here, if I may be permitted to say so, the outline of a new training, another curriculum for psychoanalyst readers of Lacan, at least if they want to read him otherwise than in an apelike, orthodox, and defensive manner. This parallels, in sum, the advice concerning a "new training" that certain of us—the rare professional philosophers who read and published on Lacan in the philosophical university (I am thinking above all of Philippe Lacoue-Labarthe and Jean-Luc Nancy)—gave to philosophers when we told them to read Lacan, which advice was then, about twenty years ago, rather rare. (If I had the time, I would explain why in my opinion all the texts of the "professional philosophers" to whom I have just referred are not read and are not readable in France, particularly by most French "Lacanians.")

### 3. *Second Protocol: The Future Anterior of the After-the-Fact*

I have said that my reading of the "Seminar on 'The Purloined Letter'" as well as what prefigured it from 1965 to 1971 in *Of Grammatology* and *Positions* did not claim to enclose or exhaust Lacan (I said so explicitly in these very texts), but only to treat a strong and relatively stabilized configuration of Lacanian displacement. The discourse of Lacan, which was always very sensitive to any movement on the theoretical scene—and who could blame him?—continued thereafter to readjust, even recast, sometimes contradict the axioms I have just mentioned. After 1968, the accent put on writing continued to become more pronounced, to the point of inverting, very "grammatologically," the utterance I cited a moment ago concerning "phonematic and even always phonetic" writing, since he could write in the seminar *Encore:* "But the signifier can in no way be limited to this phonematic support."[26] Earlier, René Major cited certain spectacular examples—there are many more beginning at this time—of this sudden substitution of

26. Lacan, "A Jakobson," in *Le Séminaire, Livre XX: Encore* 22 (1975).

the graphematic for the phonematic (which, moreover, interests me here only as a symptomatic index in the history of ideas, as we used to say, and not in itself, since what I proposed to call trace, gramme, differance, and so forth is no more graphic than it is phonematic, no more spatial than temporal; but let's drop the subject since this is not the place to take up this serious and tenacious misunderstanding). This kind of substitution of writing for speech around 1970 deserves its own history and is not limited to Lacan. Ponge told me one day, with a smile, that he was rereading his texts to see whether he had not given in too much to phonocentrism and whether he could replace speech by writing here and there without too much damage. Roger Laporte drew up a list, which I found to be as illuminating as it was remorseless, of all the places where, during the same years, our friend Maurice Blanchot, when he republished his old texts in collections, had simply replaced "speech" by "writing." I am not sure that it is a matter of a *Kehre,* as Stephen Melville put it, but if one were to open the question of the *Kehre,* then it would be very general.

All of this merely to say that the historical narration of what remained and still remains—and first of all for me—the future of Lacanian thought as it moves beyond the *Ecrits* is all the more difficult in that Lacan was an incomparable listener and his discursive machine was one of such sensitivity that everything could be inscribed there with finesse or discretion (and this is quite all right; who doesn't try to do the same?). But, what is more, it is inscribed there in the spoken words of a seminar that, by giving rise to numerous stenotyped or tape-recorded archivings, will have then fallen prey not only to all the problems of rights (which I don't want to get into here and which M. Conté will have evoked in passing the other day), but also to all the problems posed by the delays of publishing and of an editing—in the American sense—that was of the most active sort. Since all of these things hang by a hair, since the stakes get decided in a word, an ellipsis, a verbal modality, a conditional, or a future anterior, especially when one knows Lacan's rhetoric, I say good luck to any narrator who would try to know what was said and written by whom on which date: what would Lacan have said or not have said! This is also at the bottom the problem of the letter and destination that separates me perhaps most closely from [*d'avec*] Lacan.

### 4. *Third Protocol: Chiasmatic Invagination of the Borders*

Not only were my references to Lacan, and in particular to the "Seminar on 'The Purloined Letter,'" not totalizing, homogenizing, or critical, but I even conceded he was right as concerns reason, the question of reason remaining open, as well as the question of what happens when one concedes to another, that is, when one gives reason or, as we say in French, *donne raison.* In *The Post Card,* I said that he was right about "the reason for a characteristic [*trait*] that has never been elucidated, and which shows once again the depth of Freud's intuition: namely, why he advances the view that there is only one *libido,* his text showing that he conceives it as masculine in nature" (482). Saying Lacan is right (just as the signatory of the "Envois" begins by saying the beloved other is right: "Yes, you were right"), "Le Facteur de la vérité" speaks, as concerns precisely this "characteristic [*trait*] that had never been elucidated," of a trait drawn from reason or a check [*traite*] drawn on reason. "In the logic of the kettle (a check drawn on reason), reason will always be right" (482–83). By saying Lacan is right or by doing right by Lacan [*raison donnée . . . ou rendue*] makes my text still more unreadable for readers in a rush to decide between the "pro and the con," in short, for those minds who believed I was opposing Lacan or showing him to be wrong. The question lies elsewhere: it is the question of reason and of the principle of reason. Thus, not only was I not criticizing Lacan but I was not even writing a sort of overseeing or objectifying metadiscourse *on* Lacan or *on* a text of Lacan's. My writing involved me in a scene, which scene I was showing at the same time (no doubt in small phrases that no one reads) could not be closed or framed. All of this has *since* been constantly put back into play in other scenes *en abyme* that have been deployed here and there, more often there than here, which is to say once again abroad. Moreover, for all these reasons, the argument of "Le Facteur de la vérité" does not lend itself to being framed in the text bearing this title; it is played, set adrift in *The Post Card,* the book with that title, which inscribes "Le Facteur de la vérité" like a piece in a borderless fiction, neither public nor private, *with* and *without* a general narrator. It is inscribed first of all in the "Envois," of which I am not the signatory and where a little-read plot involving a wandering letter, some remarks on destination as well as on the analytic institution and what then happens, or not, demonstrate, while doing it, that which is uttered there without lending itself to some meta-utterance. I will take only one example, if I may be permitted to quote a character from this book without quoting myself (that is my excuse), from the "Envois" dated August 18, 1979:

> *18 August 1979:* Is it true that you call me only when I'm not there?
>
> One day you told me that I was a torch
>
> "come" which is not valid without the tone, without the timbre, without the voice of mine that you know. So much for the fire. They had put everything on a picture (of the one, of the other, of the couple), and then they remained attached to the betting, and they are still speculating but they are no longer there. Each of them to the other: you were in league to destroy me, you conspired, you covered all the trails, get out of it yourself.
>
> And this short philosophical dialogue for your amusement: "—What is it, a destination?—There where it arrives.—So then everywhere that it arrives there was destination?—Yes.—But not before?—No.—That's convenient, since if it arrives there, it is that it was destined to arrive there. But then one can only say so after the fact?—When it has arrived, it is indeed the proof that it had to arrive, and arrive there, at its destination.—But before arriving, it is not destined, for example it neither desires nor demands any address? There is everything that arrives where it had to arrive, but no destination before the arrival?—Yes, but I meant to say something else.—Of course, that's what I was saying.—There you are."
>
> As I gave her to understand, I don't know if she was right to write *what* she wrote, and this is quite secondary, but in any event she was right to write it. Right *a priori.* I know nothing about how it happens, how it arrives for her, and it will be a long time before I figure it out, it is only the beginning, but she cannot have been wrong to send herself that." (244–45)

This "envoi" relayed two other postscripts, one within the other (which you will pardon me for reading as well, but you may presume that they are not by me). They situated, I believe, one of the essential places in the ongoing and interminable discussion with Lacan, namely, the thinking of contingency, singularity, the event, the encounter, luck and *tukhè*, which is also a certain thinking, interpretation, or experience of death whose signifier would be the phallus; all of which could summarize the unanswered questions I am still today putting to Lacan, *with* whom it is worth discussing: questions on the subject of what he has to say on, in effect, being, man, animals (especially animals), and thus God—no less.

> P.S.: I forgot, you are completely right: one of the paradoxes of destination, is that if you wanted *to demonstrate,* for someone, that something never arrives at its destination, it's all over. The demonstration, once it had reached its goal, would have proved what it was not supposed to demonstrate. But this is why, dear friend, I always say "a letter *can* always *not* arrive at its destination, etc." This is a piece of luck.*
>
> You know that I never say that I'm right and never demonstrate anything. They put up with this very badly, consequently they would like nothing to have happened, everything wiped off the map. Wait for me.
>
> *P.S. Well a piece of luck, if you will, if you yourself can, and if you have it, luck (*tukhè,* fortune, this is what I mean, good fortune, good fate: us). The mischance (the misaddress) of this chance is that in order *to be able* not to arrive, it must bear within itself a force and a structure, a straying of the destination, such that it *must* also not arrive in any case. Even in arriving (always to some "subject"), the letter takes itself away *from the arrival at arrival.* It arrives elsewhere, always several times. You can no longer take hold of it. It is the structure of the letter (as postcard, in other words the fatal partition that it must support) which demands this, I have said it elsewhere, delivered to a *facteur* subject to the same law. The letter demands this, right here, and you too, you demand it. (123–24)

This thinking of the destination is indissociable, of course, from a thinking of death, from destination as death—and that is why I allowed myself to recall this barely private thing, between Lacan and me: the fact that, at each of our encounters, it was a question of death and that it was Lacan alone who spoke of it.

What binds destination to death is said by the signatory of the "Envois," for example:

> Murder is everywhere, my unique and immense one. We are the worst criminals in history. And right here I kill you, save, save, you, save you run away, the unique, the living one over there whom I love. Understand me, when I write, right here, on these innumerable postcards, I annihilate not only what I am saying but also the unique addressee that I constitute, and therefore every possible addressee, every destination. I kill you, I annul you at my fingertips, wrapped around my finger. To do so it suffices only that I be legible—and I become illegible to you, you are dead. If I say that I write for dead addressees, not dead in the future but already dead at the moment when I get to the end of sentence, it is not in order to play. Genet said that his theater was addressed to the dead and I take it like that on the train in which I am going writing you without end. The addressees are dead, the destination is death: no, not in the sense of S. or p.'s predication, according to which we would be destined to die, no, not in the sense in which to arrive at our destination, for us mortals, is to end by dying. (33)

Well, pardon me for these readings, which lead me to hasten my conclusion with three remarks that I will make as brief and elliptical as possible:

1. death
2. the analytic situation
3. the "is there a psychoanalysis?" in general or some properly namable psychoanalysis, namable by a proper name.

*1.* On death: *since,* since all the texts I have just mentioned, I feel increasingly tempted not to accept the discourse on being-for-death, in either its Heideggerian form or the Lacanian form in which it is linked to the phallocentered signifier, without a lot of questions in return, questions of all sorts, and without a lot of displacements that are also experiences and not only speculative discourses, discussions, or even critical objections. But I can't say more about this here; these things are happening elsewhere, in recent seminars, in relation with the questions of the animal and of God. (The remarkable things Lacan says on the animal are also in my view most problematic. In short, it would be a matter of contesting that death happens to some mortal being-for-death; rather, and this is a scandal for sense and for good sense, it happens only to some immortal who lacks for lacking nothing. I am thinking here of a certain passage in *Zarathustra* on the suffering that arises from a lack of lack and that, in the course of my seminar this year on "Eating the Other," I interpreted in a direction that perhaps intersects with what Nancy was saying the other evening.) In "Le Facteur de la vérité, at the conclusion of an analysis of "the lack that is never lacking (in its place)," I pointed out the following, which at the time seemed to be to situate very well the difference "with" Lacan: "The difference which interests me here is that—formula to be understood as one will—the lack does not have its place in dissemination" (441).

2. On the analytic situation: another recollection from my meeting with Lacan. In this case, I was not a direct witness—and the question of the archive is thus posed in yet a different manner. René Girard reported to me that after my lecture in Baltimore, when he was seeking to elicit from Lacan his own (generous) assessment, Lacan supposedly replied: "Yes, yes, it's good, but the difference between him and me is that he does not deal with people who are suffering," meaning by that: people in analysis. What did he know about that? Very careless. To be able to say such a thing, so imperturbably, and know such a thing, he could not have been referring either to suffering (alas, I too deal with people who suffer—all of you, for example) or to transference, that is, to love, which has never needed the analytic situation to claim its victims. Lacan thus made clinical treatment, institutionalized in a certain mode, and the rules governing the analytic situation into criteria of absolute competence for speaking—about all this. Here is a better known episode that occurred some ten years later after Lacan had used the future anterior several times to reappropriate by way of antedating (when he said for example that he was giving up certain concepts and words[27]—for instance, gramme and other similar things, of which as far as I know he never made any use and which, instead of giving up,

27. Lacan, "De Rome 53 à Rome 67: La psychanalyse. Raisons d'un échec," in *Scilicet*, June 17, 1968, at 47.

he should have simply taken up). In a session of the seminar in 1977 (still "l'Insu-que-sait"), Lacan made a compulsive blunder: he said that he thought I was in analysis (laughter from the audience, the sentence replaced by an ellipsis in *Ornicar*, but too late because the transcription had circulated; once again the problem of the archive, the archive that no one can master, here no more than ever because of this recording technique). The thing has now been recounted and commented on in *The Post Card* (202–4). Elisabeth Roudinesco cites it but only in the official version from *Ornicar*, with its ellipsis. Meanwhile, since the legal archive covers less and less of the whole archive, this archive remains unmasterable and continues on its way, in continuity with the anarchive.

In any case, what did he know about it, whether or not I was in analysis, and what could that mean? The fact that I have never been in analysis, in the institutional sense of the analytic situation, does not mean that I am not, here or there, in a way that cannot be easily toted up, analysand and analyst in my own time and in my own way. Like everyone else. In a remark that has been archived by the recording machines but forever withdrawn from the official archive, Lacan says this (notice and admire the syntax and the reference to non-knowledge and truth): "someone about whom I did not know that—to tell the truth I believe he is in analysis—about whom I did not know that he was in analysis—but this is merely a hypothesis—his name is Jacques Derrida, who has written a preface to this *Verbier*."[28] This non-knowledge in truth of a belief ("to tell the truth I believe he is in analysis"!), of a simple hypothesis, concerned therefore the being-in-analysis of someone whom he, Lacan, was not afraid to name, the being-in-analysis with a couple of analysts ("for he couples them," added Lacan, who was then obviously unaware of the fact that one of the two, who was my friend, was dead by the time I wrote the preface in question, which was thus written to his memory, as homage, and in his absence).

How could Lacan make his listeners laugh on the subject or on the basis of a blunder, his own, concerning a hypothetical analysand—even as he himself presented himself (and this is, moreover, one of his most

28. The reference is to Derrida's "Fors: Les mots anglés de Nicolas Abraham and Maria Torok," forword to Abraham and Torok, *The Wolf Man's Magic Word: A Cryptonomy* (Barbara Johnson trans., 1986). For an account of the episode, see 2 Roudinesco, *supra* note 8, at 602–4.

interesting assertions) as an analysand, a master of truth as analysand and not as analyst? How could he insist on two occasions on my real status as institutional nonanalyst and on what he wrongly supposed to be my status as institutional analysand, whereas he ought to have been the first to cast suspicion on the limits or borders of these sites, to pay attention to the tangled knots of this invagination?

3. This leads to my last point. However insufficient, intermittent, distracted, or floating my interminable listening to Lacan may be, what keeps it on alert is less the question of philosophy, science, or psychoanalysis than another question, which concerns a certain dominant state (meaning the dominance of the master) of the history of philosophy, science, psychoanalysis, namely, the dominant state that at a certain point I called phallogocentrism, according to a certain historical, precarious, conventional, and finite determination of the analytic situation, of its rules and its limits. To this analytic situation, it seems to me, one might aptly apply the topological expression that I ventured in another circumstance: the chiasmatic invagination of the borders. I proposed the expression in "Pas" in *Parages,* which I thank Stephen Melville for having mentioned here.

If this is indeed how things are, the question of knowing *whether or not there is* some psychoanalysis—X-ian, his, yours, mine—that can hold up or that is coming, this incalculable, unimaginable, unaccountable, unattributable question is displaced at the rhythm at which the analytic situation, and thus the analytic institution is deconstructed, *as if by itself,* without deconstruction or deconstructive project. As for the relations between this deconstruction as experience of the impossible and the "there is," I have spoken of them elsewhere; it is archived.

What will I not have said today! But if I had said that we loved each other very much, Lacan and I, and thus we promised each other very much, and that this was for me a good thing in this life, would I have been in the truth? Stephen Melville said that the promise always risked being also a threat. That's true. But I would always prefer to prefer the promise.

# Contributors

**David Gray Carlson** teaches law at the Benjamin N. Cardozo School of Law, where he is the author of numerous volumes and articles on commercial law. He is also the coeditor of *Deconstruction and the Possibility of Justice* (1992) and *Hegel and Legal Theory* ((1991).

**Drucilla Cornell** is Professor of Law, Political Science, and Women's Studies at Rutgers University and is the author of many books on postmodern philosophy, including *The Imaginary Domain* (1995), *Philosophy of the Limit* (1992), and *Beyond Accommodation* (1991).

**Jacques Derrida** currently teaches at l'Ecole des Hautes Etudes en Sciences Sociales in Paris. He is also a regular Visiting Professor at the Benjamin N. Cardozo School of Law, New York University, the New School for Social Research, and the University of California at Irvine. Among his principal texts are *Politics of Friendship* (1997), *Specters of Marx: The State of the Debt, the Work of Mourning, and the New International* (1994), *Limited Inc, ABC* (1988), *Truth in Painting* (1987), *Mémoires: For Paul De Man* (1986), *Margins of Philosophy* (1982), *Dissemination* (1981), *Spurs* (1979), *The Post Card* (1979), *Writing and Difference* (1978), *Of Grammatology* (1974), and *Speech and Phenomena* (1973).

**Peter Goodrich** is Corporation of London Professor of Law at the University of London, Birkbeck College, and is the author of *Law in the Courts of Love* (1996), *Oedipus Lex* (1995), *Languages of Law: From Logics of Memory to Nomadic Masks* (1990), *Reading the Law* (1986) and *Legal Discourse* (1986), and is the editor and cotranslator of *Law and the Unconscious: A Legendre Reader* (1997).

**Pierre Legendre** is Professor of Law at the University of Paris (Panthéon-Sorbonne), director of *La Laboratoire Européenne pour l'Etude de l'Affiliation*, and is affiliated with l'Ecole des Hautes Etudes en Sciences Sociales (Section des Sciences Religieuses). His sixteen books include *Dieu au Miroir: Etude sur l'institution des images* (1994), *Les enfants du* *texte* (1992), *Le crime du caporal Lortie: Traite sur le père* (1989), *L'empire de la vérité* (1983), *Paroles poetiques echappées du texte* (1982), and *L'amour du censeur: Essaie sur l'ordre dogmatique* (1974). He has also written the script for the film *La fabrication de l'homme occidental.*

**Alain Pottage** is a lecturer in law at the London School of Economics and Political Science and is widely published in law journals on legal philosophy and property law as well as on architecture. Pottage is cotranslator of *Law and the Unconscious: A Legendre Reader* (1997).

**Michel Rosenfeld** is Professor at the Cardozo School of Law where he specializes in constitutional law and legal philosophy. His books include *Just Interpretations* (1998) and *Affirmative Action and Justice* (1991). He is editor of *Constitutionalism, Identity, Difference and Legitimacy* (1994), and coeditor of *Habermas on Law and Democracy* (1998), *Deconstruction and the Possibility of Justice* (1992), and *Hegel and Legal Theory* (1991).

**Renata Salecl** is at the Institute of Criminology in the University of Ljubljana and currently (1997–98) a fellow at the Wissenschaftskolleg in Berlin. She is the author of *The Spoils of Freedom: Psychoanalysis and Feminism After the Fall of Socialism* (1994) and coeditor of *Gaze and Voice as Love Objects* (1996).

**Jeanne L. Schroeder** is Professor of Law at the Benjamin N. Cardozo School of Law and is the author of *The Vestal and the Fasces: Hegel, Lacan, Property and the Feminine* (1998).

**Anton Schütz** is a lecturer in law at University of London, Birkbeck College. He is coeditor with Pierre Legendre of *Le dossier occidental de la parenté.*

**Henry Staten** teaches in the English Department at the University of Utah and is the author of *Eros in Mourning: Homer to Lacan* (1994), *Nietzsche's Voice* (1990), and *Wittgenstein and Derrida* (1984).

**Slavoj Žižek** teaches philosophy and psychoanalysis at the Institute for Social Sciences at the University of Ljubljana. His many books include *The Plague of Fantasies* (1997), *The Indivisible Remainder* (1996), *Metastasis of Enjoyment* (1994), *Tarrying with the Negative* (1994), *Looking Awry: An Introduction to Jacques Lacan Through Popular Culture* (1991), and *The Sublime Object of Ideology* (1989).

# Index